I0787848

THE NATURAL HISTORY *of a* Mountain Meadow *and Its* Cirque

CHRIS MASER

LUMINARE PRESS

WWW.LUMINAREPRESS.COM

The Natural History of a Mountain Meadow and Its Cirque
© 2015 Chris Maser

Printed in the United States of America

Cover Design: Claire Last

Luminare Press
467 W 17th Ave
Eugene, OR 97401
www.luminarepress.com

LCCN: 2015938486
ISBN: 978-1-937303-52-5

Amidst the vivid imagery and intimate detail of a place virtually untouched by man lies an elegant allegorical expression of the human condition, not only through the trials of young Storm Hawk, but also the complex system of living beings inhabiting the meadow and its cirque. Glimmering in the eyes of every member of the ecosystem is a spark of humanity that will bring readers closer to the wildlife than a documentarian could ever imagine. The youth's journey to adulthood is portrayed again and again through the lifecycles of the numerous meadow dwellers, varying with each account by the creature's specific background, status, and fortune.

Chris Maser's expertly crafted book presents a 'coming-of-age' and 'finding-your-niche' narrative alongside an information-rich guidebook befitting top-tier adventurers, sportsmen, and wildlife enthusiasts. Each page is radiant with his tremendous passion for the outdoors, and I have no doubt that anyone enjoying this marvelous book will be struck with the overwhelming urge to go camping—as I was, and ultimately did—if only to re-experience nature through a newly developed lens. Truly, this work is a gift to the reader.

—Martin Now
Line Editor, Corvallis, Oregon

Contents

ACKNOWLEDGMENTS

It is with joy that I thank my friend and colleague, Dr. Nick Brown of Scottsdale, Arizona, for his wonderfully insightful review of the initial manuscript and his kind endorsement thereof.

I am indebted to Martin Now for his preliminary copyediting.

I also much appreciate the generosity of Patricia Marshall of Luminare Press for her helpful suggestions, professionalism, and patience during the publication process.

Finally, I am deeply grateful to Zane, my beautiful wife of 34-plus years, for her enduring patience with me during the many hours I spent within myself wandering about the cirque and the meadow, where I met Storm Hawk and all the creatures whose stories appear between the covers of this book. In addition, I am most thankful for her willingness to read the entire manuscript with care and insight. Although she has long been the best proofreader I know, I have now learned once and for all that she is also an extraordinary copyeditor—a realization that become clear when she gave the manuscript its final check.

Thank you all!

PREFACE

Friendship is one of the rare, beautiful gifts of life. I am fortunate to have you as a friend. Although I know the richness that your friendship gives to me, I can only guess what richness my friendship may give to you. But if I could, I know what I would give you to make your life as beautiful as mine.

I would give you the excitement of each sunrise, the birth of each new day. I would give you the seasons in all their splendor. I would give you the May perfume of a high desert morning, as the sun dries the dew from sagebrush, bitterbrush, and juniper. I would give you the July scent of ponderosa pine; the August fragrance of warm, ripe blackberries; and the October aroma of a thicket of mountain mahogany. I would give you the sharp, clean odor of spruce in the cold, thin air of a high-mountain winter. I would give you the colors of flowers and the songs of birds, the infinite beauty of the drifting clouds, the symphony of canyon winds, the percussion of thunderstorms, and the eternal tempo of the sea.

I would give you the coolness of clear mountain streams, the tenderness on new grass. I would give you the freshness of summer rains, the silence of winter snows. I would give you the wonder of rainbows and of northern lights, and I would give you the majesty of snow-clad mountains. I would give you the sun, the moon, the stars, the wind, rain, and snow. I would give you the fertility of the earth, the wisdom of eons entombed in rocks.

And, I would give you the peace of each sunset, the reflective beauty of the land at day's end.

But I cannot give you these things; they are not mine to give. So, my friend, I offer you my hand. Take it and come back in time with me as I paint for you with words the beauty and dignity of the land as I have seen it. Then, in small measure, I can share with you the richness that you have shared with me—friendship.

My friend, I once took you on a thousand-year journey through a forest. Now, come with me and witness the birth and life of a mountain meadow and its cirque.

Before we begin our journey, however, there are a few things I must explain to you. First, to fully appreciate the grandeur of the meadow and its cirque, it is vital to understand how they came into being because they represent a historical archive of events in the flowchart of time. Second, they are today a dynamic, living system—a library of Nature's wisdom wherein we can search for knowledge and understanding. Third, because Nature's creativity is ever-changing and novel in the eternal moment we call "life," what we witness each moment of each day in the cirque will be a singular, unique experience, not only in our lives and in the world but also in the universe forever. Fourth, the human heart of our story takes place in the year 1575, in the form of Storm Hawk, an American Indian. And fifth, the magnificence and wonder of Nature's creative artistry is beyond words, beyond thought, and will therefore be most fully understood in the spiritual silence that surrounds us.

PART I:

THE FLOWCHART OF TIME

If you could go back 300 million years, you would find a vastly different scene than exists today. In that far-distant time, before the first human thought arose from the ethers, the Earth consisted of a single, large continent surrounded by a fluid, worldwide ocean. The continent would remain anonymous until a man named Alfred Wegener peeked into the corridor of time in the year 1927 AD and coined the name "Pangaea," which he derived from the Greek *pan*, meaning "entire," or "whole," and *gaia*, meaning "Mother Earth."

All seemed quiet and stable for about 125 million years. Then, 175 million years ago, Pangaea began to rupture, causing it to rip in two. The growing north–south separation of the new continents was fuelled from deep within the Earth by a relatively thin layer of molten rock, which ranged from about 1,600 degrees Fahrenheit at its top to about 4,000 to 6,700 degrees Fahrenheit toward its bottom.

Time passed. Then, roughly 150 to 140 million years ago, the southern continent broke up a second time, and the pieces moved away from one another. Again, time passed, until somewhere between 60 and 55 million years ago, the disintegration of the southern continent reached its culmination, and was followed by the terminal fragmentation of the northern continent, as the jigsaw puzzle of continents began forming the final, geomorphic pattern we know as today's world.

Chapter 1:
The Wonder of
Planet Earth

B Y NOW, YOU MIGHT BE wondering what drifting continents have to do with the natural history of a mountain meadow and its cirque. Well, I'll tell you, beginning with the reason continents wander.

How and Why Continents Move

The Earth is composed of distinct layers, the deeper of which are heavier materials that are hotter, denser, and under much greater pressure than the shallower, upper layers. The Earth's surface is composed mostly of water, which covers about 70 percent of it in the form of oceans. The rest is rock that forms the continents we live on, the world, as we know it.

The jigsaw configuration of rigid, floating continents, typically 31 to 62 miles thick, is called "the tectonic plates," which drift a few inches each year atop the highly viscous (thick and sticky), mechanically weak region of the Earth between 62 and 155 miles deep. Although the source of heat is small compared to the sun's energy showering on the surface, the insulating property of the Earth's rocks is sufficient to keep this region viscous in consistency. Moreover, the deeper into the Earth one goes, the hotter it gets until it reaches the aforementioned temperature of about 4,000 to 6,700 degrees Fahrenheit around a depth of 1,700 miles. ("Tectonic" is from the Greek *tektonikos*, "pertaining to building," from *tekton*, "builder, carpenter.")

Here, very slow convection currents provide horizontal forces that move the tectonic plates, much as convection in a pan of boiling water causes something floating on its surface to be pushed sideways. Whereas the boiling water takes only seconds to move its floating material, the Earth's convection currents require 10 to 100 million years to move the tectonic plates; yet the principles remain the same.

1.1 Volcanic debris and lava in the Oregon Cascades.

In turn, "plate tectonics"—the cause of earthquakes—is the phenomenon wherein one plate crashes into and is forced under another. Ultimately, volcanoes and earthquakes are simply the surface expressions of physical dynamics occurring deep within the Earth.

The Cascade Mountains Rise

Now, jumping forward to around 36 million years ago, the oceanic plate in the Pacific was being pushed downward and forced under the continental plate of North America. As the oceanic plate was being submerged under the continental plate, some areas of the oceanic plate melted. In other regions, however, the continental plate was bent backward and upward, forming mountain ranges, a phenomenon that encircles the Pacific Ocean with "The Ring of Fire," which contains 75 percent of the Earth's terrestrial volcanoes, both dormant and active.

Volcanic activity in the Ring of Fire began forming the Cascade Mountain Range about 5 million years ago, at which time more than 3,000 volcanic vents erupted. However, it was not until 1.6 million years ago that the major peaks started growing. Today, the mountain range, usually referred to simply as "The Cascades," forms a curve that parallels the shoreline of the Pacific Ocean between 100 to 150 miles inland and stretches more than 700 miles, from British Columbia, Canada, southward to Northern California.

Within the Cascades is a string of 13 main volcanic centers and thousands of small, transitory volcanoes that have produced raised areas of volcanic debris and lava. (Photo 1.1) The Cascades of western Oregon, volcanic in origin, are composed of two distinct time frames: the Western Cascades being the older and more eroded of the two, and the High Cascades being the younger with prominent volcanic peaks. (Photo 1.2)

The volcanoes were formed as a remnant of the once-vaster oceanic plate (now largely under the continent) was forced beneath North America. As the oceanic plate moved beneath the continent, it was pushed deeper into the Earth, which caused enormous pressures and high temperatures to build, a process that, in turn, released the water within the rocks.

1.2 Prominent volcanic peaks of the High Oregon Cascades.

As the water vapor rose, it passed through the flexible layer covering the sinking oceanic plate, which resulted in some of the rock melting to form magma (from the Greek *magma*, "thick ointment"). The magma was then forced upward, erupting on the continental surface, where it created a string of volcanoes. (Photo 1.3) And the process continues, as witnessed by the 1980 eruption of Mount St. Helens in Washington State.

1.3 Tam McArthur Rim, composed of ancient lava flows, in the foreground, and the Three Sisters of the Oregon Cascades in the background.

According to Indigenous American legend, however, the Cascade Mountains were formed because Indians living in eastern Washington and Oregon beseeched Ocean to send his sons and daughters, Clouds and Rain, to bless their land. But no matter how much water was dropped onto the Earth, the Indians wanted more. Clouds and Rain were away so long that Ocean became lonely and went looking for his children. When the Indians demanded that Clouds and Rain remain over their land, an angry Ocean pleaded with the Great Spirit to punish their avarice. In answer, Great Spirit scooped up massive handfuls of earth and formed a barrier between the dry country of the ungrateful Indians and the moisture-laden riches of Ocean.

So it is today that the proximity of the Cascades to the Pacific Ocean, and its onshore-flowing westerly winds, creates the region's substantial precipitation, especially on the western slopes, where winter's snow has accumulated to a depth of 83 feet in some areas. Most of the volcanic peaks of the High Cascades are therefore white year 'round. At the same time, they puncture the clouds, causing them to drop their precipitation, which steals moisture from the mountains' eastern flanks and beyond, in what is termed a "rain shadow effect."

Birth of the Meadow

A volcano is built from within by fire and eroded from without by wind, water, and ice. It defies gravity in its growing, and yet obeys gravity in its dying. Volcanoes that form mountains are not eternal, however, but rather come and go, are born and die, in concert with all living things.

Thus, through processes of weathering, landforms are shaped by wind, water, and ice, as rock is broken down physically and chemically into smaller and smaller pieces that eventually comprise one part of the soil; plants, animals, and their interactions complete the soil's foundation. In turn, soil, which is like an exchange membrane between the living and nonliving components of Earth, is dynamic and ever-changing.

So, if you could go back 25,000 years, you would find a world in which winters grew colder and longer, while summers grew cooler and shorter. Over time, more snow was added to a high, volcanic peak in the Oregon Cascades than melted. As the accumulating weight gradually forced air out of the settling snow, it began not only to lose its light, fluffy texture but also to form dense layers of granular crystals of ice, which eventually became a glacier. Because winter storms regularly supplied more snow than melted during summer, the glacier continued to grow in both volume and weight. With time, the glacier, impelled by gravity, began to move down the mountainside over the underlying bedrock.

As it moved, the quarrying action of the glacier's base was facilitated by water entering cracks in the rocks where, in freezing, the entrapped ice expanded until it exerted a pressure in excess of 30,000 pounds per square inch, which far exceeded the strength of the rock—splitting it. Thus, small stones, sharp fragments of various sizes, and large boulders tumbled down and became embedded in the ice, thereby adding their weight to the glacier and were carried away. The abrasive action of the rocks, now frozen into the glacier's base, excavated the underlying surface, which allowed the glacier to sink ever deeper into the trench it was cutting for itself, polishing and smoothing some rocky surfaces in its passing, while gouging grooves and furrows into others.

Although covered each winter by new snow, the dirty ice deep within the glacier, now between 1,000 and 2,000 feet thick, was doing its work. Impregnated with whole rocks, sharp fragments, and grit, the blackened ice removed and transported large quantities of material, scouring the area as it bulldozed along its margins, undermining and steepening the rock walls, and gradually forming the cliffs of today (from the Old Norse "klif"). Over the centuries, avalanches of rock fell on top of the glacier, adding their weight to its cutting power.

However, the glacier did not move very far down the mountain before the climate began to change. As summers became warmer and longer, and the amount of snowfall progressively decreased, the glacier melted more each year (Photo 1.4) until it retreated into its bowl-shaped cirque and then disappeared altogether. ("Cirque" comes from the French, meaning "arena.") (Photos 1.5, 1.6)

1.4 A melting glacier on Mount Hood in the Oregon Cascades with its landscape of boulders; smaller rocks; pebbles; and fine, flourlike material created by the moving glacier and collectively called glacial till.

1.5 Cirque with minimal glacial till and no moraine, which is a ridge of loosely accumulated glacial till.

Then, one September day, 10,000 years ago, a tiny spider climbed to the top of a large boulder and raised the rear of its body in the air, almost standing on its head. From the tip of its abdomen, it ejected a mass of silken threads from its spinnerets into the breeze. Suddenly, without visible warning, the spider was jerked off the boulder and borne skyward to join other spiders riding the warm, afternoon wind flowing up the mountainside from the valley below.

1.6 Cirque on Three Fingered Jack in the Oregon Cascades, with its lake and the small stream draining it; lateral moraine, which is a ridge of loosely accumulated glacial till; talus (which is visible at the bottom of this photo) and the meadow below the lake.

If you could have traveled with that spider, you would have seen the last dirty, melting ice of the once-dominant glacier as it completed its transformation under the summer sun, not only rising skyward as water vapor to join the clouds and rivers of air but also flowing down the mountain as water in streams and rivers to join the sea. You would have seen the debris—boulders, smaller rocks, pebbles, and flourlike material, collectively called glacial till—spread several feet thick over a broad area just below the cirque to the east, south, and west. (Photo 1.7)

Water from the melting ice carved several small stream courses through the debris over the centuries, as it flowed south from the cirque, gradually forming a single stream in what would become the meadow, as the glacier, vanquished at last by the sun, gave up in total retreat. Thus beginning, growing, and ending in the same location, a place now greatly and forever changed, the glacier, as sculptor, dissolved into the ever-fading light of history.

1.7 Glacial till, minus the large boulders.

Time passed, and the seeds of such plants as fireweed, asters, and woolly sunflowers came riding winds from distant places, and parachuted out of the sky. Others, such as bedstraw and beggar-tick, came riding attached to the hair of deer and elk, as well as to the hair of their predators, pumas and wolves, and fell onto the stony debris. Although most seeds were eaten by deer mice venturing among the rocks or by passing birds, some survived to germinate and grow. Again, most were eaten, and again some survived to maturity and shed their seeds. Each year more and more seeds were sown, and decade after decade, century after century the stony surface gradually became clothed in the pioneering forbs and grasses, whose living and dying began to build the soil that supported them.

As the plants occupied the available space, they harvested the only true investment the meadow would ever know, energy from solar radiation (materialized sunlight). It works like this:

Green plants capture sunlight through chlorophyll molecules and use its energy to synthesize carbohydrates (plant sugars) from carbon dioxide and water through a process known as photosynthesis (from the Greek *phos*, "light" and *synthesis*, "putting together"). This energetic fusion, derived from the sun (an original input), combined with carbon dioxide and water, as well as nutrients from the soil in which the plants grow (already existing chemical elements), is the basis for sustaining the life processes of all plants, and thus all higher forms of life—including you and me.

Think of it this way: a plant (an array of solar panels) uses the green chlorophyll molecule (a *photoreceptor*, meaning "receiver of light") to collect sunlight (energy) within chloroplasts (small, enclosed structures in the plant that are analogous to individual solar panels). Then, the sun's light is used, through photosynthesis, to convert carbon dioxide and water to sugars (analogous to electricity) as usable energy for the plant (which is partially sustained by chemical elements in the soil, where, incidentally, most of the water is also derived). This process is comparable to converting the sun's light in solar panels on the roof of a building (derived from recycled energy in the form of already-existing materials) into electricity for our use. These plant sugars, in turn, are partly stored energy from the sun—a new input of energy into the global ecosystem—and partly the storage of existing energy from the amalgam of carbon dioxide and water, a process sustained in part by chemical elements in the form of nutrients from the soil.

Therefore, when we eat green plants, such as lettuce or cabbage, the sugars (carbohydrates)—partly new energy from the sun and partly recycled energy from the soil—are altered through digestion into the various types of energy our bodies require for their physiological functions. The *excess* energy (that which is not required for physiological functions) is expended in the form of physical motion, such as work, or expelled as bodily waste. On the other hand, it is different when eating meat because the animal has already used the sun's contribution to the energy matrix in its own bodily functions and its own physical acts of living, so all we get from eating flesh is recycled energy.

When plants in the evolving meadow died, they became organic material that, on decomposing, began lending the young soil its dark color (termed *humus*, Latin for "the ground," "soil"). The accumulating humus provided many important functions, including absorbing and holding water, which acts as a weak acid, and forming a physical structure within the soil, such as the pores that allow biological activity to exist. The porous nature of the soil also provided a mechanism for holding both water and chemicals in place, as well as air, which is required for chemical interactions. Incorporation of organic material into the surface of the soil, where the dark layer of "topsoil" forms, was rapid when considered in the scale of geological time but exceedingly slow when considered in the scale of a human lifetime.

As the glacial debris at the cirque's base became progressively inhabited by early plants that died and recycled through the rocky material, viruses, bacteria, fungi, one-celled animals called protozoa, and eventually earthworms began to play critical roles wherein they both increasingly created and maintained the biological and physical ("biophysical") integrity and fertility of the developing soil by voiding their bodily wastes into it, as well as their bodies when death claimed them.

As the total productivity and respiration of the developing soil increased, so, too, did the biological diversity within the soil's food web. The greater the number and kinds of organisms and their interactions within the circuitry of recycling organic material and mixing it into the soil through their activities, the greater became the abundance of nutrients retained in the soil. These interactions included prey, their predators, and the predators of the predators.

It was only through this belowground food web that plants were able to sustainably obtain the nutrients necessary for their growth. And so it was, that the complex, biologically driven functions of the belowground organisms, which regulated the biophysical processes that translated into a soil's productivity, developed slowly over hundreds of years to eventually become the cirque's meadow.

Part II: The Cirque

As a young man wandering the high-mountain trails, I fished, hunted, trapped and gathered much of my food, and sometimes, even with the quarry in the sights of my rifle, I went hungry.

Me at 19, living in the forest.

Shortly after I was discharged from the military at 18 years of age, I headed for the high country. I had been alone in the mountains for almost two weeks and had been subsisting on fried grasshoppers, crayfish, and trout. Game seemed to have vanished, taking their tracks with them. Finally, after three days without food, I found the fresh sign of a deer, and began tracking it. Following its trail was easy. Being quiet was difficult, however, even wearing moccasins, because the country was so dry that everything crackled underfoot.

I tracked the deer for several hours, as its trail led me up through the spruce-fir forest into clusters of subalpine firs and white-bark pine interspersed with small openings, where the lower edge of a beautiful mountain meadow met the forest. It was late afternoon when I slipped into a peninsula of firs and, peering through their boughs to the far side of a small finger of the meadow, saw the deer—a magnificent buck. I stood motion-less, watching it, feeling the warmth of the sun, seeing the wispy clouds sweeping clean the great, blue vault of the sky. Somewhere a Swainson thrush sang, its liquid melody drifting on the soft breeze. A fly buzzed. A raven croaked. I stood in a moment of Cosmic perfection, a moment in which I disappeared into the nothingness from which all creation comes and into which all creation returns.

Me at 20, in the Oregon Cascades.

"My brother," I whispered quietly, "today I go hungry, for today is yours to live. If I see you tomorrow, I will feast on your body, but not today." I then turned and walked away without the deer ever knowing I was there. And, so I came to the meadow, stream, and cirque, but I never saw the deer again.

The cirque, as it turned out, is a complex of seven interconnected habitats: the lake, cliff, moraines, and talus all surrounded on the west, north, and east by the meadow. From the cirque's lake, a stream flows southward through the meadow into the forest that borders its lower edge. It is here, among these interconnected habitats, that our story takes place.

So, let us take a journey through time.

Chapter 2:
The Cirque
and Its Talus

As the glacier melted, innumerable rocks, from the size of pebbles to giant boulders, covered the slope below the cirque's slightly semicircular portion of the cliff. And still rocks fall from the heights, adding to the growing depth of the "talus," or "scree," as such rock-strewn slopes are known. (Photo 2.1) Whereas small rocks remain near the cliff's base, larger rocks are more respondent to the call of gravity and come to rest farther down slope. In fact, the larger the rock the farther it tumbles downhill, helping to create the irregular, boulder-strewn edge of the meadow.

2.1 Talus, with water seeping into the meadow from winter's melting snow.

With the warming days of late May 1567, and the quiet melting of the snow along where the southern edge of the talus meets the meadow, western spring beauties and avalanche lilies begin to awaken from their winter sleep. Their arousal is accompanied by the first, tiny roots extending themselves into the rich soil from whence they draw life's nourishment.

As the days continue to lengthen, and the snow to melt, delicate tips of leaves become visible as tiny, green protrusions through decaying, straw-colored grasses of a bygone summer. Day by day, they reach infinitesimally higher and wider until the day they are joined by the first flower buds of the season, their tender stems reaching toward the life-giving light of the sun.

Day after day, the stems grow higher, the buds larger, and the snow melts. Finally, the time comes when the last vestige of snow disappears from the small, exposed areas flooded with sunlight. It is here that the first buds of the western spring beauty open and expose their small, oval, five-petaled blossoms of pink, with their accentuated notched tips and darker longitudinal lines. Within days, the six-petaled avalanche lilies open to mirror the color of the sun's brilliant, yellow sphere, as their slender petals curl gently backward. Thus, the first flowers of spring adorn the meadow.

Rock Rabbits

Meanwhile, activity deep within the snow-covered talus begins to increase during the second week of March, when the rock rabbits become sexually aroused. Although I will refer to them as "rock rabbits" because they belong to the scientific Order that includes rabbits and hares, their most frequently used name is "pika," from their Mongolian name, which is properly pronounced "peeka." (Photo 2.2)

An adult rock rabbit, weighing a little more than five ounces, is about eight inches long, including its tiny, inconspicuous tail. Its broad, rounded ears, a little less than an inch in width, are blackish with a distinct white margin. The soles of its feet are covered with rather stiff, woolly hair, which gives it excellent traction on and silent running over the rocks of its home. The soft fur on the upper parts of its body is uniform reddish-brown, slightly darkened over the back by black-tipped hairs, whereas the belly is tannish, and the throat is reddish-brown.

2.2 Rock rabbit, Oregon Cascades.

Largely intolerant of one another's proximity throughout much of the year, the breeding season relaxes the usual social barriers. Although three feet of snow still covers the talus, the long, inviting "songs" of the males and the short, answering calls of the females herald the onset of breeding.

This is a time when adult males and females with adjoining territories form mated pairs. However, one female becomes choosy because the territories of four males surround hers. On the 5th of April, she selects a male with whom to breed.

As the days pass, she begins feeling the babies moving inside her. This sense grows stronger until the 5th of May, when she settles into her nest of vegetation situated in a snug crevice (they don't dig burrows) two feet below the rocky surface of the talus. Here she waits for half an hour. Then, one of three little miracles of life begins to appear, each born blind and scantily furred, weighing about three-tenths of an ounce, but with fully erupted teeth.

With her babies tucked safely in the nest, the mother ventures to the meadow's edge to eat, where she, like all the pikas, selects plants that have the most calories, proteins, fats, and water. After eating for about two hours, she returns to nurse her young, thereafter going to the meadow again for another meal. This is a rhythm she will maintain all day, every day until her youngsters are weaned.

For their part, the growing babies open their eyes on the 14th of May, and become independent on May 28th, about the same time they are weaned. The breeding season now over for the female, she again practices mutual intolerance of the male, as her youngsters emerge from the inner protection of the talus. Although they stay in the general area in which they were born, they avoid their relatives as much as possible.

Elsewhere in the talus, however, a female, whose first litter was found and killed by a long-tailed weasel, has been impregnated a second time. It is mid June. The cirque and its surrounding meadow are bathed in sunlight, and the blue of the sky is reflected in the water of its small lake nestled between the cliff and the moraines, which are ridges of loosely accumulated glacial debris about 20 feet high and 43 feet wide (Photo 2.3) that embrace the east and west sides of the lake, extending outward from the cliff some 200 feet.

2.3 Lateral moraine.

At the south end of the lake, where the stream flows out of the cirque's bowl, there is a small band of streamside soil that hosts mountain willows and a sparse carpet of herbaceous vegetation in various shades of green and brown that, earlier in the year, sported the pink of spring beauties and the yellow of glacier lilies. The sides of the cirque have been somewhat softened in outline over the centuries by rocks of various sizes breaking off the steep cliffs and accumulating at the bottom in curved slopes, forming the now-clearly-visible talus.

Along the bottom of the talus, where it joins the meadow, there are small islands of finer material that pass for soil and support a meager variety of plants, such as green parsley fern, the creamy-yellow blossoms and pale-green leaves of the succulent stonecrop (Photo 2.4), and the bright yellow blossoms and dark-green leaves of cinquefoil. Where the talus meets the meadow on the south side of the cirque, there is an abundance of herbaceous vegetation surrounding the base of the rocky rubble, including mountain willows, some of which are three to four feet tall and almost as wide.

2.4 Stonecrop.

If you could be here and sit quietly atop a boulder to listen and watch, you would soon hear the nasal *waaa, waaa, waaa, oink, waaa* of a rock rabbit, and then another, as here and there they magically appear in the midst of sun-drenched boulders. The call is usually made from the top of a rock or from the doorway of a cavern between rocks. If you were to sit still long enough, you might hear a trill of alarm and catch a small, reddish-brown blur, as a rabbit dives into the protection of the nearest crevice. And occasionally, you will hear a faint call from deep within the rabbit's rocky fortress.

If you then continue to sit quietly and scan the talus, you will see a small curve on a sun-drenched boulder, and a pair of tiny, black eyes watching you. (Photo 2.5) But, to see these wee creatures scampering silently and deftly over the roughest rocks on fur-cushioned feet, you must either catch a flicker of movement out of the corner of your eye or be able to pick out the white margin of a small, round ear that is somehow out of place in this high, mountain world of jags and angles.

2.5 Rock rabbit, Oregon Cascades.

From now to early autumn, they can be seen from sunup to mid-morning and from mid-afternoon until dusk, although some activity seems to be ongoing during all hours. Their nighttime activity, however, is confined to the safety of the talus and consists mostly of calling, a vocalization that alerts other pikas of impending danger. Nighttime disturbances are instantly noted and immediately challenged vocally. During the breeding season, territorial calls are given on bright, moonlit nights throughout the talus.

These little denizens of the cirque find no discomfort in either the heat of summer or the cold of winter, for they keep cool deep in their rocky caverns during the hottest of days, and warm in their snug nests deep under the snow during the coldest of nights. The rabbits are alert, keen of sight and hearing, and quick to dive into the depths of the talus at the first hint of danger.

When active in the open, they use lookout stations between their home areas and the meadow, where they gather vegetation to carry back to their portion of the talus. If you could visit the talus today, the 13th of June, you would see adult rabbits emerge from the rocky depths with the growing light of day, and make their way to the meadow. Once there, they begin gathering mouthful after mouthful of vegetation and transporting them to their own territories within the talus, where they store it under the protective cover of the boulders. This "hay gathering" will continue until the beginning of November, unless a heavy, early snow makes the vegetation of the meadow temporarily inaccessible.

Rock rabbits eat a wide variety of plants, including parsley fern, stonecrops, grasses, sedges, thistles, fireweed, and shrubs, although subalpine lupine is especially favored. However, forbs and tall grass tend to be harvested for the "haypiles," rather than eaten directly. ("Haypiles" is a term natural historians have traditionally used with respect to rock rabbits.)

If you are observant and know something about the nutritional quality of the vegetation, you may notice that the male you are watching is harvesting the plants in a deliberate sequence that corresponds to their seasonal pattern of growth. He seems to assess the nutritional value of available food, and harvests it accordingly, selecting those plants that have the highest caloric content, the most protein and fatty substance, as well as the most water.

As you watch, the rabbits are busy carrying one mouthful of

vegetation after another from the meadow to their home areas, where it will provide their primary source of nutrition during the winter, as well as new vegetation for nests. An individual's storage area often forms a complex of haypiles, some of which may grow so large that they eventually spill out of the internal confines of the talus and become visible in the openings among the boulders. (Photo 2.6) Although they usually store enough hay for over 300 days of food, they normally use about 175 days worth in a given winter.

2.6 Rock rabbit haypile, Oregon Cascades.

In addition to the haypiles, rock rabbits also produce soft, black, shiny strings of feces that form in the *caecum*, which is a pouch-like structure between the small and large intestine. (Photo 2.7) The caecum is a specialized adaptation of the digestive system that allows the rabbits to effectively digest non-fibrous sugars, but quickly exclude from their digestive tracts the relatively indigestible fiber in their diet, while simultaneously allowing digestion of readily fermented, highly complex sugars. Therefore, because *caecal pellets* have more energy value than stored plant food in a haypile, the rabbits either consume them directly or store them for later.

They do not, however, use the same storage areas every year. Despite how the haypiles are moved around over the years, they form the center of the rock rabbits' social organization.

2.7 The round pellets are rock rabbit fecal material (waste material) and the dark material stuck to the grass are caecal pellets, most of which are reingested.

If you were to watch one particularly hungry male, you would see him make 130 trips to the meadow to eat. (Photo 2.8) His eating is rabbit-like in that a large leaf is seized at the tip and drawn into his mouth with rapid chewing motions, without the assistance of his forefeet, because Nature did not design his feet to manipulate objects. In addition to feeding, he makes just over 200 trips to gather vegetation for his haypiles during the sun's journey across the heavens.

His trips to the meadow are periodically interrupted, however, by chasing other rabbits for trespassing in his territory, being chased for trespassing in another's territory, calling, periods of observation, grooming, and heeding predator alerts sounded by rabbits elsewhere in the talus. In turn, he defends his own specific area against the trespass of others by vocalizing, consistently spacing his haypiles, chasing trespassers, fighting, and marking his territory by rubbing secretions on strategic rocks from well-developed chin glands, as well as depositing his small, hard, brown fecal pellets in certain locations to mark his territorial boundaries.

2.8 Mountain meadow in the Oregon Cascades with Mt. Jefferson in the background.

Now mid June, with haying in full progress, young rock rabbits continue to appear on the surface of the talus and display their first territorial behavior with high-pitched calls for about a week after they emerge. Within two weeks, the calls of the young are indistinguishable from those of the adults, who become intolerant of the youngsters soon after they become independent of parental care and seek territories of their own, igniting competition.

There is a clear difference between the male's territory and his home range. His territory, which accounts for just over half of the total area he uses on a daily basis, is that part of his home range he defends against the intrusion of other rock rabbits, such as the area around his nest and haypiles, as well as his route to and from the meadow and the quality of the vegetation in his designated "hay field." The rest of the area that he normally uses (his "home range") can be shared. Nevertheless, the distance between the male and his neighbors is greatest during the haying season of early and mid summer, but shrinks as late summer and autumn brings haying to an end. And it is during the waning days of autumn that the entire rabbit community fills the talus with song.

It is the first week in July, and the female who was impregnated a second time is about to give birth. Because the production of milk with which she fed her first set of four babies reduced her body's fat reserves so severely, this is the only time in her life that she has produced a second litter of two.

Time passes. July melds into August. The young rabbits from the mother's second litter start to appear on the surface of the talus and begin displaying their first territorial behavior within a week through high-pitched calls. Being new to a world that, in turn, is new to them, the young lack alertness when they first emerge, and so are vulnerable to predators.

The Long-tailed Weasel

As the high-mountain summer begins to wane, and August slips into September, and the sun floods the talus with early morning warmth, a sudden commotion erupts among the boulders. A male long-tailed weasel is chasing a rock rabbit. The rabbit runs in and out among the boulders, the weasel in close pursuit. Seemingly tireless, the long-bodied, bounding weasel closes in for the kill. Alarm calls from rabbits in various parts of the slope accompany the chase, but hunter and hunted are silent.

A massive, granite boulder looms in front of the rabbit; it turns to the right at the cost of precious distance. Coupled with its speed, precision of movement, and judgment, the weasel, now within striking distance, seizes the handiest portion of the rock rabbit's body with its teeth and quickly throws its own body in a loose, snakelike coil over the rabbit. This maneuver effectively subdues the rabbit's frantic struggling, and allows the weasel to shift its initial grip to the back of the head and neck for the killing bite, all the while arching its body around the rabbit by holding it with all four feet.

A pained, panic-stricken squeal—silence. This brief intrusion into the background of silence is the sole acknowledgment of death.

The weasel emerges and moves toward the foot of the talus and its nest, the rabbit limp in its mouth. The rabbit is no longer a rabbit. It has suddenly become a meal. And though the essence of the rock rabbit's mortal being has fled with the snap of jaws and the ensuing silence, it shall, in some ageless way, live on in the weasel and in the weasel's weasels. This rock rabbit shall influence the lives of all animals that come into contact with this weasel and the generations of weasels to come from the consummation of this life and this death. Thus, from the first breath of life until the last, all living things are part of one another.

So it is that weasels, both long-tailed and short-tailed, are the rock rabbits' main predators because they can penetrate the rocky fortress and either kill the adults or carry off whole litters of young from their nests. Even though martens, Cascade red foxes, and bobcats are too large to follow the rabbits into their talus, when the rabbits see them approaching, they still warn one another, even at the expense of being seen by the predator. The same is true for golden eagles and northern goshawks, which patrol the meadow's edge during the summer and autumn, returning to the warmer lowlands for winter. But they are markedly silent when a weasel is near because, with its snakelike body, a weasel can follow a pika anywhere, leaving little chance of escaping the sharp, needlelike fangs.

On reaching a small cavern within a clump of boulders near the meadow's edge, the weasel deposits his meal next to a commandeered rabbit's nest, renovated with fur plucked from his prey, and the renovation continues. Sitting next to his nest, he laps the blood oozing from the rabbit's wound. Once the blood is licked up, he begins pulling one mouthful of fur after another from the rabbit's body, adding each to his nest, and thus preparing it for winter's chill. With the rabbit now largely naked, he settles down for a meal. Having eaten his fill, he curls his lithe, cylindrical body into his nest, his head to his tail in the shape of a circle to conserve heat, closes his eyes, and goes to sleep.

He is almost 20 inches long, of which about 7 inches is tail, and weighs just over 11 ounces. He is, however, about twice the size of most females.

Weasels, one of the smaller predators in this high-mountain world, have long, slender, sinuous bodies; hairy, slightly bushy tails; and short legs. Their heads are small, horizontally flattened, and taper to a blunt nose. Their ears are prominent, round, and hairy, and their feet terminate in five toes, each of which has a small, curved, sharp claw. All together, their bodies are perfectly formed for pursuing prey into surprisingly tight spaces.

Their pelage is short, moderately fine, but not thick. In summer, they vary from brown to yellowish-brown on the back, sides, and the outsides of the legs, including the feet, but are darkest on the face and tail, the latter terminating in a distinct black tip. There may be some white hairs on the face. The throat, chest, belly, and insides of the legs vary from yellowish-white, light yellowish, dark yellowish, to orange. Although long-tailed weasels in the lower elevations west of the Cascades retain essentially the same color of their pelage throughout the year, those inhabiting the talus, meadow, and forest edge are entirely white in winter with the exception of their eyes, nose, and black tip on their tails. Occasionally, as winter progresses, the underside and the tail may show some sign of a yellowish stain.

As a predator, the long-tailed weasel is well adapted for either an open chase or pursuit of its prey in a burrow, such as gophers. In the open, its long, bounding, tireless pursuit can wear down prey to a point the outcome is without question. The same weasel can wend its way through any burrow system wide enough for its head to enter.

On the 6th of May, about the same time the baby rock rabbits were coming into the world, a female weasel is giving birth to seven babies in a clean, snug nest of vegetation in the belowground, food-storage chamber of a Mazama pocket gopher located about 50 yards into the meadow from the end of the western moraine. The female keeps the natal nest clean by using another of the late gopher's food-storage chambers some distance from the nest as a latrine in which she defecates and urinates.

Each baby arrives pink and wrinkled with a few sparse, rather long, white hairs on the head and back. They have very long necks, resembling those of their parents, and weigh about one-tenth of an ounce when a day old. Their fur grows rapidly, and by May 20th they are covered with silky, white fur, which is longest on the back of the head, neck, and over the shoulders.

Although their eyes will not open until the 11th of June, they begin eating meat on May 23rd and will be weaned on the 20th of June. Meanwhile, their mother will come into heat on the 3rd of August, 90 days after giving birth, and will remain in heat for several weeks if she is not bred.

The young females, of which there are four, will become sexually mature by the time they are three months old, and will be bred by adult males during their first summer of life. Although the gestation period ranges from 205 to 337 days, females have what is known as "delayed implantation," which means an embryo is not implanted until 27 days before birth, after which its development is rapid.

The three, young males, on the other hand, will not become sexually mature until the following spring, when they are 10 to 11 months old. Their testes will begin to grow actively with the onset of their first spring molt, at which time viable sperm will be produced.

Thereafter, their testes will begin to enlarge in late March, reach their maximum size in April, but will shrink again rapidly during August and the first of September, reaching their minimum size by mid-September. The increase and decrease in the size of the testes correlates with the onset of the spring and autumn molts. Adult males have sperm in their testes and are fertile from April through August, but most females are probably bred during July.

Now, as mature adults, both the males and females have the ability to "weasel" their way in and out of almost anywhere they want to go, in addition to which these sinuous-bodied carnivores are exceedingly quick in their reflexes. When hunting, they seem to use the senses of smell, sight, and hearing, which undoubtedly aid them in capturing a wide variety of prey under varied circumstances. Depending primarily on mammals for food, insects and birds are also captured and eaten, as well as an occasional Cascade frog or a western terrestrial garter snake.

But for now, the late afternoon sun is approaching the western horizon, and haying is in full progress. Here and there, a rabbit calls from the talus, then another, and another. It is a quiet afternoon with clear, blue skies and light breezes that dance and whirl over the meadow on their way to the talus and the small lake in the cirque, rustling the dead stalks of summer's grasses in their passing. The breezes skip and skidder over the surface of the water, ruffling it hither and yon as they dart back again to the meadow along the stream flowing out of the cirque.

Bushy-tailed Woodrats

As night approaches, there is a quiet rustling in the cliff above the talus, as a female bushy-tailed woodrat awakens and moves around in her nest of vegetation tucked into a small, cave-like crevice 20 feet up in the cliff toward the eastern edge of the talus, where a variety of vegetation is growing amid the scattered boulders. (Photo 2.9) To enter her cavern, she must go through a crevice so small that she barely fits; however, the entrance protects her open, cup-like nest, which is a little over six inches in diameter, from every predator—except a weasel.

2.9 Bushy-tailed woodrat.

Although the actual nest of the male living toward the upper end of the talus is similar to that of the female, it is nearly eight inches in diameter. Situated on a pile of smaller rocks within the talus, where three boulders form a semi-enclosed cavity, his nest is protected by a fortress-like pile of middens (= rubbish) across the entrance. To create his midden pile, the male collects debris from neighboring areas—which he considers "collectables." After all, he and his kind are not called "packrats" for nothing.

In addition to the "collectables," he adds the remains of plants and his feces to the growing pile. Speaking of feces, I once watched a male bushy-tailed woodrat in his nest. Shortly after going to sleep, he defecated, but instead of soiling his cuplike nest, he grasped each fecal pellet with his front teeth as it was expelled and, with a flip of his head, tossed it away from the nest. By all appearances, this procedure did not interrupt his sleep.

As well as his feces, some of which is soft and tar like, he urinates on his middens, which not only infiltrates but also crystallizes and solidifies the middens as he builds it, forming the protective "fortress." The crystallization is due to the large amounts of dissolved calcium carbonate and calcium oxalates contained in his urine. The high oxalate content comes from many of the succulent plants he eats and progressively adds to the middens over the weeks and months.

Because the woodrats have a penchant for collecting objects that strike their fancy, as they move about their home ranges, it is not surprising that both sexes help themselves to the various haypiles of the rock rabbits in obtaining cured vegetation for their loosely constructed inner nests, as well as vegetation gleaned from within certain areas of the talus and the sparse vegetation growing along the base of the cliff.

With darkness settling over the meadow, the female moves eastward and downward toward the boulder-strewn edge of the meadow to forage, while the male goes to a different border of the talus, where an island of vegetation is flourishing. Although they are difficult to see in the gathering darkness, the growing light of the moon allows a great horned owl, who has both excellent night vision and color vision, to see the scampering rodents, ranging in body size from 13 to almost 19 inches long, with tails from 6 to just over 9 inches, and weighing from 6 to almost 16 ounces, with the female on smaller end of the scale.

As the moonlight brightens, the owl sees two large woodrats with long, bushy tails, large ears with little hair, long whiskers, and a soft, almost woolly pelage. Their backs vary from a dark grayish-brown to a somewhat reddish-brown, being darkest along the middle from the head to the base of the tail. Their sides are lighter and more brownish, and their underside varies from gray to light gray with areas of clear white. The tail has two types of hairs: short, light-gray woolly hairs and long, straight hairs, which are dark gray to blackish. On the underside of their tails, the hairs vary from light brown, to light gray, to white. The tops of their feet and toes, including the claws, are white.

What the owl cannot see, however, is the prominent gland in the skin of each woodrat near the lower middle of the belly (technically "abdomen"), where the shorter hairs are stained yellowish. This gland, which is most prominent in the male, is used for scent marking both to attract reproductively active females and to mark his territory and thereby establish his dominance. However, physical confrontations between males can erupt, consisting largely of biting and scratching, and may result in serious injury.

2.10 Urine territorial post of a bushy-tailed woodrat.

In addition, both males and females use "urinating posts." They appear as white streaks and blotches on the rocks, which harden and can accumulate to a thickness of several inches over many years and generations. (Photo 2.10) This "whitewash" is the result of microcrystalline encrustations consisting primarily of calcite, particularly calcium oxalates.

Despite being vulnerable to predation while foraging along the edge of the talus, they must eat. Being primarily vegetarians, they select a wide variety of plants, including truffles (the fleshy, edible, underground fruiting body of a fungus) when such are available, carrying some to the area of their nests, where they build food caches to use during the winter months because they do not hibernate. (The word "truffle" is derived in a round-about way from a modification of Middle French *truffe,* from Old Occitan *trufa,* from Vulgar Latin *tufera,* which is akin to Latin *tumēre,* "to swell.") (Photo 2.11)

2.11 A truffle, the fleshy, edible, underground fruiting body of a fungus.

Although usually solitary and territorial, except with close rela-tives, they communicate with one another by thumping their feet on the substrate when alarmed. At times, however, they will also drum when undisturbed, producing a slow, tapping sound.

About the time both the rock rabbit and the weasel are giving birth, the female woodrat is being bred. Because gestation takes from 27 to 32 days, she gives birth on June 4th. To give birth, she sits in a crouched position with the top of her head against the rocky bottom of her rocky home. With the onset of labor, her whole body trembles spasmodically until a youngster appears, after which the trembling stops for two to three minutes while the newly born baby creeps under her body and attaches itself to a nipple. Then her body begins to tremble again and continues until the next youngster is born, when it too attaches itself to a nipple. The process is identical for the birth of each baby, which, in a litter of four (three males and one female), takes a total of about 15 minutes. After the last baby is attached to a nipple, the mother rises and pulls them into the nest. The only sign of the birthing process is a small, wet spot.

The babies are born naked, blind, and helpless. The eyes of the first two open on June 17th, while those of the third open on June 19th, and those of the fourth open on June 20th. The babies remain firmly attached to their mother's nipples. Although the males will gain an average of about thirteen one-hundredths of an ounce per day for the first 25 days, the single female will gain a little less.

Before they are weaned, during the first week in July, the babies continue to remain firmly attached to their mother's teats most of the time. Such attachment is possible because of the development of the deciduous front teeth (termed "incisors"), which curve sideways as they grow out from the jaws, forming a diamond-shaped opening when they are brought together, a natural "locking mechanism" around the mother's teats. The locking nature of the front teeth has definite survival value in that a mother can carry her babies wherever she goes. ("Incisors" are the flat, sharp-edged teeth in the front of the mouth used for cutting food.)

Whereas the males will leave their mother in mid August, each to establish his home range and territory, the female will stay in the same area as her mother, and the two will share overlapping home ranges. The daughter will also share food caches with her mother, increasing her likelihood of survival. Moreover, a higher density of females in the talus may help attract males from other places along the cliff. Although the mother was bred again within 12 hours of giving birth and thus pregnant with a new litter while nursing the current one, the young female will not breed until she is a year old. During that time, this young, adventurous female will explore the cliff along the western edge of the talus above the lake.

Chapter 3: The Lake

Over the centuries, the hot east winds and rising thermals of summer and autumn have blown dead leaves and fine grasses into the lake from the meadow, talus, and cliff, as well the seeds of rushes, sedges, and mountain willows from the stream, some of which have landed on the lake's shore and grown. As the plant detritus cycled through the bottom sediments, it nourished algae, which, in turn, nourished a growing number of aquatic insects that followed the stream to its source. One of those insects is the water skater.

The Water Skaters

The surface of the cirque's lake is mirror-still; the world seems to momentarily hold its breath. If you were sitting quietly on a boulder along the lake's shore, watching the water, you would soon notice insects making little dimples on the surface as they zip around hunting for food and socializing in the style of water skaters.

A water skater (also called "water skipper") is really a predaceous bug, and like all true bugs, it has piercing-sucking mouthparts. What sets the water skater apart from all other insects is their ability to literally move about on top of the water's surface in any pond, river, lake, and even the open ocean. Watching them, you would soon have the feeling they were "born to skate."

The lake's water skaters have small bodies that are long and narrow, and in common with other insects, they have three pairs of legs. The first pair is the shortest and is equipped with retractable claws in the middle of each leg that are adapted to capture and puncture prey. The middle legs are longer than the first pair, but shorter than the last pair, and are adapted for propelling the skater through the water. The hind pair is the longest and is used for spreading the skater's weight over a large area of the water's surface, as well as steering it where it wants to go.

In addition, water skaters have piles of minute hairs covering their entire body at a rate of 1,000 hairs for each ⅒oth of an inch. These specialized hairs are called "hydrophobic" (from Greek *hudōr*, "water" and *phobos*, "fear of") because they repel water, and thus prevent waves, rain, or spray from sticking to the skater's body and weighing it down, a hindrance that would inhibit the skater's ability to keep its entire body on the water's surface. But, if a skater were to accidentally become submerged by a large wave, the hairs would trap air in tiny bubbles over its entire body. In turn, the bubbles not only provide buoyancy, bringing the skater to the surface again, but also provide air that allows it to breathe underwater.

Accordingly, water skaters use their long, hydrophobic legs to help them stay above water by taking advantage of its high surface tension. The surface tension is created by water molecules becoming attached to one another, thereby forming a film-like layer at the top of the water. This layer is strengthened not only by gravity pulling downward on the surface molecules in general but also by the lower water molecules pulling the upper ones downward from below.

The lake's skaters use the surface tension to their advantage through their long, slender legs that allow them to distribute their weight over a large area. Their legs are both strong and flexible, a combination that allows them to keep their weight evenly distributed and flow with the water's movement. The tiny hairs on the legs provide a hydrophobic surface, as well as a larger area of distribution for the skater's weight over the water's surface.

The middle legs are used for rowing and have particularly well-developed fringe hairs on that part of the leg in contact with the water, which helps to increase the skater's momentum. When the rowing stroke begins, the "feet" of the middle legs are quickly pressed down and backwards to create a circular surface-wave in which the crest can be used to propel the skater forward. The circular wave is essential to the skater's ability to move rapidly because it forms a "backstop" to push against. As a result, skaters often move at a rate of three feet a second, or even faster, all the while using their hind legs for steering.

If I were watching the skaters zip around on the lake, it would take me back to my childhood ditch, my friend Billy, and the skaters' secret we could never unravel. We spent many hours harassing water "skippers," as we thought of them, by poking them with long pieces of grass, or tossing little pebbles at them, just to watch them speed skate. Although we often wondered how they found the ditch each spring after winter's floods had swept away everything belonging to the previous seasons, we never discovered their secret.

We did learn through observation, however, that they were attracted to whatever new object landed suddenly on the water's surface and floated. So if our initial attempts at capturing one were unsuccessful, we threw a small piece of dry wood onto the water. As the skippers congregated about it and fought over it, we would drop a large rock into their midst, trying to disorient, and perchance stun, one or two so we could nab them.

Having caught a few, we transferred them to the livestock watering trough near Billy's house, and watched closely as their feet, surrounded by little, round shadows, made tiny dimples in the water's surface.

Although we loved watching them skate, they did not like the trough, and seldom stayed long, despite the fact that the trough was surrounded by dry pasture a goodly distance from the ditch and even farther from the creek behind Billy's house. Yet, no matter how hard we tried, we could not figure out where they went because we never saw one leave, albeit they were always gone by the next day.

One day, some years ago, while working many miles from the open water in the hot, sagebrush-covered hills of southeastern Oregon, I parked my blue-green pickup truck in the middle of nowhere, and ate lunch while sitting in the cab. All of a sudden, literally out of the blue, a funny, dark object crashed onto the hood. Without a second's thought, I leapt from the cab and caught it as it bounced around, trying to get a grip on the smooth metal with its long legs. And there, of all things, I held in my fingers a water skater that must have thought the pickup's hood was an inviting pool on whose waters it could skate!

"A water skipper! Well, I'll be.... All these years I've wondered how they find water. Billy, I know how water skippers find water! I know how they left the trough! They can fly!" Some things simply cannot be rushed, like the water skater's secret.

As it turns out, when Billy and I tossed a small piece of dry wood onto the water of our ditch and watched the "skippers" congregate about it and fight over it, we were unknowingly witnessing their feeding behavior. Skaters feed on invertebrates, primarily spiders and insects that fall on the surface of the water, where the ripples produced by the struggling prey attract the skaters.

A skater uses its front legs as sensors for the vibrations produced by the ripples in the water, after which it grabs the insect, punctures its body with its claws, and then sucks out the nutriments with its piercing-sucking mouth parts. Consequently, living prey is preferred, although skaters are opportunistic predators when it comes to the type of terrestrial insect they encounter.

On the other hand, when skaters encounter predators, they either dive into the water or fly to a neighboring pond, such as the one in the cirque's meadow that is home to the Cascade frog. Coincidentally, the latter behavior aids the skater's dispersal over a larger area of land.

Although you would not detect it by observing them on either the lake or the frog's pond, the skaters are territorial, and make it known by their vibrational patterns. Whereas adult females and males hold separate territories, the male's is usually the largest. Male skaters emit warning vibrations through the water during the mating season, and defend both their territory and the female in it.

Despite the fact that skaters are conspicuous on the water's surface and make their presence known through signals to repel other skaters, they often live in large groups. These groups usually form during the non-mating season because there is less need to compete, so they cooperate in obtaining nutrition and shelter. If, however, the group becomes overpopulated, they disperse either by flying away or by participating in cannibalism. Today, the western toad provides another means of controlling the skater's overpopulation, but it was not always that way.

Western Toads

There is a stream on the far, eastern side of the meadow that flows from a spring at the base of the cliff through the meadow into the forest, where it enters a small lake 200 feet below the cirque on a drier, southeast-facing slope. Somewhere in the silent annals of the cirque is recorded the journey of the western toad from this stream to the skaters' lake at the upper, western edge of the meadow.

If you could cut a section out of the 250-year-old Engelmann spruce that fell under the weight of snow and ice in the winter of 1570, its rings would reveal a severe drought in the year 1300. The drought, which all but dried up the small, east-side lake, sent the western toads on a journey of survival up the meager trickle from the lake's inlet up through the forest and the meadow to the cirque's northern border at the base of the cliff. The trip was leisurely, however, because they move slowly, and tend to walk, or hop, rather than jump (like frogs).

Fortunately for the toads that reached the northern edge of the meadow in 1303, it was a wetter year with good winter snows, which allowed them to begin dispersing westward along the base of the cliff, where they took advantage of the frequent seeps, and the scattering of small, temporary snowmelt ponds. Finally, in 1336, the first toads arrived at the lake on the western side of the cirque and quickly began to populate it. In the interim, others increasingly occupied the available habitat throughout the meadow. However, because they have a limited rate of dispersal, particularly in rugged terrain, it would be nearly 50 years, 1386, before the toads could take full advantage of the ever-changing habitat conditions within the cirque. By this time, the lake annually had many hundreds of breeding toads.

Western toads are a medium-sized to large toad, two to five inches long from the tip of their nose to the end of their spine. They have a blunt head, stout body, broad waist, and short legs. They are various shades of green or brown on top, with a white, cream-colored, or yellowish stripe down the middle of their backs from about the level of their nostrils to their rear end. They have a light underside with irregularly distributed, dark markings. The skin on their backs and upper legs is covered with small, rounded or elongated wart-like bumps. Two yellow, rounded knobs, called tubercles, exist on the underside of the hind feet. (Photo 3.1)

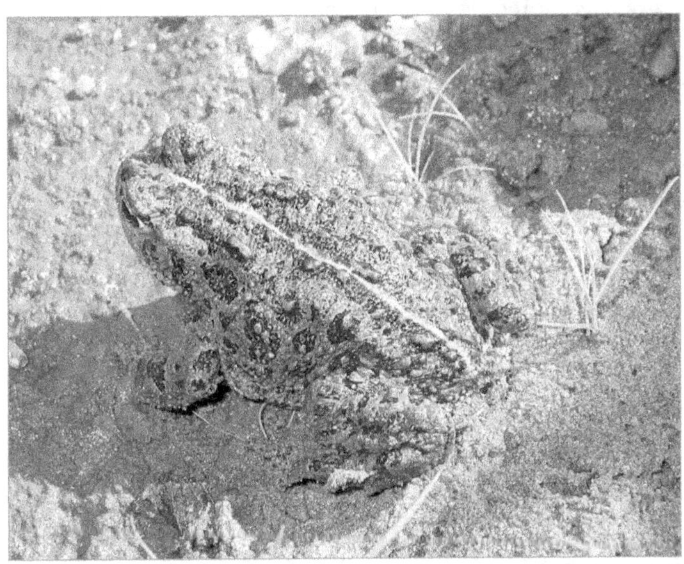

3.1 Western toad. Note the small, rounded or elongated wart-like bumps.

They have horizontal pupils, and behind each eye is a large, oval swelling somewhat larger than the eye, called a "parotoid gland." The "parotoid glands" are external skin glands that secrete a milky, alkaloid substance to deter predators, called "bufotoxin," which acts like a nerve poison. Nevertheless, the cirque's ravens prey on the toads by eviscerating them, thus leaving them partially eaten, presumably to avoid the toxins in their skin. In addition, this toxin is secondarily deposited in the female's reproductive cell, or "ovum," and is thought to afford some protection to newly laid, fertilized eggs, although the toxicity may decrease as the fertilized eggs develop.

Males have smoother skin than the females during the breeding season, as well as reduced dorsal blotching. Moreover, during the mating season, males develop "nuptial pads," which are especially prominent as horny or thickened skin on each thumb. The nuptial pads assist the male in grasping the female during the sexual *amplexus* (meaning "embrace" in Latin) as he extrudes sperm over the eggs being ejected by the female.

Toads give voice day and night to what sounds like a mellow "chirruping" or soft, high-pitched "plinking," like the peeping of a chick. You must, however, be less than 100 feet away to hear them.

The toads in the cirque hibernate during the winter in small, natural, rock-lined cavities near the streams and under boulders among the seeps along the base of the cliff, where the water is constantly flowing, and deep winter snow maintains the air temperature slightly above freezing within the cavities, or "hibernacula" (*hibernacula* is the plural of *hibernaculum*, which in Latin means, "tent for winter quarters"). Others either dig their own burrow in loose soil or use the burrows of small mammals, such as the water vole or Mazama pocket gopher. Those living at the interface of the meadow and the forest take refuge under the root systems of the trees.

Freed from hibernation as the cirque warms in spring, they travel to breeding pools, then move to terrestrial sites during the summer, and return to their hibernacula in the autumn, a journey of roughly 3,000 feet there and back again. Within this cycle, they are active during the day in spring and autumn, but mainly at night during hot, summer weather. Being cold blooded, they depend on basking in the sun and resting on warm surfaces to increase their body temperature, and on evaporative cooling and resting on cool surfaces to lower their body temperature.

Unlike frogs, a toad's skin appears to be dry. To avoid dehydration during hot weather, they usually spend the daylight hours on the forest floor, where they seclude themselves in the soil under rocks, fallen trees, stumps, and other surface objects, or in rodent burrows, depending on which part of the cirque they are in, and use the same retreat repeatedly. This behavior is called "aestivation" (from the Latin *aestas*, meaning "summer").

On the other hand, in locations, where little or no hiding cover exists, they either spend most of the day in the water or they bury themselves in loose soil and volcanic ash by shuffling their back legs and digging with the aforementioned tubercles on the bottoms of their hind feet, a process that can take half an hour or more.

With respect to diet, western toads wait for their prey on the surface of the ground or in shallow burrows dug by other animals. The intended meal is snapped up by a quick extension of the tongue, after which it is swallowed. Such meals include bees, beetles, bugs, ants, spiders, grasshoppers, mayflies, flies, butterflies, and moths. In short, they eat any kind of flying insect, as well as Cascade earthworms.

The dispersing toads of 1303 required open water for breeding, at which time males were three years old and females four to six years old. Although they used some snowmelt ponds and a spring along the base of the cliff, it was not until they reached the lake in 1336 that they had a reliable breeding site. Once established, all members of the local population returned year after year to the same clumps of submerged mountain willows near the lake's outlet. In addition, they bred in the quiet pools of the stream between the lake and the forest.

The onset of warming weather and the melting of winter's snowpack in late May or early June was, and is, the determining factor in the cirque for the beginning of breeding, which nevertheless varies from one to three weeks each year, depending when and how quickly the snow melts. Males gather at the lake days to weeks before breeding commences, at which time they may rest quietly or swim vigorously toward one another and release frequent, bird-like, twittering calls in response to the nearness or actual touching of another male. They may even wrestle briefly with a newly arriving male.

Females, on the other hand, are much more cryptic and secretive, normally waiting until breeding is about to commence before arriving. In addition, while males breed every year, females reproduce less often, depending on their individual condition and the rigors of the previous year's experience.

There are more than 1,000 toads in the lake at once, of which the males normally outnumber the females. Thus, the males actively search for gravid females (those carrying eggs) during the night. Once found and accepted, the male mounts the female from behind. However, both males and spent females give a "release call" when grabbed by an indiscriminant male. This call, a rapid chirping, is accompanied by a pulsing of the body.

Females usually deposit their eggs in shallow water between 6 and 12 inches deep in both the lake and quiet pools in the stream. The warmth of shallow water in the lake increases the rate at which development occurs, whereas the water temperature in the stream is less influenced by depth because it is constantly flowing in and out of shadows in areas both shallow and deep.

Each female lays up to 17,000 eggs per clutch in two gelatinous strings of 13 to 52 eggs per inch, one strand from each oviduct, a tube through which eggs are expelled into the water. Because the pair moves about somewhat during the egg-laying process, the strands become entangled with one another and around submerged parts of the shrubby mountain willows growing along the water's edge. In essence, western toads are explosive breeders, laying all their eggs within a week.

From the time the eggs are laid until they hatch is usually less than two weeks. Tadpoles are about four-tenths of an inch long when they hatch, but grow rapidly once they begin feeding. They are uniformly dark, appearing black in the water, although there are varying degrees of fine, lighter flecking on their bodies, which are horizontally flattened, the underside being slightly paler than the upper surface. A vertically flattened fin with a rounded tip borders the dark tail muscle. The fin is slightly pigmented, with the top being darker than the bottom. Their eyes are situated relatively high on the head. The spiracle (a small hole through which a tadpole breaths) is on the left side of the body, and the anal opening is in the middle of the underside at the tail-body juncture.

The tadpoles form dense aggregations during the day, each composed of thousands of siblings from the same clutch. They generally seek the warmer, shallower areas of the lake by day, and retreat to deeper waters as temperatures drop. If disturbed by such things as gray jays or spotted sandpipers, which prey on them, they swim to rocks, vegetation, or shadows, each of which acts as hiding cover. On the other hand, the larvae of the large, predaceous diving beetle, which often lurks in submerged vegetation, can grab a tadpole and eviscerate it in the blink of an eye.

When undisturbed, the swarms of tadpoles move from place to place around the lake's shore with a constant seething movement of individuals within the mass. What's more, the temperature within such an aggregation can be nine-tenths of a degree Fahrenheit higher than the surrounding water. There are also smaller groups of tadpoles, which can extend for two-tenths of a mile, that follow one another in a wandering course through the water. All tadpoles, however, seek the warmer temperatures within the lake, increasing the speed of their growth.

The tadpoles feed on filamentous algae and by filtering suspended plant material in the water, as well as consuming detritus on the lake's bottom. At times, they may even scavenge carrion.

As the mountain summer fades into August and early September, the tadpoles, having grown to approximately two inches in length, form aggregations numbering in the thousands of metamorphosing toadlets (transforming from tadpoles into miniature toads) along the lakes gradually sloping, open shores. Ultimately, they emerge from the lake by the thousands, dominating the lake's margin like a live, moving carpet for a week or two, as they disperse along the moistest avenues leading toward the meadow. At times, they not only cover the ground but also gather in huge piles while basking in the sun.

Juveniles in the process of changing from one form to another emerge from the water with remnants of the tail and dark skin. Within days, however, they look like miniature adults except that the parotoid glands are less obvious, and the dorsal stripe may be subtle or absent.

Because of their minute size, newly transformed toadlets can use small cracks in the soil and other tiny, protected refuges in which to spend the winter, while adults typically use larger burrows of small mammals or other underground hibernacula. Nevertheless, the mortality rate between hatching and returning as adults in two, three, or even four years to breed is well over 99 percent. Those that do survive, however, keep the cirque well supplied with western toads, considering that just 400 females annually lay at least 4,500,000 eggs.

Although the cliff, talus, and lake form a reclusive part of this high-mountain world, wherein life may seem confined, the stream is flexible, busy, and talkative, as it spills over waterfalls and rushes around rocks, only to become silent where its channel deepens and the water slows. Thus flows the stream from the cirque through the open meadow, where its graceful curves and intermediate riffles add beauty and song to the ever-changing colors of flowers and butterflies—until it enters the forest, where it seems to disappear, swallowed by the trees.

Chapter 4: The Meadow and Its Stream

The meadow is somewhat marshy in late spring and early summer along the base of the talus, as water from the melting snow forms seeps and rivulets (bordered by scattered, shrubby mountain willows) that flow toward the stream with which they coalesce. (Photo 4.1) The silence of the ages is entombed within the rushing stream of spring, as melting snow from the cliff and talus feeds its escalated voice (Photo 4.2), but its flowing is silent to the human ear under the late summer sun, as its water is progressively sucked up by the meadow's growing thirst. (Photo 4.3)

4.1 Springtime water seeping out of the talus.

4.2 Rushing, noisy stream of spring.

Where the stream leaving the lake receives water from the last rivulet, and becomes a single entity flowing through the meadow, is a small waterfall made by two, large, flattened boulders whose upper surfaces appear, at first glance, to be polished. Closer inspection, however, reveals fine striations, evidence of the glacier's millennial march toward the valley below—really more of a millennial marching-in-place. Under the boulders, behind the waterfall, is a small, protected hollow with a gravel bar that slopes into the cold, clear water. The waterfall is further protected by low, shrubby mountain willows growing on both sides of the stream around the outer edges of the boulders.

4.3 Slow, quiet stream of summer.

4.4 Overhanging banks of the steam as it flows through the meadow.

The damp gravel takes on a dull luster as the setting sun penetrates the veil of cascading water. The sides of the stream leading into the hollow are protected along the water's edge by the overhanging banks with their rank growth of meadow vegetation, which has developed well past the pioneering stage into a plant community whose strong, intertwining roots hold the soil firmly in place along the banks. (Photo 4.4)

Water Shrews

As the sun's light begins to fade from the pebbles, there is a sudden bustle of activity. Two water shrews race over the gravel bar amid much shrill squeaking. And just as suddenly as they appeared, they disappear into the water.

The water shrew, weighing up to one-half of an ounce, is exceeded in size only by the marsh shrew that lives in the marshy areas at lower elevations in the forest and along the big river in the valley bottom. The water shrew is about six inches long, of which about half is tail. It has a long, pointed, flexible nose; minute eyes; and short, wide, round ears that are almost concealed in the fur.

The fur itself is dense, soft, and velvety. The upper parts are dark gray to blackish, lightly frosted with paler hairs, whereas the underparts, from the throat to the base of the tail, are whitish tinged with gray or brown. The tail is blackish above and whitish below.

Water shrews have fringes of short, stiff, silvery hairs on the margins of their hind feet, including the toes. The fringe, usually referred to as a "swimming fringe," is most noticeable on young animals. It appears to sustain much wear during a shrew's life, and is not replaced as a shrew ages.

At this moment, daylight continues to glide silently westward with the setting sun. The fading light is replaced in the eastern sky by the dark line of night—an arched curtain pulled across the great vault of the heavens as the stars begin to twinkle and planets to stare at the small, spinning sphere called Earth.

As the sun sets, the silvery edge of the full moon begins to show over the cirque's stony brow. The rising moon floods the meadow with its soft glow, casting shadows behind the boulders and mountain willows along the stream's course and behind the deer and elk feeding on the lush vegetation. The moon, reflecting the light of the sun, is a symbol of both day and night, of light and darkness, of heat and cold. Its gentle light shrouds the meadow in the mystery of the half-seen, shadowy silhouettes of what is and what might be.

Where the stream slows, deepens, and meanders in the flatter, more level portion of the meadow, the water flows from the darkness of the banks' shadows into the mercurial light of the moon, gliding like quicksilver from shadow to shadow. If you were to sit motionless on the bank of the stream, you would soon see the small, dark form of a water shrew appear from the shadows, only to dive beneath the surface of the water in search of food.

The water shrew is the most skilled swimmer in these swift, cold, mountain streams. Its fur is so thick and soft that it traps and holds air, which allows the shrew to sit on the surface of the water and float like a duck. Were you to continue watching, you might see one walking on the surface of the water.

Because the shrew's fur gives it such buoyancy, it must force its way to the bottom of the stream, where it literally stands on its long, flexible nose, searching the bottom for food, its hind feet kicking rapidly to maintain this position. To change direction, it twists its body, and to come to the surface, it simply stops kicking and rises like a cork, bursting to the surface with dry fur.

Wherever the shrew goes under water, it is trailed by a row of bubbles rising out of its fur. In fact, the shining layer of air that clings to the surface of its fur as it swims makes the shrew resemble a silvery fish.

Although a water shrew's fur is remarkably resistant to wetting, water does begin to penetrate after several minutes of aquatic activity. Therefore, a shrew leaves the water and dries its fur by rapidly and thoroughly working over its body with its hind feet. During this process, which lasts from 10 to 30 seconds, fine droplets of water are thrown off. The stiff hairs of the swimming fringe along the margins of the hind feet function almost like a comb that helps to dry the fur.

One shrew, startled by the sudden appearance of a water vole, which is really a semi-aquatic "meadow mouse," darts out from the shadow of the stream's bank and runs across the surface of the water, only to disappear in the shadow of the opposite bank. (Unlike the shrews, which feed mainly on insects, the water vole is a rodent and, therefore, a vegetarian.)

The stiff hairs of the swimming fringe trap air that allows the shrew to literally walk or run on the surface of the water. In short, the northern water shrew is a truly remarkable mammal; it can swim, dive, float like a duck, and walk both on the surface of the water and on land.

Water shrews in the stream feed mainly on invertebrates, such as the larvae of aquatic insects (dragonflies, caddisflies, stoneflies, mayflies), earthworms, and the larvae of terrestrial insects (crane flies and beetles) found along the edge of the meadow by the stream, as well as on snails, spiders, beetles, and centipedes. In addition, they catch and eat immature rainbow trout and, when possible, trout eggs, as well as larvae of the long-toed salamander and Cascade frog. Because water shrews have very high metabolic rates, they not only spend a large portion of their active hours searching for prey but also consume over half of their weight in food daily (approximately 100 insects).

When hunting young rainbow trout or the larvae of the long-toed salamander, a shrew dives to the bottom and, finding its prey, bites it somewhere around the head, which seems to paralyze it. The shrew then pops to the surface and swims to a preselected site, gripping the fish or salamander larva by the head while its body trails alongside that of the swimming shrew. Once out of the water, the shrew bites its prey through the head with its front teeth (incisors) to kill it.

One female shrew, hunting trout in the shallow water of the stream's edge, rushes about the rocks, stopping frequently to elevate her flexible nose, as if trying to detect a scent. She then plunges into the water and swims beneath the surface. In this case, young trout are not moving, so she has difficulty finding them, until she bumps into five seemingly by accident. Startled, the fish scatter, but she has little difficulty catching a couple of them, which she carries to a chosen spot to kill. She then eats one and stores the other for later use in a tiny cavity, where the stream has undercut its bank. The cavity is protected from view by low mountain willows growing immediately above the undercut on the east side of the stream and by rushes intermixed with tufted hairgrass growing along the stream's west bank.

Solitary by nature, a shrew may be abroad at any time during the 24-hour cycle. However, their activity patterns are generally characterized by two periods: one between sunset and eight o'clock in the evening, the second occurs one hour prior to sunrise. For every 30 minutes of activity, a shrew spends the next hour resting.

Thus, after catching the trout, the female, holding it with her forefeet, tears off pieces by using her teeth and an upward thrust of her head. Having finished her meal, she retires to her burrow to relax in her spherical nest, constructed out of dry vegetation. She had dug her tunnel and nest chamber under a large rock in the meadow about two feet from the edge of the stream's bank.

After selecting the place to begin, she used her forefeet to dig with and her hind feet to expel the soil. Once the excavation was completed, she collected dry vegetation and carried it into the chamber. She then shaped her nest with her feet and legs, after which she formed the inner depression and walls with her nose and face.

Yesterday, however, she simply stopped and fell asleep in a crouched position under the waterfall. From time to time, a shrew goes to sleep on a rock under the protection of the overhanging bank along the stream's edge, loses its balance, and falls into the water—a rude awakening!

Male water shrews, which are larger and heavier than females, are born in the late spring and summer (as are the females) and do not become sexually active until the December or January following their birth, when their testes enlarge, after which reproductive activity continues until August. Females, on the other hand, are either pregnant or raising young from February until August, and may produce several litters during the breeding season. Litters normally range from five to eight young, but six is most common, and the usual lifespan is about 18 months.

Being active throughout the year, the shrew's major activity is confined to the banks of the stream, despite Nature's seasonal variations. For example, the stream does not freeze solid under the insulating cover of winter's snow, although a small shelf of ice forms along its banks, and in some places, across the entire stream. As the top of the lake freezes, the level of water along the stream drops, forming a space between the bottom of the ice shelf and the water's surface, becoming the winter domain of many a water shrew.

4.5 Subnivean refugium of winter in the meadow.

As the water along the edges of the stream freezes, snow gradually covers the meadow (Photos 4.5 and 4.6) and stream margins to a depth of 10 feet (Photo 4.7), creating a "subnivean" refugium (from the Latin *sub* "under" and *nives* "snow") that provides not only insulation from tissue-damaging cycles of freezing and thawing brought on by inclement winter weather but also protection from predators for those mammals that do not hibernate, such as the water vole, montane vole (meadow mouse), long-tailed weasel, short-tailed weasel, Mazama pocket gopher, and wandering shrew.

4.6 Snow encircles the islands of trees interfacing with the meadow.

4.7 Snowpack along the stream in the forest.

The warmer, more stable conditions within the subnivean refugium are driven principally by the depth, density, and duration of the snowpack. Falling snow is light and fluffy (low in hardness and density) with many easily distinguishable forms of fragile snow crystals. The flakes age, however, as the winter continues, and change into rounded grains of ice within the snowpack as a result of wind, weight, and the temperature gradient between its bottom and top. This gradient is composed of an interconnecting system of pore spaces within the snowpack that changes its vertical structure as water vapor migrates upward. Thus, over the winter, as the snowpack ages through the process of melting and freezing under the increasing pressure of its weight, the grains of snow grow together and bond, thereby greatly increasing the strength of the pack.

Temperature within the snowpack varies, approaching air temperature near the surface and warmest near the ground, where mammals burrow or bed down, taking advantage of the snowpack's insulating qualities. In the meadow and along the edge of the forest, the subnivean zone, where the meadow and snow meet, maintains a temperature of close to 32 degrees Fahrenheit once the snow cover has reached a depth of six inches or more, regardless of the temperature above the snow.

But for now, the shrews are bathed in the quiet light of the September moon as they alternately swim, dive, and float along the stream through the meadow; meanwhile, rainbow trout keep a wary eye on them from below.

Rainbow Trout

Rainbow trout have very small, fine scales on their torpedo-shaped bodies. Their name is derived from their beautiful, multi-hued coloration, which consists of blue, green, or yellowish backs and sides shading to silvery white on the underneath. They have a pronounced, horizontal, pinkish-red stripe along the upper-middle part of the body from the gills to the tail, though the intensity of this stripe can vary. In addition, there are clearly visible black spots along their backs and sides, as well as on the tail fin, which is slightly forked. (Photo 4.8)

Centuries ago, rainbow trout migrated from the large river in the valley bottom, upstream in its tributaries through the forest, into the small, clear, cold headwater streams of the meadow, but due to the local structure of the lake's outlet, none have managed to enter it. Their migration was made possible by the gradual modification of the waterways.

4.8 Rainbow trout.

Over time, the development of riparian vegetation (that grows along a river or stream), such as trees, shrubs, rushes, sedges, grasses, and forbs, created shade that moderated the water's temperature and provided a source of protective cover in the forest when limbs and trees fell into the stream. Roots of riparian vegetation, such as willows, also helped to stabilize stream banks, thereby maintaining the water's quality. In addition, undercut banks, overhanging vegetation, turbulent or deep water, submerged or semi-submerged wood, beds of aquatic plants, root masses, and large rocks also contributed to the habitat diversity not only for the trout but also for the other life important to the aquatic food chain.

By the year 1575, the ideal distribution of habitat components, from the river in the valley bottom, through the forest, to the outlet of the lake in the cirque, and the collective seeps along the cliff, consists of a well-connected complex of undercut banks with overhanging, soil-stabilizing vegetation; slow-flowing, shallow to deep pools; riffles with their shallow, rapidly flowing, choppy water; one- to three-inch-diameter gravel for spawning; beds of aquatic plants; submerged or semi-submerged trees or branches; in-stream boulders and piles of rocks, as well as root masses that provide shelter. Moreover, the often-extreme winter conditions in and around the cirque make the deep, mountain-willow-bordered pools, which serve as refuges in the iced-covered streams, critical for the trout's winter survival.

Because the trout living in the cirque's drainage basin are largely solitary by nature, the overall abundance of such well-connected, complex habitat components both partition and reduce the size of their individual territories, allowing more trout to inhabit a given stream. For example, the two main streams draining the cirque (one on the west side of the meadow, the other on the east) support numerous trout with relatively small territories because food is plentiful, but a stream's smaller side-branches, which produce less food, not only support fewer trout but also require larger feeding territories. In addition, high-elevation streams, like those in the cirque, are oligotrophic (from the Greek, adjective *oligos*, "few," and *trophikos*, "feeding"), which means these streams have meager supplies of available food and thus produce smaller fish than do downstream habitats.

Their solitary nature becomes evident as soon as they hatch and emerge from the gravel, at which time they are referred to as a "fry." From then on, there is little communication among them—other than hostility as they compete with one another for the best habitat, namely, the sides of streams, where shading is prevalent, the water is less swift, and protection is greatest. Nevertheless, there is a size hierarchy among all trout, wherein larger fish usually dominate the best habitat and food sources.

The cirque's trout are visual predators, relying on a keen sense of vision to detect prey. However, they serve not only as important predators in their own habitats but also as critical sources of food for other predators, both small and large.

Trout inhabiting the main streams within the forest and meadow, which have significant amounts of riparian vegetation, feed heavily on terrestrial insects, such as grasshoppers, ants, and beetles, that fall into the streams and drift with its current. On the other hand, the slower, deeper water, such as the caddisfly pool and the big pool in the forest, offer a variety of foods: larval and aquatic stages of dragonflies, mayflies, caddisflies, and stoneflies; worms, including the occasional earthworm; and snails. As opportunists, the trout remain, for a time, in stream riffles to feed on bottom-dwelling insects and crustaceans, such as fairy shrimp. In addition, young trout include algae in their diet, which grows on rocks along the stream's bottom.

Rainbow trout spawn in main river channels and their tributaries, like the streams coming from the cirque. Tributary streams containing gravel between one-half and three inches in size are the most suitable spawning habitats for resident fish. Generally, spawning in the spring and early summer, the trout most commonly use stream riffles located downstream from pools as spawning areas.

Potential mates communicate before spawning with visual cues. Thereafter, the female digs a nest in the gravel with her anal fin, while her mate guards the site (a depression, technically termed a "redd") from other interested males and predators. (The "anal fin" is a single fin on a fish's underside situated between the anus and the tail, which helps the fish to maintain its balance.)

Her nest completed, she descends on it to position her vent and anal fin into the deepest part of the nest. (The vent is the opening between the anus and the anal fin through which fish secrete either eggs or sperm.) The male joins her in a parallel position so that their vents are opposite each other. Then, with mouths open and backs arched, they simultaneously deposit eggs and milt (white, milky fluid containing sperm). The eggs are fertilized, as a cloud of milt envelops them. Only a few seconds elapse between the time the female drops into the nest and fertilization occurs. The fertilized eggs are covered by gravel, as the female excavates yet another nest just upstream, repeating the process until she has deposited all her eggs.

Here, it is critical to understand that trout deposit their eggs within a range of water depths and velocities that minimize the risk of desiccation as seasonal water levels recede, especially during exceptionally hot summers and autumns. Sediment-free spawning gravels at a sufficient depth are critical to ensure that the stream's water can percolate through the spaces in the gravel, bringing oxygen to the eggs while removing metabolic wastes associated with incubation and hatching. The eggs require continuous oxygenation. At temperatures of about 55 degrees Fahrenheit, the eggs will hatch approximately 21 days after they are laid.

The eggs hatch in the gravel, and at first the fry, which are three-quarters of an inch to one inch long, can move very little. They do not feed, but rather absorb the nutrients from their attached yolk sac. Remaining in the protective gravel for two to three weeks, they shed their yolk sacs, wiggle through the gravel, and emerge into the stream, although they tend to remain in areas of shallow water, often along the side of the stream, where there is protective cover and slow-moving currents. After the fry absorb the yolk sac, they begin feeding on plankton (from the Greek *planktos*, meaning "wanderer"). Plankton are a diverse group of microorganisms, both plants and animals, that live in the water, but cannot swim against a current.

4.9 Juvenile rainbow trout showing its "parr marks."

As the fish grow, they develop 8 to 13 "parr marks" on their sides, which are vertical, color bars. Consequently, they are called "parr," which is the life stage extending from the time a trout begins feeding until it becomes sufficiently pigmented to obliterate the parr marks, usually by the end of the first year. (Photo 4.9)

Predation is severe during a trout's early life, and less than one percent of the hatchlings survive their first year, thanks in part to the water shrews. Survivors, however, have a usual lifespan of four to six years.

Chapter 5: Where the Meadow Meets the Forest

As a youth, I saw, and felt with my heart, the forest through which I so often traveled, and I found in it nurturance and safety. Today, I see the forest not only through my training as a research scientist in natural history and ecology but also through the experience of more than 50 years with the heart of one in love with its song and mystery. As a youth, I felt enveloped in its rhythms. Today I marvel at the fluid dynamics of its pulsating cycles, the interplay of it parts, and the mystical union of its apparent opposites: life and death, animate and inanimate.

As a young man in the 1950s and earliest years of the 1960s, I could stand on the shoulder of a mountain in the High Cascades and gaze upon a land clothed in ancient forest as far as I could see into the blue haze of the distance. My sojourns along the trails of deer and elk were accompanied by the wind, as it sang in the trees and by the joy of water bouncing along its rocky channels. At others times, the water gave voice to its deafening roar as it suddenly poured itself into space from dizzying heights, only to gather itself once again at the bottom of the precipice and continue its appointed journey to the ocean, the mother of all waters.

Throughout those many springs, summers, and autumns the songs of wind and water were punctuated with the melodies of forest birds. Wilson warblers sang in the tops of ancient firs, while the plaintive trill of the varied thrush drifted down the mountainside, and the liquid notes of winter wrens came ever-so-gently from among the fallen monarchs, as they lay decomposing through the centuries on the forest floor. From somewhere high above the canopy of trees came the scream of a golden eagle, and from deep within the forest there emanated the rapid, staccato drumming of a pileated woodpecker. (Photo 5.1) And on a still day in winter, I could hear the "swish" of snow flakes as they drifted past me to add their beauty to the 15 feet of snow on which I was standing.

5.1 The dead tree on which the pileated woodpecker was drumming as it searched for carpenter ants, which are its main food.

These were the sounds of my youth. This was the music that complemented the forest's abiding silence, a silence that archived the history of centuries as the forest grew and changed, like an unfinished mural painted with the novelty of infinite Creation.

While my youth has fled with the passing years, today I behold an even greater wonder as I once again hike the high mountain trails. Now I see the infinite, creative novelty of the forest.

But, if it were the year 1000, you would see that, except for a few remnants on the north-facing slopes, winter's snow is about gone, and the meadow is resplendent with mid-June flowers that nod and sway in gentle breezes. Fluffy clouds drift slowly across a sky of deep blue, followed always by their shadows. The shadows glide silently up one hill and down another, grow large and shrink, combine, dissipate, and reform in some new shape. The shadows can only reflect the clouds that, in turn, can only reflect the constantly changing Universe.

An Indian youth of sixteen summers lies in the new grasses amidst the flowers of the meadow. His vision drifts idly with the clouds until it is riveted on a small, dark speck in the vast sweep of blue.

The midday sun warms the youth as he watches the speck sailing effortlessly in and out of cloud canyons and around cloud peaks. In his mind, he journeys to the dark speck, the great golden eagle riding the currents of warm air reflected from the earth into the sky, into the immensity and freedom of space, where there is no beginning and no end.

He soars wingtip to wingtip with the great bird. One with the eagle, one with the air, the warmth, the earth, the clouds, the sun, one with the Spirit that is the unity of all things. He is the Spirit, and the Spirit is he.

Looking down, the youth sees that the meadow on which he was lying has become a riot of color surrounded by the cliff and dark green of the forest, which together enclose the brighter green with its splashes of yellows, reds, and blues. Looking toward the forest, he sees the avalanche track left over from the ice age that formed the glacier responsible for the stream, and he watches its sparkling water, which chronicles the events of that ancient time, disappear into the tangle of mountain willows that gradually give way to Sitka alder, as the stream penetrates deeper into the forest.

The alders, 10 to 15 feet tall, have strongly bowed stems from the gravitational pressure of the snow as it creeps down the steep slope against their bases. Here, 50 yards below the meadow, the stream picks up an added volume of water that, moving slowly downhill below the soil of the meadow, seeps out of the ground in an area of small, flattish slabs of basalt, about one and a half feet square, with a smattering of mountain willows.

Over the centuries, this area, kept moist by the slowly trickling water, has become overgrown with mats of various kinds of mosses. Interspersed among these mats are mountain willows, grasses, rushes, sedges, and such flowering plants as the purple-blossomed alpine shooting star and white marsh marigold. It is here, where their burrows are protected from erosion by the vegetation, that the life cycle of the ancient dragonfly begins and ends.

DRAGONFLY SEEP

The dragonfly inhabiting the seep by the alders is one species in a tiny remnant of a great group whose abundant fossil remains show that they flourished on Earth as the dominant group of dragonflies during Jurassic times (between 180 and 135 million years ago). The ancient dragonfly of the seep is large, about three inches long, and blackish with a stout body, clear wings, and a rather rugged appearance. Although it lacks the finish of form and coloration that characterizes modern dragonflies found everywhere along the streams, the ancient dragonfly does have spots of yellow and half-rings of orange on its body.

The ancient dragonfly, like all dragonflies, possesses a similar design of a head, a thorax (sturdy midsection), and a long abdomen. Their head contains two compound eyes with as many as 30,000 lenses or facets in each eye. And, each lens has its own nerve going to the brain, which means that a dragonfly "sees" 30,000 images in concert. These sight-based creatures are able to scan 360 degrees, as well as above and below, with a quick turn of the head. Moreover, their acute vision probably allows them to discern individual wing beats, which to us would be nothing but a blur. They can see ultraviolet and polarized light, and many species also see well in dim light. Thus, like us, dragonflies use their eyes as the primary means of assessing the environment.

In addition, there are two inconspicuous antennae, which seem to act as a speedometer. Dragonflies can reach a top flying speed of 37 miles per hour. They have two pairs of large, veined wings about equal length attached to the thorax. The abdomen is long and narrow with 10-segments. Their six legs are not used for walking. Instead, they are important for perching, as well as scooping up and handling prey. In addition, many species have spines on the legs that form a type of basket in which prey is caught. The front two legs are also used for grooming the eyes and face. This basic design has produced such a finely tuned aerial predator with superb vision and unmatched aerial agility that it has undergone no significant modifications for millions of years.

Because it is the 5th of September, 1247, the very end of their period of flight, which normally occurs between the beginning of July and the end of August, only one or two old adults of these rare dragonflies can be seen sitting flattened on the dry, warm, sunny surfaces of low pieces of basalt, with their wings and legs widely outspread. One takes off suddenly in a low, uneven flight. It flits back and forth until, reaching about 20 feet above the ground, it ceases to flap its wings and glides for a short time before returning to its rock. However, had it been a hot day in July or early August, rather than the 5th of September, the spectacle of the ancient dragonfly would have been very different.

If you could return to the first of July, you would see the males leave the protective coloration of the forest trees on which they have been resting and arrive at the seep between eleven o'clock in the morning and four o'clock in the afternoon. Each male then selects an oblong area four to six feet long and two to three feet wide and begins to patrol it; a patrol lasts but a few seconds, after which the dragonfly finds a tall stalk of grass on which to perch. (Photo 5.2) The perch is chosen not only to offer a clear flight path but also to allow the dragonfly to orient himself in a way that he receives the maximum sunlight. From his perch, he can fly out and capture food, such as mosquitoes, small craneflies, and alderflies, or he can defend his territory against the encroachment of other dragonflies.

5.2 A dragonfly (not the ancient dragonfly) resting on a piece of grass.

A territorial male is intensively aggressive against intruding dragonflies of all kinds and both sexes. When a dragonfly is spotted within three to six feet of an occupied perch, the male quickly flies to meet the intruder. Both dragonflies then hover face-to-face about six inches apart for a second or two before the defending male flies at the interloper. There ensues a great crashing of wings and bodies, after which the trespasser tries to escape by flying in an ascending vertical spiral that often terminates 18 to 20 feet above the seep, as the defending male again attacks with a clashing of wings and bodies. Although the chase lasts just 30 seconds, it covers about 30 yards before the stranger is escorted beyond the boundary of the seep.

Females, having been bred beyond the seep in the edge of the forest, occasionally stray into a male's territory, at which time the male either ushers her out of his territory or attempts to copulate with her. Most females, however, arrive undetected at the seep between three o'clock and five o'clock in the afternoon and quickly descend to the ground, where they enter the thick vegetation's protective cover. Here, a female walks for a few seconds and then probes the wet, spongy mosses with her ovipositor, which is located near the tip of her long, slender abdomen. Preferring to lay her eggs in an organic substrate, the probing helps her to select just the right spots. She may spend five minutes to more than half an hour dipping her abdomen into the wet, spongy vegetation as she lays her eggs. (Photo 5.3)

Photo 5.3 A female dragonfly (not the ancient dragonfly) laying eggs.

One female lays her tiny, ovoid, light brown eggs in the water under the moss on the 8th of July, but does not attach them to the plants. Sixteen days later, on the 24th of July, the young dragonflies are well along in their development. The eggs begin to hatch on the 3rd of August, after 26 days of development, but some do not hatch until the 8th of August, 31 days after being laid. This may have something to do with differences in the temperature of the water in which the eggs were deposited.

The young dragonfly inside the egg is called a *pronymph*, which simply means "before the nymph," and "nymph" means an immature stage (following hatching) of an insect that does not have a pupal stage. On hatching, the ancient dragonfly is transparent and has very long upright hairs on the upper surface of the abdomen. The tips of these hairs are curved downward toward the body and pick up debris as the nymph moves through the muck of its surroundings, which makes it indistinguishable from its habitat, and thus helps to protect it from predation by such creatures as water shrews.

Upon hatching, a nymph crawls through the mucky, watery habitat until it finds just the right spot, a place where the muck is deep enough for it to construct its burrow. A burrow normally consists of an opening at the top of a vertical section, which descends to a right-angle turn into a horizontal compartment.

The diameter of its burrow varies from three-eighths to one-half of an inch. The vertical section is three to four inches long, and the horizontal section is also three to four inches long. At times, the first portion of the burrow is not strictly vertical, but passes downward at an acute angle. There are even some burrows that have their openings under the edge of the basalt slabs and follow the rock along its projection for eight inches or more. These burrows always face upslope, perhaps to ensure an adequate flow of oxygenated water.

Occasionally, an additional short, horizontal section is made in the opening of the burrow just under the surface of the water. Here a nymph lies in wait for its prey, completely submerged in a shallow pool and completely camouflaged by the accumulation of debris held in the long hairs of its body. Most of the time, however, a nymph simply lies in wait for its prey near the opening of the vertical section of its burrow. Even though such a nymph is vulnerable to predation, it is well protected because, in addition to the camouflaging debris, it "plays dead" when touched, and so blends almost perfectly with its background.

Although nymphs are active throughout the 24-hour cycle, they are most active in the evening and during the night when they appear at the openings of their burrows in the greatest numbers. Here, a nymph lies facing the opening of its burrow as it waits for prey, such as passing spiders, small ground beetles, and leaf beetles. Although they usually hunt from within the protection of their burrows, a nymph will occasionally leave its burrow and forage in the open.

By the time a nymph reaches its last molt, it has a rough-hewn exterior and short, somewhat twisted legs. Its eyes are prominent at the front angles of a squarish head, and its body, which is not quite cylindrical, is hairy and is so encrusted with mucky debris that its coloration is obscured.

The seep is an ideal habitat for the nymphs of the ancient dragonfly, because the supply of water tends to be continuous within and between years, and flows slowly. If the supply of water is not permanent, it will take several years for a nymph to develop. Moreover, the water must flow slowly because the nymphs do not swim and are relatively slow moving. If, on the other hand, as occasionally has happened over the centuries, the seep largely dries out, the nymphs turn upside down in their burrows, with their heads in the receding water but with their abdomens above it. In this position, they can breathe air, an activity that they can sustain for days or even weeks without an increase in water, until more favorable conditions return.

With the advent of August, the fully developed nymphs leave their burrows and climb a short way up nearby vegetation, where they become quiescent. Here, their outer skins split and the newly formed adults emerge. (Photo 5.4) They remain for a time sitting on their cast skins while their wings straighten and dry. Then, with seemingly effortless grace, they greet the hot breezes rising from the valley below. By the end of August, all adults have abandoned the nymphal skins, and the cycle of the ancient dragonfly continues.

Once the stream is 100 yards below the lower end of the dragonfly's seep, the number of its small waterfalls and pools increases because some of the larger branches, broken off the 260-year-old trees over the last decade by heavy snows and ice, have fallen into the stream and formed small dams. There are fewer boulders in the ancient forest, and the stream's channel, now gentler than it was immediately below the meadow, is deeper and narrower in some spots, and shallower and wider in others.

5.4 The discarded exoskeleton of a dragonfly nymph, but not of the ancient dragonfly.

If you went a quarter of a mile to the west of this spot, you would find a stream flowing from a spring hidden behind the huge, partly buried Douglas-fir tree that fell diagonally across its mouth in the winter of 900. The stream, six inches wide as it leaves the spring, flows freely for 20 feet or so before two Douglas-fir trees that sprawl across its channel back it up. They fell 113 years ago during the winter of 1134, when wet snows turned to freezing rain in March and toppled the 800-year-old trees. Below the dam with its steep, overhanging banks and long, quiet pool is a tear-shaped gravel bar that extends partway across the stream, where the water has undermined the roots of a large fir that has grown for centuries along its bank.

On this 5th of September 1247, there is a soft, cool breeze blowing up the small stream that flows from the spring in the ancient forest. It's a gentle afternoon as shafts of sunlight peek through gaps in the towering firs that enfold the pool in their protective shade. This pool is home to the northern caddisfly.

Caddisfly Pool

Caddisflies in general are small to medium-sized insects that somewhat resemble moths in appearance. The four membranous wings, which are rather hairy, occasionally have scales, and are usually held roof-like over the abdomen when the insect is at rest. The antennae are long and slender. Most caddisflies are rather dull-colored, but a few have bright patterns. Caddisflies undergo complete metamorphosis, and have aquatic larvae.

The northern caddisfly is so named because it is adapted to the cold water, like the springs and small streams of the ancient forest. The eggs are laid in masses that most often are suspended to the undersides of large trees that have fallen across a stream, but remain above the water. Because females concentrate their egg-laying activities, most of the egg masses are aggregated on a few fallen trees at each stream. The masses are arranged in rough rows within a clear, tacky, gelatinous matrix that usually contains between 50 and 600 eggs per mass. Developing larvae remain in the egg mass for three to five days, when it begins to liquefy and the larvae are "dripped" into the stream or onto its banks. Periodic rainstorms during this time seem to facilitate the escape of larvae from the gelatinous matrix.

The larvae are caterpillar-like, with a well-developed head and thoracic legs, and a pair of hook-like appendages at the end of the abdomen. They breathe with filamentous gills that are attached to the abdominal segments.

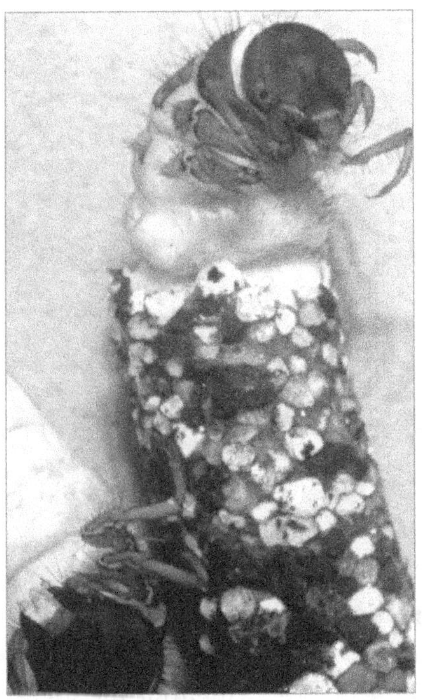

5.5 Caddisfly nymph with a case of sandgrains.

The larvae construct slightly curved, cylindrical cases from grains of sand (Photo 5.5) or the needles of the forest's Douglas-fir and mountain hemlock—western hemlock in the lower elevations. (Photo 5.6) Additional material is added when the larvae are actively growing, which results in a long, tapered case. The larval diet differs, depending on where the larvae are. For example, those in the spring spend much time on the sides of wet rocks, where they scrape bits of mosses and filamentous algae off the rocks, but those living in the pool below the spring feed primarily on the needles of Douglas-fir and mountain hemlock, and on decomposing wood. A little further down the mountain, on the other hand, where the first big pool occurs in the main stream, the larvae feed primarily on the fallen leaves of red alder, when they are available. In turn, the larvae are critical to the stream's aquatic food web.

5.6 Caddisfly nymph with a case of conifer needles.

The larvae in the forest below the meadow have a two-year cycle. Completing its growth, a larva fastens its case to some object in the water, seals the case's opening or openings, and pupates inside. When the pupa is fully developed, it chews its way out of the case, swims to the surface, crawls out of the water onto a stone, stick, or some other object, and emerges as an adult. (Photo 5.7) Although most caddisflies are rather weak fliers and usually live about a month as adults, northern caddisflies overwinter in the canopy of the ancient forest along the stream and start the cycle over again the following year.

Below the pool of the caddisflies, the stream weaves its way through tangles of wood with their swirling eddies to flow serenely under the interlaced branches and green, filtered light of vine maples, only to bounce and churn in riffles, to cascade in small rapids and over low waterfalls, and then to flow again for a time in silent, reflective pools.

5.7 Adult caddisfly.

Thus, the streams descend toward the valley, the one from the cirque for about a mile, and the one from the spring for about half a mile, before they meet in the 260-year-old forest that grew out of the ashes of the fire of 987. Here they join and become a larger stream that varies from about four feet wide during the period of low water in summer to about 16 feet wide during periods of high water in winter and spring.

Where Streams Join

Today, June 5, 1575, there is a small, triangular area of gravelly-sandy-looking sediments located in the fork of the "Y," where the two streams join and become one. The opening in the canopy of the

---

Note: Until now, the reference to time, as we humans think of it, has somewhat been general because humans have not been part of the landscape, other than my brief sojourn to the meadow, which will actually take place centuries from now. However, Storm Hawk's entrance into the evolutionary history of the cirque brings the human dimension of time momentarily to the fore. Thus, an event that took place prior to Storm Hawk's entering the scene is written in past tense, those taking place while he is in the cirque are written in present tense, and those that will take pace after his departure are written in future tense.

---

forest created by this joining of the streams has greatly increased the amount of light reaching the ground. As a result, a thick bed of herbaceous plants, such as Oregon oxalis and Indian lettuce, covers the bank between the forest edge and the bar. In addition, three vine maples have stretched a couple of their limbs over the gravelly area. The surface of the gravel is dry on this warm, sunny, early-June midday, as Storm Hawk, an Indian youth of 19 summers, stops to examine its surface, the high spot of which is about three inches above the level of the water.

Storm Hawk is intent on finding the meadow he has been told about. Having seen from a high point approximately where the meadow is, he decides to take a shortcut through the forest instead of following the stream. To do so, however, he must cross the stream.

Standing on the bank opposite the gravelly-sandy-appearing bar toward the far side of the confluence of the two streams, he searches it for the tracks of animals. He sees none; yet he saw the tracks of deer crossing to the other side just upstream from the bar. He thinks about it for another minute or two. It looks solid, so he backs up and takes a running leap. Landing in the middle of the bar, he instantly sinks to the middle of his waist in what turns out to be sandy-clayey sediment deposited by the streams at the fork.

Storm Hawk, blind with panic, struggles, and thus sinks further into the sucking grip of the ooze. During his struggle, his right hand brushes against one of the out-stretched limbs of the vine maple. He stops struggling and looks up. Seeing the limb, he reaches for it only to find that he has settled too deeply in the ooze to grasp it with more than the tips of his fingers. The harder he tries to reach up, the further his thrashing body sinks away from the limb. Then he remembers his short hunting bow in its carrying case slung over his back.

Still fighting the panic welling up in waves from the pit of his stomach, he manages to get his bow out of its case. Reaching upward with the bow, he carefully slides it over the limb and slowly works the limb downward, closer and closer to his free hand.

"It's almost in reach. I must be patient. I must swallow my fear.

If I get in a hurry, I'll just sink deeper and deeper and maybe lose the limb forever. I must do this myself. The Great Spirit has given me a test, and I must succeed."

Finally, the limb in the grasp of his right hand, he begins to work himself upward out of the ooze. After minutes that seem like hours, he can reach the second limb; now he spans both limbs with his bow to even his weight and to add the strength of the limbs to one another. The vine maples are springy with much give, so they easily bear his weight without breaking, as he wiggles and pulls, slowly and steadily, always working his body toward the maples' main stems.

An hour passes, then another, and another. At last, a tired, triumphant, and far wiser Storm Hawk pulls himself free of the clutching, viscous tentacles embodied in the suspension of sediments in the fork of the two streams.

Once free from the bar, he goes downstream a quarter of a mile, and finds a big pool caused by a dam across what is now a single stream. Taking the case for his bow, quiver of arrows, and backpack off his shoulders, Storm Hawk wades into the cold water, where he washes himself thoroughly. There is a deep, warm feeling in his chest and in the pit of his stomach. He knows that he has accomplished a great feat by mastering his fear; he knows that he is both humbler and wiser than he was in the morning of this day. For now he knows that any gravelly-sandy-appearing bar at the confluence of small streams that does not have the tracks of animals, especially of the larger animals, such as raccoon, wolf, deer, or elk, is not safe to step on.

The Big Pool

Contemplating the complexity of the dam, he wonders how it came into being. If he could have gone back in time, he would know that the upper dam of three, old Douglas-firs has been in place for 25 years, since the violent winter storm in 1222 that had blown them down.

One had been a 600-year-old tree that died 50 years earlier and had stood as a barkless, whitened snag, having been severely injured by the falling of another fir 75 years earlier. The year following the injury had been the beginning of a three-year drought that had so stressed the old fir that it could neither acquire nor mobilize sufficient resources to heal its injuries and sustain its life.

The other two had been live trees, one 635 years old, and one 641 years old. It was not wind alone that felled these trees, however. The stream had been undermining their roots for decades. And then in March, the heavy winter snows became saturated with rain, which turned to freezing rain, and then had frozen almost solid. The final blow came suddenly, when a violent storm blew in from the Pacific Ocean, and combined with the other factors toppled the ancient trees.

The dam at the lower end of the pool has been in place only a decade and is formed by a single, old fir that was weakened over many years by a root rot fungus. It was blown over by gusty winds that preceded a thunderstorm in late July of 1237. As these trees fell into and across the stream, they smashed other vegetation that, in turn, opened a relatively large hole in the canopy of the forest, called a "light gap." With the sudden increase in light reaching the stream and its banks, there came a dramatic shift in vegetation. There was an immediate explosion of herbaceous vegetation: sedges, common monkey flower, and coltsfoot, and such woody vegetation as devil's club and vine maple. The warming of the water also increased the potential for algae to grow on the rocks of the stream bed, and Sitka alder to quickly seed itself and spread, adding not only leaves to the detritus-base energy system of the stream but also hardwood twigs and branches. (Detritus means dead, decomposing, and disintegrating organic materials, such as leaves, needles, twigs, bark, and wood.)

Although Storm Hawk washed in the pool, he does not see most of the aquatic life hidden there, each in its own tiny recess. Could he have seen into the large pieces of submerged wood that made the dam on which he now sat, he would have seen the larvae of wood-eating craneflies and small flies, called "midges." Some of the wood-eating larvae inhabit sound wood that fell into the water and has been only slightly decayed by fungi; others inhabit wood that started its decomposition process on land, and was well rotted before it fell into the water.

MIDGES

Midge larvae inhabiting the more rotten wood are those that burrow the deepest into it. Not all larval midges are eaters of wood, however. Most larvae associated with wood are collector-gatherers. Some are predaceous and capture live animals as prey; others are herbaceous and feed on living plants, such as algae and diatoms. (Diatoms are a large group of single-celled algae that are encased in a cell wall of silica.) In fact, not all larval midges are aquatic in their habitat requirements. A few live in decaying vegetation, under bark, or in moist soil along the edge of the pool. Most of them are scavengers. The larvae of some species are red because of the presence of hemoglobin in their blood; they are known as blood-worms. (Hemoglobin is an iron-containing protein in red blood cells that combines with oxygen and transports it—in humans, for example—from the lungs to the tissues of the body.)

Aquatic larvae of midges in the big pool live in tubes or cases. The larvae swim by means of characteristic whipping movements of their bodies, something akin to the movements of mosquito larvae, often called "wrigglers" because of the way they swim. Mosquitoes are also flies.

Adult midges are small and delicate, somewhat mosquito-like in appearance, and the males usually have feathery antennae. Midges often occur in huge swarms, usually in the evening, and the humming of such a swarm can be heard for a considerable distance. Storm Hawk, who often has seen and heard swarms of midges, neither knows nor probably cares that some larvae are actually eating the ancient Douglas-firs, whose slowly rotting stems form the dam of the pool.

STONEFLIES

The pool is also the home of stoneflies and mayflies. Stoneflies are medium-sized, somewhat flattened, soft-bodied, rather drab-colored insects. (Photo 5.8) They are poor fliers and are seldom found far from the stream. They have four, rather long, membranous wings, of which the hind wings are slightly shorter than the front wings. Stoneflies at rest hold their wings flat over the abdomen. The antennae are long, slender, and many segmented. Cerci, a pair of appendages at the end of the abdomen, are present and are usually long. Stoneflies, the nymphal stages of which are aquatic, undergo incomplete metamorphosis.

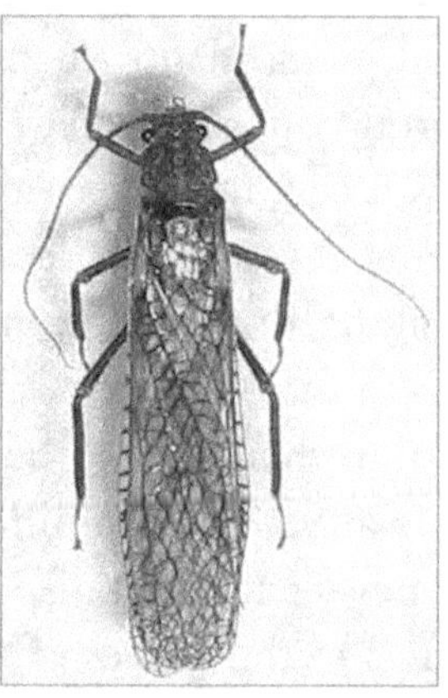

5.8 Adult stonefly.

Females lay from about 90 to over 800 eggs at a time. Some females fly over the surface of the water and dip their abdomens into it as they extrude their masses of eggs that seem to explode in the water as the gelatinous masses expand. Others alight on the surface of the water and extrude their masses of eggs at or below the waterline, where the masses separate and the eggs sink. The eggs have a sticky coating, which attaches them to the bottom of the stream, where they hatch after an incubation period that may be as short as three weeks to as long as seven months.

Stonefly nymphs are somewhat elongated and flattened with long antennae and long tails, called "cerci." They are similar to mayfly nymphs, but lack a middle tail—that is, they have only two tails, whereas mayfly nymphs have three. The gills are also different in that mayfly nymphs have leaf-like gills along the sides of the abdomen, whereas stonefly nymphs have branched gills on the thorax and about the bases of the legs.

Stonefly nymphs often are found under stones in the cirque's streams and along the shores of its lake, hence their common name, but they can also be found in other lakes and streams wherever food is available. Some species feed on plant material in the nymphal stage; others are predaceous or omnivorous.

Mature stonefly nymphs crawl out of the water when they are ready to emerge as adults; although some remain close to the water on vegetation or stones above the surface, others may crawl as high as eight feet up into trees. Some emerge, feed, and mate during the autumn and winter. The nymphs of these species generally feed on plants, and the adults feed chiefly on blue-green algae during daylight hours. Those emerging during summer, however, vary in nymphal feeding habits, and many do not feed as adults.

Mayflies

The mayflies of the pool are small to medium-sized, elongated, very soft-bodied insects with three long, threadlike tails. Adults have membranous wings with numerous veins. The front wings are large and triangular, whereas the hind wings are small and rounded and may be vestigial or absent in some species. ("Vestigial," from the Latin vestīgium, meaning "footprint" or "trace," represents the last small part that remains of something that existed earlier and performed a useful function.) The wings at rest are held together above the body. (Photo 5.9) The antennae are small, bristle-like, and inconspicuous. The immature stages are aquatic, and the metamorphosis is simple.

Some mayfly nymphs are streamlined in form and very active, while others are burrowing in habit and rather sedentary. They can usually be recognized by the leaf-like gills along the sides of their abdomens and by their three long tails. Stonefly nymphs, on the other hand, are similar but have only two tails, and their gills are on the thorax (only rarely on the abdomen) and are not leaf-like.

5.9 Adult mayfly.

Nymphal mayflies feed on algae, leaves that fall into the water and sink, fungal mycelia (the non-reproductive part of a fungus, consisting of a mass of thread-like filaments), and a variety of spores (the fungal analogue to "seeds"). The larvae of some species also ingest many tiny particles of wood in their feeding, but this may be incidental to feeding generally on decaying plant materials. The fungal mycelia, which can be a high proportion of the diet in some, are probably gleaned from the surfaces of the rotting leaves and wood.

When ready to transform to the winged stage, a nymph rises to the surface of the water, molts, and flies a short distance to the shore, where it usually alights on the vegetation. At this stage, the mayfly is rather dull in appearance, and is more or less hairy; it molts once more, usually the next day, and emerges as an adult. The adult is smooth and shining with longer tails and legs than the previous stage. Mayflies are the only insects that molt after the wings become functional.

The aquatic stages require a year or more to develop, but the adults, who have vestigial mouthparts and do not feed, seldom live more than a day or two. Adults often engage in spectacular swarming flights, during which mating takes place. The individuals in a swarm are usually all males that often fly up and down in unison. Sooner or later females will enter the swarm, at which time a male will seize a female and fly away with her.

The eggs are laid on the surface of the water, or are attached to vegetation or stones in the water. In cases where the eggs are laid on the surface of the water, they may be simply washed off the end of the abdomen a few at a time, or they may all be laid in one clump. In one case, a female lays her eggs in a milky mass and dies immediately. Once laid, the eggs sink and often adhere to objects on the bottom of the stream. The number of eggs laid by a female varies from as few as 50 to over 7,500.

These are only a few of the aquatic organisms that inhabit the stream from the lake in the cirque, the seep, and the pool between the large, fallen trees, where Storm Hawk baths himself. And yet, even among these few organisms, there is already an incredible partitioning of the available resources, even if food habits are the only consideration. For example, in the pool are immature dragonflies, stoneflies, midges, mayflies, and caddisflies. These insects can be separated into four functional feeding groups: shredders, grazers, collectors, and predators.

The shredders are dependent on large pieces of organic material, such as leaves, needles, wood, and other plant parts that are derived primarily from the margins of the stream, including the top of the forest canopy. Grazers are adapted for removing attached algae, especially where it grows on the surfaces of rocks and fallen trees in the current. Collectors use minute particles of organic matter, generally less than one-sixteenth of an inch in size, which they glean either by filtering the materials from the passing water or by actively gathering the chosen materials from deposits in the sediments of the stream bottom. Predators, on the other hand, are adapted through behavior and specialized body parts for capturing prey.

Because predators feed somewhat non-selectively on all functional groups (including other predators), their behavior indicates little about the stream-streamside interactions. For example, in the small- and medium-sized streams of the ancient forest, almost 58 percent of the aquatic insects are shredders, about 23 percent are collectors, 12 percent are grazers, and 7 percent are predators. This combination of functional feeding groups is capable of using the entire input of organic materials that fall into the stream as it flows through the forest toward the big river in the valley below.

As for Storm Hawk, thinking to himself that it's a good day to be alive, he takes off his fringed buckskin shirt, breechclout, and leggings and washes himself, after which he carefully cleans his bow, quiver of arrows, obsidian hunting knife, and the outside of his backpack, which houses his light bedding, an extra pair of moccasins, flint for sparking fires, and a meager amount of dried meat for emergencies. Then, sitting for a time in the afternoon sun, he idly watches the fallen leaves of Sitka alder and the dead needles of Douglas-fir and mountain hemlock float in lazy circles in the small eddies at the lower edges of the pool in which he had just bathed. Feeling light of heart and at one with the forest and the streams, he starts to climb toward the meadow where, according to the village elders, there is an ancient campsite of his people hidden in a clump of subalpine fir.

Chapter 6: Arriving at the Cirque

As he considers what to do next, his inner sense is to follow the stream upward, feeling it will surely lead him to the meadow, where legend says a young boy soared with a golden eagle in the land of far-distant memory. It was the image of this boy soaring with the eagle that dominated his dreams for several nights. When he discussed his dream with the elders, they not only told him that the Great Spirit was sending him on a vision quest but also assured him that he could recognize the meadow by the isolated clump of subalpine firs, where the ancestors had their hunting camp in the days of old.

In Storm Hawk's last dream, there was a man walking quietly along the edge of the meadow in early autumn toward an old burn, looking for signs of elk, which he had come to hunt. He pauses, climbs a small, rocky promontory, and surveys the ancient forest and the burn. He remembers how it looked when he had first seen it in his 16th summer (in the year 1000), and had laid in the meadow and soared with the great eagle. Now in his 36th summer (1020), the burn looks very different, its changes dramatic. He thinks how both he and the burn have grown and changed since that day in his youth, and how the ancient forest seems not to have changed at all.

Gazing at the meadow, he sees that a few reddish orange paintbrushes still grace moist places along the stream, and asters, in their blue autumn glory, dot the meadow. Dry, golden seed stalks of summer grasses resist the breeze that tries to bend them, and butterflies search for waning flowers. A bull elk bugles and is answered. A varied thrush calls, its trill floating on the September breeze. Flies buzz.

Storm Hawk, with his dreams vividly in mind, begins to follow the stream as it wends its way through the forest. Climbing over large, fallen trees, the grandparents and great grandparents of the forest's younger generation, he makes his way toward the meadow. Then, about 500 yards below the edge of the forest, he comes to a trail used by deer and elk. Turning to his left, he follows the well-defined trail as it winds around a small rocky outcrop and continues upslope. Finally, as the curtain of night begins to claim heaven's vault, he enters the finger of subalpine firs into which I will track a deer 345 years later, when in my 18th year. As darkness settles over the land, he builds a small fire and, taking some dried meat from his leather backpack, he prepares to spend the night serenaded by a distant chorus of frogs.

June 6th

The 6th of June is greeted by a faint glow in the east that gives portents of the rising sun. Minutes pass, the east grows brighter, and the first rays of light touch the meadow. The coming of dawn is accompanied by a symphony of bird voices, some singing and some seeming to measure the cadence with chattering.

Storm Hawk lies listening to Nature's music, as the first beams of sunlight touch his face. Still resting, a gentle, inner voice nudges him to rise and greet the day, the first in his search for the old campsite. Getting up, he picks up his bow and quiver of arrows and ventures quietly along the meadow's edge in the direction of the stream he left yesterday. Once there, he washes his face and has a drink.

Suddenly, out of the corner of his eye, he sees a slight movement under an alder at the stream's edge. Turning his head slowly, he focuses on the ground next to the movement, because he knows that, whatever the animal is, it could "feel" his direct stare. There, he detects a ruffed grouse feeding under the alder. (Photo 6.1) Slowly, carefully, he draws an arrow from his quiver and fits the arrow's notch to the bow's sinew string. Watching the grouse with his peripheral vision, he turns slightly to the right, waits until the grouse is eating in a small opening with its head down, then draws back his bow and shoots.

6.1 Ruffed grouse.

The arrow impales the grouse, which flops briefly, as its spirit departs the body. Storm Hawk walks over and, kneeling down by the fallen bird, apologizes for taking its life, and thanks the Great Spirit for guiding his arrow that he might have food. He then plucks the grouse, removes the intestines, and cleans its body in the stream, including the heart, lungs, liver, and kidneys, which he will eat.

With grouse in hand, he walks back to his camp, where he kindles a small fire, makes a spit with which to secure the bounty of his hunt, and cooks his meal. Having eaten his fill, he puts the remainder in a small pouch, which he puts into his backpack with the rest of his belongings, and sets off into the meadow in search of his ancestor's campsite.

He has not gone far beyond the upper-most subalpine fir of the small grove in which he spent the night when he notices some small, rounded, tube-like ridges running in various directions on top of the growing spring vegetation. Here and there they crisscross one another. As he walks along studying them, he finds a small boulder against which a soil ridge abruptly ends, then moves slightly to the left and continues around it. Elsewhere, he sees a larger boulder with one of the soil cylinders going over the top of it. Sitting on the boulder, looking at the meandering ridges, he wonders what kind of animal could have made such a complicated maze.

While contemplating the mysterious ridges, he notices a tentative movement of the soil about 10 feet in front of him. *There!* The soil bumps upward again, this time a little higher. The movement stops. *There it is again!* All is quiet. Suddenly, a small, reddish-brown head with noticeably large front teeth and two beady, little eyes erupts amidst a load of soil being pushed to the surface of the meadow. (Photo 6.2) Then another load, and another, until, finally, the small, reddish-brown body emerges far enough above the ground to arrange the soil in the characteristic, fan-shaped design of its burrow entrances.

6.2 Mazama pocket gopher excavating its burrow.

Having no idea what this secretive creature is, he has no clue how important this small mammal is to the long-term, biophysical integrity of the meadow. Storm Hawk is witnessing the activity of what today is known as the Mazama pocket gopher.

Mazama Pocket Gopher

An adult Mazama pocket gophers ranges in length from about seven to nine and a half inches and weighs from almost two ounces to a little over three ounces. Its back varies from reddish-brown to dark reddish-brown, whereas the nose and cheeks are somewhat darker and less reddish, and there are black patches around the ears. The underside is somewhat yellowish, and the feet and tail are a soiled whitish to gray. Moreover, their soft, loose fur enables them to move backward through the narrow tunnels as easily as it enables them to move forward.

Primarily inhabitants of the meadow, they dig two kinds of tunnels: shallow ones for gathering food, such as roots and tubers, and deep ones for shelter. ("Tubers" are the short, thick, round stem of certain plants, such as the potato, that grows underground and can produce a new plant.) The deep tunnels include separated chambers for nesting, food storage, and toilets. The burrow systems are marked by a series of earthen mounds on the surface of the ground, where they expel the excess earth through inclined, lateral shafts that result in fan-shaped mounds. In the process of constructing a burrow system, each gopher is capable of turning over three to seven tons of soil per acre per year.

Although gophers dig primarily with the strong claws of their front feet, they use their large, front teeth (incisors) to loosen soil and rocks, as well as to cut roots. They can use their incisors in this fashion because their lips can be closed behind them, preventing soil and other materials from getting into their throats.

They hold the loose earth between their chest and forelegs and push it to the surface. They plug the exits of their burrows with soil, thus creating an effective air-conditioning system and some protection against unwanted visitors.

Gophers are solitary except during the breeding season, when mating takes place and the young are reared. In fact, they are not only solitary most of their lives but also pugnacious. Their loose, flexible skin, thickest in the region of the head and throat, is advantageous both when they fight over home territories and when they try to fend off their main enemy, the long-tailed weasel, who hunts them in their burrows.

In winter, however, they sometimes dig shallow tunnels in the upper surface of the soil and the lower surface of the snow and find that sufficient. (Photo 6.3) At other times they pack soil into the snow to line their tunnels, creating a protected, winter subway. They do not, of course, go straight, but rather spend a day or two here and a week there, as they explore and hunt for food.

6.3 Winter burrow under snow. Note opening at bottom of tunnel.

The spring thaw reveals their winter travels recorded by the solid cores of soil, which Storm Hawk sees lying on the surface of the ground. (Photo 6.4) These cores are solid because the soil-lined tunnels collapsed inward as the snow melted. The cores also reveal where one tunnel went from belowground in one spot, up into the snow in another, and over an adjacent tunnel somewhere else. The latter is evident where one earthen core lies over another. Moreover, the gophers occasionally bumped into rocks, which they either climbed over (Photo 6.5) or went around. (Photo 6.6)

6.4 Winter burrows in snow revealed after snow melts and tunnels cave in on themselves.

6.5 Winter, earth-lined tunnel in snow going over rock.

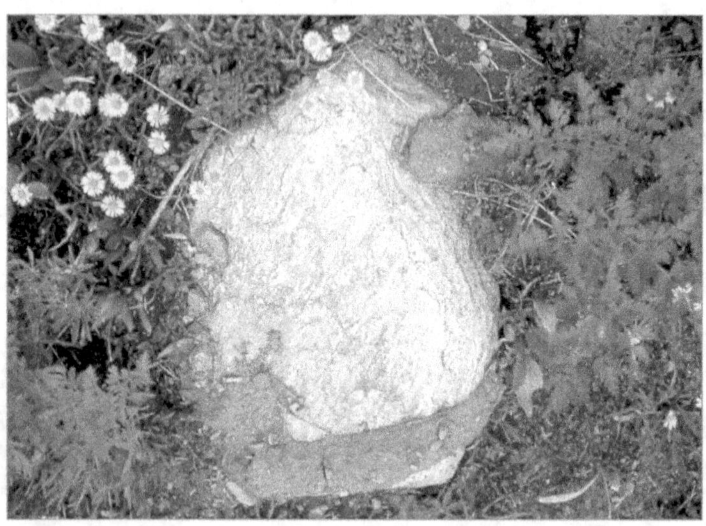

6.6 Winter, earth-lined tunnel in snow bumping into and going around rock.

In addition, one gopher built a nest on the surface of the soil with a toilet (a short tunnel filled with elongated fecal pellets) next to it. (Photo 6.7) These fecal chambers, when created below ground in the meadow, are an excellent source of subterranean fertilizer, a critical component in keeping the soil mellow.

6.7 Winter, earth-lined tunnel leading into nest chamber and toilet under the cover of snow.

Their mounds cover five to ten percent of the surface in some areas, and their burrows, six inches to a foot below ground, are so numerous that deer and elk can't help breaking into them. The tunnels are constantly extended and gradually fill up as they are abandoned and the old nests, pantries, and toilets are buried well below the surface; meanwhile, the mounds are constantly burying surface vegetation deeper and deeper. The soil thus becomes friable and porous due to the ever-changing network of underground burrows. So it is that a greater part of the snowmelt and rainfall not only penetrates the soil but also is held in the ground instead of running over the surface, where it is likely to cause erosion.

Although the gophers are active above ground primarily from the evening, throughout the night, into the early morning, they are active at any time on warm, overcast days. Underground activity seems to be almost continuous and is often heralded by muffled gnawing or scratching. The sound ceases and the stem of a lupine, or other favored food plant, begins to wiggle, as a small, brown nose appears. The hole is quickly enlarged to allow the gopher's head to emerge in the plant. A stem is cut off and drawn below ground. A good meal is gathered within a minute, and the hole securely plugged with soil.

While gathering food in the evening, a gopher is alert and stays close to its burrow. It cuts vegetation quickly, crams as much as possible into its external, fur-lined cheek pouches (hence the name "pocket gopher"), and disappears below ground. It reappears in a few minutes and gathers more food, which it takes into its burrow for storage in its food chamber. Although a gopher can withdraw food at will from its belowground pantry, much of the stored food is not eaten and decomposes, fertilizing the soil from within.

In addition, their burrowing not only helps air to circulate within the soil but also mixes the soil and thus distributes chemical nutrients from the soil's deeper layers to the surface and vice versa. What's more, their abandoned tunnels provide homes for a variety of animals, including salamanders, frogs, toads, and other, small denizens of the meadow.

As mid July approaches, seed heads of the grasses form into a soft "dough" stage, and the gophers remain outside next to their burrows for long periods. They sit on their haunches in twilight and deftly and systematically bend down one grass stalk after another with their forefeet. The soft, green heads are cut off, stuffed into cheek pouches, and transported below. The cheek pouches, extending from the lower portion of the face back to the shoulders, are turned inside out, emptied and cleaned with use of the forefeet. They are then pulled back in place by a special muscle. Thus, in their own inimitable way, the gophers are caretakers of the meadow.

However, gophers living along the southern edge of the meadow often visit the forest, where they dine on truffles, after which they move back into the edge of the meadow, and deposit spore-laden feces in their fecal chambers, thus inoculating the soil with mycorrhizal fungi—you will learn more about the role of these fungi on June 8th. With time, seedlings from the forest become established in the meadow. As the forest has gradually migrated upslope over the decades and centuries, gophers have been progressively displaced farther into the meadow. (Photo 6.8)

6.8 Winter evidence of a gopher's helping to establish young trees in the meadow at its interface with the forest.

On the other hand, the deep burrows along the lower end of the meadow cause the gophers to bring fairly deep subsurface soil to the surface. Because deeper soil contains few spores of mycorrhizal fungi compared to the topsoil, gopher mounds are often bare of plants because there are not enough spores of the necessary mycorrhizal fungi in this deep soil to inoculate the roots of plants and allow them to become established. In turn, however, this bare soil is vital to the survival of the Cascade tiger beetles, predacious beetles that prey on ants.

Tiger beetles appear to have rather shiny, bright-green wing covers and legs. The under surface is also green toward the head, becoming violet-blue in the middle, and green again toward the tail end. The wing covers have delicate, slightly curved, white markings on the shoulders and mid-wing, going from the outer margin of the wing cover across to the inner margin. In addition, there is a white spot at the rear of each wing cover. In reality, however, they are devoid of pigment and yet are arrayed in brilliant, metallic hues. *But,* you might wonder, *how can that be?* Well, rather than pigment, the colors exhibited by tiger beetles are created by light refracted off the minute structural topography of their wing covers and external skeletons.

If you now leave the tiger beetles to their daily rhythms and go back to the 10th of March, you would find the meadow still covered in deep snow, under which a male gopher finds a receptive female and mates with her. She conceives, and gives birth to a litter of five, naked babies in a warm, belowground nest on the 7th of April, 28 days after impregnation. By mid July, the rapidly growing youngsters leave their place of birth and establish their own burrow systems. At which time, they are about two-thirds grown and resemble their parents.

Returning to the present (June 6th) Storm Hawk, after watching the gopher's activity for an hour or so, continues his quest for the campsite. But before leaving the boulder, he climbs on top of it and surveys the meadow, which today is dotted here and there with the yellow of avalanche lilies, the pinkish of spring beauties, and red of Scarlet gilia, all embraced by the spring green of newly emerging grasses.

Despite how diligently he surveys the meadow, he fails to see the clump of trees within which the camp was reputed to have been. Therefore, reasoning the camp was probably near water, he decides to follow the stream through the meadow. Having thus made up his mind, he leaves the gopher to its work and walks farther into the meadow to locate the stream.

He moves slowly, quietly through the meadow enjoying the beauty surrounding him. Overhead a highly vocal flock of geese is winging its way north, flying in a V-shaped formation. Storm Hawk has always loved the airborne flocks of geese, and has often wondered why they insist on this basic pattern of flight.

If he could talk to the geese, they would tell him it's because flying in formation is easier and less tiring when they remain close to the wingtip of the bird in front of them, than if they were to fly solo. In essence, flying in a V-formation takes advantage of the aerodynamic uplift created by the wing beat of the bird in front, while simultaneously counteracting its downdraft. Moreover, they take turns leading so that each bird can experience a more restful pace, thereby preventing any one bird from having their energy reserve unfairly depleted.

This combination of aerodynamics not only reduces the energy expended by each bird but also reduces the rate at which its heart beats thus conserving the energy stored in its body fat. Conserving energy is an important function on long, migratory flights because it means a goose can reduce the number of necessary stopovers to replenish its fat reserves.

Watching the geese brings a smile to Storm Hawk's face, as he wishes them well on their journey and, looking skyward with outstretched arms, he thanks the Great Spirit for the gift of their company. Continuing his search, he stops to admire the flowers and examine a bustling mound of ants. Looking closely at the mound, he notices that the north side is still relatively devoid of vegetation while the south side is covered with small plants. (Photo

6.9) Although he has seen this sort of thing before, he does not understand the dynamics of its creation because his view is a simple snapshot in time from a single vantage point. Even if he had been one of the ants, however, and shared their experienced, he would still have missed the larger picture.

6.9 Ant mound showing seasonal microclimate—vegetated on the warm southern exposure and relatively bare on the colder northern exposure.

The snow, melting by mid-May, gradually exposed the top of the ant's mound, and the ants within began to feel the receding chill of winter. As winter's withdrawal from the meadow continued, the south-facing slope of the mound became increasingly visible, accompanied from within the mound by the growing warmth of the sun's southern traverse of heaven's azure vault. Spring's progression toward summer saw the days lengthen in accordance with the sun's migration northward, an event that daily melted the snow on the mound's southern slope, while leaving the northern slope untouched until the sun was sufficiently high in its northward journey to rise above the mound and begin to melt the snow on its north-facing slope. What was taking place on the ant's mound, as the sun daily climbed the heavens, was a mirror image of what was simultaneously occurring on the mountain of which the meadow is a part.

Meanwhile, the ants, feeling the accumulating heat within the mound, were becoming increasingly active, to the point of warming themselves in the sun on the mound's south-facing side. As the daily temperature increased, they began to forage in the meadow, following the snowmelt from the mound's south side, to the north, and then into the meadow in whichever direction they chose.

The few ants Storm Hawk sees reflect the personality of the whole colony, in fact, the personality of every colony of ants in the cirque. They are "risk takers" when it comes to foraging, and respond more aggressively to intruders than ants in more southern climes. This behavioral pattern coincides with the short time they have following snowmelt to acquire the total amount of resources needed to reproduce, and thus maintain the population and integrity of their colony.

So, while the ants are warming themselves, Storm Hawk, setting off once again on his quest, continues eastward into the meadow. Although his inner need to find the old campsite is urgent, the indescribable beauty surrounding him captivates his heart. Again he pauses and thanks the Great Spirit.

Continuing, he hears a raven call, and then another from somewhere along the eastern side of the meadow up toward the cliff. Finally, after an hour of slow progress, he hears the faint sound of water tumbling over a small blockade of rocks. Quickening his pace, he arrives at the stream a short distance above the forest.

Cascade Frog

Turning upstream, he comes to the waterfall. Rapid melting of snow in the meadow during mid-May has once again created the annual, temporary pond in a low area of the meadow, which acts as a nursery for the Cascade frog, a regular denizen of the area. (Photo 6.10) This year, being somewhat warmer than usual, sees the pond's water warm enough by the last week in May to stimulate not only the vocal abilities of the male frogs but also some of the females to lay the season's first egg masses along the bottom of the pond's sloping sides. Although females breed only once a year, they can lay up to 425 eggs in a single, gelatinous mass that is roughly the size of a grapefruit. The females often lay their eggs in a communal fashion, sometimes as many as 50 or more females depositing their eggs next to or on top of the eggs of other females. Egg-laying will continue through the 1st of July, after which the pond will have shrunk enough to preclude further deposits.

6.10 Cascade frog.

Some of the eggs began hatching by the second week in June. Therefore, as Storm Hawk reaches the waterfall, his attention is drawn to the pond by the multitudinous voices of the male frogs. Walking the short distance to the pond, he finds it alive with small, black creatures. They have oval, rather bulbous bodies with a pair eyes on their backs, and relatively long, fin-like, pointed tails. The wriggling creatures are tadpoles, the frog's immature stage. Although the mass of tadpoles seems to be in constant motion, some stop now and then to rest on the meadow's submerged vegetation.

Because Storm Hawk's visit to the pond is but a brief inter-lude in his day, he will not see the change from their current black coloration to a metallic silvery or brassy tone. Nor will his short sojourn in the meadow allow him to witness the tadpoles commence their metamorphosis from the immature stage to that of adult frogs. Moreover, it will be three years (until 1578) before most attain their full size, after which they become fertile and can begin to mate and lay their eggs in this same pond.

On reaching adulthood, a Cascade frog is two to two and half inches long from its nose to its tail end. It has a slender body, relatively smooth skin, two distinct parallel ridges of skin along the upper sides of the body, and blackish eye masks. Its back is tan, brown, or olive-brown with inky-black spots with distinct margins. The undersides of the legs and margin of the abdomen are a dull yellowish. The sides of its body and groin are black with cream to greenish-yellow mottling. It has long legs and webbed toes, which aid it in swimming. Juveniles resemble adults, but may not have the distinct yellow coloration on the undersurfaces. Mature males have gray, swollen "nuptial" pads on the thumbs, which aid them in clasping and holding the females during breeding. As for their diet, adult Cascade frogs are generalist predators, feeding primarily on grasshoppers, spiders, ants, larval insects in general, and craneflies.

After watching the tadpoles for about half an hour, Storm Hawk goes back to the stream and continues a little farther toward the cirque, when a small, blackish mammal arrests his gaze as it floats past while sitting on the surface of the water. Not sure if he is really seeing what he thinks he is, he moves slightly for a closer look. The water shrew, seeing the movement, dives into the stream and disappears.

Shortly thereafter, he sees a large mouse scurry out of the water, head up the bank to a well-worn runway, dash along it, and disappear into a burrow. (Photo 6.11) Looking around, he discovers runways extending here and there from the stream bank into the meadow, where some terminate in burrows, a few in globular nests of vegetation, and some seem to just peter out. This is the closest Storm Hawk will get to experiencing the life and times of the water vole.

6.11 The bit of stream out of which Storm Hawk saw the water vole scurry. You can see where the voles have been going in and out of the stream in the lower right-hand corner of the photograph.

WATER VOLE

The largest member of the "meadow mouse" group in North America, adult water voles range from about 8 inches to 10¾ inches in length, of which about one third is tail. Their large hind feet are almost an inch in length. Adults may weigh as much as four and a quarter ounces, males being larger than the females.

The pelage is long and rather coarse. The back and sides are dark reddish-brown to dark grayish-brown, and the underparts are washed with whitish hairs over a dark-gray underfur. The tail is bicolored, dark grayish above and lighter grayish below.

More than any other species of North American "meadow mice," these big, long-tailed, large-footed water voles are semi-aquatic in habits. Excellent swimmers and divers, they depend in part on the stream's water for protection. Although active throughout the 24-hour cycle, their peak of activity occurs during periods of darkness, but they are often abroad on sunny afternoons, like today, dashing along a runway between two burrows or swimming from one side of the stream to the other.

Most of the water voles live in burrows within 15 to 30 feet of the stream's banks and even have the entrances to some of their burrows under the surface of the water (Photo 6.12), much like their larger cousins, the muskrats of the lowlands. Some, however, live in more outlying wet areas in the meadow, such as the occasional seeps along the lower margin of the talus, where their large, well-worn trails, usually four inches wide or even wider, are conspicuous during the snow-free time of the year and are often strewn with the stems of grasses and sedges cut for food, as well as small piles of fecal pellets. (Photo 6.13) Along the stream, however, their trails commonly enter the water, where it is swift.

*6.12 A water vole's aquatic runway to its underground burrow
and up the stream bank into the meadow.*

6.13 A water vole's runway and burrow (bottom of the photograph) in a wet area of the meadow.

Their burrows, many of which are dug beneath large rocks, are about three inches in diameter and, constructed with no effort at concealment, often have large mounds of earth at their entrances. (Photo 6.14) Freshly dug burrows are sometimes so abundant that it seems likely more are dug than are used at any one time.

6.14 Water vole burrows in a wet area of the meadow.

The water voles' belowground passages and nest chambers are excavated and re-excavated between June and late September. The voles dig their tunnels immediately below the 1½- to 2½-inch-thick network of plant roots and mosses that cover the overhanging stream banks. Short segments of belowground tunnels, three to nine feet in length, and surface runways form branching travel lanes that lead to nest chambers, feeding areas, and the stream's edge.

The belowground burrows are about three inches in diameter, whereas the chambers are about four inches high, about six inches long, and about four inches wide. The nest chambers are dug inside small rises in the micro-topography of the stream's bank and the wet areas in the meadow, which keeps the nest above the water table and dry most of the year. Each vole completely fills its chamber with a large, dome-shaped nest made from short segments of leaves, grasses, sedges, and other vegetation from the meadow, and a single vole occupies each nest. The numerous burrow openings in the stream's banks and on the meadow along the stream's edge allow easy access to areas both below ground and above ground.

In winter, the voles spread out over much of the meadow under the cover of snow, where they live from seven to eight months of each year. Their tunnels are dug through the snow along the surface of the ground, but do not lead to the surface of the snow. In fact, no vole activity will be seen above the snow once the first two and a half to three inches have fallen without melting. The voles even make bulky nests of autumn's dry grasses under the cover of snow—the ones Storm Hawk saw on the surface of the ground. These nests, which are loosely built and fall apart soon after the snow melts, may be used throughout the winter or only during the period of melting snow when the soil becomes saturated with water and the voles' belowground tunnels and nests are flooded.

The voles' food consists of such things as the green leaves and stems of grasses, sedges, clovers, and numerous other meadow plants, including some of their seeds during the short seedtime of the mountain summer and autumn. Roots, bulbs, and bark of mountain willows and other plants, such as bear grass, which is a lily, are eaten during winter under the cover of snow.

Their breeding season begins in late May or early June and lasts until late September. The onset of the breeding season coincides closely with the appearance of the first new growth of the herbaceous vegetation as melting snow banks recede. The minimum gestation period is 22 days, after which two to 10, but usually five to six young are born in belowground nests. The young are able to swim by the time they are 17 days old, are fully weaned by 21 days of age, and are sexually mature after two months.

Those adults that survived the last winter are responsible for most of the reproduction because youngsters generally do not appear above ground until after the 1st of July and only about 25 percent of them will breed in their first year. Although most voles will survive only one winter and die during their second autumn or winter, a few will survive two winters. Of the many causes of death, short-tailed weasels and long-tailed weasels account for most. Even though the number of voles in the meadow fluctuates over time, there is, at present, a good population.

It is midday when Storm Hawk approaches the bottom of the cirque's moraine. Resting momentarily, he examines the eastern moraine, and decides to climb it for a wider view of the meadow. (Photo 6.15) Once on top, he surveys the lake, cliff and its immediate talus, and the meadow. Wherever he looks in this rocky terrain, his gaze is greeted by a loosely knitted flock of bold, gregarious gray-crowned rosy-finches that show no sign of fear, despite the fact that he is but two to three feet from where some of them are feeding.

6.15 The moraine.

The cliff, he discovers, curves north and east about a quarter of a mile to the east of the cirque, and extends another half mile eastward before it reaches a point where the meadow gradually slopes down to meet what looks like a fringe of trees. Between the moraine on which he is standing and the distant line of trees, the meadow shows no hint of what might have been the campsite for which he is searching. Nevertheless, Storm Hawk remains atop the moraine for another hour, scrutinizing the gently waving grasses and nodding flowers for any irregularity in the outline of the meadow's surface that might hint of a place worth examining.

Finding none, he decides to go back to his camp for the night and move to the far-eastern side of the meadow the next day.

Once back in camp, however, he realizes that he is already in a finger-like peninsula of trees, in addition to which there are three islands of firs, making him wonder if the old campsite could be somewhere in this side of the meadow. With this in mind, he decides to search this side of the meadow before considering the eastern side. Then he remembers the birds he saw in and around the cirque earlier in the day, and he wonders about their fearlessness.

Cascade Gray-Crowned Rosy-Finch

A migrant from Asia somewhere in time, the vast majority of Cascade gray-crowned rosy-finches still migrate south with the advent of autumn and north with the promise of spring. Whereas the majority of the rosy finches that Storm Hawk saw arrived in the cirque as winter's blanket of snow was beginning to melt with the growing warmth of May, a small population remains in and around the cirque throughout the year, roosting in old cliff swallow nests during the cold, winter nights.

These hardy finches have a stout body 6 to 6½ inches long with a nine-inch wingspan, and weigh from a little over 7/10 to 9/10 of an ounce. Adult males of the cirque have a gray body and variable gray cheeks. The forehead and throat are black; the back and top of the head is gray—hence the name "gray-crowned." There is, however, some variability in the amount of grey on the head. In addition, a faint-gray ring exists around each eye and a white patch at the base of the bill, which is black during the breeding season and yellow otherwise. The dark wings and tail, the latter being forked, are variable white and pink, and a pink wash can be seen on the underparts. Their flight feathers appear pale from below, giving the underwings a "frosted" appearance that helps identify rosy-finches as they fly about the cirque. Adult females are similar, but have less pink and white in the wings and tail. Moreover, males typically outnumber females throughout the year.

Rosy-finches are gregarious birds that form large flocks in

winter and even remain in loosely associated flocks during the breeding season. They communicate with a call that can sound like a buzzing *chew* or raspy *twew chirp* that is regularly repeated in a long series. Bold and fearless, the tone of their call can change pitch to designate aggression, a warning, or to note other situations.

Ground-feeders, the finches often forage in small flocks, walking along on winter's white blanket looking for whatever food they can find. With the increasing warmth of spring, they wander along the edges of the melting snow, as it gradually exposes the meadow's cloak of new grasses, low shrubs, and rocky areas, where they search for the minute seeds of alpine plants. Although their main diet is the seeds of grasses in season, they also eat insects that are wind-borne on updrafts of warm air from the valley and foothills, some of which become frozen in whatever snowfields might still be in existence. However, the finches also fly to catch airborne insects.

Gray-crowned rosy-finches breed in alpine regions at a higher altitude than any other bird in North America. The finches Storm Hawk observed are in the beginning phases of building their bulky, cup-shaped nests in rocky crevices, on cliff ledges, and under overhanging rocks that will completely hide them from view. As long as the appropriate rocks are available, some of the finches will nest near the moist seeps at the base of the cliff along the meadow's upper edge.

Being monogamous, the mated pair collects the nesting material of grass, roots, lichen, and moss, but only the female builds the nest, lining it with fine grass, hair, and feathers. Moreover, the male defends his mate's territory and nest during the breeding season, but not only that, he also defends her wherever she goes. (A lichen is formed by the composition of two plants in a mutually beneficial symbiotic relationship, where the outer plant is a fungus that houses an inner alga, and the alga captures energy from sunlight through photosynthesis, which then feeds itself and the fungus.)

Nest completed, the female that Storm Hawk first noticed will lay a single clutch of three to five eggs, beginning on June 8th, and will incubate them for 14 days, until June 22nd, when the helpless babies hatch. By that time, both parents will have grown a pair of "gular pouches," opening from the floor of the mouth, wherein they carry food to their nestlings. (A "gular pouch" is derived from the gular skin, which is the area of featherless skin that joins the lower part of the beak to the bird's neck, forming a flexible, flap-like pocket in which food can be stored.) The young birds will leave their nest (termed "fledging") somewhere between July 10th and July 29th, after Storm Hawk will have departed the cirque for home, at which time, the young birds will look quite different from the adults.

They will have light gray to gray-brown bodies, no black forehead, and no rosy wash, as well as having creamy-buff wing-bars and patches, but that will all change by the time they return in the spring. Nevertheless, they will continue to be fed by their parents for another two to three weeks, well into August.

With the breeding season drawing to a close and the young birds assuming their independence, some of these summer visitors will begin gathering into a large flock. As the frosty chill punctuates the autumn air, they will commence their departure from the cirque for warmer climes, leaving behind the small, resident flock.

Cliff Swallows

Although cliff swallows, one of the most social land-birds of North America, normally stay at lower elevations than the cirque, a few have followed the thermals to this high world over the years, arriving in early to mid-May, depending on the year, and normally depart in early to mid-August for South America, where they spend the winter from Venezuela southward.

Only peripherally aware of the swallows flying around the cliffs, out over the talus and meadow and along the edge of the forest, Storm Hawk is unaware that two kinds of swallows are sharing the cirque. Those flying around the cliffs, talus, and lake are cliff swallows, whereas those along the lower meadow and the forest are predominantly tree swallows.

Compact birds, the cliff swallows of the cirque are about 5½ inches long, including their tiny, black beaks. They have pointed, triangular wings with a 12-inch wingspan, a small head, and a medium-length tail with a square end. In the early light of morning, before the sun has fully risen, the swallows look brownish with dark throats and white underparts. As the sun clears the horizon, however, their iridescent, dark-blue backs and dark caps, which extend below the eyes, are clearly visible. Their cheeks, sides of the neck, and throats are chestnut brown. They have pale, pumpkin-colored rumps and white underparts. Their faces are brick red with a bright, buff-white forehead patch that resembles a headlamp.

Looking toward the cliff, Storm Hawk sees the swallows zooming here and there, hither and yon, in intricate, aerial patterns to catch insects on the wing, and he faintly hears their constant, subdued, squeaky twittering and chattering, but not their typical alarm call, which sounds like a sharp *keeer*.

Cliff swallows preen, feed, drink, and bathe in groups, and they continue sticking together in large flocks during migration and on their wintering grounds. Although they sleep in the few trees growing near the cliff, a breeding bird will start sleeping in the nest as soon as the structure is partially finished.

Cliff swallows eat flying insects, particularly swarming species, foraging during the day in groups while on the wing along the cliff, over the talus, lake, and meadow, and along the edge of the forest, often taking advantage of the warm air currents that collect and bring dense swarms of insects upslope from the valley, which the tree swallows of the forest also benefit from. There is, however, little competition between the two species because the cliff swallows forage some distance above the tree swallows. As such, the cliff swallow's diet consists of bugs, flies, bees, wasps, ants, beetles, lacewings, mayflies, butterflies, moths, grasshoppers, crickets, dragonflies, and damselflies.

Although sharing information about food at the colony appears unintentional, when a swallow finds food away from the colony during the poor weather conditions that occasionally descend on this high mountain world during the swallows' seasonal visit, it may give a specific call to let others know that food is available. By alerting other swallows to a large swarm of insects, an individual may ensure that the swarm is both tracked and can be followed.

On the other hand, in cool or rainy weather, when insects are scarcer and thermals weaker, the colony serves as a foraging information center, as parents make trips back and forth to feed nestlings. In this case, unsuccessful hunters follow their successful neighbors to food sources.

With the beginning of the nesting season, which commenced around May 10th this year, each pair of cliff swallows would either take over an existing nest or select a space within the colony to build a new nest. During the search, females spent more time than the males scoping out a suitable nest site before they settled on one under an overhang on the cliff face. However, an unmated male could choose a site on his own and begin building a nest before he attracts a mate.

One pair, having found a site on the 15th that suited them, flew to the seep along the base of the cliff, where they collected pellets of mud in their beaks, which they carried to the chosen location. In past drought cycles, however, they would have to fly a few miles from the cirque to obtain mud—but not this year.

While collecting mud pellets, the pair, having bred on the 18th, fluttered their wings up high in an apparent attempt to prevent forced copulation, because extra-pair copulations are common. Beyond that, they carried the mud pellets to their chosen location in their beaks, and molded them into place with a shaking motion, beginning by dabbing a circle of mud onto the selected area of the cliff face. From there, they added mud-balls to the bottom of the rim in an upward and outward direction, eventually forming a gourd-shaped nest made of 900 to 1,200 individual mud pellets. (Photo 6.16)

6.16 Cliff swallow in a partially built nest; note mud on its beak.

During the construction of their nest, they were obliged to fight for their chosen site by grappling with others to prevent a hostile takeover of their half-built nest. Moreover, they will also have to continue defending their completed nest by sitting in the entrance, where their bright foreheads glow in its dim light, as they puff up their head and neck feathers to look larger when they lunge at intruders.

They finish constructing their nest on the 19th at which time it is about eight inches long, six inches wide, and 4½ inches high, with walls ²/₁₀ to ⁷/₁₀ of an inch thick. Its entrance, which they have elongated into a tube, is about 1⁷/₁₀ inches high and two inches wide. The pair then lined their nest with dried grass and feathers, after which they will make repairs as necessary throughout the breeding season by patching it up with mud.

These enclosed, globular nests along the cliff share common walls, which not only strengthen the nests but also keep the peace by preventing the inhabitants from peeking into one another's abodes. If, however, a hole is made in the common wall and the swallows can see each other, they bicker and squabble until the hole is repaired, which immediately restores tranquility.

Their nest completed, the female laid six pinkish eggs with brown speckles. Both parents incubated the eggs for 14 days, until June 2nd, when the naked, pink-skinned babies hatched, weighing less than a tenth of an ounce each.

Here, there is a caveat termed "brood parasitism." The pair's neighbor could only lay one egg, but returned from feeding to a nest with two eggs in it because another female had snuck in during her absence and laid another. But that is not all. Three days later, when she returned to her nest, it contained three eggs because yet another female had carried in her beak one of her own eggs laid in her own nest, and left it.

Be that as it may, this year both parents will feed their youngsters for 21 days before they fledge and leave the nest. Two years ago, however, a long, cold, rainy spell occurred while the youngsters were still in their respective nests, which caused widespread mortality throughout the colony because the adults were unable to obtain enough insects to feed them.

Then, on June 23rd, the nestlings, now juveniles, leave their nest, the same day Storm Hawk will acquire a snowshoe hare from a weasel. At this juncture, they are essentially brown above and whitish below, except for the buff rump and dark face. In addition, they have varying numbers of small white spots on their forehead and throat. And it is at this time that they begin to congregate with other juveniles in a large group, called a "crèche," wherein parents must use a sophisticated vocal-communication system to locate their own young.

As the days and weeks pass, the juveniles begin to look more like their parents. Finally, cooling days and colder nights herald the beginning of the cliff swallow's long migration from the cirque to the southern parts of South America, where they will spend the winter, until, once again, the cirque calls out for them to return.

Tree Swallows

Although Storm Hawk sees the tree swallows as they pursue insects along the lower part of the meadow and over the forest, he does not recognize them as different from the cliff swallows because, while they were flying lower in the sky than the cliff swallows, when seen together from below, they appear to be a singular flock of feeding birds.

The cirque with its forest, lake, streams, and marshy areas constitutes an ideal habitat for the tree swallows Storm Hawk casually observes. Having spent the winter along the Caribbean coast of Central America, they begin arriving at the forest along the meadow's edge somewhere between the latter part of April and the beginning of May, at which time they once again enter the biophysical drama of the cirque. How? They do so by affecting the population dynamics of the insects they eat, as well as providing food for their predators, such as sharp-shinned hawks. They will remain in the cirque until the end of July or the beginning of August, depending on the hospitality of the year, after which they will again follow the airways to the sunny climate of the Caribbean for the winter.

The tree swallows return to the cirque before the cliff swallows. They do so because they can eat plant foods in addition to their normal insect prey, which helps them survive the cold snaps and wintry weather of early spring.

Handsome aerialists, they have deep-blue or blue-green, iridescent backs that flash in the sunlight, and clean, white fronts. Seen in profile, both sexes have a sharp line of demarcation between the dark of the head above the eye and the pure white of the rest of the face and underparts. Although males and females in adult plumage look similar to each other, they are unique because first-year females, although reproductively mature, have a different plumage from older birds. Their first-year plumage is similar to that of juveniles: non-iridescent brownish-gray above with a grayish-white belly. However, juveniles have a grayish breast-band that first-year females lack.

Small birds, tree swallows range from 5 to 6¼ inches in length and weigh about 7⁄10 of an ounce. They have long wings; tiny, black beaks; small legs; small dark reddish-brown or brownish-gray feet; and moderately forked tails. Their voice is a cheerful series of liquid twitters.

The cirque, with the forest of large, old trees that contain myriad cavities in close proximity—by swallow standards—to the meadow, lake, streams, and marshy areas, forms an ideal habitat for the nesting swallows. In addition, they are primarily insectivorous, and thus require an abundance of flying insects as food. This requirement is fulfilled by the local bodies of water, which produce multitudes of winged insects, coupled with the thermals that bring swarms of flying insects from the lower elevations into the cirque.

Although flying insects account for most of their diet, the swallows also eat berries and the seeds of various plants when insects are not available. This allows them to survive cold spells better than other swallows, which in turn allows them to overwinter farther north than other swallows.

They feed from dawn to dusk in sheltered areas full of flying insects, usually foraging no more than 40 feet above the ground. Before eggs are laid, a pair may travel up to 37 miles to acquire food. After the eggs are laid, however, until the nestlings fledge, they stay within roughly three miles of the nest site.

They eat a variety of flying insects (dragonflies, damselflies, flies, mayflies, caddisflies, true bugs, sawflies, bees, ants, wasps, beetles, stoneflies, butterflies, and moths, as well as spiders), some smaller than a grain of sand, others up to two inches long. Chasing prey in the air, with acrobatic twists and turns, they sometimes converge in large numbers on an insect swarm. However, they can also glean insects from the surface of water or vertical surfaces. During the breeding season, they eat high-calcium items like the bones of fish and discarded eggshells of other birds.

Agile fliers, they tend to glide more than the cliff swallows, which would have helped Storm Hawk separate the two species in flight, had he known this. In addition, they bathe by flying low over the lake and skimming their bodies against the surface, then rising quickly, as they shake off droplets. They also bathe by preening extensively during summer's rainfall, using it as a shower.

Beyond bathing, they like to play with feathers. In doing so, a swallow flies up with a feather held in its beak. Sometimes this leads to chases. At other times, the feather may simply be dropped, causing an aerial free-for-all to see who retrieves it.

Tree swallows communicate primarily through the use of sounds and physical displays. Although both sexes use calls to communicate, only the males sing, apparently to proclaim their territory.

At least 14 different calls have been identified. The apparent purposes of these calls range from signaling distress, anxiety, pleasure, submission, and begging for food. Body signals, such as crouching and wing-fluttering, are also used to convey a variety of messages, including aggression and the invitation to copulate. In addition, tree swallows respond to predators, such as the great horned owl, by gathering in large numbers, then swarming and dive-bombing the predator one of the swallows has found, all the while giving alarm calls.

Tree swallows are mainly monogamous, but copulating secretly outside the pair is common, with as many as 50 percent of the nests in a given population possibly containing young that were fathered by an individual other than the resident male. Consequently, there are times when a male attends two mates in separate nest sites. Though an individual swallow may have the same mate for several years, it may be more faithful to the site than to its mate.

They nest in tree cavities, such as old woodpecker holes, appropriate hollows in standing dead trees (snags), and even in hollow tree stumps invariably located in the immediate vicinity of water—in this case, one of the streams. Although tree swallows are highly social outside of the breeding season, being hole-nesters, they often face a housing shortage and must fight, not only to get into a sought-after nest site but also to keep it for the duration of the nesting season.

This being the case, it is little wonder they are so strongly territorial during the breeding season, at which time a pair defends a 33- to 50-foot radius around their nest against both their own kind and other nest-site competitors. Such competition for nest sites may be the underlying motivation behind sexually selective infanticide, as well as frequent copulation and their strongly aggressive responses to nest-site competitors.

On the 30th of April, a pair of tree swallows located a vacant cavity in a large snag that once belonged to a pileated woodpecker. Having thus procured their nest site, the male began collecting nest material on the ground, within 100 feet of the snag, and brought it to his female partner, at which time she commenced to build the nest, an undertaking that would last eight days, until the 8th of May. When available, a nest is made entirely of grass, but in this case it included mosses, rootlets, and animal hair in addition to some grass.

Within the cavity, the female pressed her body against the nest material, shaping it into a cup two to three inches across and one to two inches deep, after which she lined it with numerous feathers from various kinds of birds. At times during this process, the male gathered most of the feathers; at others times, both birds shared the responsibility.

The nest completed on May 13th, the female laid four eggs. The eggs, pale pink when first laid, turned to pure white within 4 days. Once laid, she incubated her eggs until the 28th of May, when the helpless nestlings hatched, with their eyes closed and pink skin that was sparsely covered in down. From this day until the 18th of June, both parents feed the youngsters. Although they leave the nest as juveniles on the 19th, as Storm Hawk continues searching the eastern side of the meadow for some sign of his ancestor's campfire, their parents will continue to feed them until the 22nd, despite the fact that they are already good fliers.

The juveniles are similar in appearance to adults, but are brownish rather than greenish blue. They also have a hint of grey across their white chests. Further, they will be able to breed the next summer, 1576, if they can find and establish a nest site. Whereas their lifespan may be somewhere between 8 and 10 years, their longevity will more likely be around three years.

Nesting season over, the tree swallows begin forming a flock that spends a few more days in and around the cirque before leaving to join a flock of migrants in the low country numbering in the hundreds of thousands. Before they leave for their southern wintering areas, they gather about an hour before sunset and form a dense, swirling cloud, reminiscent of a dynamic tornado, above a roosting site, such as a cattail marsh or grove of trees. With each pass, more birds descend until they are all settled for the night. And then, one day, they are gone.

THE EVOLUTIONARY MIRACLE OF A BIRD'S EGG

The shell of a bird's egg is a complex, multifunctional, bioceramic structure that is far more sophisticated in its functional dynamics than it would appear on the surface. ("Bioceramic" is a ceramic compound composed of calcium and phosphates that is compatible with the spark of life in a bird's egg. The dentine in our own teeth is another example of a bioceramic.)

In this sense, a bird's eggshell simultaneously represents a highly evolved physical structure (thickness) and chemical structure (pigment concentration and shell reflectance) that actively shapes the developmental environment of the bird's embryo by protecting it from both mechanical damage and too much ultraviolet light, facilitating gas exchange, and providing calcium for the growth of its bones. ("Pigment" is a natural substance in the tissue of plants and animals that provides their color.)

Considering the millions of years it has taken for birds' eggs to evolve the various shell components necessary for the survival of the babies inside under so many different circumstances, you might wonder what the value of laying eggs is to begin with. The answer to this question might well be another question: Can you imagine what a handicap it would be for a mother bird to fly with the seasonal bulk and weight of a whole clutch of egg-encased babies inside her?

That said, the most obvious characteristic of an eggshell would seem to be its coloration. Ancestrally, birds' eggs were probably white and immaculate, a characteristic that has been retained by species whose nests are safe from attack by predators. Today, many cavity-nesting birds, such as the flammulated owl, lay eggs that are not only pure white but also round—protected from rolling out of the nest by the cavity's walls. (Photo 6.17) On the other hand, birds that historically moved to increasingly vulnerable nesting sites are today more likely to lay brownish eggs that are both covered in speckles and smaller at one end, which keeps them rolling in a small circle, thus preventing them from rolling away from the nest. (Photo 6.18) This evolutionary dichotomy is the result of ancient diversification in nest-site selection, and thus in the clutch's vulnerability to predation. Yet, even blue eggs might be hidden in a nest built under certain conditions within vegetation.

6.17 Eggs of a cavity-nesting flammulated owl.
Note that the eggs are both white and round.

6.18 Eggs of a ground-nesting killdeer in gravel. Note the speckled pigmentation and the fact that one end is larger than the other. .

Then there are the brood parasites, birds that do not raise their own young but rather lay their eggs in the nest of another species of bird (the host). The European common cuckoo is a classic example. In this case, the shells of the cuckoo's eggs are usually thick with an outer chalky layer thought to resist cracking when a cuckoo drops its egg into the host's nest. Once there, the cuckoo's egg hatches earlier than those of the host's own young. In addition, the cuckoo chick not only grows faster than the host's young but also instinctually evicts the eggs or young of its host. Thereafter, the chick encourages the host to keep pace with its fast growth through its rapid begging call and open mouth, which together serve as a stimulus to keep it fed.

Most likely, these parasite-host dynamics have influenced the diversity of colors in birds' eggs, and so the resultant appearance. Both parasite and host have long driven the evolution of coloration and pattern on one another's eggs. To whit, the host species attempts to avoid exploitation by rejecting odd-looking eggs from its nest, while the brood parasite attempts to outwit its host by laying eggs that will escape detection.

In addition to such deceptive camouflage, adaptations in the concentration and thickness of the shell's pigment allow the right amount and wavelength of light to pass through the eggshell in a particular nest location and reach the embryos inside. Put succinctly, embryos require a certain amount of exposure to ultraviolet light—too little and it not only prohibits the embryo from metabolizing enough calcium for normal growth but also allows harmful micro-organisms to grow on the eggshell; too much and it damages the developing embryo by producing DNA lesions. This simply means that birds whose nests are exposed to the sun and those with simultaneously long periods of incubation have eggshells containing more pigment, thus limiting the embryo's exposure to potential tissue damage by allowing less ultraviolet light through the shell. In essence, the concentration of pigment on an eggshell determines the amount of light that can pass through it—the more pigment the less light the shell allows inside the egg.

6.19 Note the amount of pigmentation on this killdeer's egg and the camouflaging effect of its coloration, as well as the fact that one end is significantly larger than the other, a structure that keeps the egg rolling in a small space, even on a flat, unobstructed surface. Note also, how well the three chicks blend into the background of their nest.

Here an example might be the killdeer, which nests on the ground in open depressions in gravel that are exposed to the variability of Nature's weather patterns, including the damaging component of the sun's ultraviolet light. This being the case, their eggs contain extra pigment that helps control the amount of light entering through the shell and thus reaching the embryo, regardless of the shell's thickness. (Photo 6.19)

In contrast, eggs belonging to species that nest in burrows (such as burrowing owls) and cavities (such as flammulated owls and pileated woodpeckers) are pure white, and thus allow a greater transmission of light through the shell to assist embryonic development under the low-light exposure of the nest's surroundings, regardless of the shell's thickness.

There is yet another hidden aspect to the coloration of birds' eggshells: a light-inducing, anti-microbial protection against certain, damaging bacteria, such as those in the genus *Micrococcus*. For example, birds' eggs are susceptible to microbial attack in a number of ways once the eggs have been laid and are exposed to contaminating microorganisms in the surrounding environment from such things as feces, dust, and soil.

Of the several hundreds to millions of bacteria typically inhabiting the surface of a domestic chicken's eggshell, for example, the most common are species of *Micrococcus*, which are resistant to drying out. On the other hand, bacteria that are susceptible to drying out find it difficult to grow on an eggshell's surface.

As it turns out, birds' eggs are equipped with both physical and chemical defenses against microbial infection, defenses that have evolved to protect the developing embryo. Collectively, therefore, pigments have evolved into a natural, eggshell-defense system in the form of a light-induced, anti-microbial overlay against certain infectious bacteria.

Nevertheless, even if both kinds of bacteria have the same probability of entering an egg's interior through pores in the shell, the multiplication of those resistant to drying out will be prevented from multiplying by anti-bacterial proteins present in the egg's albumen. "Albumen" is the clear, water-soluble protein surrounding the yolk of an egg that provides the embryo with nutrition—also called "egg white."

While perhaps not as obvious to the human eye as is coloration, the role of eggshell thickness is every bit as important. There are two reasons for this. The first is the weight of the bird resting on the egg during its incubation. The larger the bird the thicker, and thus stronger, the shell needs to be, such as the North African ostrich weighing an average of 245 pounds *versus* a rufous hummingbird weighing between ⅒ to ²⁄₁₀ of an ounce.

The second, and perhaps less obvious reason, is the length of the incubation period. That is, after taking the initial weight of the parent bird into account as it rests on the egg, the length of time the bird incubates its egg, which bears the bird's weight, must also be accounted for—35 to 45 days for the ostrich, but only 15 to 17 days for the rufous hummingbird. In essence, the longer a bird of a given body weight sits on an egg, the greater the cumulative stress the shell's thickness must be able to withstand as the bird gets on and off the egg and shifts its body around while on the nest as the hours and days pass.

There is yet another aspect to the miracle of birds' eggs, and that is the long, transformative journey of the huge, meat-eating, land-living dinosaurs of old changing into the light, winged birds of today by constantly shrinking in size through 50 million years in the evolutionary corridors of time. Technically known as *theropods*, (Greek for "beast-foot") with strong, hind legs on which they walked and short front limbs (such as the carnivorous *Tyrannosaurus rex*), they shrank 12 times, the last time from the 359 pounds (as the "bird line" of dinosaurs evolved closer to true birds) to 1⁸⁄₁₀ pounds with the arrival of modern birds.

What, you might wonder, *has this to do with a bird's egg?* Try to imagine how big the egg of a 5- to 7-ton *Tyrannosaurus rex* would have to be compared to that of modern birds—from an ostrich egg (weighing from 3½ to 5 pounds) to a hummingbird egg (weighing from ⁷⁄₅₀₀ to ½ of an ounce).

The distinct, prolonged phase of shrinking in size along the route to becoming modern-day birds would have facilitated the evolution of many novelties associated with a smaller body size, such as reorientation of body mass, increased aerial ability, and "paedomorphic" skulls (from the New Latin *paed*, "child," and the Greek *morphosis*, "a variation in the pattern of development"). In other words, skulls of the adult dinosaurs evolving toward today's birds retained the characteristics of young dinosaurs, but with reduced snouts and enlarged eyes and brains. So it was that shrinking in size and new, bird-like traits jointly influenced the transition of dinosaurs into birds—including the one Storm Hawk will meet tomorrow during his sojourn to the forest.

June 7th

Entering the trees, Storm Hawk pauses, quietly looking around, but sees nothing that would constitute a meal, although he hears a low-frequency, thumping sound somewhere in a distant part of the forest, which begins slowly and speeds up—*thump.....thump.... thump...thump..thump.thump-thump-thump-thump*. Listening intently, he realizes that he is hearing the territorial drumming of a male grouse like the one he shot and ate yesterday.

Ruffed Grouse

An inhabitant of the forest, a male grouse, standing on top of a fallen tree 12 inches above the ground, makes the "drumming" sound that Storm Hawk hears. Although the grouse is in an area of moderately dense forest shrubs, where he can maintain unrestricted surveillance over the terrain for a radius of about 60 feet, he is out of Storm Hawk's view.

This drumming is the male grouse's non-vocal declaration of his presence, and is produced as he quickly rotates his wings forward and backward. The air that rushes into the temporary vacuum beneath his wings creates a deep, thumping sound wave that carries up to a quarter of a mile. (Photo 6.20) Moreover, one grouse's drumming will often trigger a defensive, territorial response in a nearby male because they are all aggressively territorial throughout their adult lives, each defending his exclusive, life-long use of a piece of forest 6 to10 acres in extent—that is, with the exception of one or two females he is willing to share his territory with.

6.20 Male ruffed grouse drumming.

Ruffed grouse are chunky, medium-sized birds that weigh from a pound to a little over 1½ pounds. They are 16 to 20 inches long and have a span of 20 to 25 inches across their short, strong wings. They also have short legs and a crest of feathers on top of their heads that sometimes lie flat.

In general, those living in and around the cirque have intricate patterns of dark bars and spots on a brownish-gray background. Dark bars extending down the side of their necks continue and widen on the belly. The tail is finely barred, with one wide, black band near the tip. This pattern of light and dark coloration on their feathers helps to "fragment" a bird's visible silhouette, and is known as "disruptive" or "cryptic" coloration. (Photo 6.21)

6.21 Female ruffed grouse.

More specifically, they have brownish-gray heads, necks, and backs, and their breasts are light with barring. There is much white on the underside and flanks. Overall, the birds have a variegated appearance, with throats that are often distinctly lighter. Although their broad, flat, fan-shaped tails are essentially the same brownish-grey, the pattern of alternate, irregular dark and light markings on the tail feathers is unique to each bird, including the broad, black band near the end of the tail.

The name "ruffed" is derived from some long, shiny, black or chocolate-colored neck feathers, which are most prominent on the male. Concealed under normal circumstances, the ruff is erected in full display when a male is either defending his territory or showing off for an interested female. When completely erected while a male is drumming, the feathers extend into a spectacular ruff that, together with his fully fanned tail, makes him look twice his normal size.

The feathers on their heads cover their nostrils, and likely warm the cold air the grouse breathe in during the winter in this high mountain world. In addition, they grow comb-like fringes on their toes that, like snowshoes, allow for easy travel on snow.

Ruffed grouse spend most of their time on the ground, often running and hiding to avoid detection. And like other forest-dwelling creatures, they maintain trails through the underbrush. Although they spend most of their time quietly on the ground, when severely threatened, they explode from their hiding places into flight, beating their wings loudly. Though good fliers that can hover and make complete turns in the air when flying through thick brush, they seldom go more than a couple hundred yards before landing either on the ground, where they run into a thicket and hide, or in a tree. On landing in a tree, they sometimes back up and stretch their necks flat against the tree's trunk in an attempt to camouflage themselves from predators.

Like other gallinaceous birds, they dust their feathers to rid themselves of skin pests, such as feather lice. Their dusting places usually consist of soil trapped among the roots of an upturned tree that was blown over by the wind. They return to these spots during the late afternoon to bathe in the dust, socialize with an individual of the opposite sex, including copulation, leaving behind visibly disturbed areas of soils along with some feathers.

During winter, the grouse burrow or dive into soft, powdery snow when it is available. This behavior helps keep them warm in times of extremely cold temperatures when the snow, which is an excellent insulator, can be as much as 25 degrees Fahrenheit warmer than the air above. Moreover, it hides them from predators. If approached too closely, however, they suddenly burst out of the snow and fly away.

As it turns out, the most productive ruffed grouse are those living in areas where they spend most of the winter burrowed into 10 inches or more of soft, powdery snow, and emerge for only a few minutes once or twice a day to make a meal of the male flower buds of the aspen, which occur predominantly east of the Cascade-Mountain crest. They tend to be less numerous and less productive, however, if they live in regions where they cannot burrow into snow.

Whereas, populations of ruffed grouse rise and fall in roughly a decadal cycle, short-term fluctuations in their abundance appear related to trends in the weather and variations in the quality and quantity of available food. As with everything in the cirque, weather and food resources are interrelated.

Ruffed grouse feed almost exclusively on vegetation, including leaves, buds, and fruits of ferns, shrubs, and woody plants—bitter, often toxic plants that many birds cannot eat. In autumn, soft fruits, such as huckleberries, become an important part of the diet. In winter, they feed on buds and twigs of such shrubs as mountain willows.

Moreover, the grouse have an advantage over many of the other birds in and around the cirque because they can consume and digest large volumes of fibrous vegetation thanks to extra-long, paired pouches at the junction of their small and large intestines. In addition, they have the ability to digest foods high in cellulose, which makes it possible for them to survive harsh winter conditions in the cirque. ("Cellulose" is an insoluble substance that forms the main constituent of plant cell walls and of vegetable fibers.)

There is, however, a third aspect relevant to the interrelationship of their population and their habitat, one that is superimposed on the preceding two, and that is predation—predators taking advantage of grouse during times of unfavorable weather and inadequate food. In addition to predation, females who are forced to spend the winter eating poor-quality food or have to use excessive amounts of energy to keep warm may not have sufficient reserves to produce a clutch of viable eggs, let alone vigorous, healthy youngsters come spring.

With respect to reproduction, drumming occurs throughout the year, so long as a male's "drumming tree" is not too deeply buried under snow. Nevertheless, given the opportunity to display his magnificence for a female, especially in late April (the peak of the mating season when his drumming increases), he stands on his fallen tree with crest, ruff, and tail erect, puffing up to nearly double his normal size, while beating his wings to create a rapid-fire drumming sound.

Following the elaborate display, mating lasts but a few seconds to a minute, which, in this case, took place on April 27th. Immediately thereafter, without the development of a pair bond, the female went her own way to build a nest at the base of a tree and raise her young as a single parent, having no further association with the male.

She constructed her nest half a mile from where she copulated. Her nest, located at the base of a tree, was in an area that allowed her to maintain a clear view as she watched for the approach of potential predators. It was a simple, hollowed-out depression in the leaves on the forest floor, reaching up to six inches across and three inches deep. She then lined her bowl-shaped nest with vegetation plucked from the edge of the nest site.

Her nest completed within three days, April 30th, she laid 11 milky-white eggs with a few dull-brown spots. Laid at the rate of one each day to a day and a half, beginning May 1st, it took 18 days, until May 18th, for her clutch to be completed. (Photo 6.22)

6.22 Ruffed grouse nest with 11 eggs.

Incubation commenced when the last egg was laid, and will take another 23 days before the eggs hatch on the 10th of June. (Photo

6.23) The chicks, seven females and four males, each covered in down ranging from sandy to brown, will have a triangular patch of black feathers around their ears, and they will be able to walk and feed themselves within 24 hours after hatching.

6.23 Female ruffed grouse on her nest.

Not much larger than Storm Hawk's thumb, the chicks will be precocial, which means they will be ready to leave the nest and start feeding themselves just as soon as they have dried following hatching. Once out of the nest, they will be surprisingly mobile and moving more than a quarter of a mile a day by the time they are three or four days old. They will begin flying when about five days old, at which time they will resemble giant bumblebees. Their mother will lead them as far as four miles during the first 10 days of their lives, from their birth place to a special habitat for the summer.

The chicks will need a prodigious amount of animal protein early in life for the development of muscle and feathers. This requirement will be satisfied by feeding mainly on insects and other small animals for the first few weeks, before gradually shifting to a diet of green plants and fruits. They will grow rapidly, increasing from about ½-ounce miniatures when hatched to 17- to 20-ounce, fully-grown young birds 16 weeks later—a 38- to 46-fold increase in weight by the 4th week of September. Moreover, they will almost reach their maximum size and weight during the following week, at which time they pass out of adolescence and leave in search of their own home ranges. This is the second and last time in their entire lives they will be highly mobile.

The four young males will be the first to depart, seeking a vacant drumming territory wherein they can claim a fallen tree as a drumming stage. Of those, three will find a suitable drumming site within two miles of the place where they grew up, although one will have to go as far as 4½ miles before finding a vacant territory. Nevertheless, each of the males will claim a drumming tree by the time they are 20 weeks old, the 3rd week in October. And, having done so, they will spend the remainder of their lives within a 200- to 300-yard radius of their drumming tree.

The seven young females, on the other hand, will begin dispersing a week later than their brothers, and they go about three times as far. Of these, four will move between 8 and 10 miles, whereas two will move 15 miles, and one will travel 17 miles before finding the place where they each will spend the rest of their lives.

Although a few of the ruffed grouse in and around the cirque will live two to three years, most die a violent death through which they provide a meal for one of the cirque's predators because, in Nature's interactive dynamics, the grouse are a critical link in the cirque's complex food chain. In addition, some die from disease and parasites, whereas others die from exposure to severe weather or from accidentally hitting trees or branches while in a panicked flight after being frightened.

Meanwhile, as the time is fast approaching when the grouse eggs will hatch, two days hence (the 10th of June), Storm Hawk, going deeper into the forest, comes to a bend in the stream, where it has created a small, gravel bar on its east side in the process of carving out a foot-deep pool under the roots of an ancient mountain hemlock growing along its western bank. Laying his bow on the ground, he takes off his quiver of arrows and lays it next to his bow. Then, creeping softly to a flat spot next to the hemlock's roots, he lies down carefully on the bank. Being downstream from the tree's trunk, he slowly puts his right hand, palm upward, into the water, which is swiftest in the curved channel under the tree's exposed roots. Moving his hand slowly upstream, he feels for the body of a rainbow trout.

Slowly, slowly, he feels around in the pool until his hand brushes against the tail of his quarry. He pauses to let the fish get accustomed to the slight touch. He then gradually lowers his hand and moves it gently under the trout's belly. The fish moves slightly. Storm Hawk freezes. The trout relaxes, and Storm Hawk moves his hand along its belly until he reaches the area of the trout's gills, whereupon he thrusts his thumb and first finger into the fish's gills and, with a swift jerk, flips the 12-inch rainbow trout onto the stream's bank, where he quickly dispatches it with a blow to the head.

Retrieving his bow and arrows, he moves downstream to another overhanging part of the bank, where he repeats the procedure. Thus occupied for a little over two hours, he is rewarded with three more fine trout, enough for a meal. So he heads diagonally upslope through the forest toward the trail leading to his campsite in the firs.

Once in camp, he lights a small fire and cooks the fish, after which he sets off to begin exploring the peninsula of trees wherein he is camped, as well as the three adjacent islands of subalpine firs. He begins by spending the day examining the area surrounding his camp.

Finding nothing of interest, he stands at the meadow's edge and watches the sun descending below the western rim of the cirque. As the arched curtain of night moves westward, the insect patrol over the cirque changes from cliff swallows and tree swallows to a host of bats, while the dancing light of Storm Hawk's small fire greets the first twinkling of stars in the east. Night cloaks the cirque, and the complex interaction of bats begins in which Nature has scripted how the different species use the airspace within and around the cirque.

Bats of the Cirque

The scientific name "Chiroptera," the taxonomic Order of bats, is derived from the Greek words *cheir* (hand) and *pteron* (wing) and refers to the four greatly elongated, slender, finger-like, bony structures of the forelimbs between which are stretched thin, delicate membranes. The membranes, composed of a double layer of skin, are also attached to the sides of the body, the hind legs, and the tail, forming wings. In this sense, bats are unique among mammals in that they have true powers of flight. (Photo 6.24)

6.24 Townsend big-eared bat.

In fact, bats and birds share the same basic aerodynamic characteristics. Among bats, the structural differences and the resultant aerodynamic characteristics of their wings are extremely important because they are directly related to the effectiveness with which various sources of food can be exploited.

Coupled with aerodynamic characteristics are the time, location, and altitude of flight. These factors interact to maximize the effectiveness with which bats can use a given source of food. At the same time, variations in these factors minimize direct competition among and within species.

The bat's ear is a specialized organ adapted not only for hearing but also for maintaining balance or equilibrium. Although it is true that bats depend on echolocation (sonar) for guidance, and thus have acute hearing, they are not blind, as implied by the phrase, "blind as a bat."

To account for the extremely accurate directional-focusing system of bats, one must assume that their sense of hearing is highly directional in both horizontal and vertical planes. Sonar signals emitted by bats are brief and must be perceived and interpreted within milliseconds. Within a given species of bat, different signals indicate that prey is being sought, pursued, or captured. Some species emit sonar signals through their mouths; others, through their noses.

The external ears of bats exhibit great differences in size, shape, and elaboration of accessory structures. Insectivorous bats, such as the Townsend big-eared bat (see photo 6.24), which can hunt insects resting on vegetation or solid objects, usually emit faint sonar signals and have enormously large ears. Fast-flying bats, such as the hoary bat, emit loud sonar signals within high frequencies and have relatively small ears. And, both occur within the cirque and its surrounding habitats.

Evening bats are in the scientific family "Vespertilionidae," to which the bats around the cirque belong. The familial name is derived from the Latin word *vespertilio* ("animals of the evening") and the Latin suffix *idae* (which designates it as a family).

Evening bats alight initially with their heads up. Once alighted, they quickly shuffle around and hang by their toes with heads down and wings folded along their bodies. Although some hang from vertical surfaces, such as little brown bats and big brown bats, others crawl into small crevices in the cliff face or under loose bark on standing dead trees (snags) in the forest, like the California bat, long-eared bat, silver-haired bat; and some, namely the hoary bat (Photo 6.25), hang freely suspended from limbs of trees amid the foliage.

6.25 Hoary bat in day roost.

Members of most species roost in small groups or large colonies, but those roosting in foliage are solitary by nature. Colonial species normally return to the same roosting site annually. Some remain in colonies throughout the year; some congregate only in winter. Cave dwellers become torpid in winter, periodically changing locations within the cave. Members of a few species, such as the silver-haired bat, migrate south in autumn to milder climates and return in spring.

The bats of the cirque use habitats in their nighttime feeding that are similar to those used by birds in their daytime feeding. The bats, however, are strictly insectivorous and eat a variety of insects and their relatives (such as spiders). Although the foods eaten by bats of the cirque are greatly influenced by availability, there often are considerable differences in the prey selected by the different species. For instance, the little brown bat, Yuma bat, and California bat feed heavily on flies; the Townsend big-eared bat, long-legged bat, long-eared bat, and silver-haired bat feed primarily on moths; the big brown bat concentrates on beetles, when moths are unavailable.

Some of these differences in food items reflect not only differences in the availability of insects at the time and place where the bats are feeding, such as different heights above the ground in different areas of a given habitat, but also their tendency to select for certain groups of species within the insect-spider fauna. These behavioral differences allow maximum effectiveness in the utilization of available habitats and the source of food (listed in a descending order from generalist to more specialized), as well as their adaptability toward the capture of certain groups of prey:

Big brown bats of the cirque are usually associated with the forest. They emerge early, frequently before the swallows have ceased to feed, 30 to 40 minutes before full darkness. They usually forage high over the forest, in great sweeping circles, sometimes well over 150 feet above the ground. As dusk deepens, however, they often descend to within 40 to 50 feet of the ground. When feeding along the forest edge, big brown bats normally fly only 20 to 30 feet high and tend to fly relatively straight, as they garner moths, scarab beetles, and other kinds of beetles in the various aerial habitats within the cirque.

California bats are not generally active until after dark, and feed on midges, flies, and craneflies along the streams within the forest and the lower part of the meadow, as well as along the cliff.

Little brown bats exhibit an affinity for the forest. They usually emerge about 20 to 30 minutes before full darkness, and forage in and out among scattered trees along the meadow's edge, where they feed on midges, and the internal organs of large insects.

Yuma bats are closely associated with the streams and the lake. They normally emerge 20 to 30 minutes prior to full darkness and often feed just a few inches above the surface of the water, flying regular routes up and down the streams in relatively straight patterns, feeding on midges, winged damp-wood termites, and moths. Over the lake, however, where midges predominate, they fly in circular patterns.

Long-eared bats are associated with the forest, where they emerge from 10 to 40 minutes after full darkness and feed on moths, flies, and spiders among the trees.

Long-legged bats are generally distributed in the forest. On warm, overcast evenings, they feed along the edge of the forest and among the trees on moths, winged damp-wood termites, and spiders. On cold, clear evenings, they feed among the trees within the forest, and emerge as much as 45 minutes earlier on heavily overcast evenings than on lightly overcast evenings.

Hoary bats are large, swift, late-fliers associated primarily with the airspace above the forest, where they forage on mosquitoes and moths well after full darkness (see photo 6.25, page 139).

Silver-haired bats are associated mainly with the forest. They emerge from 15 to 45 minutes prior to full darkness. The slowest-flying bat around the cirque, they frequently hunt in sweeping circles, often 100 yards or more in diameter, as they catch moths over the forest. But they also forage on winged damp-wood termites and flies within the forest. Adults generally feed singly, but occasionally in groups of three to four.

Townsend big-eared bats normally feed on moths around the cliffs, where they rely on crevices as daytime roosts (see photo 6.24, page 137).

By emitting ultrasonic sounds through their mouths, evening bats avoid flying into objects as they locate and pursue prey. Such echolocation brings a bat within capturing distance of its prey. Although a bat may capture some insects directly with its mouth, the majority are "netted" with a wingtip and immediately transferred into the cupped tail membrane, which is formed by curling the tail forward under the body. The prey is then grasped with the teeth.

Small prey are eaten in flight, but large prey are consumed at a resting site. The remains of large prey may occasionally be found under such sites.

Many evening bats pause during feeding to rest at night roosts, which are specific places in which bats hang up to allow their food to digest, and accounts for the accumulation of feces under such resting stations. Feeding appears to take place in definite areas, and resting at definite sites. In contrast, day roosts are where bats spend the daylight hours sleeping.

In colonial species, such as little brown bats, which also hibernate, the females segregate into maternity colonies to bear and raise young. Males do not associate with the rearing of offspring. However, breeding takes place from August through October and often again in the spring. Sperm deposited in the females' reproductive tracts in the autumn is stored through the winter. The combined periods of breeding produce a single litter in spring, because that is when ovulation and fertilization occur. The gestation period of most species ranges from 40 to 70 days, but is 100 or more days for the Townsend big-eared bat. Litters range from one to four young.

As the time of birth approaches, an expectant mother, who has been hanging quietly from a vertical surface, suddenly becomes restless and changes position frequently. She is nervous, irritable, and reluctant to eat. She periodically grooms her underside, genitalia, and tail membrane; this behavior lasts from a few minutes to an hour.

Just before the onset of labor, a fetus changes from a horizontal to a vertical position. Thus an expectant mother also reverses her position until, head up, she is suspended from the vertical surface by her thumbs and feet. Her hind legs are spread, and her tail is curled forward over her vaginal opening, forming a "cup" into which the youngster is born. During labor, the mother cries, closes her eyes, bares her teeth, and makes chewing motions, indicating that labor is probably painful.

In normal labor, there may be as few at 10 muscular contractions. The babies are usually born in a breech position. Unlike most mammalian offspring, a baby bat starts to grope with its feet and hind legs as soon as it is freed from the birth canal. The feet grasp whatever they encounter, usually the fur or leg of the mother.

After securing a foothold, the baby pulls vigorously with its hind legs and helps to draw its body from the vagina. In a few seconds, the body is freed up to the head, which remains momentarily inside the vagina. The baby may continue to pull with its legs or may bring them forward and brace its feet against its mother's body to push vigorously. Pushing or pulling by the baby, coupled with the muscular contractions of the mother, frees the head suddenly. The mother then tears the birth membrane off her baby with her teeth. A single birth is usually completed within 30 minutes; double births often take longer.

After delivery, the naked, blind baby remains attached to the afterbirth (placenta) by the remarkably elastic umbilical cord. In members of some species, the expulsion of the placenta with its attached umbilical cord is delayed, and the cord functions as a "safety line" after the birth. Should a baby fall off its mother, it remains suspended close enough to her to be able to secure a firm grip on her with its well-developed thumbs and feet.

Free circulation of blood continues through the umbilical cord for 3 to 10 minutes and then begins to blanch as circulation ceases. The delicate cord dries rapidly. If the umbilical cord ruptures too early, the baby bat bleeds to death in minutes. After its expulsion, the mother may eat the placenta.

During or shortly after birth, the mother resumes her normal head-down position. She then grooms her baby until it is clean and dry, after which she cleans herself, using her wings to shift the baby around.

Most bats probably live at least four to eight years in the wild, but some banded individuals have exceeded 21 years of age.

June 8th

The 8th of June finds Storm Hawk up with the sun. Taking his bow and arrows with him, he sets off to see if the mushroom he found lodged on the tree limb, where the small peninsula of trees hosting his camp meets the forest, is still there. It is. (Photo 6.26) How, he wonders, did it get there? Then, he sees another and another. Still wondering, he sits down in the sun at the base of a mountain hemlock, when he notices that some small pits have been dug in the soil of the forest floor.

6.26 A mushroom stored on a tree limb by a chickaree.

His curiosity aroused, he gets up to investigate, and finds more pits, some with small, elongated droppings next to and in them. Still pondering what he sees, a movement in the peripheral vision of his right eye catches his attention. A "chickaree" (also known as a Douglas squirrel or pine squirrel) is busy sniffing the ground. Moving his head slowly, he turns to look at the chickaree, but not too directly.

The chickaree suddenly stops digging and pokes its head into the hole, coming up with a small, roundish, potato-like truffle (Photo 6.27), which is the fruiting body of a mycorrhizal fungus, like the ones eaten by the Mazama pocket gophers living along the forest edge. Truffle in mouth, the squirrel heads up a tree, where it sits on a limb and eats the truffle, after which it retrieves one of the mushrooms from the fork in a limb, and disappears into the tree's top.

6.27 A truffle left by a chickaree alongside the pit it had dug to get the truffle.

From somewhere in the treetop, Storm Hawk hears a low "chirr," which suddenly turns into an explosive "bauf, bauf, bauf," as the resident chickaree detects an interloper with its mushroom. Two vociferous chickarees are suddenly engaged in a noisy, territorial dispute. Although the interloper leaves, the resident chickaree throws a "temper tantrum." In fact, it is so "irritated" by the trespass that it bounces up and down on the top of its nest with such vigor that the whole nest is knocked out of the tree. After a "cooling off period," the chickaree retrieves its nest, to the last twig, packs it all to the original site, and rebuilds it, an episode that leaves Storm Hawk convulsed in laughter.

Living at a lower elevation, Storm Hawk is fascinated by everything he sees and hears in this high-mountain world, all of which is new to him. In this lies a danger, however. When everything is new, it is virtually impossible to read those nuances that are out of place, and thus signify danger. To live safely in the wild, he has to meld into the benign rhythms of the present moment while simultaneously being alert to what does not belong and thus stands out—a slight sound, a slight movement caught from the corner of his eye.

Of Chickarees, Flying Squirrels, and Truffles

Be that as it may, the wonders of Nature he is daily witnessing do not begin to tell the story of life in the cirque, such as the relationships of chickarees, northern flying squirrels, truffles, and the forest they inhabit, including where Storm Hawk is camped.

The Chickaree

The chickaree is a lively, noisy, little squirrel that ranges from 10 to 14 inches in length and weighs between 5 and 10 ounces. (Photo 6.28) Its eyes are encircled with short, orange hairs, and the small ears have short tufts of blackish hair at the tips. In summer, the back varies from slightly reddish brown to slightly grayish brown with many orange- and black-tipped hairs. There is a short, blackish stripe on each side, extending from the forelegs to the hips. The underside and the tops of the feet are light to dark orange; however, there occasionally are white patches on the throat, chest, and near the forelegs. The bushy tail is wide and somewhat flat. In winter, the squirrel's coat is slightly grayer than in summer, and the black stripes on the sides are less apparent. Many gray-, brown-, or black-tipped hairs obscure the orange of the underside. The tops of the feet are dark gray. The short, sharply curved claws vary from brown to dark gray.

6.28 Chickaree.

Chickarees are well adapted for life in the forest, especially climbing. These adaptations include an excellent perception of distance, which aids their ability to jump from limb to limb and even from one tree to another, strong claws that can grip bark, hind feet that can be rotated 180 degrees so they can descend trees head first, and tails that supplement their balance as they navigate their forest environment. In addition, they have whiskers above and below their eyes, as well as on their noses and chins, which allow tactile perception (touch or feeling) of their environment. They also have very good vision and hearing, and a keen sense of smell.

These noisy forest denizens are solitary and, as Storm Hawk witnessed, exceedingly territorial, which often includes loud disputes between individuals. A single squirrel will occupy a territory 2½ to a little over 3½ acres. With the onset of breeding, however, a mated pair will "team up" and defend a single territory.

These inquisitive little characters arise at dawn to begin their day and usually retire with the setting sun. Active daily throughout the year, except when nest-bound by inclement weather, they are one of the main sentinels in the forest, where little escapes their attention, a circumstance that is clearly evident not only by their noisy chattering at intruders but also by their oft-repeated calls, which seems to ring throughout the forest every minute or so. During much of the year, their vociferous commentaries call attention to such things as a western screech owl trying to sleep, a hunting weasel, or a puma (also known as a cougar or mountain lion) abroad during the day.

Much of their time is spent climbing up and down trees, searching the ground for truffles and other foods, keeping watch, minding the affairs of others, or just sitting quietly on a branch next to the trunk of a tree with their tails over their backs. Hence the familial name Sciuridae, from the Greek word *skiouros* ("shade tail"), which in turn is derived from *skia* ("shade") and *oura* ("tail") plus *idae* (denoting the scientific family). However, they were known as "Pillillooeet" to the Indigenous Americans of Kings River in California, which is an imitation of its characteristic alarm call.

When building a summer nest of twigs, the squirrel cuts live twigs and carries them to the selected site, where in a short time it constructs a loose nest, which is then lined with soft, dry mosses, lichens, or shredded inner bark from western redcedar for its sleeping quarters. Summer nests may also be merely large balls of mosses, lichens, or shredded bark, sometimes interwoven with grass, into which the squirrel burrows a hole and makes its sleeping quarters. They also take over and remodel abandoned nests of hawks, owls, and flying squirrels.

Winter nests are usually located in hollows in trees, frequently abandoned pileated woodpecker nest-cavities 60 or more feet above the ground. When nests are constructed on limbs, however, they are well within the tree's crown and are bulkier and much thicker than summer nests.

When it comes to diet, chickarees are omnivorous, and eat whatever is available. Although their main diet in the cirque consists of seeds, berries, truffles, and mushrooms (including those in the genus *Amanita*, which are poisonous to humans), being more carnivorous than other squirrels, they also devour insects, spiders, and centipedes, as well as the eggs and young of nesting birds when such are readily available. But, lacking cheek pouches in which to hold food, they normally have to eat close to where they obtain the food, with the exception of transporting the cones of forest trees to scattered storage areas.

During early spring in the cirque, they frequently cut the newly active terminal shoots of Douglas-fir from which they eat the developing inner bark and needles, but discard the old ones. When available, sap is also eaten. Now and then, an individual consumes mature pollen cones in great quantities, resulting in yellow feces because of the high pollen content. During summer, they dine on some green vegetation and various ripening fruits, such as huckleberries from the bushes growing in various spots along the meadow's edge.

Their main food during spring, summer, and autumn is truffles that are detected by odor and dug out of the forest floor in a manner similar to that of the flying squirrel and other forest rodents, although chickarees also eat and store mushrooms in forked limbs, especially in autumn, where they dry and so can be eaten during the winter (see photo 6.26, page 144). When a chickaree, flying squirrel, or other forest rodent eats a truffle and defecates near the boundary of its home range, the spores may germinate and ultimately form a fruiting body (a truffle) that is subsequently eaten by some other rodent that, in turn, deposits feces somewhere else. So it is that the fungi's genetic material is continually moved throughout the forest to combine and recombine with that of other colonies of fungi within the same species.

The diet of chickarees, which Storm Hawk usually associates with them from his sojourns in the low-elevation forests, consists of the cones of such coniferous trees as Douglas-fir, Engelmann spruce, grand fir, and noble fir, and they are indeed an important part of the chickarees' diet. When seed-bearing cones near maturity in early autumn, the squirrels cut them off branches, extract the ripening seeds, and eat them. A cone is held with the forefeet, and individual scales are cut off the central core of the cone with the squirrel's sharp incisor teeth. Good seeds are eaten and defective ones discarded.

A chickaree normally eats in one or two selected places near its food storage area. The discarded scales of the cones (middens) accumulate on the ground under a low branch, or on a stump, fallen tree, large rock, or other elevated feeding perch, from which they can maintain an acute awareness of their surroundings. The discarded scales may accumulate into piles more than three feet across and two or more feet high as the years pass and the site is used by succeeding generations of squirrels.

As the majority of the cones ripen, the chickarees ascend to the tops of the trees in the early morning, cut the cones off, and let them fall to the ground. The cones are then collected one at a time and carried to a storage area, such as an underground burrow, hollow stump, or hollow fallen tree. (Photo 6.29)

6.29 Cones of lodgepole pine stored in a hollow log.

Cones are normally cached in a moist place to prevent them from drying out and shedding their seeds. At times a squirrel may store cones in a small stream or spring, where they remain fresh for a year or more, while those stored on land often become moldy and spoiled. This kind of aquatic cache is made possible by the squirrel's ability to both swim and dive. (Photo 6.30)

6.30 Spruce cones stored in a small stream.

An examination of a chickaree's kitchen middens in the winter will usually show whether the cones were stored on land or under water. Cones stored under water often have the scales pulled off, whereas those stored on land are hard and the scales have to be chewed off. (Photo 6.31)

Chickarees not only protect their caches of cones but also access them throughout the winter by burrowing through the snow. In addition, they usually store more food than they consume during a winter. There is survival value in this excessive harvesting of cones. Should there be a failure in the next year's crop, a chickaree can rummage through its unused stores of cones and often find enough good ones to augment the inadequate harvest.

The chickarees in the cirque are sexually active from late March through May, as exemplified by mating chases in which males and females call to and chase each other, which ultimately lead to the formation of a mated pair. Each pair then remains monogamous through that year's breeding season.

6.31 Top cone was stored under water and has the scales pulled off, whereas the bottom cone was stored on land and has the scales chewed off.

A female, in estrous for a single day, was bred on the 1st of April. On the 7th of May, after a gestation of 36 days, she gave birth to six babies, three females and three males, in a cozy nest situated in an abandoned woodpecker nest cavity 53 feet above the forest floor not far from the edge of the meadow. Often thought of as "kits," the babies were born naked and blind, weighing between $\frac{4}{10}$ and $\frac{6}{10}$ of an ounce. Within 18 days, the 25th of May, they were covered with fur. Then, between June 7th and 8th, just after Storm Hawk arrives in the cirque and sets up his camp, the youngsters' eyes open. Although their weaning will begin on the 17th of June, it will not be completed until July 4th. Thereafter, the juveniles will remain in their mother's nest until mid-July, when they will be one-half to two-thirds of her size.

When first out of their nests, siblings will stay close together and be tended by their mother. The family will remain together until mid-September, when they shall become independent, although they will remain relatively close through December, at which time the juveniles will have attained both their adult size and sexual maturity. They will not mate, however, until the coming spring of 1576.

Chickarees are both alert and fast, which helps them evade such predators as the long-tailed weasels, martens, bobcats, and northern goshawks. They are, nevertheless, part of the cirques' food web. Beyond that, in eating the fruiting bodies of fungi, they disseminate the fungal spores through their feces, many of which germinate and form critical mycorrhizal associations with the forest trees—to be discussed in detail shortly.

THE FLYING SQUIRREL

Flying squirrels of the cirque range from 9 to 17 inches long and weigh from a little over 1½ to 6½ ounces. In essence, they are not only the smallest of all squirrels but also the only nocturnal tree squirrel.

They have long, very fine, soft hair. Their pelage is not separated into guard hairs and underfur because all the hairs are about the same length, which gives their coat a sleek appearance. One of the distinctive features of this squirrel is the loose fold of skin that stretches from the wrist of the foreleg to the ankle of the hind leg, forming a gliding membrane. (Photo 6.32)

6.32 Adult northern flying squirrel. Note the gliding membrane down its side.

The hairs on the back are bicolored; the shafts are dark gray, and the tips are dark reddish-brown, giving the back a predominantly dark reddish-brown appearance. The cheeks are light grayish-brown, and dark gray hairs encircle the large eyes. The top edge of the gliding membrane is dark gray, and the hairs along the margin of the membrane are tipped with light tan, giving the appearance of an almost whitish stripe. The underside is tannish. The tail is relatively wide and horizontally flat; the hair of the tail is dense and of the same texture as that of the body. The top of the tail is dull; it is brownish-gray along the basal one-third, becoming dark gray toward the tip. The hairs on the underside are gray, tipped with light to dark tan, and give a tan appearance. The underside of the tail is dark tan with a dark gray margin.

Flying squirrels *cannot* fly; they can only glide downward. They climb to an elevated point and launch themselves with impetus. As they leap into space, they extend their legs outward from the body. Such action erects the cartilaginous projections on the outside of each wrist. These projections spread the large, loose folds of skin along the sides of the body so that a monoplane is formed, allowing the squirrel to glide gently and quietly with good control. They accomplish steering by raising and lowering their forelegs. The tail, flattened horizontally, is used as a stabilizer to keep them on course.

Before a squirrel starts its glide, it carefully examines the chosen landing site by leaning to one side and then to the other, a maneuver that possibly acts as a method of triangulation in measuring the distance. As a squirrel reaches a landing point, normally the trunk of a tree, it changes course to an upward direction by raising the tail. At the same time, the forelegs and hind legs are extended forward, which not only allows the gliding membrane to act as a parachute and slow the glide but also allows the legs to absorb the shock of landing.

The instant the squirrel lands, it races around the trunk of the tree, thereby eluding any predator, such as an owl, that may be following it. Then, to make another glide, it dashes to a higher position with incredible swiftness and agility and again launches itself into space. From a height of 60 feet, a squirrel can glide gracefully about 160 feet at a rate of almost six feet per second.

The flying squirrels of the cirque and the mountain in general have home ranges that vary from 2 to 77 acres, depending on the quality of their habitat. While the females are territorial because they are responsible for the young, males are not. Moreover, where the habitat offers ample food and shelter, up to 10 squirrels may occupy a given acre.

They generally nest in hollows in large-diameter trunks of both alive and dead trees and in abandoned, woodpecker nest cavities. However, they also build outside nests (referred to as "dreys") constructed on the limbs of trees composed of shredded bark; Fremont's lichen, which is dark brown, hair-like, and grows hanging from trees; mosses; dry leaves; and other soft materials. Except for females rearing young, the squirrels frequently shift from nest to nest. Regardless, they keep their nests clean.

On the other hand, females rearing young usually commandeer available woodpecker nest cavities, relegating any inhabiting squirrels to less-well insulated and protected hollows, or even to outside nests. Under these circumstances four to 10 evicted males may aggregate in a nest. During the winter, however, "aggregate nests" (those shared by related and/or unrelated individuals of a single sex, including juveniles) are normally located in tree cavities, including those made by woodpeckers.

Shared nests are critical at this time of year if the squirrels are to maintain their body temperatures, because northern flying squirrels neither hibernate nor enter states of torpor. (Torpor—from the Latin *torpēre*, to be motionless—is a state of lowered physiological activity typically characterized by reduced metabolism, heart rate, respiration, and body temperature.)

Because they are active at night, often in dense forest, they need a way to make sure they know where they are within the boundaries of their home range or, in the case of females, within their territory. One way the squirrels mark their home areas is with scent glands, of which there is one in each corner of their mouth. As they move about their home areas at night, they find an appropriate place, twist their heads, and drag one side of their face across the object. They generally mark with one side only, but on some occasions they mark with both. Such scent marking is done primarily at sites of grooming, feeding, and resting and probably acts to keep a particular squirrel reassured that it's within its home area.

They communicate with one another by emitting a soft, low *chirp* or a *cluck* when distressed. In addition, they use scent and touch to interact with one another.

6.33 Adult northern flying squirrel eating a truffle.

These bright-eyed squirrels of the night feed mainly on truffles during spring, summer, and autumn. They thus descend each night to the forest floor and dig out truffles, which they detect by odor. (Photo 6.33) Truffles are abundant in and around the large, fallen trees from the ancient forest that lie decomposing on the floor of the forest. In addition, the decomposing trees situated a ways within the forest are protected from drying winds of summer by the forest's canopy, and thus act as reservoirs that hold water all year, prolonging the fruiting season of the truffles well into the summer, and even the autumn. Flying squirrels are therefore most abundant in those areas that have large numbers of slowly decomposing ancient trees. In winter, the squirrels both eat Fremont's lichen and use it, moss, and shredded bark to build their nests.

Because these squirrels get most of their food from below the surface of the forest floor, they are vulnerable to predation while on the ground, which explains how pumas, bobcats, long-tailed weasels, and marten are able to catch them to eat. Being vulnerable to predation makes it imperative that flying squirrels are familiar with their home areas.

Courtship begins in March and April, and may continue until late May. One female conceives on April 21st and immediately establishes a territory around the pileated woodpecker cavity she and three others occupied throughout most of the winter. (Photo 6.34) Finally, after a gestation period of 40 days, three babies were born on the 31st of May—two females and one male—in a snug, soft, warm nest. Naked and pink, their eyes and ears were closed, their toes were fused, their tails were cylindrical, and they weighed about two-tenths of an ounce.

On the 5th of June, as Storm Hawk arrives in the cirque, their toes separate, but their eyes will not open until the 1st of July, when they are 31 days old, by which time they are fully clothed in exquisitely soft fur. Although they will begin leaving their nest for short periods when they are about 40 days old, the 10th of July (the day Storm Hawk leaves for home), they will not be fully weaned until the final days of July. (Photo 6.35) Thereafter, they will remain with their mother, until the end of August, at which time they become fully independent. They will be reproductively mature in the spring of 1576, and may live to be four years old.

6.34 Abandoned nest cavity of a pileated woodpecker.

Because they must be well developed to successfully cope with the hazards of an arboreal and gliding life style, their development is correspondingly slow when compared with that of many ground-dwelling mammals of similar size.

6.35 Baby northern flying squirrels in their nest.

The Truffle Dance

Truffles are the predominant food of the cirque's chickarees and flying squirrels. *But what, exactly,* you might wonder, *is a "truffle?"* Truffles are the reproductive bodies of belowground-fruiting fungi, termed mycorrhizae, which literally means "fungus-root" and denotes the mutually beneficial symbiotic relationship between certain fungi and plant roots, a phenomenon that can be traced back some 400 million years to the earliest known fossils of plant rooting structures.

Mycorrhizal fungi absorb nutrients and water from soil and translocate them to a host plant, such as Douglas-fir, mountain hemlock, and subalpine fir. In turn, the host plant provides sugars from its photosynthesis to the mycorrhizal fungi. Fungal hyphae (the "mold" part of the fungus) extend into the soil and serve as extensions of the host's root system and are both physiologically and geometrically more effective for nutrient absorption than the roots themselves.

Moreover, nitrogen-fixing bacteria, which occur inside the mycorrhiza, use a fungal "extract" as food and in turn fix atmospheric nitrogen. (To "fix" nitrogen is to take gaseous, atmospheric nitrogen and alter it in such a way that it becomes available and useable by plants.) Nitrogen, thus made available, can be used both by the fungus and the host tree.

In effect, mycorrhiza-forming fungi serve as a highly effective extension of the host root system. Many of the fungi also produce growth regulators that induce production of new root tips and increase their useful life span. At the same time, host plants prevent mycorrhizal fungi from damaging their roots. Mycorrhizal colonization enhances resistance to attack by pathogens. Some mycorrhizal fungi produce compounds that prevent pathogens from even contacting the root system.

Truffles are the initial link between belowground mycorrhizal fungi and the two kinds of squirrels, both of which nest and reproduce in the tree canopy and come to the ground, where they dig and eat truffles—the chickaree during the day and the flying squirrel at night. As a truffle matures, it produces a strong odor that attracts the foraging squirrel. Evidence of a squirrel's foraging exists as shallow pits in the forest soil, such as those seen by Storm Hawk, and occasional partially eaten truffles.

When the squirrels eat truffles, they consume fungal tissue that contains nutrients, water, viable fungal spores, nitrogen-fixing bacteria, and yeast. Pieces of truffle move to the stomach, where fungal tissue is digested, then through the small intestine, where absorption takes place, to the cecum. The cecum, a pouch in which the large intestine begins, is like an eddy along a swift stream; it concentrates, mixes, and retains fungal spores, nitrogen-fixing bacteria, and yeast. Undigested material, including cecal contents, is formed into excretory pellets in the lower colon; these pellets, which are expelled through the rectum, contain all the viable elements necessary to inoculate the root tips of trees with prolonged life. (Photo 6.36)

6.36 Fecal pellets from a northern flying squirrel.

A fecal pellet is more than a package of waste products; it is a "pill of symbiosis" dispensed throughout the forest. Each fecal pellet contains viable spores of the mycorrhizal fungi. (Photo 6.37) Each also contains the entire nutrient requirement for nitrogen-fixing bacteria, as well as "antifreeze" that protects the bacteria during the cold of winter. Without the antifreeze, the bacterial cells would rupture and die when feces deposited during winter thaw in spring. Yeast, as a part of the nutrient base, has the ability to stimulate both the growth of, and nitrogen fixation in, the bacteria. Abundant yeast cells may also encourage spore germination because spores of some mycorrhizal-forming fungi are stimulated into germination by extractives from other fungi, such as yeast.

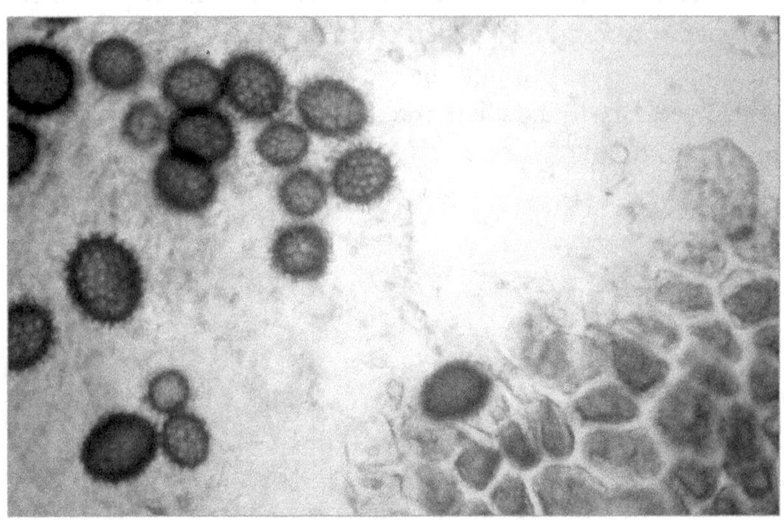

*6.37 Spores of a mycorrhizal fungus on the left and plant tissue
in the lower, right-hand corner.*

The whole squirrel-fungal-forest feedback loop is complex beyond imagination. To put it simply, the squirrels eat the truffles, the truffles germinate and feed the trees in which the squirrels live, and the trees feed the fungi that feed them. In this sense, the squirrels take care of the trees and the trees take care of the squirrels—with the mycorrhizal fungi taking care of both as the intermediary.

In addition to chickarees and flying squirrels, other animals that either live in or visit the cirque also depend to some extent on truffles for food. These include: deer mice, western red-backed voles, Townsend chipmunks, mantled ground squirrels, and even rock rabbits, heather voles, Pacific jumping mice, black-tailed deer, Roosevelt elk, and black bear.

Already humbled by everything he is seeing, if Storm Hawk could witness the entire, interrelated scope of the squirrel-truffle-tree feedback loop, his sense of Nature's sacredness would ascend beyond thought. At this moment, however, he can only approach the spiritual gate of Nature's mysteries, as they are revealed to him.

After watching the chickaree, Storm Hawk spends the rest of the day scouting the extent to which the peninsula of trees wherein he is camped penetrates into the meadow. He also takes a brief survey of the three islands of trees around the upper end of the peninsula before returning to camp for the night.

6.38 Douglas-fir with its outer bark striped away in years past by a black bear so it could scrape the living, inner bark or cambium off the trunk with its lower teeth and eat it.

June 9th

The rising sun finds Storm Hawk hunting the mule deer of which he caught a glimpse yesterday near one of the islands, where he also found several places they had bedded down during the day among the trees. Having already gone to the upper edge of the peninsula, he stands next to the trunk of a Douglas-fir, where a black bear had stripped off the outer bark in years past to reach the cambium or "inner bark." (Photo 6.38)

Black Bear

Bears are related to the dogs and wolves, but their exact line of descent is uncertain. Although black bears have better eyesight and a better sense of hearing than humans, their keenest sense is that of smell, which is about seven times greater than a dog's.

Black bears are massive, heavy bodied, with moderately sized heads; their facial profile is rather straight. Adults are approximately 3 feet high at the shoulder, and from 50 to about 75 inches long from nose to tail. Their short tails are hairy and inconspicuous, varying from three to seven inches in length. In addition, they have great physical strength. Even bear cubs can turn over flat rocks weighing 310 to 325 pounds by flipping them with a single foreleg.

A black bear's weight varies according to age, sex, health, and especially season. In autumn, their pre-hibernation weight tends to be 30 percent higher than in spring, when they emerge from their dens. Adult males (generally referred to as "boars") typically weigh between 126–551 pounds, while females (referred to as "sows") weigh 33 percent less or 90–375 pounds. Moreover, they are sexually "dimorphic" (from the Greek *di*, meaning "two" and *morphe*, "form, shape"), highlighting the fact that adult males are larger than females, as evidenced by the fact that a large male can exceed 600 pounds, while females seldom go beyond 200 pounds.

They have small eyes and small, round, erect ears. Their tapering nose has a broad pad and large nostrils. The soles of their feet are black or brownish, naked, leathery, and deeply wrinkled. Their broad feet terminate in five digits, each with a non-retractable claw that is typically black or grayish-brown. The claws are short, rounded, thick at the base, and taper to a point. Those on the forefeet are sharply curved, providing an excellent ability to climb trees, an ability that declines as age progresses. When starting to climb, a bear stands full length at the base of a tree, reaches up with both forefeet and grasps the tree with its claws and legs in a series of bounds. They cannot, however, climb small trees.

Their fur is soft, with dense underfur and long, coarse, thick guard hairs. Although different color phases exist in various parts of their geographical distribution, the bears of the cirque are indeed black.

The setting sun in late afternoon and early evening usually brings the bears out to forage. Normally remaining active throughout the night and into the early morning, they may occasionally be seen during the day, at which time they can appear awkward and comical. A bear lumbering along a trail in full flight, its head swinging from side to side and its hind feet stretching past its forelegs, may indeed be amusing to some people, but a bear's speed is deceptive. They move in a rhythmic, sure-footed way, and can run at speeds of 25 to 30 miles per hour.

Typically shy and easily frightened, black bears tend to be solitary, with the exception of a mother and her cubs. Easily alarmed, a bear will rise onto its haunches, sniff loudly, and look around for the source of the disturbance.

The average length of a female black bear's home range is around one and a half miles, whereas that of a male is in the neighborhood of four miles, but may be as much as 15 to 80 square miles, especially if food is scarce. Home ranges of adult males may overlap with those of females, but there is minimal overlap between the home ranges of two adults of the same sex. Home ranges of subadults, on the other hand, may overlap considerably with those of adults. Moreover, as an individual matures, its home range may increase in size.

Although bears usually forage alone, they will tolerate one another and eat in groups if there is an abundance of food in a given area, such as the annual run of salmon in the valley's river below the mountain. Being excellent swimmers, they capture the salmon in the water. But, there is a caveat. When such a group forms, dominance hierarchies also materialize, with the largest, most powerful males dominating the best feeding spots, which they mark by rubbing their bodies against trees and clawing the bark. In addition, they express aggression with growls, woofs, snorts, bellows, and roars. In contrast, they express contentment with mumbles, squeaks, and pants.

Here, it might be noted that black bears simply enjoy water. In the hot, summer landscape of the High Cascade Mountains, a bear often bathes and wallows in shallow pools. Through regular use, such pools become know as "bear wallows." I have, in decades past, seen bears immersed in these muddy pools. In fact, I once watched a large mother as she wallowed for three hours on an extremely hot summer afternoon, but she did not share the wallow with her three cubs. Every time a cub tried to enter the water, she would throw it out with a single swipe of her forepaw.

Black bears are typically omnivorous, meaning they not only eat grasses and other succulent plants, roots, berries, and the cambium or "inner bark" of Douglas-fir but also eat insects (such as yellow jackets, ants, and their larvae); fish; the eggs and nestling of birds; and mammals, such as the montane voles. Using surprise whenever possible to ambush their prey, they can even kill adult deer and elk. When they initially emerge from hibernation, however, they seek carrion from winterkilled animals, as well as vulnerable, newly born deer and elk.

As the spring temperature warms the cirque, they seek the new shoots of grasses, forbs, and wetland plants in the seeps along the base of the cliff. Young shoots and buds of the trees and shrubs are especially important, as they assist the bears in rebuilding their muscles and strengthening their skeletons, in addition to which they are often the only digestible foods available at this time.

As well, the bears hook their claws under the outer bark of young Douglas-firs and pull it off in great strips. (Photo 6.39) They then scrape the cambium off the trunk with their lower, front teeth and eat it. (Photo 6.40) On flat ground, a bear has to work hard to get around the low limbs and reach open areas of bark (see photo 6.38, page 163). On the steep slopes, however, a bear might climb a 50- to 80-year-old fir to eat the cambium on the open, downhill side of the trunk, at times, two-thirds or more of the way up the tree.

6.39 Strips of Douglas-fir bark stripped off the trunk by a black bear with its claws to get at the tender, inner bark or "cambium."

6.40 Young Douglas-fir tree with its cambium stripped off by a black bear within the past 48 hours by using its lower front teeth to scrape with.

When a nursing deer is killed in spring, a bear often begins feeding on the udder, but normally prefers flesh from the viscera. Whereas, a captured fawn is frequently torn apart alive as the bear feeds.

Although black bears prefer to eat in seclusion, the vegetation around the carcass of a yearling doe, which Storm Hawk will discover on his way home, will be matted down, and the nearby droppings will clearly spell out the killer's identity. Moreover, he will find the skin has been stripped back and turned inside out, whereas the skeleton has been left largely intact. The remains Storm Hawk will see are partially covered with vegetation, a practice much more common to pumas than to bears.

Black bears do compete with pumas over kills and will sometimes steal them. Though fights between the two species are rare, they can be violent, fatally injuring both parties. At other times, a bear may kill a puma, and vise versa.

Despite the fact that a black bear is more powerful than a wolf on a one-to-one basis, packs of wolves kill the bears in disputes over carcasses. Most of the bears killed by wolf packs, however, take place when the large animals are in hibernation.

During summer, the bears' diet is comprised largely of fruits, especially huckleberries, and soft buds. As summer matures into autumn and eating becomes a full-time occupation, the bears add to their larder of stored fat that will nourish them throughout the winter. Now, the seeds of whitebark pine, growing along the rocky ridges on either side of the cirque, form one of the most important components of their diet, in addition to which they raid the food caches of the cirque's various squirrels—when they can find them.

Throughout the summer and autumn, beds or shelters are merely concealed places a bear scratches in the ground among dense vegetation, by a rock, or under the branches of a fallen tree. Resting places may be lined with bedding materials and are fairly neat, even though its owner does not habitually clean it, primarily because the bear goes some distance from its resting place to defecate or urinate.

In late autumn, bears in the terrain surrounding the cirque construct their winter dens in a variety of places, such as the base of large trees (Photo 6.41), the undersides of large fallen trees, in rock caves, or holes dug in the ground either totally by the bears or enlarged by them. Females, however, are pickier than males in their choice of dens.

6.41 Winter den of a black bear dug into the rotten center of a dead Douglas-fir.

Although the bears tend to make hollows inside their den in which to lie, only about a third of them are motivated to move bedding materials into their dens. One female makes a large bed out of bark she strips from cedar trees in the immediate vicinity of her den, and she locks the entrance to her den with bedding materials. In addition, she habitually rearranges her bed during the winter.

Late-autumn and early winter weather greatly influences the onset of hibernation. Prior to that time, a bear can put on 30 pounds of body fat to get through the months during which it fasts.

Bears in the cirque usually enter their dens by late October, but during prolonged periods of Indian summer, the onset of dormancy may be delayed until early November. The first heavy snowstorm generally sends the bears into their winter quarters, where they will go without food for 5 or 6 months, depending on the winter's severity. During that time, their heart rate drops from 40 to 50 beats per minute to just 8 beats per minute.

Although I was taught that black bears were not true, or "deep" hibernators, discoveries concerning the metabolic changes that allow black bears to remain dormant for months without eating, drinking, urinating, or defecating, have fostered the redefinition of mammalian hibernation as *specialized, seasonal reduction in metabolism concurrent with scarce food and cold weather*. Black bears are now considered to be truly effective hibernators, consuming 25 to 40 percent of their body weight by digesting their stored fat. This notion is considered true in part because a special hormone, leptin (from the Greek *leptos*, meaning "thin"), is released into a hibernating bear's system, suppressing its appetite. Because they do not urinate or defecate during dormancy, the nitrogen waste from a bear's body is biochemically recycled into its proteins, thus preventing muscle loss by processing the bear's waste products into muscle during the long periods of inactivity.

Indians of several tribes thought bears ate the skin off their feet during winter and so had sore feet in spring, when they emerged from dormancy. This belief was carried forward by the early European colonists and gave birth to an old saying that I often heard used by back-country folks when I was a young man: "He's as angry as an old sow with sore feet!" Well, bears do indeed shed the hairless pads (soles) of their feet during winter dormancy. The newly forming pads are tender until they harden. Some bears do in fact have tender feet upon emergence from their dens in spring. In addition, droppings near the entrances of the bears' winter dens normally contain portions of their footpads—not surprisingly, the Indians were correct.

Testes begin to enlarge before the males arouse from winter sleep and contain mature sperm before and after the period in which females are receptive, but by the time a male enters dormancy, the testes have again shrunk drastically and are nonfunctional. Females normally breed and produce litters every other year, provided available food is sufficiently plentiful. In times of scarcity, a female may skip an additional year or two between litters.

Females in the cirque come into estrous by the last week in May and remain in estrous until about the second week in August. The peak of the breeding season, however, is usually from mid-June through mid-July. A female remains in estrous until she is either bred or her ovaries become reproductively nonfunctional. Last year, 1574, a female was bred in the cirque and conceived on the 11th of June.

Although both sexes are promiscuous, a dominant male may violently claim a female if another mature male comes near. For their part, females are inclined to be short tempered with their mates following copulation.

Ovulation is induced through copulation, after which development of the fertilized eggs either ceases or is considerably slowed. Consequently, they do not become implanted in the wall of the uterus until about the 1st of December. The process of delayed implantation allows the female's body to physiologically "assess" her condition prior to the actual implantation and the subsequent beginning of the 235-day gestation period leading to the birth of cubs. This delay allows the female to conserve her store of body fat and energy if a pregnancy would have little chance of success because of her poor physical condition.

Three embryos were implanted on the 11th of October 1574, in the female, whose den is under the roots of an ancient western redcedar about a quarter of a mile below the edge of the meadow. They began to develop rapidly on December 11th, seven weeks before their birth, on the 29th of January in this year of 1575.

Her three cubs—two females and a male—were born while their mother was deep in her winter sleep. They were about 8 inches long and weighed around 12 ounces. Their eyes were closed, and they were sparsely covered with fine, gray, down-like hair. In addition, their back legs were only slightly developed.

Development was slow the first few days after birth, but sufficiently nourished by their mother, the young grew rapidly thereafter. They opened their eyes when 29 days old, on the 27th of February, at which time they were covered with short, fuzzy, brownish hair, even though they will be black adults. The cubs began walking about the time they were six weeks old, around the 8th of March, at which time they weighed two pounds. By the time they were eight weeks old, the 22nd of March, they weighted 5½ pounds.

Their mother was very attentive and protective of her young during this time, and would have moved to a new home if she had been unduly disturbed, carrying each baby to the new den by the nape of its neck. As for the cubs, they commenced playing by themselves in April, before they were three months old, but they were carefully watched and guarded by their mother.

Having nursed them in the den until spring, mother and cubs emerged on the 21st of May in search of food, at which time she frequently vocalized, calling her cubs with a whimpering sound. However, on this day, the 9th of June, the sow and her cubs are in the forest adjacent to the peninsula when she catches the odor of Storm Hawk, as he hunts for deer, and she warns her cubs with a loud "woof-woof," urging them deeper into the forest.

The youngsters will weigh 40 to 60 pounds by the beginning of August, when they are six months old and able to fend for themselves, but will remain with their very-protective mother for a year or more, either sleeping with her or near her during their first winter.

In the spring of 1576, when the cubs will be 1½ years old, they will go their separate ways, and their mother will breed again. The youngsters will reach sexual maturity at the age of three years, in 1578, and attain their full growth in 1580, when they will be five years. Somewhere between 1578 and 1580, the two females will have their first litters.

The potential longevity of black bears in the wild is about 30 years, but they normally live in the neighborhood of 20 years. (Photo 6.42) Other than humans, they have few outright enemies.

6.42 Carcass of a black bear partially eaten by turkey vultures.

With no thought of bear in mind, Storm Hawk peers through the boughs and scans the meadow, as the first rays of light touch the vegetation, causing the droplets of moisture to shimmer with rainbow hues.

Seeing no deer, he is about to step into the open, when his gaze is arrested by a spider web at just the right angle between two blades of grass to reflect the rainbow's pallete of brilliance. Never before has he seen such a dazzling spider web.

He looks up just as a yearling deer comes into view from his blind side, created by the tree's trunk. Still within the boughs of the fir, he moves to the left, away from the trunk, just enough to slowly place an arrow against the bow's string, raise the bow, draw it back, and release the arrow. The deer, a scant 20 feet away, jumps as the arrow strikes it behind the right shoulder, and crumples to the ground. Putting another arrow to the bow's string, Storm Hawk watches the deer.

Seeing no movement, he walks to it. Looking at the deer, he apologizes for killing it and thanks both the Great Spirit and the deer for the gift of its life. Putting his bow and quiver on the ground, he draws his hunting knife and cuts the deer's throat to drain the carcass of blood. He then cuts it open and guts it, keeping the heart, liver, and bladder each attached in its place in the carcass. Being hungry, however, he slices off a chunk of the liver and eats it, thoroughly enjoying the flavor, as blood covers his hand and runs down his chin. While he is savoring the flavor, the ruffed grouse eggs are beginning to hatch 3½ miles away in the forest below the meadow.

Finished eating the liver, he stoops over, picks the deer up and puts it over his shoulders, then squats and collects his bow and quiver and heads back to camp. Once in camp, he puts the carcass down and goes to the stream to wash his face and hands. Returning to camp, he removes the bladder, liver, and heart, after which he skins the deer, cuts off its hind quarters, front quarters, and backstrap (a strip of muscle along each side of the spine), all of which he lays on the flesh side of the deer's skin.

He then cuts four strips off the hide on the opposite side, ties one end of each strip around the leg portion of a quarter, and ties the other to the branch of a tree, suspending each in turn. Although they will attract flies and yellowjackets, the outer surface will dry and protect the meat, allowing Storm Hawk to have a goodly number of meals, such as the one of backstrap he will be eating shortly.

Finally, he cuts the backbone in two just behind the rib cage. Picking up the two pieces of backbone, he carries them into the meadow and deposits them between the peninsula and the western island of trees to share the cirque's bounty with its creatures and ultimately with the soil of the meadow.

BLACK-TAILED DEER

Black-tailed deer (a subspecies of the mule deer) found west of the crest of the High Cascades, where the cirque is located, have black on the tops of their tails, as opposed to the larger, lighter mule deer found east of the crest of the High Cascades, with tails that just have a black tip.

Black-tails are well-muscled animals, the females of which are nearly 4 feet long and weigh around 100 pounds, whereas the males are 4½ to 5 feet in length, 3 feet high at the shoulder, and weigh from 150 to 200 pounds. They have large ears that can move independently of each other and pick up any unusual sounds that may signal danger; long, slender legs; and slender, pointed hoofs.

Their coats, which are composed of hollow hairs, vary from dull yellowish-brown to reddish-brown in summer and dark grayish to rich brownish-gray in winter. The upper throat, insides of the ears, and insides of the legs are whitish; the belly varies from white to tannish. The nose, forehead, and chest are dark brown to blackish. The rump patch is white, and the rather bushy tail is black on top. Youngsters are thickly spotted with white over tannish to reddish-brown upper parts. The females lack antlers, but the males grow branching antlers each summer, only to shed them in winter.

Male deer (bucks) communicate with the aid of scent and pheromones from two forehead glands, one located on each side of the head between the eyes and the base of the antlers. In addition, there are two different glands located on the lower, hind legs, and one between their toes. (A "pheromone" is a chemical compound produced and secreted by an animal that influences the behavior and development of other members of the same species.)

Whereas, only males have the forehead glands, both sexes have "tarsal" glands, which are longitudinal glands located on the insides of the hind legs in the area of the hock or heel (visible as tufts of long, stiff hairs) that serve for mutual recognition. Moreover, there are "metatarsal" glands situated on the outside of the lower leg near the ankle that produce an alarm scent. And there are "interdigital" glands between the toes of all four feet that release "trail phero-mones," which leave a scent trail when deer travel and serve to guide other deer along a certain route, such as to the location of food.

Most black-tailed deer in the cirque live primarily along the edge of the meadow and forest, but some live deep in the forest. They seem most at home, however, in the small fingers of trees, like the one in which Storm Hawk is camped.

In essence, deer occur wherever there is enough cover to protect them from the heat of summer and from predators. Because they are not herd animals, they require only scattered cover of sufficient size to safeguard a small family group, which includes at least a doe and a fawn—at most a doe, two fawns, and two yearlings.

One such family started with a doe that conceived along the river in the valley on the 25th of November 1574. She nurtured her embryos throughout the winter. Then, she, along with other deer, followed the spring of 1575 upward through the forest to the edge of the cirque's meadow during the beginning of May. On the way, they ate Douglas-fir, western redcedar, huckleberry, salal, deer fern, mushrooms, and lichens growing on trees.

Chiefly browsers, the tender forage of woody plants annually supplies about three-fourths of their diet, especially in winter. In spring and summer, however, the tender growth of forbs and grasses may furnish up to half of their diet.

Being somewhat warmer than usual this year, the deer, arriving at the meadow on May 17th, had an early opportunity to graze on the newly growing grasses and emerging forbs, which they normally do mainly at daybreak and nightfall. When feeding at night, they gravitate toward wide, airy settings.

Now early in the afternoon on the 28th of May, the doe walked into a thicket of alder along the stream and lay down in the bed she used yesterday. She lay quietly for 15 minutes, and then commenced labor. A male fawn was born within 10 minutes and was immediately licked clean by his mother. Fifteen minutes later, a female was born, and she was also licked clean. They weighed between 6 and 8⁹⁄₁₀ pounds. Their mother was alert, and stayed with her youngsters for some time.

The fawns had no detectable scent for the first week or so, which enabled her to leave them hidden while she went off to eat and replenish her body after giving birth. She also had to consume enough food to produce the required amount of milk to feed her fawns.

When she finally left in late afternoon, the fawns lay flat against the ground with their necks outstretched and their ears laid back against their heads. This flat, immobile posture, their white spots that disrupt the outlines of their body contours (Photo 6.43), and the fact that they had no discernable odor all served as protection from potential predators.

6.43 Young black-tailed deer in an immobile, protective posture to avoid detection by potential predators.

Mother and young learned to recognize each other by sniffing one another's tarsal glands, the aforementioned longitudinal glands located on the insides of the hind legs in the area of the hock, or heel. While the fawns bleated for their mother during the day, at night they "rub-urinated" to communicate, as well as to give a distress signal. (Rub-urinating is ritualized in that the hocks are rhythmically rubbed together as urine is slowly released over them.)

Meanwhile, unknown to the mother and her fawns, Storm Hawk enters the cirque on the 5th of June, as the youngsters are beginning to practice the use of rub-urinating in a defense manner. Smelling of the metatarsal glands is normally the first stage of aggressive behavior. As the young male matures, he erects and rhythmically moves the long hairs around his tarsal glands, exposing the scent, and he often combines this with rub-urination.

Two yearling females periodically try to rejoin their mother only to be rejected because of her new offspring. They are finally accepted, however, during the last week of June, and the family group is complete.

Mutual grooming, licking one another, begins between the mother and her newest young, forming the initial ties within the family group. Grooming helps to establish strong bonds among members of a family and reestablishes them if they are weakened by frequent contact with a relatively large number of deer during the gregarious wintering period in the valley. In addition to grooming, members of a family group sniff the tarsal glands of one another's legs once or twice an hour during the day, and as often as six times an hour during the night.

Adult females are mutually antagonistic toward one another much of the year, and conflicts may arise when they come together. Such antagonism results in a fairly regular spacing of the females' centers of activity. A female occasionally remembers a conflict and avoids the area of another female, even if she is dead. Although family ties weaken during late winter and spring, when fawns have been weaned and females congregate in a choice feeding area, the birth of new fawns renews the mutual antagonism, and thereby spaces the females throughout the available habitat.

Most males are solitary, but some have a strong tendency to congregate throughout much of the year. They usually disperse with the onset of the breeding season, which occurs at lower elevations than the cirque during November to early December, but many gather into groups again during winter and spring. Several families and groups of males may come together in spring and form large feeding bands. Although these bands resemble a social herd, each small group retains its integrity. Conflict often arises when these small groups approach one another too closely. No permanent, social herd forms, however, because each group goes its own way as the feeding period ends.

The males' centers of activity are often clustered, and other than maintenance of social rank and sexual aggressiveness, no antagonistic behavior occurs. Neither the maintenance of social rank nor sexual aggressiveness seems to have any effect on the spacing among individual males, which remain aloof from one another.

The bucks rub their forehead glands, which are located between their eyes and the base of their antlers, against signposts (trunks of trees, branches, twigs, and occasionally other things) throughout the year, forming an intricate system of communication detected through sniffing established signposts. The material from the these scent glands is apparently washed off the signposts by rain and melting snow because there is an increase in rubbing activity following precipitation.

Males share rubbing sites, as well as having some that are strictly their own. Rubbing sites are established at strategic places, such as resting areas and along commonly used trails. Males apply scent on signposts, and both sexes sniff them. There is a correlation among males between marking shared signposts with scent and sniffing them. The dominant buck frequently marks rubbing sites but seldom sniffs, whereas lower ranking males sniff more and mark less, depending on their social status.

From spring to autumn, there is an increase in the frequency and intensity with which males mark shared rubbing sites and a decrease in the number of exclusive signposts that an individual maintains. Rubbing reaches its peak during the breeding season and seems to advertise the presence and physiological state of a particular male. During this time, both females and males sniff signposts more frequently than at other times. In addition to absentee communication, forehead rubbing, including thrashing vegetation with the antlers, may be one method by which breeding males establish both dominance and express a threat, while simultaneously avoiding unnecessary conflict.

Yearling and mature males begin growing antlers from April until August, when day length reaches an exact number of hours and minutes. This timing insures the maturation of antlers in time for the breeding season and also that the young will be born within a certain period in the spring.

Growing antlers are encased in a thin layer of skin covered with short, fine hair called "velvet." They are soft, tender, and well supplied with blood. Antlers attain maximum size by late summer, when the supply of blood gradually decreases, then terminates. The velvet dries, loosens, and drops off. By this time the antlers are hard and dead. Once the velvet is off, the antlers serve as sexual characteristics, as well as weapons. (Photo 6.44) Antlers are shed on the winter range only to begin to re-grow the following April.

6.44 Adult male with fully developed antlers.

Antlers, containing much calcium, fall to the ground during a hard time of the year for most active rodents. So it is a fortunate deer mouse, chickaree, or flying squirrel that finds a discarded antler on which it can not only sharpen its ever-growing front teeth but also obtain a welcome supply of calcium and other minerals. (Photo 6.45)

Satiated from his meal of venison, Storm Hawk goes to the stream and has a leisurely bath, as the sun reaches its zenith and the meadow becomes pleasantly warm. Thereafter, he sits on a rock along the bank, allowing the warm breezes and sunshine to dry him. He then puts on his cloths and finds a shady spot under a tree along the peninsula's edge near his camp and takes a peaceful nap.

*6.45 Fallen antler of a black-tailed deer gnawed on by rodents whereby
they not only sharpen their ever-growing front teeth but also obtain
calcium and other dietary minerals.*

It is mid-afternoon when he awakens. Getting up, he wanders
to the stream and follows it toward the forest, stopping in an area
of scattered, frost-tolerant, mountain huckleberry bushes, most
about 12 inches tall interspersed here and there with a few that are
20 years old and almost four feet high. (Photo 6.46) New, yellow-
green twigs are visible among the thin, 1½- to 2-inch membranous,
oblong leaves with their serrated edges. Solitary, bell-shaped flowers
occur in the leaf axils, each a little more than a quarter of an inch
long, and creamy-pink. Bees are pollinating the flowers, each of
which will produce a single berry.

Bending over to inspect the shrubs in anticipation of ripe berries later in the summer, he sees a couple of small burrows under the
bushes. Curious about their owner, he begins searching the huckleberry patches for more burrows. After an hour or so of searching,
he finds a few more, where the berry bushes, the stream, and the
forest come together, as well as small fir stripped of its bark about
a foot above the ground. One of the burrows has a pile of small,

reddish, elongated droppings in close proximity (Photo 6.47), as well as a rather bulky nest of grass.

6.46 Scattered bushes of mountain huckleberry.

6.47 Fresh fecal pellets of a heather vole on top of older pellets, which are the dark ones that show around the margin of the pile, both deposited under the cover of snow.

By now, the afternoon is fast waning, so Storm Hawk decides to make his way back to camp, with every intention of returning tomorrow to make a more thorough investigation.

June 10th

Storm Hawk awakens as the sun warms his face. Although the voice of his heart tells him that he came to find the campsite of his ancestors, he can't let go of the mystery surrounding the little denizen of the huckleberry patch. With this in mind, he eats the remainder of the meat he cooked last night, then goes to the stream, where he washes his face and fills a deer bladder with water before heading to the berry patch.

Arriving at the place where he saw the burrows and nest yesterday, he sits cross-legged on the ground and simply watches and listens to Nature. Somewhere a Steller jay chatters, a chickaree scolds, and a rufus hummingbird visits the huckleberry blossoms.

Time passes. A beautiful, white cloud drifts overhead, then another and another. A little, gray face appears for an instant in one of the burrows close to where Storm Hawk is sitting.

Again, time passes. The heather vole (a little mammal that resembles a "meadow mouse") pokes its head out of the burrow and looks at Storm Hawk, who remains still. The vole ventures out of its burrow, scoots along a runway and disappears into the bushes, only to reappear again within minutes. It stops in front of Storm Hawk and looks at him.

For a reason he cannot fathom, he slowly extends his left hand toward the wee creature. The vole sits rooted to the spot. Storm Hawk's hand is now but an inch away, and yet the vole remains motionless, making no attempt to escape, even as Storm Hawk gently picks it up and looks at it. For its part, the vole sits quietly in his hand. After a minute or so, with a deep sense of mystical love in his heart, Storm Hawk puts the back of this hand on the ground, and the vole departs, entering its burrow without the slightest sign of fear.

Heather vole

Heather voles, active on a 24-hour cycle, range in total length from 5½ to 6 inches, their tails varying from 1 inch to 1⁹⁄₁₀ inches. Adults weigh from 1²⁄₁₀ to 1⁴⁄₁₀ ounces. A heather vole's back is grayish to brownish gray, and its underside is whitish or light brown. There are moderately stiff, orange hairs in the peripheral half of the inside of the ears. The tail is grayish to brownish gray above, whitish below. Their feet are light brown to whitish on top. Juveniles may be duller and darker in all respects.

Heather voles are active year round, and thus have different nesting areas, depending on the time of the year. Their winter nests are built on the ground under the cover of snow; they are thick-walled, well insulated, and usually made of grasses, but lichens and other materials may also used. Usually situated under the cover of shrubs or fallen trees, the inner-nest chambers are warm, soft, and accommodate a family group that huddles together for warmth. Nevertheless, the nest is clean since these voles deposit their feces in specific, blind-ended tunnels in snow outside of the nest. Thus, by spring, when the snow melts, the accumulation of fecal pellets becomes apparent.

Newly exposed toilets are light reddish and appear fresh (see photo 6.47, page 182). Those that have been exposed for some time, however, are dark and beginning to break down, as the surrounding vegetation is growing up around and through them. (Photo 6.48)

6.48 Old fecal pellets of a heather vole deposited under the cover of snow.

Their summer nests are also made of grasses and mosses and may be situated on the surface of the ground under the cover of vegetation. However, those in which young are born and reared are usually located eight inches or so belowground.

Although runways are characteristically used under cover of snow, as the snow disappears these small voles take up predominantly subterranean abodes. Sometimes, however, their faint runways are evident as they connect one burrow entrance with another. At other times, their dropping-studded runways can be found in thickets of huckleberry. More often than not, there is scant indication of runways in summer when the voles are freed of winter's constraining snow.

Heather voles seem to be strict vegetarians. They eat such plants as mountain willow, huckleberry, and bear grass. In summer, they eat mountain huckleberry by cutting off the terminal twigs in lengths of 1½ to 3½ inches and pull them down into their burrows, where they eat the leaves and discard the twigs as refuse. At times, several uneaten twigs are left in a burrow entrance, which the occupant saves for a later meal.

In winter, under the cover of snow, heather voles gnaw the bark off sapling firs and lodgepole pine, a few of which adorn the huckleberry patches, and occasionally climb up five or more feet into the snow and eat the needles off the terminal shoots and lateral branches of the pines. Sometimes they even kill young trees. (Photo 6.49) And all around these trees are their telltale toilets.

6.49 Young tree girdled and killed by a heather vole eating its needles, twigs, and bark within a deep blanket of winter snow.

Heather voles usually lead solitary lives, except during breeding season. Although they may have several estrous periods from May through August, one female, bred on May 13th, gives birth to five males and two females 24 days later, on June 5th, the day Storm Hawk arrived in the cirque. Although the babies are born blind and deaf, they will wander out of their nest when they are about three weeks old, during the last three or four days of June.

Even in the short summer of this high-mountain cirque, adult females have more than one litter, usually consisting of five to six babies each. The two juvenile females will reach sexual maturity at the age of four to six weeks, between the 5th and the 18th of July. While they may reproduce, their litters will be limited to three or four young. Males, however, will not become sexually mature until the spring of 1576.

Storm Hawk spends the next several hours exploring the berry patch and its surroundings, where he observes other burrows, scat piles, faint runways, and winter nests, but does not see another heather vole. Feeling a deep sense of peace and oneness with all Nature, he walks slowly along the stream on his way to camp, when he startles a pair of Oregon juncos that suddenly erupt from the path in front of him, flashing white tail feathers as they flee. These are not the first juncos he has seen, however, because they frequently visit the vicinity of his camp.

Oregon Junco

Oregon juncos are neat, flashy, dark-gray little birds that flit about the forest floor. Males have a black hood, brown back, reddish-brown sides, white underparts, and gray wings, whereas females have a gray hood and are less colorful. They both have a dark-gray tail with white, outer tail feathers that flash distinctively in flight and while hopping on the ground. Their bills are pale pinkish. In addition, they are 5$\frac{1}{10}$ to 6$\frac{9}{10}$ inches long, have a wingspan of 7$\frac{1}{10}$ to 9$\frac{8}{10}$ inches, and they weigh from $\frac{3}{5}$ to 1$\frac{3}{5}$ ounces.

Their calls include what sounds like *tick* and very high-pitched *tinkling chips*, with a slight metallic trill on the same pitch. Moreover, members of a widely spread flock may keep in contact by constantly calling *tsick* or *tchet*, in addition to a soft *buzzy trill* in flight.

With the advent of mid-March, these lively, ground-dwelling, territorial birds leave their lowland wintering areas and migrate to the cirque, where they breed, usually arriving around end of April or the beginning of May. Living in flocks, they have a distinct social hierarchy, which they exercise by frequently chasing one another. Those arriving in the cirque first each year tend to rank higher in the group than later arrivals. Further, males are not only decidedly territorial but also extremely agile, chasing off intruders in rapid flights accompanied by excited call notes.

In flight, juncos flap continuously and pump their tails so the white outer tail feathers flash, as they maneuver in and out of thickets and around the trees. Flashing their white, outer tail feathers while in flight and moving about on the ground serves two purposes. First, because their overall coloration blends into the background, the sudden flashes of white disrupt a would-be predator's focus in a case of, "now you see me, now you don't," and is thus called "disruptive coloration." And, second, flashing white tail feathers serve as a signal to alert others when the one flashing is alarmed.

Although they spend most of their time on the ground, they also move about the lower branches of the trees and seek shelter in the dense tangles of shrubs. When foraging, juncos typically hop (rather than walk) on the ground, pecking and scratching with their feet at the leaf litter, or flitting low in brushes, where they glean food from twigs and leaves. Sometimes, they even fly up and catch insects on the trunks of the trees.

While in the cirque, about half of the juncos' diet is made up of such insects as beetles, moths, butterflies, caterpillars, ants, wasps, and flies, as well as centipedes. The other half consists of seeds.

On the 11th of May, a male, having established his territory, sang from a high perch in the upper island of trees on the west side of the meadow to attract a mate. Seeing a female responding to his song, he flew to the ground, where he fanned his wings and flicked open his tail because females seem to prefer a male that shows a considerable amount of white in the tail. In addition, he hopped up and down and picked up pieces of nest material. Having been accepted by the female, the pair hopped about on the ground with their wings drooping and their tails spread, showing off their white, outer tail feathers.

Once mated, the female chose a nest site on the ground in a cup-shaped depression well hidden by grass. Meanwhile, a female nesting at the base of the cliff chose the protection of an over-hanging rock, whereas those in the forest select protected areas under fallen trees or amid their tangled roots.

Having selected a site under the large clump of grass at the interface between the trees and the meadow, on the 13th of May, she built her nest, using her beak to weave together grass, bits of moss, and rootlets, and lined it with fine grasses and hair. She then moved her body around in the cup to give the nest its shape. Finish-ing her nest on the 20th of May, it measured 5 inches across, with an inner diameter just over 2½ inches, and a depth of two inches.

However, a nest can be quite variable, depending on where it is built. Nests built on the west side of the meadow and in the forest are often placed on a foundation of twigs, leaves, and moss, then lined with grasses, ferns, rootlets, hair, and fine pieces of moss. Those on the east side of the meadow just get a fine lining of grasses or pine needles, and sometimes feathers.

Beginning on the 21st, she laid 3 of 5 eggs; the last 2 arrived on the 22nd. The slightly glossy eggs were pale bluish-white with variegated, pale-purplish blotches concentrated at the larger end. She incubates them until the 7th of June, when the chicks hatch naked, except for dark-gray down on their backs, with eyes closed and clumsy movements.

Thereafter, both parents feed the chicks, which leave the nest on the 7th of June, the day following Storm Hawk's first full day in the cirque. At which time, the juveniles' bills still have conspicu-ous yellowish edges that border the interior of their open mouths, in addition to the remains of the fleshy margins that guided their parents when they fed them as nestlings. Beyond that, they will have pale streaks until they acquire adult plumage sometime between late August and mid-September, but their heads are generally quite uniform in color.

Her first family gone, she will lay a second clutch of eggs by the 15th of June, and raise another brood. However, as is the way of juncos, she will build a new nest in a different location, rather than reuse the previous one.

By late September and the first part of October, the cirque's juncos are beginning to migrate to lower elevations, where they often arrive by late October or early November, depending on where they go. Their journey over, their diet shifts toward seeds and berries, which are more readily available in their lowland, winter habitats.

Arriving at camp still in the cradle of profound peace, Storm Hawk kindles his evening fire, eats a leisurely supper, and watches as the sun's light—Earth's daytime star—is gradually replaced by nighttime's myriad stars whose light took thousands of years to reach Earth and gladden the heart of a young man on a sacred quest.

June 11th

The day begins cloudy, and there is a decided chill in the air. Despite having again cooked enough meat for breakfast and lunch, Storm Hawk builds a fire by which to warm himself. Seeing the clouds are going to dominate the heavens for some time, he adds more wood to the fire and cooks more meat. Toward afternoon, however, it begins to look and feel as if the cold, cloudy weather will remain throughout the rest of the day, which it does, so Storm Hawk stays close to his fire.

June 12th

By morning, the sun and warmth have returned to the cirque, but Storm Hawk is having a challenge waking up because the inner voice of his heart is urging him to search the peninsula and islands thoroughly for the old campsite, rather than becoming so entranced with the life of the cirque.

Finally awake enough to get up, he eats and begins a thorough search of the peninsula, which takes the rest of the day, but once again fails to find anything of interest with respect to the old campsite, much less a concrete clue to its whereabouts. Along the way, however, he sees the hind leg of a deer poking out from a clump of young firs and huckleberry bushes.

Walking carefully, with bow and arrow at ready, he circles the bushes and finds the mostly eaten carcass of a doe covered with leaves, sticks, and other debris from the ground. (Photo 6.50) Having seen this scenario before, he recognizes it as a puma's recent kill (later to be called a "mountain lion" by the Europeans who invade his people's land).

6.50 A puma killed this doe and has eaten most of her over a period of days.

Puma

Pumas apparently disappeared from North America during the massive, late Pleistocene extinction-event—between 11,500 and 10,000 years ago—that eliminated 80 percent of the large vertebrates, and thus may have extirpated pumas. Shortly thereafter, a genetically uniform population of pumas, derived from a small number of genetic ancestors, began to re-colonize the continent.

Moreover, the ancestors themselves originated from a center of puma genetic diversity in eastern South America between 200,000 and 300,000 years ago. So it was, there existed three wildcats in the northern part of North America during the days Storm Hawk's tribe lived in dignity on and with the land: the bobcat, lynx, and largest of all—the puma.

Today, the slim, agile puma occupies the most extensive range of any New World, terrestrial mammal, spanning 100 degrees of latitude from the Canadian Yukon to the Strait of Magellan. The Strait of Magellan is one of the world's most important, natural waterways, linking the Pacific and Atlantic Oceans. The strait passes below Chile and above Tierra del Fuego and Antarctica, and is named after Ferdinand Magellan, who not only was the first person from the Old World to navigate the waterway but also was the first person to circumnavigate the entire globe.

The scientific name *Puma concolor* means "cat of one color." Indeed, their coloration is such that it readily blends into the landscape through which they travel and in which they hunt. They are large, slender cats with smallish heads; noticeably long, cylindrical tails that account for about one-third of their total length; and short, coarse fur. Their heads, backs, sides, and the outsides of their legs are dark tannish to reddish-brown, but can appear gray or almost black, under certain conditions of lighting. The tops of their tails are darker brown than the back, darkening to a relatively long, blackish tip. The backs of their ears are black. They have a pinkish nose with a black border that extends to their lips. Their throat, chest, belly, and insides of the legs are whitish. Their short, muscular limbs terminate in broad feet, with four digits on the hind feet and five on the forefeet. In addition, their retractable claws are sharp and curved, excellent for grabbing prey. The eyes of mature animals are grayish brown to golden. (Photo 6.51)

6.51 Adult puma.

Pumas range in size from 5 to 9 feet in length, stand 2 to 2 $\frac{9}{10}$ feet tall at the shoulders, and weigh from 80 to about 210 pounds. Males are larger than females. The overall size of pumas varies with location; they are smallest close to the equator and largest toward the north and south poles.

A puma's normal walking gait is a rather long-stride. Yet, these cats can leap as high as 18 feet in one bound, and as far as 40 to 45 feet horizontally. A puma's top running speed ranges between 40 and 50 miles per hour, but is best adapted for short, powerful sprints, rather than long chases. It is adept at climbing, which allows it to evade canine competitors, such as wolves, which kill one now and then. Although it is not strongly associated with water, it can swim. Regardless of what a puma is doing, it is always the epitome of grace and strength welded into fluid beauty.

Solitary by nature, only mothers and kittens live in groups, with adults meeting just to mate. Pumas are also naturally secretive, and thus most active during the night, with peak activity at dawn and at dusk. The dawn-and-dusk pattern is known as "crepuscular" activity.

Although most resident, adult pumas confine their movements to specific areas year after year, there is also a contingent of younger, transient adults. Resident pumas occupy fairly distinct, contiguous winter-spring and summer-autumn home ranges. The use of these areas, however, varies not only with season but also with time and individuals. Generally speaking, resident pumas use larger areas in summer than they do in winter. A male's home range can vary from 54 square miles to 293 square miles, whereas that of a female can vary from 10 square miles to 135 square miles. The tendency of pumas to increase their movements during late winter is a result of the scarcity of food. Pumas hunt almost continuously, rarely spending more than one day in the same location. Except for the longer periods of heavy rain in spring and autumn, the activity of pumas seems largely independent of the weather.

During winter, a male puma ranges over a minimum area of about 64 square miles, whereas a female ranges over a minimum area of about 13 square miles and a maximum area of about 50 square miles. Although resident males occupy areas that are distinct from one another, a male's area overlaps with those of females. Females, on the other hand, share common areas, and transients of both sexes move freely through occupied areas. Pumas have a high degree of tolerance for other pumas in their areas, but are decidedly unsocial in that they avoid contact with one another. That pumas seldom defend an area is a behavioral mechanism of mutual avoidance that keeps them distributed without injury.

Pumas rely mainly on vision, smell, and hearing to navigate within their home ranges. They use low-pitched hisses, growls, spits, purrs, yowls, and piercing, drawn-out screams in different circumstances.

Although pumas use all their senses on a daily basis, scent marking is particularly important in advertising territorial boundaries, as well as an individual's reproductive state. Urine, "scrapes," feces, and scent from anal or other glands advertise a puma's presence, either bringing pumas together or maintaining the distance between them. Puma scrapes are areas where the cats scrape soil, or litter, or both, into a pile in one to six places usually less than three feet apart. The cats may deposit feces, urine, or both in or on the pile. All pumas make these marks, but males mark more frequently than females, and the marks are more numerous during periods of high populations.

A puma's land tenure is based on prior rights, and home ranges are well covered. Because males disperse earlier and farther than females and also compete more directly for mates and territory, they are most likely to be involved in conflict. When males encounter each other, they hiss, spit, and may engage in violent combat if neither backs down. Male territorial competition even extends to the young; for example, the father may kill a juvenile-male offspring if he fails to leave his maternal range.

Nevertheless, home ranges change after deaths or movements of the residents. Young adults establish home ranges only as vacancies occur. The land-tenure system acts to maintain the density of breeding adults below the carrying capacity of the available supply of food. (Carrying capacity is the maximum number of pumas that their prey base can sustain without altering the integrity of the ecosystem that supports them.)

In the short term, a puma's home range is in a state of constant change created by the availability of prey. Over the long term, however, the conditions in certain parts of the home range are such that a cat tends to be more successful there in making kills, and, as a result, will spend more time in those parts. There is a definite advantage for a puma to be thoroughly familiar with its home range, especially for a female in the process of rearing kittens.

Deer and elk, but primarily deer, are the pumas' staple diet in this high-mountain world, although they also eat snowshoe hares, flying squirrels, chickarees, the occasional porcupine, ruffed grouse, and other animals. The male, whose home range encompasses the cirque, normally zigzags back and forth through the thickets, around the meadow, and under the overhang of the cliff. He goes up and down the small draws and back and forth across the creeks. This method of travel better enables him to detect prey and to stage a successful attack.

He does not, for example, try to capture deer indiscriminately wherever he finds them, but, being a stalker, he searches for a deer in a location where he can employ his stealthy approach, which may require more than an hour of patient stalking to get close enough for a successful attack. In addition, having high visual acuity, he notices which deer is least attentive to what is going on, which often is a sign of sickness or extreme old age, and thus he chooses that animal for his next meal.

When in a favorable position, he leaps suddenly from the ground onto the shoulders and neck of the deer. Holding the deer's head against the ground with a forepaw, he bites down through the back of the neck, near the base of the skull, and sometimes even through the skull. At other times he kills with a "choking" bite that crushes the windpipe. After killing the deer, he drags it as much as 1,200 feet from where he killed it and scrapes a mound of leaves, sticks, and conifer needles over it, after which he may leave, only to return nightly and eat as much as nine pounds of meat in a meal (see photo 6.50 on page 191).

He remains in the immediate vicinity of his kill, ostensibly guarding it against scavengers, while he eats it over a period that may last 19 days, depending on its size and age. He eats any young prey that he kills almost entirely, including the spinal column, skull, and feet, but he eats only about 70 percent of older prey. The 30 percent that is left includes the rumen (the large, first chamber of the deer's stomach), some viscera, larger bones, feet, and some of the hide. (Photo 6.52)

6.52 The inedible remains of a puma's kill and the track of the departing cat.

If his caches are left intact for him to eat, 14 to 20 average-sized deer would sustain him for a year. Not all of them are left unmolested, however, despite his presence, because a pack of wolves periodically roams through the cirque. When they find one of his cached deer carcasses, they not only scavenge it but also may kill him, should he attempt to claim the carcass while it is in possession of the wolves. Therefore, he only reclaims what is left after the wolves have departed.

Wolves are not the only scavengers in the cirque, because the resident puma also scavenges carcasses when available, and their condition does not seem to bother him. In fact, he treats each scavenged carcass as he does his own kills, dragging it to a preferred site, caching it, depositing scats, and making scrapes in the area. Thus, over the years, he has eaten carcasses that ranged from frozen and fresh to rotting and maggot-infested.

With respect to pumas in general, each large animal they kill has some physical or behavioral anomaly that affects its long-term survival and is thus most vulnerable to predation by the big cats, which ultimately culls them from the population. In addition, predation by the pumas keeps the deer and elk moving, especially on the lower-elevation winter range. The mere presence of a puma does not usually alarm deer or elk, but when a kill is made, the reaction is striking. Deer and elk immediately leave the area, crossing to the far side, or even move into a different drainage. This forced redistribution helps to prevent their overpopulating an area and causing severe damage to their habitat.

As far as the occasional porcupine is concerned, one entered the cirque a year ago (1574) this summer and was flipped on its back by the resident female puma. Although she managed to avoid most of the quills, some got in her paws, shoulders, face, and mouth. Over the next few weeks, she pulled some out, others fell out, and those under her skin gradually dissolved.

Having secured her meal, she ate everything except the head, beginning with the porcupine's underparts. Despite a quill puncturing her stomach wall and working into her abdominal cavity, she suffered no apparent ill effects before it dissolved. Moreover, once eaten, the quills in her stomach began to soften within an hour.

Reproduction is confined to the resident pumas. The male breeds two of the females whose home ranges overlap with his. Since the transient pumas are nomads, the reproductive phase of their lives is restricted until they find vacancies and establish their own home ranges. Because the land-tenure system of the pumas is dynamic and flexible, a home range is not inherited intact but involves a re-sorting of living space. This re-sorting takes place first among the older cats, so the younger ones must accept what is left.

A puma will not mate until it has established a home range, but then commonly breeds sometime between December and March, although mating can happen at any time of the year. Individual females, however, breed only every other year. Just before and just after the young become independent, a female associates with, or perhaps only tolerates, adult males and even adult females more frequently and for longer periods than at any other time. Such tolerance reaches its peak during estrous when a pair remains in one another's company, traveling together for 8 to 16 days.

While in estrous, she vocalizes freely, and frequently rubs against nearby objects. The male responds with similar yowls and sniffs the female's genital area. A single act of mating lasts less than one minute, but can occur several times in an hour.

The male bred the female, whose home range includes the cirque, on the 28th of March, shortly after she had left her three kittens (one male and two females), which had been with her for the previous 17 months. On the 1st of July, after a gestation period of 95 days, she goes to a shallow cave in the base of the cliff and gives birth to four kittens, each weighing between 14 and 16 ounces. Her newly born, helpless kittens are covered with short, soft hair that is dull tannish with darker blotches on their bodies and bands on the tails. Their eyes are closed and their ears folded over. On the 11th of July (the day after Storm Hawk leaves the cirque), the kittens' eyes will open, at which time their eyes will be blue, and their ears will become erect. (Photo 6.53)

6.53 Puma kittens.

The kittens will grow rapidly and weigh between 8 and 10 pounds by early September. After nursing them until the second week in September, she moves with her family to another cliff about a mile away. Even though the kittens are weaned by the first of October, their mother will be restricted in the use of her home range, and her pattern of movement will be more complex until the kittens are one year old. She will leave her kittens in a protected place for a day or two at a time while she hunts in a loop away from them and back again. They, in turn, will call to her with loud, chirping whistles, in addition to which touch will be an important language of bonding between the kittens and their mother.

As the kittens mature, their coloration will pale, but the dark spots will remain on their flanks, only to fade as the juveniles move toward adulthood. During the next months, the family will wander proportionately farther, as she teaches them to hunt, by selecting young deer as prey and taking her offspring to visit the kill sites. By the time they are six months old, the first week in December, they will begin to hunt small prey on their own. And by the time they are two years old, their juvenile spots will be completely gone, and they will begin to cover their mother's entire home range.

They will become independent during their second winter (1577) and will finally break the family ties with their mother in March in some southeastern portion of her home range, where they will have spent considerable time earlier in the winter. Their mother will leave them at a kill and simply not return. The siblings, in turn, will remain together for a while, and then will meet for short periods before going their separate ways.

The young independents become transients and wander about until they find a vacancy, take up residence, and thus achieve breeding status. Thereafter, the male will reach sexual maturity when he is 3 years old, and will remain reproductively active at least to the age of 20. His two sisters, on the other hand, will reach sexual maturity when they are 2½ years old, and will remain reproductively viable at least until they are 12 years old.

At the moment, however, the light of day is dissolving into darkness, as the shadows created by the setting sun coalesce into the black velvet of night, and the pumas begin to prowl the cirque.

June 13th

Waking just as the curtain of night rises enough to acknowledge the coming day, Storm Hawk quiets his mind and becomes aware that sounds are coming from every direction all the time—some quiet, some loud, some soft and gentle, some harsh, some beautiful, and some not so. He also realizes that how he interprets each sound depends on his state of mind at the time he hears it.

Getting up with a deep sense of oneness with the cirque, he eats and departs for the western island, having decided to search one each day. Thus, to honor his commitment, he spends the entire day walking back and forth throughout the trees and around them, where they join the meadow, often accompanied by the chattering of Stellar jays.

Steller Jay

Storm Hawk vaguely hears the jay's harsh-sounding *SHACK-Sheck-sheck-sheck-sheck-sheck* background call and their periodic alarm call, which is a harsh, nasal *wah*, as he concentrates on his mission. In days past, however, he marveled at their beauty and enjoyed their constant company around his camp, where they spent much time exploring and patrolling the treetops, periodically scolding some perceived irregularity.

One of the most vocal species within the cirque's forest, they keep a running commentary on events, and often instigate mobbing of predators or other possibly dangerous intruders. At other times, they give forth with a variety of loud, raucous calls that are repeated in patterns of three.

A large, striking bird 11 to 12 inches long with a 17-inch wingspan, the Steller jay has a deep blue and black plumage and a prominent, shaggy crest on its head that often stands nearly straight up. The front of its body is black, and the rear is deep blue. The black extends midway down its back and down its breast. This dark coloring gives way from the shoulders and lower breast to a silvery blue. Its body is all blue (lightest, almost sparkling, on its wings, which have dark bars). Adults have blue, vertical "eyebrows" above each eye. Its bill is long, straight, and powerful, with a slight hook. (Photo 6.54)

6.54 Steller Jay.

In addition to the jays' appearance, Storm Hawk was captivated by their graceful, seemingly patient flight with its long swoops on their broad, rounded wings, as they made their way to the ground, where they investigated his camp. Moving with bold, decisive hops on their long legs, they searched for food. At other times, seeing what they perceived to be a scrap of food, they would swoop down from a tree, grab it, and fly off screaming a loud victory call! He was also amused by the jay's ability to mimic the vocalizations of a goshawk or golden eagle, causing other birds to seek cover, thereby abandoning feeding areas to the jay's benefit.

Highly social, Steller jays usually travel in pairs or family groups. They have a complex communication system, with a variety of calls, postures, and displays. For example, a spread wing indicates submission; an erected crest might mean attack, while a folded crest indicates retreat, all part of their strict, social hierarchy and patterns of dominance. Traveling in groups outside of the nesting season, they occasionally fly in single file across the meadow, sometimes playing with or chasing one another, or joining mixed-species flocks.

Omnivorous, they move with bold hops on their long legs, both on the ground and among the main branches of forest trees, often pausing to eye their surroundings, cocking their heads suddenly this way and that. These intelligent, opportunistic birds are quick to take advantage of newly discovered food sources, both in the trees and on the ground.

About two-thirds of their diet is derived from plants and one-third from animals. The vegetable portion of their diet consists of conifer seeds, nuts, and berries, whereas the animal portion consists of invertebrates, bird eggs and nestlings, small rodents, reptiles, and carrion.

With respect to plant food, conifer seeds are a staple during the non-breeding season, of which the jays carry several at once in their mouth and throat, and cache them one by one in the ground or in trees to be eaten at a later time. Then, because they raid the caches of Clark nutcrackers, which consist of 1 to 15 seeds from the cirque's white-bark pines, they place special emphasis on making sure that their own food store is covered and hidden from all directions. Once hidden, they depend on their incredible, spatial memories to retrieve the store of food.

Habitual nest-robbers, they are highly vocal when not nesting, but exceedingly quiet and inconspicuous when engaged in raising their own young or when robbing the eggs or young from nests of the Clark nutcracker, among a variety of other species. In addition to robbing nests, they occasionally attack and kill small, adult birds, such as red-breasted nuthatches and Oregon juncos.

Like the deer, Steller jays follow spring from their lower, winter habitat to the high world of the cirque, where they reside until late autumn or early winter impresses on them the avian wisdom of returning to the milder winter conditions at a lower elevation. Once in the cirque, however, they, like the cliff swallows, are being prepared by Nature for the forthcoming nesting season that begins as late May slips into June.

This year a pair of jays began building their nest in an Engelmann spruce on two closely spaced, horizontal branches close to the trunk near the top of the tree. Being a monogamous pair with a long-term, year-round bond, they selected their nesting site together. Having made their choice, they began gathering twigs, small plants, leaves, and moss, which they crafted into a bulky cup held together with mud. They lined the inside of the cup with soft rootlets, animal hair, and other fine materials. Their finished nest is a bulky 15 inches in diameter, 7 inches tall, and 3 inches deep on the inside of the cup.

Having finished their nest on the 29th of May, the female laid 4 oval-shaped, bluish-green eggs with a somewhat glossy surface and purplish speckles. Having laid her last egg on June 2nd, she incubates them for 16 days, until June 18th, when the chicks hatch naked and helpless. And the male has been feeding his mate during this entire process.

Both parents are silent and shy near their nest, as they feed their babies for the next three weeks, until July 9th when they fledge the day before Storm Hawk leaves the cirque, at which time they appear similar to their parents, but have slightly browner heads and lack the blue eyebrows. They will begin making short flights within a few days of fledging and sustained flights by the time they are 30 days old on July 18th, which is about when they will begin to find their own food. Nevertheless, their parents will continue to provide them with some food for another month, until mid August.

The family will remain in the cirque as summer wanes. Only the growing cold of early October will induce the family to abandon their summer home and fly to a lower elevation for the winter. They will, however, return to the cirque with the coming of spring.

Meanwhile, the afternoon grows late. Finding no hint of the old campsite, Storm Hawk returns to his own camp and prepares for the coming night.

June 14th

Arriving at the northern island in mid-morning, Storm Hawk begins to search it in the same way he did the one yesterday, and with the same results, but does find himself periodically being watched from the shadows by small, striped squirrels, which are today known as "Townsend chipmunks."

Townsend Chipmunk

A large chipmunk, they range in total length from 8½ to 11 inches and weigh from 1½ to 3½ ounces. Moreover, the females are slightly larger than the males, giving them dominance in the population.

Townsend chipmunks have a moderately long, lax pelage and rather diffused coloration. They undergo two annual molts, shedding their winter pelage in May and their summer pelage in August. Their summer pelage is lighter, brighter, and more contrasting than that of winter. Juvenile pelages are similar to that of the adults.

They have two gray and three brown stripes on their faces. There are three black stripes on the back. The middle one extends from between the ears almost to the base of the tail, while the outer two extend from about the shoulders to the rump. There is an additional, short, dark-brown strip along each side of the back, extending from behind the shoulders almost to the rump. Between the dark stripes are four lighter ones that vary from light brown, to yellowish-brown, to whitish. The stripes on the sides of the head are lighter than those on the back, and their ears are black in front and gray behind.

Their sides, below the short, brown stripes, vary from brown to slightly yellowish-brown. Their undersides are creamy white to gray. They have a long, rather bushy tail, which they hold erect while running. It is blackish above, with many white-tipped hairs, while the underside is bright reddish-brown with a black margin and a "frosted" edge of white-tipped hairs. (Photo 6.55)

6.55 Townsend chipmunk.

These chipmunks live in burrows up to 33 feet long, which are located within the cover of shrubs or under fallen, decaying trees and large stumps within the forested islands and the forest itself. A few make it to the talus, however, where they live under the protection of the boulders along its margin.

Being solitary by nature, they are fairly aggressive toward others of their kind within their home ranges, which can reach a little over an acre. They are particularly assertive within a 30- to 40-foot territory around their burrows. But, females, being bigger than males, tend to have larger territories.

Although they move about from dawn until dusk, their primary activity occurs in the late morning and early afternoon. While above ground, they perceive their environment through sight, hearing, and smell, but communicate using vocalizations, threat displays, and touch.

These shy, wary chipmunks are normally heard, rather than seen. Their calls are quiet, birdlike, and often muted by the rank vegetation in which they tend to live. The calls usually emanate from shadowy undergrowth in which their diffused coloration blends with the ever-changing lights and shadows of their surroundings. And they tend to "freeze" or crouch when they hear a sound or see a movement.

Nevertheless, they give alarm calls to warn others of their kind, compromising their own survival, a phenomenon that seems to be most important when the chipmunks are genetically related. This recognition comes about when young siblings engage in mutual sniffing and grooming.

Their unique, but quiet, alarm call can be simulated by forming a rigid "O-shape" with the lips, and then, placing the little finger inside the mouth so that the back of the hand is toward the face, sliding the finger out of the mouth, all the while pressing firmly against the taught cheek. The sound produced is high and crisp and may be written *po*, with the sharpest accent on the beginning of the sound. When emitted by a chipmunk in the wild, it sounds like, *po, po, po.*

When startled, these silent, graceful, softly colored denizens of the forest usually dash quietly for cover, but are just as apt to scurry up a tree, where they are difficult to locate. Expert climbers, they often forage, hide, or sun themselves in bushes and trees.

From late spring through autumn, their activity consists mainly of feeding and gathering food, such as the seeds of grasses, Douglas-fir, mountain hemlock, and Engelmann spruce. Stuffing their cheek pouches, they carry food from their foraging areas to their burrows, where they cache it as reserves for the winter and early spring.

In summer and autumn, the chipmunks eat a variety of fruits, being especially fond of huckleberries, which stain their mouths purple. In late autumn, they concentrate on eating and storing the seeds. Their diet during the spring and autumn is augmented, as much as possible, with the fruiting bodies of belowground mycorrhizal fungi (truffles), which they detect by odor and dig out of the soil. In addition to vegetable foods, the chipmunks also consume insects, primarily beetles, and occasionally the eggs of such ground-nesting birds as juncos. While foraging, however, they expose themselves to potential predators, and thus select paths within cover so they can stay hidden.

In the autumn, before winter blankets the cirque with deep snow, they accumulate body fat and remain throughout the winter in their burrows, where they hibernate. Emerging from hibernation, as the late-spring sun vanquishes most of the snow, they commenced their breeding season, which took place on the 26th of April in this year of 1575, and continued until the 10th of May.

Townsend chipmunks breed only once a year for a two-week period. This concentration of their reproductive activities provides the young with the best chance of maturing when food is available and the cirque's weather is most favorable, allowing them to prepare for their first winter's hibernation.

The chipmunks are promiscuous in that a female mates with several males, each of which, in turn, mates with several females. One of the females Storm Hawk sees became pregnant on the 1st of May and gave birth to 6 youngsters, three females and three males, in her burrow on May 29th.

They were born naked, blind, with folded ears, webbed feet, and toothless. Weighing about 1/10 of an ounce (roughly as much as a dime), they were between 2 and 2½ inches long. Their loose skin was so translucent that milk could be seen in their stomachs just after they had been fed.

By the time they were 10 days old, on June 1st (just four days before Storm Hawk arrives in the cirque on June 5th), hair had begun to grow on their backs, but their eyes were still closed. Not totally helpless, they could move about by pulling and pushing with their front legs.

Twenty days old on June 11th, their lower front teeth begin to erupt, they have fur, and are more active. The canal leading to the inner ear will open two days from now, on June 16th, and their eyes will begin to open on June 18th, at which time their upper front teeth will begin to erupt.

By this time, they will be fully furred, and their pelage will be bright and fuzzy with markings more distinct than those of the adults. The young will begin eating solid food when they are 39 days old, on July 7th (three days before Storm Hawk leaves the cirque). But even then, they will continue to nurse until mid or late July or early August, when they will weigh a little over an ounce, and will be scampering about in the islands of trees, where a young Indian teen, named Storm Hawk, once stayed while he searched for the fabled hunting camp of his distant ancestors.

Although the chipmunks will reach adulthood by the end of August, when they are three months old, they will not be sexually mature until the following breeding season in 1576. Those that survive their potential predators, mainly the cirque's long-tailed weasels, goshawks, and occasionally a great-horned owl, may live to add their kind to the cirque's population for six to seven years.

During this time, some of the chipmunks will serve as meals for their predators, whereas others will disperse the seeds in their feces from earlier meals that are not readily digestible. Moreover, some of the seeds stored in the shallow parts of their burrows might germinate and penetrate the soil to reach the light. They also disperse fungal spores not only by carrying them on their feet but also by eating the fungal fruiting body or "truffle" and eliminating the spores in their feces, which germinate, grow, and inoculate their host plants, wherein the mutualistic symbiosis of life is formed.

June 15th

The eastern island is not only a little farther into the meadow from the peninsula but also somewhat larger and slightly closer to the stream from the lake. This being the case, Storm Hawk leaves camp earlier than yesterday and repeats his method of searching. As the day wears on, he has the growing sense that any more time spent in the western part of the meadow looking for the fabled campsite is a waste of time.

Thus, having conducted his search by late afternoon, he is about to go back to camp when a female rufous hummingbird buzzes past his head and disappears into the low branch of a lone Douglas-fir about 15 feet away. Storm Hawk, without a moment's hesitation, follows it, but sees nothing. So, he stands still and watches. Minutes tick by, then more. Suddenly, the hummingbird seems to be in Storm Hawk's face, as she leaves her newly constructed nest atop the fir's lowest branch, which just so happens to be at Storm

Hawk's eye level. He walks to the limb and, after a brief search, sees the tiny nest made from plant fibers held together by spider webs and well camouflaged with bit of lichens, within which are cradled two eggs. (Photo 6.56)

6.56 Nest of a rufous hummingbird with eggs.

Rufous Hummingbird

Rufous hummingbirds are about three inches long with a wingspan of about four inches, and a long, straight, very slender bill. (Photo 6.57) They weigh from $7/10$ to almost $8/10$ of an ounce—the weight of one and a half pennies. The female is slightly larger than the male. Their tails are nearly straight, coming to a point when folded, and their short wings do not reach the end of their tails when the birds are perched.

6.57 Young rufous hummingbird. Note straight, slender beak.

In bright light, adult males glow like embers with bright orange on the back and belly and a vivid, iridescent-red throat patch, termed a "gorget." Females, on the other hand, have green upperparts with some white, rufous-washed flanks, some iridescent orange feathers in the center of the throat, and a dark tail with white tips and a rufous base. Both males and females have a white spot behind their eye, and a mix of black and green feathers in addition to their mostly rufous coloration.

Rufous hummingbirds make a clockwise circuit of western North America each year, moving up the Pacific Coast from the wooded areas of the Mexican state of Guerrero, where they spend the winter. Having migrated more than 2,000 miles in late winter and spring, they reached the cirque in early May, as the meadow's flowers began blooming. Once there, they drank nectar with their long, extendible tongues and progressively pollinated such flowers as scarlet gilia, penstemon, monkey flower, paintbrush, lilies, fireweeds, and huckleberries as each came into season. The ability to beat their wings 52 to 62 times per second allows them to hover in place while feeding.

The first birds to arrive in the cirque and discover patches of blooming flowers, these hummingbirds not only claim them as their source of food but also defend them against others of their kind. Even when satiated, a male of these pugnacious, little birds will perch nearby and intercept intruders in the air with angry buzzing. Having the gift of fast, darting flight and pinpoint maneuverability, they are tireless when chasing away other hummingbirds.

In contrast, if a female is disturbed when feeding, she gives a "no trespassing" signal by fanning and waving her tail. Females, therefore, have developed distinct tail patterns, whereas males, facing the opponent, signal with their brilliant throat patches, the aforementioned "gorgets."

Although nectar makes up a large part of the diet, these miniature birds get protein and fat from eating insects, particularly gnats, midges, and flies caught in midair; aphids taken from plants; and from other insects entangled in spider webs. When nectar is scarce, they make use of holes pecked into the bark of trees by sapsuckers, so named because these woodpeckers eat the sap that oozes from the wound.

Moreover, they require frequent feeding while active during the day because of their high rates of metabolism, and become torpid at night to conserve energy. Nevertheless, rufous hummingbirds are exceedingly cold hardy.

Arriving in the cirque as the flowers bloom in early May, a male established his feeding and breeding territory, performing a few displays of flying talent when a female entered it. These performances included steep, oval or J-shaped courtship flights. When the female perched, he switched to low, horizontal figure-8s, copulating with a female on the 17th.

Thereafter, the female built her nest with soft plant fibers that were held together with spider webs. She then camouflaged the outside with bits of lichen. Completing her nest on the 20th, it measured about two inches across on the outside, with an inner cup width of about an inch. The thick wall will not only insulate the nest's cup, keeping the hatchlings protected and cozy, but also compress, allowing the nestlings to grow with the same sense of secure confinement as the day they hatched. (Photo 6.58)

6.58 Hummingbird nest on fir branch. Note the thick wall of plant down held together by spider webs, camouflaged with lichens.

6.59 Newly hatched rufous hummingbird.

She laid two, white eggs on the 21st of May (see photo 6.56, page 210). She incubated them for 16 days, until the 7th of June, when they hatched—two days after Storm Hawk arrived in the cirque. At this time, they are helpless and naked except for sparse, gray down along their backs, and their eyes are closed. (Photo 6.59) Moreover, nights in the high-mountain world can still send temperatures close to freezing, which makes the insulation of the nest's thick wall all-the-more important for the hatchlings' survival.

They grow rapidly (Photo 6.60), and are getting ready to leave the nest by the time they are 13 days old, on the 20th of June. (Photo 6.61) However, they must wait until the 25th before they can fledge, two days after Storm Hawk will have departed the vicinity to investigate the eastern side of the meadow. Now fledged, the young will choose a perch nearby, from which their mother will feed them.

6.60 Baby rufous hummingbird beginning to fill the nest.

6.61 Young rufous hummingbirds about to fledge. Note how thin the wall of the nest has become as the young birds grew.

Often described as "feisty," rufous hummingbirds may have the ideal size-to-weight ratio among North American hummingbirds, in addition to which they not only outfly all other species but also have the longest migration route of hummingbirds inhabiting the continent. And, as the flowers begin to wane in the cirque and other high-elevation meadows during the latter part of July and beginning of August, they will begin their 2,000-mile-plus return journey by traveling over to and down the Rocky Mountains to their winter habitat in Mexico, only to return again along the Pacific Coast to the cirque in the spring.

As they travel, they will drink nectar and pollinate the flowers (particularly nectar-rich, tubular flowers) just as they did throughout the thousands of miles of habitat they visited since they left the cirque in the autumn of 1574. Having an excellent memory for specific locations, they return to once-visited feeding areas and flowers from day to day and from year to year. Yet, even en route, both sexes and all ages demonstrate their aggressiveness during the brief one- to two-week stopovers, at which times they may commandeer and defend feeding areas by chasing off resident broad-tailed, broad-billed, violet-crowned, and black-chinned hummingbirds.

For his part, Storm Hawk has spent much of the day feeling it is time to leave the western side of the meadow and move eastward, when he has second thoughts. He has not examined the stream from the cirque's lake to the forest. "What if," he wonders, "the camp was somewhere along the stream, and the trees have blown over and are lying on the ground rotting?"

June 16th

Thus thinking, he decides to stay a while longer, and spends the day tidying up his camp, gathering more firewood, and determining how many more days the venison will last before it is too ripe for him to eat. Upon examination, he determines that it will be good for five more days.

But for now, the curtain of night is pushing the light of day westward. As the sun sinks below the horizon, the pack of gray wolves begins to fill the cirque with its canine "song." (Photo 6.62) When howling together, the pack actually harmonizes rather than voicing the same note, thus creating the illusion of more wolves than there actually are.

The Wolf Pack

The gray wolf (or timber wolf as some people think of it) is the only member of the dog family (wolves, coyotes, and foxes, among others) to have originated in Eurasia during the Pleistocene and colonized North America, giving it a range that encompasses both the Old and New Worlds. (The term "Pleistocene" is derived from two Greek words, *pleistos*, meaning "most," and *kainos*, meaning "new" or "recent," which may seem strange to some people, considering that it spanned the human concept of time beginning 2.6 million years ago and ending just 11,700 years ago.) Today, the gray wolf is the largest living member of its family, with males weighing an average of 95 to 99 pounds and females averaging 79 to 85 pounds.

6.62 Wolf howling.

Gray wolves are slender, powerfully built animals that, on aver-age, are 41 to 63 inches long, with 11- to 20-inch-long tails, and shoulder heights of 32 to 34 inches, as measured from the base of the paws to the top of the shoulders. Males have large, deeply descending ribcages, sloping backs, and heavily muscled necks. Their legs are moderately longer than those of other kinds of dogs, enabling them to move swiftly and to navigate deep snow. Females, on the other hand, tend to have narrower muzzles and foreheads, thinner necks, slightly shorter legs, and less massive shoulders. The heads of both sexes are large and heavy, with a wide forehead, strong jaws, and a long, blunt muzzle (nose and jaws). The ears are relatively small (3½ to 4³⁄₁₀ inches in height), triangular, covered in short hair, and project above the fur. (Photo 6.63)

6.63 Gray wolf.

Their coat is composed of a combination of short underfur and long, coarse guard hairs. Most of the underfur and some of the guard hairs are shed in the spring, but grow back during the autumn in time for winter. The fur is longest on the back, particularly on the front quarters and neck. In fact, especially long fur occurs on the shoulders, where it almost forms a crest on the upper part of the neck. Moreover, hairs on the cheeks are elongated and form tufts.

Females tend to have smoother furred limbs than males, and generally develop the smoothest overall coat as they age. Older wolves have more white hairs in the tip of the tail, along the nose, and on the forehead.

Over the years, the coats of wolves roaming the mountains that include the cirque have been characterized by varying mixtures of white with shades of black, gray, cinnamon, and brown on the upper parts. Their backs have usually been blacker, with their muzzle, ears, and limbs exhibiting a cinnamon coloration as well. In addition, their under parts have been whitish, and their tails have been conspicuously black over the "tail gland," and paler below to the tip, which has been nearly pure black. The tail gland—also known as the "violet gland"—is an important scent gland located on the top of the tail near the place where it joins the back and is used for communication among pack members.

Their winter coats have a very dense, fluffy layer of underfur that is highly resistant to cold. This insulation allows them to rest comfortably in open areas at 40 degrees below zero Fahrenheit by placing their muzzles between their hind legs and covering their faces with their tails. In addition, their fur does not collect ice when their warm breath condenses on it. The winter fur is retained longest in nursing females, though some hair is lost around their nipples.

They have large, heavy teeth that are better suited to crushing bones than other, living members of the dog family, although their teeth are not as specialized as those of hyenas. However, the gray wolf's jaws can exert a crushing pressure of around 1,500 pounds per square inch compared to the 750 pounds per square inch for a German shepherd. This force is sufficient to crush open most bones.

The gray wolf is the most specialized member of the genus that includes dogs, as demonstrated by its structural adaptations for hunting large prey. As such, a wolf usually carries its head at the same level as the back, raising it only when something causes it to become alert. Beyond that, it normally travels at a loping pace, placing its paws one directly in front of the other, in a gait it can maintain for hours. It can leap 16 feet horizontally in a single bound, and can maintain rapid pursuit for at least 20 minutes.

Although they normally travel at night, wolves can cover up to 125 miles in 24 hours at a normal pace of 5 miles an hour. What is more, they can run at speeds up to 44 miles per hour. It is also more gregarious than other species within its genus, living and traveling in packs.

In July of 1563, a dispersing two-year-old female chose an unrelated dispersing three-year-old male, and they mated for life. Then, in June 1564, after traveling together in search of an available area, they came upon the cirque with its summering deer and frequent visitations by Roosevelt elk (known prior to the European invasion as "wapiti," which is a Shawnee word meaning "white rump"). At that time, the cirque was devoid of a hostile, neighboring pack, so the pair claimed it by remaining in the area and beginning a family. Their initial territory encompassed a mere 15 square miles from the cirque to the valley of the big river, where the deer and elk wintered.

Being monogamous, they spent a great deal of time together over the next five and a half years, until December 1569, when the male died, whereupon the dominant male among their offspring quickly re-established the pair. However, the female died six months later, in June of 1570. Only this time, the male next in line was already eight years old and easily displaced by a four-year-old male. Two years later, in the winter of 1572, a rutting bull elk with fully developed antlers mortally injured both of them. Thereafter, a new breeding pair took over the leadership of the pack, whose reign is still viable in 1575.

As the years passed, and the age and number of offspring increased, the pack expanded its territory to include an 87-square-mile area, which is larger than the pack requires for survival, but which assures a steady supply of deer and elk. Once established, the pack developed both a stationary phase and nomadic phase. The stationary phase includes the cirque during the spring and summer, while pups are being reared and large prey is plentiful. Whereas the nomadic phase takes place during the autumn and winter, when the pack follows the deer and elk to their winter ranges in the lower elevations.

On the 5th of June, 1575, when Storm Hawk first arrived at the cirque, the pack consists of 11 members: the mated pair, this year's six pups born on the 11th of May, and three yearlings—the nuclear family. As soon as the pups of the year can travel, the pack will resume its widespread search for prey, covering about 13 miles a day of their territory. However, at least half of their time is spent within the 21-square-mile core of their territory, despite the fact that prey density tends to be much higher in the territory's surrounding areas. The pack avoids hunting in these fringe areas, however, unless they are desperately short of prey, because there is always the heightened possibility of a fatal encounter with a neighboring pack.

In like measure, the pack defends its own territory from other wolves through a combination of scent marking, howling, and direct attacks when necessary. However, the sense of smell is perhaps the wolf's most acute sense, and thus plays a fundamental role in communication. Therefore, scent marking, including raised-leg urination, is the most important form of scent communication in part because it reflects the height of the marking wolf. Only the dominant male uses raised-leg urination while subordinate males continue to use the juvenile standing posture throughout adulthood. Urination aside, the other forms of scent marking are defecation and ground scratching, but all three are used to advertise territorial boundaries.

Pack members have a large number of specialized glands on their face, lips, back, and between the toes. The odor produced by these glands varies according to the pack member's live-in microscopic organisms and diet, which gives each member a distinctive "odor fingerprint." In addition to the aforementioned glands, there is another kind of gland on the feet, which allows pack members to deposit their scent as they scratch the ground, something they usually do after urination and defecation, especially during the breeding season.

Scent marks are generally left every 800 feet or so along regular routes of travel and their junctions throughout the territory. Such markers can last up to three weeks, and are typically placed near rocks, trees, and the skeletons of large animals.

Within the pack, there is a strong hierarchy, wherein the breeding male is the leader and thus dominant over all other individuals. The next in line is his mate, who is subordinate only to the dominant male. Moreover, rank within the hierarchy determines which members of the pack mate and which eat first. Rank is communicated through body language and facial expressions. For example, when the pack's breeding male encounters a subordinate family member, he stares at it, while standing erect and still with his tail held horizontal to his spine.

When a pack member is simply feeling neutral about a situation, its legs are relaxed, its tail hangs down loosely, its face is smooth with relaxed lips, and its ears point in no particular direction. In contraposition, a pack member who is feeling aggressive or self-assertive displays slow and deliberate movements, a high body posture with stiffened legs and raised hackles (hair on the back of the neck and along the spine), whereas a submissive member carries its body low, its fur sleek, and lowers its ears and tail.

With respect to submissive behavior, there are two forms: passive and active. Passive submission occurs when a dominant member of the pack approaches a subordinate member, and consists of the submissive wolf lying partly on its back allowing the dominant wolf to sniff its anal-genital area. Active submission often occurs as a form of greeting, in which the submissive wolf approaches another in a low posture, and licks the other's face.

When the cirque's pack members are together, they frequently indulge in nose pushing, jaw wrestling, cheek rubbing, and licking each other's face. The mouthing of each other's muzzles is a friendly gesture, while clamping bared teeth on another's muzzle is a display of dominance. However, because of the strict, hierarchical nature of the pack, should the acknowledged leader become injured or otherwise unable to maintain his dominance, the next male in line will take his place, at which time the ex-leader would most likely leave the pack, as happened in the year 1570.

Beyond body language, vocalizations, such as howling, allow pack members to communicate with one another about where they are during a storm or in unfamiliar territory and to communicate across great distance. Howls are also used for calling pack members to a kill; these are long and smooth. But when pursuing prey, the wolves give forth a higher-pitched howl that vibrates on two notes. When closing in on their prey, they emit a combination of a short bark and a howl. Under certain conditions, their howls can be heard for 50 square miles, which helps to inform other wolves of the boundary locations surrounding the pack's territory.

Other vocalizations among members of the pack include growls, barks, and whines. Startled wolves usually bark a few times, and then retreat from perceived danger. Growling among adults usually occurs during food challenges, whereas pups commonly growl while playing. One variation of the howl is accompanied by a high-pitched whine, which precedes a lunging attack. Whining is also associated with situations of anxiety, curiosity, inquiry, and intimacy, such as greeting one another, feeding pups, and playing.

As far as the pack's diet is concerned, the wolves are "apex predators," dominated only by an occasional confrontation with the land's Indigenous people. When hunting as a pack, the wolves normally pursue deer and elk. By selecting weak, old, and immature individuals, they keep both deer and elk within the sustainable bounds of the available habitat, to the long-term benefit of the populations of prey animals, the wolves themselves, and the Indigenous human hunters.

The pack hunt, itself, has five stages: (1) locating the prey, (2) stalking the prey, (3) encountering the prey, (4) rushing the prey, and (5) chasing the prey.

The pack locates prey by its windborne odor, tracking, or a chance encounter. The wolves' best chance of locating a deer or elk is to be directly downwind of it. When the wolves detect a breeze carrying the prey's scent, they stand alert and focus their eyes, ears, and nose toward their intended target. In open areas, such as the meadow, the wolves may stand nose-to-nose and wag their tails before heading toward their intended prey.

Coming within a certain distance of a deer or elk, the wolves attempt to conceal themselves as they continue their approach. As they narrow the gap, they quicken their pace, wag their tails, and focus intently, endeavoring to get as close as possible without causing the deer or elk to flee.

Whereas deer flee when they detect the wolves, an adult, bull elk with mature antlers usually stands its ground. In this case, the wolves either ignore it or attempt to intimidate it into fleeing because they require the stimulus of a running animal to proceed with their attack.

If the elk attempts to flee, the wolves immediately pursue it. This is the most critical stage of the hunt, because the wolves may never catch up with an elk fleeing at top speed. If, however, there is a group of elk, the wolves either attempt to fragment it or simply isolate one or two individuals.

When chasing deer, the wolves attempt to catch up with them as soon as possible, but with adult, bull elk sporting mature antlers, the chase is prolonged in an attempt to wear down the elk. Nevertheless, the wolves usually give up a chase within a mile and a half.

Once a deer or elk is down, the wolves attack its rump, flanks, and shoulders. Thereafter, a feeding frenzy begins with the wolves ripping and tugging at the carcass in all directions, and bolting down large chunks of it.

Although the breeding pair typically eats first in order to continue producing pups, they usually work the hardest in killing prey and may rest after a long hunt, thus allowing the rest of the family to eat unmolested. Once the breeding pair is done feeding, the rest of the family tears off pieces of the carcass and carries them to secluded areas, where they can eat in peace. However, when the larger, internal organs, such as the heart, liver, lungs, and lining of the stomach, are exposed, the wolves focus on them, followed by the kidneys, spleen, and finally the muscles.

Although a single wolf consumes up to 20 pounds of meat at one meal, the pack normally devours the entire carcass, including some hair and bones. Because they digest a meal within a few hours, wolves can feed several times a day, making quick use of large quantities of meat.

In addition to hunting as members of the pack, individual wolves hunt on their own, pursuing such prey as snowshoe hares, squirrels, montane voles, heather voles, Pacific jumping mice, Mazama pocket gophers, and weasels, as well as grouse and their eggs. Smaller prey often accounts for a substantial part of their diet. In addition to hunting, the wolves steal food from other predators, such as the puma, as well as scavenging whatever carrion is available. They also dine on huckleberries in season and thus encounter heather voles and jumping mice, which they catch when they can. When pack members are well fed, they store fat under the skin, around the heart, intestines, kidneys, and bone marrow, particularly during the autumn and winter.

The first time gray wolves breed and rear pups depends largely on when food is plentiful, which can be as young as two years of age, allowing them to better exploit abundant resources. Females are not only capable of producing at least one litter of pups every year but also are reproductively active throughout their adult life. While the onset of breeding typically occurs in late winter, older females, who have borne litters, mate two to three weeks earlier than younger females.

During pregnancy, females remain in a den located well within their territories to avoid violent encounters with other packs. Old females usually give birth in the den of their previous litter, whereas younger females typically dig a den near their own birthplace.

So it is that, on March 1, 1575, the female wolf, who became part of the breeding pair controlling the pack in 1572, became pregnant. Thereafter, she selected a site with a view in a secluded part of the meadow and dug the den in which to give birth. The den's entrance opened down slope and then went upward to the chamber in which she would house her family. With the den completed on May 1st, she gave birth to six pups on May 11th, 72 days after their conception, just as the black-tailed deer were arriving in the cirque from their low-elevation winter range.

The pups, three females and three males, were born blind, deaf, and covered in short, soft grayish-brown fur. Because they ranged in weight from 10½ ounces to just over 1 pound, they depended on their mother for warmth. Four of the pups had their eyes open May 21st, the fifth on May 22nd, and the last pup's eyes opened on May 23rd, all of which were blue. Their milk teeth, however, will not begin to erupt until June 11th.

Although the pups had control only over their front legs and thus had to crawl about the den, they could all stand, walk, and use their voices by the end of May. Until then, the pups were reliant on their mother for milk, and she, in turn, was reliant on their father to bring her food, after which both parents began feeding their youngsters solid, regurgitated food.

Despite their mobility, the pups will remain in the den until the first week in July, at which time they will get their first glimpse of the meadow. Then all members of the pack will feed them regurgitated food until the 25th of July, when they will be 45 days old. Thereafter, the pack will provide them with meat. And it's during the first four months of life that the pups grow fast enough to increase their weight nearly 30 times.

Once out of the den, they will learn to play fight, although their bites will be restrained at first. Actual fights to establish their place in the pack's hierarchy begin taking place by the time the pups have been out of the den for a week or two. The pup's interactions at this time, as well as the dominance status of their mother, will ultimately determine their position in the pack's hierarchy.

By autumn, the pups will be mature enough to accompany the adults hunting for large prey. Their rapid development in this arena will be critical because they must be large enough and accomplished enough to actually hunt with the pack by the onset of winter.

The young will leave the pack when they are between one and three years old. Although an occasional wolf may live thirteen years in the wild, adults usually die from old age or from injuries received while hunting or fighting with other wolves between the ages of five and six. But for now, the pack is sharing the cirque with a young Indian teen who is on a spiritual quest.

June 17th

Vowing not to be distracted, Storm Hawk begins his search. From dawn to dusk, he walks up and down the sides of the stream, examining everything that might conceivably harbor evidence of a campsite, especially the rotten tree toward the lower end of the meadow in proximity of the forest's edge—but nothing.

In the process, however, he manages to flush a spotted sandpiper father and his five juveniles, entrusted solely to his care since they hatched. Although he barely notices the birds, so focused is he in his search for clues to the whereabouts of the old campsite, he is aware that others along the stream constantly bob their rear ends up and down, a trait that centuries later would earn them the nickname of "teeter-tail." (The teetering gets faster when the bird is nervous, but stops when it is alarmed, aggressive, or courting.) Nevertheless, his attention is briefly arrested when they suddenly erupt into flight with short bursts of quick, snappy wing beats interspersed with brief glides in which the wings are kept below the horizontal position.

Spotted Sandpiper

Having spent the winter with others of his kind on the beaches of South America, the father sandpiper and several other males flew both during the day and at night in between stopovers, arriving at the cirque not long after the snow had melted off the meadow, but later than the females.

The spotted sandpiper is about 6 to 7 inches long, with a wing-span of almost 15 inches. Females are 20 to 25 percent larger than males, weighing 1³⁄₁₀ to 1½ ounces in comparison to the males' 1 to 1½ ounces. They are brown to olive gray on top of the head, back of the neck, back, and wings, and they are bright white on their face, throat, chest, and belly. Their white undersides are decorated with bold black spots, of which the females' tend not only to be larger but also to extend lower on the belly than those of the male, hence their common name. In their winter plumage, however, spots are lacking in both sexes.

Due to their overall coloration, they exemplify Nature's counter-shading with brown plumage above and white below sporting dark-brown spots on the chest and belly. (Counter-shading is a reversal of how an artist uses darkened areas to create a sense of shadows, and thus of roundness, which gives the bird a flat appearance when seen from the side or above, making it difficult for predators to detect it.)

In addition, they have a white line over their eyes, an orange bill with a black tip, and long yellowish or pinkish legs. While in flight, spotted sandpipers display a white wing-stripe and a plain rump and tail.

They can sleep anytime, day or night, but generally sleep whenever it is dark. Solitary birds, they spend some time on daily self-maintenance: preening, head scratching, stretching, and bathing. With respect to getting around, they walk, hop, climb, and fly, as well as occasionally swim and dive for prey.

Their calls are primarily variations of a *weet*, which is repeated at different pitches, intensities, and rates to communicate such things as alarm, maintain contact with chicks, during courtship, and to distract predators from a nest. In addition, physical displays are employed to threaten others, solicit a mate, and show submission.

Beyond being the larger of the two sexes, females take charge in life by arriving at the cirque earlier than the males, establishing and defending a territory of up to 215,000 square feet, and attracting males. Females do the courting via elaborate, swooping flight patterns with their wings held open while they voice a *weet-weet* song. They may also give a strutting display on the ground. During these performances, they look for mates over a wide area.

Even if Storm Hawk had been in the cirque early enough to find the nest with its eggs, there is a caveat of which he would have been totally unaware. Namely, while females begin the breeding season by copulating with one male, as additional males arrive, they are allowed to remain in her territory and mate with her, but disinterested males are evicted. Females mate with up to four different males, leaving each the duty of incubating the eggs and caring for the chicks, in a process called "polyandry" (from the ancient Greek *polys* "many" and *anēr* "man").

Males that mate with the same female set up smaller territories within her territory and defend them aggressively against one another. Territorial disputes typically involve pecking at the head and eyes of the opponent while trying to mount their back. In essence, the males use their legs, wings and bills to fight.

Male parents of the first one or two clutches may be the genetic fathers of chicks in a later male's nest (such as the one in the clump of Davidson's penstemon along the lake's shore, Photo 6.64), due to sperm stored within the female's reproductive tract for up to a month. Such storage of sperm is common in birds. Females that fail to find additional mates usually help to incubate and rear the chicks.

6.64 Davidson penstemon.

Despite the gender roles, male spotted sandpipers have 10 times more testosterone than the females, but only in absolute terms. During the breeding season, on the other hand, mated females see a sevenfold increase in their level of testosterone (over unmated females), which may account for their aggression, as well as the overall role reversal between male and female, particularly since the level of testosterone declines substantially in males during the incubation process. Moreover, males tend to have more of the pituitary hormone *prolactin* than females. Prolactin promotes parental care, which may augment the role reversal that develops each breeding season.

The female who established the nest that hosted the family Storm Hawk disturbed did so on the 5th of May in a semi-open area with a small gravel bar along the water's edge and patches of dense vegetation for sheltering the chicks. The actual nest, built after the initial pair's courtship had ended, was a depression two to three inches wide scraped out in the soil and lined with dead grass under a clump of pink monkey flowers along the stream's bank.

Although the female began building the nest, the male completed it on the 8th of May, the day after which she laid five, pale-greenish eggs speckled with brown. During the egg-laying process, the female increased her food intake to offset the energy spent producing the eggs. And the male almost doubled the time he dedicated to finding and catching prey while incubating the eggs.

The chicks hatched 22 days later, on the 31st of May, just five days before Storm Hawk arrives in the cirque. At that time, they were downy, coordinated, had their eyes open, and weighed $5/100$ of an ounce. (Photo 6.65) They began teetering nearly as soon as they hatched, and began walking, stretching their wings, and eating within 24 hours. Moreover, they were hunting for immobile food by the time they were two days old, on the 2nd of June, and were stalking moving prey a day later. By the 11th of June, they are beginning to lift off the ground in their first attempts to fly. Within four more days, the 15th of June, they are weak fliers, but can completely lift off the ground and fly a significant distance by the 17th, as demonstrated by Storm Hawk's unconscious intrusion into their living space. Although three will die within a year, the other two will survive and breed next spring.

*6.65 Newly hatched spotted sandpiper chicks along the stream flowing through the
meadow from the cirque's lake.*

The sandpipers of the cirque are active, opportunistic carnivores
well equipped to forage on the ground and even in water. In addition to probing into the mud along the stream's banks and the lake's
shore with their bills like most sandpipers, they also walk quickly,
crouching low, and dart at moving prey, pick insects off plants, and
snap at airborne insects. Visual hunters, their diet is comprised
primarily of such organisms as midges, mayflies (particularly their
aquatic larvae), flies, grasshoppers, crickets, beetles, spiders, worms,
snails, small crustaceans, as well as tadpoles of the Cascade frog,
but not those of the western toad. They also eat small fish, and may
pick at dead fish as well.

Spotted sandpiper eggs are vulnerable to predation by deer
mice and weasels, among others, and chicks are in danger of being
killed by weasels and ravens. Adults are susceptible to capture by
weasels and the goshawk, as well as any other raptors that happen
to be in the area.

When threatened, the sandpipers perform a defensive display
by positioning their body upright and their bill forward, in addition
to which they extend their wings outward and upward, raise their

breast feathers, open their bill, and fan their tail. In addition, nesting sandpipers may pretend to have a broken wing as a means of drawing predators away from their nest. The broken-wing display is performed by a bird crawling low to the ground with flapping wings, a tail spread and lowered, squealing all the while.

Feeling somewhat discouraged, Storm Hawk makes his way back to camp, vowing once again not to be distracted from his search.

June 18th

So it is that he sets out with the rising sun to begin his daily search, only to have it disrupted nonetheless by startling a small herd of elk, which bolts, as he walks out of the upper-most end of the eastern island of trees into the meadow on his way to the stream. Having spent the last two hours searching among the trees for some sign of his ancestor's campfire, his focus is such that he is equally startled when the elk suddenly bolt on detecting his presence. Storm Hawk stops, and the elk stop. He marvels at their size and beauty.

Chapter 7: The Ancient Campsite

Having found no sign of a campsite despite having spent 16 days looking, some more diligently than others, Storm Hawk awakens with the feeling that it is time to search the eastern side of the meadow. But, first he must replenish his food supply because the remaining venison is now rotting too fast for safe eating. So he takes the meat down, carries it to the edge of the meadow, and lays it on the ground for the turkey vultures, ravens, golden eagles, and any other of his brothers who might want to eat it. He then goes to the stream, where he washes his hands, after which he follows it to the forest in search of fresh food.

Entering the forest, he catches three trout (Photo 7.1), and is about to head back to camp when he hears a commotion on the far side of a large fallen tree, which has lain on the ground over 70 years, as it slowly decomposes. He stops and listens—nothing. *What*, he wonders, *is going on?*

About 10 minutes ago, a hungry long-tailed weasel detected a female snowshoe hare feeding peacefully alongside the fallen tree. Sensing something ominous, the hare froze. Too late! The bounding weasel leapt onto the snowshoe's head, rendering her helpless with a bite at the base of the skull, a feat accomplished without tearing the hare's skin. Today, the weasel's good fortune is the hare's misfortune because its proximity to the fallen tree hampered its maneuverability, but not that of the weasel.

Although a long-tailed weasel can kill a young snowshoe in an open chase, the story is different with an adult, which ranges in length from 15 to 17 inches long from the tip of its nose to the tip of its tail and weighs from 2 to 3 pounds, such as the one eating by the fallen tree. In that case, a hare can kill a weasel by kicking it with powerful hind legs and their sharply clawed hind feet. (Photo 7.2)

7.1 Rainbow trout.

7.2 Adult snowshoe hare.

Storm Hawk puts the fish down and draws an arrow from the quiver, placing the notch against the bow's sinew string. Going through a break in the trees some 13 feet away, he sees the weasel still holding the dead but quivering snowshoe by her head.

Without a second's hesitation, Storm Hawk rushes the weasel, while yelling and slapping his arms against his sides. Startled, the weasel drops the hare and dashes into a cavity under the tree—but not for long!

Recovering from its startled reaction, the weasel reemerges, but clearly without the slightest intention of sharing its kill, despite the fact that Storm Hawk picks up a handy stick with which to confront the weasel. His attempts to get the hare are repulsed, however, by a stamping, sputtering weasel with a stiff, oversized tail. As the minutes pass, a thoroughly irritated weasel, its tail twice the usual size, as all the hairs stand straight out, stamping its front feet, voices an explosive hiss, while forcibly emitting "musk" from its anal glands, and appears ready to attack. The weasel's attitude is an unmistakable communiqué that, if necessary, it would take even more drastic action. The confrontation continues. Time passes. The weasel finally relents and disappears under the tree, having earned Storm Hawk's respect, but not possession of the hare.

Snowshoe Hare

Holding the three-pound, 20-inch-long snowshoe in his hands, Storm Hawk marvels at her beauty. Her back and sides are covered in a long, thick, soft, relatively light, reddish-brown coat with a few intermixed black-tipped hairs. Her throat is also reddish-brown, as are her ears, with their blackish tips and white margins. The reddish-brown gives way to clear white on her chin, belly, the insides of the long legs, and the tops of the large hind feet, whereas her inconspicuous tail is blackish on top and light whitish-gray underneath. Her broad hind feet are $5\frac{7}{10}$ of an inch long and densely furred, with stiff hairs, forming the "snowshoe."

The clear white of her underside, unbeknownst to Storm Hawk, is Nature's "reversed coloration," a genetic adaptation that makes the snowshoe appear two-dimensional and thus aids her ability to blend into her surroundings and so be less conspicuous to predators. To fully understand this, you could paint a snowshoe hare in a conventional manner, which means making the hare lightest on top, guided by the source of light, and darkest underneath, where the deepest shade is. The object of such a strategy is to make the hare appear three-dimensional, and thus stand out in your painting, a strategy evolution has reversed as an aid to the hare's survival in Nature.

While examining the snowshoe, Storm Hawk wonders what her life was like. Going back to the 15th of May a year ago (1547), a female snowshoe hare emerged from a thicket of young grand firs near the edge of the meadow. Heavy with young, she moved cautiously along the edge of the thicket. She paused and tested the breeze with her keen, blackish nose and long, delicate ears. All was still except for the croak of a raven and the high whining of a hovering, yellow and black syrphid fly. She hopped further, following a faint trail through the growing grasses between the huckleberry bushes and the thicket, until she came to a jumble of five fallen trees that formed a protected alcove open to the warmth of the May sun shining through a snowberry bush. She entered the alcove and became quiet. She was a different hare than she was 38 days ago on the 12th of April when she was bred.

The 12th of April was clear and balmy, and the dirty snow lay melting, as winter retreated northward. While the sun slid silently below the western rim of the world, two hares, a male and a female, met in a small clearing between the shrubs and the thicket. They sat quietly for a time. Then the male began to chase the female, running beneath her as she leapt into the air and, in midair, urinated on him. She then ran beneath him and he leapt into the air and, in midair, urinated on her. They played for a while, and the time came when she was ready to receive her mate.

Then, as the sun graced the western tops of the trees and shrubs on the 17th of May, the last of three babies, two males and a female, were born. Each baby (called a leveret) was fully clothed in soft fur; its eyes and ears were open. Each could hop around within a few minutes after birth. They began to nurse after their mother had completely cleaned them, and they were soft and fluffy. Thereafter, they hid in separate locations during the day, coming together for only 5 to 10 minutes at a time to nurse.

They grew rapidly throughout the summer with their mother's tender care, and were fully weaned and had dispersed by mid September, which sees days becoming shorter and a sun that rode lower and lower in the southern sky. Each hare now had its own area or home range, wherein it knows all the safe places, all the trails, and had a number of hidden, shallow nests or "forms." On a typical day, they spent time grooming, taking fitful naps, and just sitting quietly watching and listening without being seen or heard.

With the lessening daylight of early October, a change was triggered in the snowshoes, and they began to shed their summer coats of soft brown fur and became mottled for a time as their first winter coats of white replaced the brown. They would become all white except for blackish tips on their ears as winter progressed, but for now they were increasingly mottled in transition.

Hunger induced the mother snowshoe to leave the alcove, where her youngsters were born five and a half months earlier. She hopped into the light mist on a cold afternoon in late October. She sat listening intently. The wind shifted. She "froze." She sat absolutely motionless for several minutes. The wind shifted again, and she began to relax. Suddenly, she panicked and screamed the peculiar distress cry of the snowshoe hare. A blurred shape sprang from behind; sharp claws gripped her right hind leg; fangs pierced her skull. Her life's blood trickled down her fur to mix with the mist and wet soil at the edge of the snowberry, 10 feet from the hidden alcove. Alive or dead, the mother snowshoe was an eternal link in the unbroken chain of ancestry from the hares of the past to the hares of the future.

The mother snowshoe's death meant life to the young bobcat that, driven by extreme hunger, almost muffed his chance for a meal. He caught the snowshoe by two outstretched claws and then almost lost her because of youthful ignorance and impatience. He wasted little time nosing her, but picked her up and carried her into the gathering darkness.

Mist turned to rain. The wind grew stronger and moaned through the thicket. Night claimed the land. The mother snowshoe's youngsters waited out the night, each alone in its own shelter and unaware that their mother had joined her ancestors in time beyond the world.

In another part of the forest, the young bobcat ate the snowshoe, cleaned himself, and lay down. The mother snowshoe lived on in the bobcat, sleeping soundly while the wind howled around his hollow, fallen tree. Her life had helped to ensure that his seed would pass to yet another generation of bobcats, and another, and another as the cosmic dance of life and death and change would continue to unfold in and around the meadow.

By mid morning, the sun was shining, the sky was blue, and wispy fog was rising in long fingers from the warming land. Leaving the shelter of a fallen tree, the daughter snowshoe hopped along the faint trail toward the alcove. In so doing, she passed the place where, less than 18 hours ago, her mother's life suddenly ended. She knew nothing of the event, however, because rain had erased all signs of it. It was as though neither the mother snowshoe nor the event had really existed. The only proof of the mother's existence is her three offspring, and the only proof of the bobcat's successful kill is the absence of the mother snowshoe.

So it is today that a particular, female snowshoe becomes hungry and ventures from her shelter under the ground-sweeping boughs of a grand fir to the log five feet away, where fate awaits her in the form of a long-tailed weasel. And it is the weasel's destiny to go hungry while providing a young Indian teen named Storm Hawk with a meal. Thus, continues the cycle of life in all its myriad, interwoven strands.

With snowshoe in hand and the arrow back in its quiver, Storm Hawk retrieves the trout and continues to the trail leading to the firs and his camp. Reaching his camp just as the sun touches the western horizon, he kindles a small fire, cooks the trout one at a time, and eats them. His hunger temporarily satiated, he gathers a little more wood and prepares for the coming night.

The flicker of Storm Hawk's fire, on which he is already roasting the hare, greets the faint light of dawn. Done to his satisfaction, he eats half of the snowshoe and saves the rest for his journey in search for the ancient campsite.

Before leaving his night's abode, however, he douses the dying embers with the last water in his deer-bladder container, after which he stirs them with a small stick to confirm their demise. Then, having attached his quiver of arrows to the left side of his backpack, he puts it on, picks up his bow, and begins walking to the stream, which he will follow to the eastern moraine and the cliff leading toward the rising sun and the fringe of trees along the far side of the meadow.

Reaching the stream, he washes his hands and face, fills the deer bladder with water, and munches some Indian lettuce growing along the stream's bank. Turning north, he follows the stream toward the lake, accompanied now and then by curious dragonflies. (Photo 7.3)

7.3 Dragonfly.

On reaching the south end of the eastern moraine, he climbs to its highest point from which he charts his course along the cliff. Although much of the cliff beyond the immediate talus, from which come the early morning calls of rock rabbits, appears to be rather sheer, there is a scattering of boulders that clearly defines the uppermost edge of the meadow.

Within this long, narrow boulder field is a rock of enormous size that Storm Hawk decides to use as a preliminary landmark by which to guide his steps. Descending the moraine, he heads slowly toward the boulder, enjoying the infinite facets of Nature's beauty as he goes, including a moth hovering next to a flower on which it is feeding.

Finding the moth's ability to hover fascinating, he stops to watch it. What he cannot see, however, is the slight angle at which the moth holds its wings to deflect the air downward. It is the downward stroke of the moth's wings that provides the thrust. Deflecting air downward causes it to flow faster over the top of the moth's wings than it does underneath them, thereby causing air pressure to build up beneath the wings, while the pressure above the wings is reduced. This contrast in air pressure is what produces the lift that keeps the moth airborne.

By moving its abdomen up or down, the moth adjusts the direction of the thrust and the consequential lift that its wings produce. Then, by changing the angle of its wings in concert to the position of its body, the moth is able to create the delicate balance between the power pushing it forward and the air's resistance pushing against it, which not only keeps it in the air but also allows it to hover while feeding.

Storm Hawk is still marveling at the moth's ability to hover, as he approaches the boulder, just in time to see a raven grab a small, dark rodent and fly to a nest, which is just visible on a small ledge high on the cliff's face. Intrigued, he goes to the place he first noticed the large, black bird and finds a series of runways and burrows, as well as clippings of grass stems and small piles of greenish fecal pellets.

Astonished by the maze of runways and burrows, he stops momentarily to examine them. To his surprise, he sees several small, montane meadow voles racing along the runways, only to disappear into burrows. He is witnessing a peak in the vole's population cycle, something that happens roughly every four years or so, when they seem to overrun the grassy areas of the cirque because there are 1,000 or more individuals for every 2½ acres of meadow.

Montane Vole

Although he caught only glimpses of them, they appeared to be somewhat different in color and size. Part of the size difference is sexual in that males are 30 percent larger than females. Thus, the voles Storm Hawk sees range in length from 5½ to 8½ inches in length and weigh from 2 to 3 ounces. Their backs seemed to vary from light grayish, to brown, dark brown, reddish-brown, and sometimes blackish-brown. Their sides are a little lighter, and their undersides are whitish, sometimes washed with light brown. Their tails are distinctly bicolored, grayish to brownish or blackish above, whitish below, while their feet are grayish above. (Photo 7.4)

7.4 Montane vole.

Good swimmers, these voles like to live along water, such as the stream, where they would have to compete with the water vole.

The density of their current population, however, has forced many of them to live throughout the meadow (Photo 7.5), particularly in the moister areas, such as the boulder field.

7.5 Meadow habitat of the montane vole.

Active year 'round and throughout the 24-hour cycle, they can be seen at almost any time. Although they are sociable and friendly with one another, they will fight savagely with anything they feel threatens them, biting quickly and severely with their sharp front teeth.

Like other meadow voles, they make elaborate systems of runways that become visible with the melting of snow in spring, as now seen by Storm Hawk. Their abandoned runways are lined with food refuse and droppings (Photo 7.6), and their grass nests, constructed above ground under the cover of snow, are scattered here and there. (Photo 7.7) With the advent of summer, their runways will become more difficult to find, especially during the height of the meadow's vegetative cover. (Photo 7.8)

7.6 *Winter runways of the montane vole constructed under the cover of snow and abandoned as the snow melted.*

7.7 *Winter nest of a montane vole built under the cover of snow.*

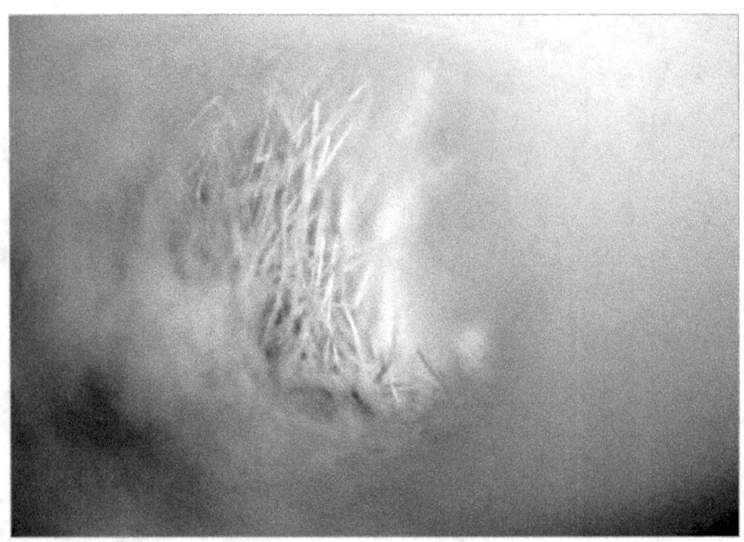

7.8 A vole's-eye view of its summer runway.

Although summer runways may also have food refuse and feces in them, all growing vegetation will be kept neatly clipped in a currently used runway. (Photo 7.9) Abandoned runways, on the other hand, will appear unkempt, and their current grass nests will be constructed below ground.

Grasses seems to be the principal food for these voles, but with it are sedges, rushes, and a great variety of meadow plants, including the edible parts of green leaves, stems, roots, and seeds. They eat by cutting the stem or plant off at the base and then eating the desired part or parts.

7.9 A neatly groomed runway, which shows that it is in use.

In the case of grass seeds, a vole cuts the stem off and, once down, pulls the stem toward itself, cuts off a section, then pulls it again and cuts off another section. (Photo 7.10) The process is repeated until the seed head is reached, which leaves a little pile of cut stem segments one-and-a-half to two inches long. In addition, roots and bulbs are dug up and eaten, as are the belowground runners between adult plants and their connected offspring. Normally, more than half of the vegetation cut is left as refuse, which is recycled into the soil of the meadow.

7.10 Grass clippings left by a vole in its runway.

The number of young per litter ranges from four to eight, with eight being the full complement for mature females. Although there are several litters per year, it's doubtful that breeding takes place during winter in this high meadow.

Engrossed in watching the voles, a shadow glides over his head. Looking up, he sees the raven descend into the midst of the vole's activity a scanty 20 feet away, where it becomes still. Without warning, it grabs a passing vole and takes off for its nest.

The Raven

If the raven Storm Hawk sees could trace its ancestry, it would learn that its origin is in Eurasia and that its ancestors were crossing the Bering land bridge (also known as the "Beringia") between Siberia and Alaska at the same time Storm Hawk's ancestors were, between 22,000 and 17,000 years ago. During that time, massive ice sheets covered much of North America and Europe, which caused the sea level to drop more than 300 feet for thousands of years, thus allowing the land bridge to become grassland 1,000 miles wide from south to north in a benign climate.

Among the smartest of all birds, they not only have coexisted with humans for thousands of years but also work together to solve novel problems. It is little wonder, therefore, that Indigenous Americans of the Pacific Northwest revered ravens as being the creator of earth, moon, sun, and stars, while simultaneously being an incurable trickster, bringing fire to the people by stealing it from the sun, and stealing salmon only to drop them in rivers all over the world.

Then, around 15,500 years ago, the rising ocean flooded the land bridge, reopening the Bering Strait, but it took another 9,000 years or so for the coastlines to assume an approximation of their present configurations.

As with many of its kin, the raven that caught the vole is slightly over 27 inches long, with a 50-inch wingspan, and weighs just over 3 pounds. Its tail is relatively long and wedge-shaped. Although its plumage is iridescent black, the throat and neck feathers are a pale brownish-grey, and its wing feathers make a sound reminiscent of rustling silk when the raven is in flight.

Just over 13 years old, this magnificent black bird will live in and around the cirque until it is 21, stretching its large wings across the sky with slow, easy, flowing wingbeats interspersed with soaring and gliding, as it fills the empty spaces with an echoing croak. The time of its passing will be archived for all eternity in every lifecycle of every living thing with which it interacted.

The raven, along with its life-long mate, attempts to hold the cirque as its territory by excluding all other ravens throughout the year. In winter, however, young ravens sometimes find a carcass and call other ravens to the feast, thereby overwhelming the local territorial owners by the sheer force of numbers, and so gain access to the food.

The pair built their currently used nest two years ago, in 1573, on a ledge two-thirds of the way up the cliff face. During that endeavor, the male brought some sticks to the nest, but mostly his mate built it with sticks around three feet long and up to an inch thick, which she broke from live plants to create the nest's base, as well as a few sticks she scavenges from one of their old nests.

The sticks and some bones from old deer and elk skeletons in various parts of the cirque were piled on the nest platform and woven together into a basket. The female then made a cup from small branches and twigs and lined it with soft vegetation and the hair of deer and elk killed by the resident wolves. The whole process took nine days and resulted in an uneven nest that was five feet across and two feet high. The inner cup was 12 inches across and 6 inches deep.

Extremely devoted to each other, they mated, and the female laid three pale, bluish-green eggs covered with brown blotches on March 24th in this year of 1575. The eggs are well suited for being in a nest on a cliff because they are relatively pointed on one end and rather bulbous on the other, which causes them to roll in a tight circle, thus helping to prevent them from falling off cliff ledge, should they accidentally be knocked out of the nest.

The eggs hatched on the 18th of April, after the female had incubated them for 25 days, at which time the chicks were naked, except for sparse tufts of grayish down. Their eyes were closed, and their movements were clumsy. The nesting period encompassed 45 days, until the 2nd of June (three days before Storm Hawk will arrive in the cirque), when the curious juveniles left the nest, and began exploring the wider world by picking up and examining almost anything new they came across, as they commenced learn-ing what is useful and what is not.

During the nesting period, however, the parents defended their chicks vigorously by flying at potential predators, such as owls, and lunging at them with their large, pointed beaks—at times with the aid of other ravens. Sometimes, they even drop stones on potential predators that venture close to their nests. On the other hand, ravens themselves are smart, which makes them dangerous preda-tors because they can often "read" the vulnerability of other animals.

Because of the family bond, the parents and their offspring will reside together for another six months, until December, when the young will be old enough to fend for themselves. At this time, they will wander off and form gregarious flocks, but only form breeding pairs when they are between two to four years old.

Part of the ravens' success as residents of the cirque and its habitats is due to their omnivorous diet, in which they are extremely versatile and opportunistic, eating such things as carrion (already-dead animals), insects, grass seed, buds, berries, small mammals (as Storm Hawk witnesses with the vole), birds, fish, and even wolf dung. They are not equipped, however, to tear apart large-bodied carrion, like deer or elk, because they lack the hooked beaks of the turkey vultures that ride the thermals over the cirque and its various habitats. So, they must wait for the prey to be torn open by another predator before they can eat. To this end, they manipulate other parties, such as calling the wolves to the carcass so they will open it and leave scraps more accessible to the manipulative ravens.

The ravens also store extra food and steal from one another. They are so intelligent they watch where others bury their food and remember the locations so they can steal it from them. This theft occurs so regularly that the birds fly extra distances from a source of food to find better hiding places for their stash, especially if it contains fat. They also pretend to make a cache without actually depositing anything, presumably to confuse onlookers.

Ravens are also among the most playful of birds and not only slide down snowbanks in various parts of the meadow for fun in winter but also by breaking off twigs to engage one another in play. They even participate in such games as catch-me-if-you-can with the wolves. In addition, they perform spectacular aerobatic displays by flying in loops, interlocking talons with each other in flight, doing sudden rolls, wing-tucked dives, and somersaults in the air, as well as flying upside down for half a mile or more. What's more, even the young birds are fond of playing games, carrying sticks aloft and repeatedly dropping them, only to dive and catch them in midair.

In addition to being playful, they lie on anthills and roll around so the ants swarm over them, or alternatively chew the ants up and rub the squashed insects all over their feathers, in a ritual called "anting." Because ants secrete formic acid, the effects of anting might act as a deterrent to feather lice, mites, fungi, or bacteria.

Leaving the raven to its daily rhythm, Storm Hawk continues along the cliff toward the line of trees, which is growing ever closer. He is so engrossed in the wonder and beauty of his surroundings that it is mid-afternoon before he even realizes that he still has some food left.

Reaching the stream on the far side of the meadow, which he discovers is flowing from a spring at the base of the glacier-sculpted cliff, he stops to eat. (Photo 7.11) Now much closer to the eastern edge of the meadow, he sees three or four small islands of subalpine fir and a few white-bark pine and lodgepole pine just this side of the forest. "Could one of these be where my ancestors had their hunting camp?" he asks himself, as Clark nutcrackers swoop here and there among the whitebark pines, flashing white in the tails and wings while voicing their *khraaaa-khraaaa*.

7.11 The glacier-sculpted cliff and its stream.

The lodgepole pines and nutcrackers are in this part of the meadow, as well as a few other species, because the glacier was situated so close to the crest of the High Cascades that the resulting outwash of glacial till that formed the meadow, as it was expelled from the receding glacier, created an interface with the vegetation and some of its fauna from the east side of the mountain's crest.

CLARK NUTCRACKER

The Clark nutcracker is a medium-sized, compact bird (about 11 inches long, weighing around 5 ounces) with a long, black, dagger-like bill used to rip into pinecones and extract the large seeds. Its plumage is light gray and loose in texture. It has long, glossy black wings that almost reach the tip of its tail when they are folded. The tail has glossy black feathers in its center, whereas the outer feathers and the undersides of the tail are white, and there are white patches at the trailing edges of the wings, which are clearly visible when a nutcracker is in flight. The legs and feet are black, the latter with heavy, sharp, curved claws. Males are slightly larger than the females. (Photo 7.12)

7.12 Clark nutcracker.

Like the deer, elk, and Steller jays, Clark nutcrackers spend the winters at lower elevations, where they forage and retrieve caches of seeds hidden the previous summer and autumn. With the coming of spring, they migrate to their preferred habitat, which is semi-open, mixed stands of pine, fir, and spruce growing on steep slopes and ridges interspersed with meadows and streams—the cirque, where they will remain as long as food is available.

Gregarious birds, they typically travel in small flocks—except while depositing seeds in or retrieving seeds from their caches—calling back and forth with rolling, far-carrying calls. Despite producing a great variety of sounds, their most frequent call is *khraaaa-khraaaa*.

A nutcracker's distance flight is strong and direct, but when swooping among the pines of the cirque, flashing the white tail and wing feathers, their flight pattern is similar to that of a woodpecker, alternating between flapping and gliding. On the ground, they hop, turning their heads from side to side, as they harvest seeds. In addition, they appear to play by flying wildly in high winds and by provoking and chasing small raptors, which they can easily outmaneuver. On the other hand, when the threat of a potential predator arises, flocks of nutcrackers react by mobbing it, be it a golden eagle, goshawk, or great horned owl.

Although the vast majority of their diet in the cirque is seeds of whitebark pine, being omnivorous, they also dine on other seeds, nuts, berries, a wide variety of insects, eggs and nestlings of other birds, and occasionally carrion. With respect to insects, nutcrackers hack into rotten, fallen trees to locate large beetle grubs, and they occasionally flip over animal dung in search of insects.

Food is gathered both from the ground and from trees, where a nutcracker is exceedingly agile among the branches. The pine seeds are extracted by clasping cones in such a way that they are held in either one or both of the bird's feet. Using its long, sharp, sturdy bill, it breaks open the unripe cones and removes seeds. It then shells the seeds by cracking them in its bill or by holding them in its feet and hammering them. Thereafter, the nutcracker tests the seeds for soundness by moving them up and down in its bill while quickly opening and closing its mouth, in a motion known as "bill clicking." It also chooses good seeds by color. Selected seeds are then eaten on the spot or stored for later use.

Ounce for ounce, the whitebark pine seeds harvested by the cirque's nutcrackers have more calories than chocolate. It is not surprising, therefore, that one nutcracker may fly toward another that is harvesting or digging up stored seeds and try to confiscate them by pushing the bird out of the way.

When harvesting pine seeds, a nutcracker enlarges a special pouch behind its tongue, wherein it can store 100 or more seeds and carry them to a spot nearby or up to 15 miles away, including as much as 3,000 feet in elevation up or down slope to cache them.

Selecting a likely spot, it makes several sideward swipes with its bill to create a trench for burying the seeds, and then coughs up three to five seeds at a time, before carefully covering them with soil. Alternatively, it pushes individual seeds into gravelly soil, pumice, or crevices in wood.

Nutcrackers migrate up or down the mountain throughout the year, as food becomes available. Starting off in the cirque, they begin eating the seeds of whitebark pine around mid-July and start caching them by mid-August. Thereafter, they gradually travel downslope to find the seeds of ponderosa pine, lodgepole pine, and Douglas-fir.

Nutcrackers are extremely intelligent and have excellent spatial memory, which enables them to cache thousands of seeds in the autumn, and then locate a large percentage of those during the winter in their lower-elevation habitat and again in the cirque when they arrive the following spring. In fact, one nutcracker stored 35,000 seeds in 9,500 different locations in one season.

Actually, the birds regularly store more seeds than they require for nutritional survival as an insurance against seed theft by such animals as chickarees, chipmunks, and Steller jays, as well as to offset potentially low availability of alternative foods. Moreover, surplus seeds left in a cache may germinate and grow into new trees. And because not every seed buried over the centuries has been recovered, virtually all the whitebark pines in the cirque and surrounding landscape come from those planted by succeeding generations of nutcrackers. So it is that nutcrackers perpetuate their own habitat through their widespread over-storing of seeds.

During both winter and spring, stored seeds are located again by remembering where they lie in relation to such nearby objects as rocks, fallen trees, and trees, even when the cache is buried under as much as three feet of snow. The birds can find their cached seed more than nine months after hiding them, even though their accuracy declines after about six months. This ability allows some nutcrackers to remain at high elevations year round, and to start their breeding season very early.

Clark nutcrackers are monogamous and pair for life. Consequently, courtship displays occur throughout the year, but are most intense in the breeding season, which begins as early as December downslope from the cirque, at which time a pair of newly committed birds begin flying together with fast dives and swoops, feeding each other, and holding twigs in their bills. As the days passed, courtship led to nest building by the onset of January. Having established a defensible territory around their nest site, the pair will hold it for several years and occasionally have to defend it by locking bills and claws with intruders.

They not only selected a site located 69 feet above the forest floor in the forks of the outer branches of an old Douglas-fir on a south-facing slope but also on the leeward side of the tree to shelter it from the wind. In addition, it was near seed stores from the previous autumn. And so the pair began gathering material on January 7th.

They gathered twigs of Douglas-fir at a rate of one twig every three to four minutes, sometimes collecting material 500 yards or more away from the nest. The twigs and some bark were initially woven into a platform 13 inches across and secured to forks of the branches, on top of which they built a cup of bark strips and grass 11 inches in diameter. The cup was well insulated within by a layer of rotten-wood pulp four inches across and three inches deep that was subsequently lined with dried grass, fine strips of bark, moss, and animal hair.

The nest was finished within eight days, on January 15th, at which time the female began laying three, pale-greenish eggs flecked with brown. With the last egg laid on the 17th of January, both parents incubated them for 19 day, until the 5th of February, when they hatched. In fact, the male actually developed a naked, incubation/brood patch on his chest just like the female, and took his turn keeping the eggs and newly hatched babies warm while his mate went off to get seeds out of her caches.

The helpless young, hatching almost simultaneously, were sparsely covered with down and had a salmon-red hue on the inside of their mouths. Both parents tended to their nestlings for the next 21 days, until the 26th of February, when the young fledged. Nutcrackers can nest as early as January or February, despite the harsh winter weather in their mountain home, because the young are fed from their parents' stored seeds, an adaptation that could provide more time for young birds to learn from their parents.

Snow in the meadow is all but vanquished, as the nutcracker family migrates upward, arriving in the cirque on the 5th of June, the same day Storm Hawk makes his appearance. Here, the parents uncover last year's larder of whitebark seeds to feed their noisy, begging youngsters.

Now juveniles, the young will follow their parents around for three or four months while they learn the complex, seed-storage strategy, preparing them for independence by late summer when it is time to start harvesting and caching their own seeds. In essence, juvenile independence corresponds with the year's seed crop becoming available and their ability to create their own caches for the coming winter. Thereafter, they will become sexually mature the following year, and may live as long as 17 years.

Not only do the lives of Clark nutcrackers revolve around their pine-seed diet but also pines within and beyond the cirque have been shaped by their relationship with the nutcrackers. Whitebark pine, limber pine, Colorado piñon pine, single-leaf piñon pine, and southwestern white pine depend on nutcrackers to disperse their seeds. Over the centuries, this interaction has changed the pines' seeds, their cones, and even the trees' overall shape in comparison to pines whose seeds are dispersed by wind.

While the nutcrackers are going about their own lives, Storm Hawk is wondering if the stream, which is slightly larger and deeper than the one draining the lake, is big enough and deep enough to harbor trout. Could he return to the scene of a certain mid-September afternoon in the year 1020, he would see two young boys competing with each other to see who could catch the most fish and win their father's praise. As it is, he has not the slightest idea of just how close he is to fulfilling his quest, when a yellow-pine chipmunk, dashing across his path, averts his attention, only to see another in pursuit.

Yellow-Pine Chipmunk

The yellow-pine chipmunk is a small, richly colored squirrel with a slender tail, pointed face and ears, and is from 7⁹⁄₁₀ to 8⁹⁄₁₀ inches long with a tail from 3⁹⁄₁₀ to 4 inches in length. They weigh between 1 and 2½ ounces, with the females being slightly larger than the males.

In summer, their coloration is bright. They have five, black, evenly spaced, longitudinal stripes down the back that are about equal in width. The three central stripes extend from shoulder to rump, whereas the two outer stripes extend only to mid-body. The pale stripes in between the black ones along the back are usually white or grayish. In addition, they have three dark and two white stripes on the sides of their head. The backs of their ears are mainly black. Their sides, shoulders, and lower surface of the tail are a rich reddish or orangish-brown, whereas the top and margins of their tail are black, overlaid with tannish. Their undersides are whitish. In winter, their pelage is slightly duller and more grayish.

Yellow-pine chipmunks are solitary by nature, except momentarily during the breeding season. A male's home range may be seven acres in extent, whereas those of females may encompass a little over 2½ acres. Despite being solitary in demeanor, they are not territorial and may have overlapping home ranges, with the exception of the immediate vicinity of their burrows.

Their daily activity normally extends from just before sunrise until mid-morning, when they return to their burrows, where they remain until mid-afternoon, when they are once again active above ground until a little after sunset. On cloudy days, or days with light rain, however, they may be active above ground all day.

Most of their day is spent foraging in areas of shade within the cover of shrubs or grooming by brushing their fur, taking dust baths, and washing their faces. When in motion, their movements are short and jerky. In addition, their seemingly ever-moving tails are held horizontally or erect when they are running, but swing from side to side when they are sitting.

Their homes are usually in burrows that range from six inches to four feet below ground, where they not only spend considerable time but also seek refuge from perceived danger. In addition, they establish nests in the hollows of fallen trees and in cavities within standing trees as high as 50 feet above the forest floor. They also nest in clefts and crevices in rocky outcroppings, rockslides, and lava fields.

Although expert climbers, often running about in trees, these delightful little squirrels generally scamper over fallen trees and rocks or climb in bushes. Yellow-pine chipmunks are adventuresome, often exploring far from their home bases, all the while keeping close to cover.

I remember one particularly bold little fellow who had the audacity to climb up my body to my shoulder, thence out my arm and onto the lens of my camera, where upon it reached over the lens and ate the huckleberries I was trying to photograph. I say "trying," because every time I got ready to shoot, my lens darkened with a wee head and the berries disappeared. I never did get a picture!

Their bright colors are often seen flashing through the leaves and bushes and their shrill chirping of alarm or curiosity is heard in various parts of the cirque. Sometimes a slow, soft *chuck, chuck, chuck* emanates from a distance, as a chipmunk calls quietly to its friends far and near—most often to warn of danger. Their voices have many degrees of pitch, timing, and quality that may mean much to members of their own clan, but little to uninitiated ears.

When greeting one another, they first touch noses, then sniff the sides of each other's face and neck, and lastly they sniff each other's anus. Visual signals, such as body posture, are also important in communication.

When it comes to eating, these independent, omnivorous, little chipmunks gravitate to open, sunny areas, favoring seeds, and using their cheek pouches to carry food to their nest, where it is stored for winter. One food cache weighed 6⁷⁄₁₀ ounces, as much as four chipmunks, while another contained upwards of 68,000 items, ranging from seeds to bumblebees.

As omnivores, they eat a wide variety of foods, including seeds, berries, flowers, green foliage, bulbs, corms (the short, underground, vertically swollen, nutrient-storage organ of a plant's stem), tubers (the short, thick, round stem of certain plants, such as the potato, that grows underground and can produce a new plant), insects, birds' eggs, small animals, and fungi. In fact, the belowground fruiting bodies of mycorrhizal fungi (truffles) are very important in their diet, just as they are in the diets of the northern flying squirrels and chickarees detailed earlier.

Chipmunks have been recognized as fungus eaters for almost 50 years. In Oregon, in the early 1940s, for example, my friend and graduate advisor, professor Kenneth Gordon, was undoubtedly observing such behavior in yellow-pine chipmunks, which he dearly loved, when he noted in reference to its sense of smell, "They often can be seen quartering the ground, as if trying to smell out food. At intervals, they dig little pits in search of some underground object."

Many of the large truffles are associated with the interior shade of the cirque's forest, where they fruit in and under large, rotting trees, and thus retain moisture long into the dry summer period. Such moisture retention may actually extend the truffle-fruiting season and thereby be an advantage to both the fungus and the chipmunk, in whose diet the truffles are an important source of both nutrients and water during July and early August, when succulent vegetation dries up in the more arid parts of the cirque and grass seeds and berries are not yet abundant.

Although a yellow-pine chipmunk probably needs only a single, large truffle per meal, it is possible for a foraging animal to find up to nine truffles in one "dig" because they frequently fruit gregariously. Truffles are thus an energy-efficient source of nutrients and water in terms of the foraging-time required by such a small squirrel.

Unlike most other chipmunks, yellow-pine chipmunks do not accumulate a thick layer of fat in preparation for winter, despite being in a state of dormancy (a period of low activity) beginning when the temperature drops below 73 degrees Fahrenheit and the length of daylight begins to decrease in autumn. Once in their burrows, they enter a state of torpor that lasts between four to five months, depending on the weather, waking every five to seven days to eat seeds stored in various caches. Moreover, they may become lethargic during the occasional bouts of cold, summer weather in this high-mountain world.

In early spring, as the deep snow begins to melt, these little squirrels tunnel up to the surface and begin to explore their world. Soon, however, the males are searching for mates.

This year, 1575, a male emerged through the snow on the 16th of April, a bright, sunny day. Seeing no others of his kind, he returned to his nest. The next day was cloudy and cold. So, after a few minutes on the surface, he returned to the warmth of his nest, where he remained for the next two days. Emerging again on the 19th, he heard the vocalizations of several females attempting to attract the attention of males in preparation for the onset of estrous.

Then, on the 26th, he encountered a female ready to mate just before noon, and impregnated her with five embryos. However, being promiscuous and in estrous for a single day, she was pursued by and copulated with three other males that afternoon, in what might be called a "mating chase."

After a gestation period of 33 days, she gave birth to five babies (four females and one male) on the 29th of May in her nest of leaves, grass, lichens, and feathers three feet below ground. The young were virtually helpless and totally dependent on their mother until they emerged from the burrow on the 3rd of July, when they were 6 weeks old. They will disperse around the 17th (seven days after Storm Hawk will have left the cirque) to find suitable areas in which to create their own burrows and nests for the coming winter. Thereafter, both sexes will reach reproductive maturity somewhere between one and two years of age.

During that time, the black and white stripes on their backs will help to camouflage them in the open forest, where the sun casts sharp, contrasting areas of light and shadows. They will also have a system whereby one chipmunk watches for predators and warns the others with alarm calls, primarily in open areas, where they are more exposed to danger. Nevertheless, one female will fall prey to a long-tailed weasel, and the male will be taken by a goshawk before the end of September. The other three will have the potential to live between three and five years, throughout which they will perform the vital function of dispersing seeds from trees in the cirque's forest and spores from the truffles through their feces, as well as carrying on the wonder of the millennial, unbroken, genetic experiments they each represent, as they grace the cirque with the simple presence of their being.

Although the two chipmunks reappear suddenly in the present moment, racing in the opposite direction, Storm Hawk's hunger commands his attention, and he follows the stream toward the bottom of the meadow in search of pools deep enough in which to catch trout. He has not gone quite mid-way to the forest when such a pool presents itself because the stream is now larger than it was in 1020, when the boys had to go almost to the forest to find fish-bearing pools.

Setting aside his backpack, quiver, and bow, he gets down on his hands and knees and slowly, carefully approaches the pool, where the stream has undercut its bank. Then, like before, and like the boys in 1020, he proceeds to feel under the bank for trout. Within two hours, he has nine trout, enough for an excellent supper and good breakfast when mixed with some of the Indian lettuce growing along a low, centuries-old ridge of rotting wood from an ancient subalpine fir that once graced this part of the meadow. Looking at the trout and the lettuce, he thanks each and the Great Spirit for the gift of their life, after which he blends for a moment into the deep quietude of the land.

Supper in hand, he retrieves his backpack, quiver, and bow and makes his way into one of the islands he saw earlier in the day. Depositing the fish, lettuce, and his bow on clean grass, he removes his quiver and backpack, after which he gathers wood for his fire. His spirit overwhelmed by the beauty of Nature in all her various forms, colors, and interactions causes him to lay aside the wood and watch the golden orb of the sun slip quietly, slowly under the western horizon, as twilight gradually creeps over the land.

From somewhere in the gathering darkness a great horned owl hoots. A wolf howls and the pack's chorus ensues. The rising moon's soft light casts gentle shadows, as Storm Hawk's fire dies to embers, and finally goes out.

June 24th

The nightly noises fade as sleep envelops Storm Hawk. He rests peacefully until the gentle warmth of the new day touches his face with the sun's early light. Rising, he goes to the stream and washes his face, after which he eats the last of the trout, picks up his bow and quiver, and begins to explore the islands of subalpine fir.

Although positive he'd seen four islands when he first reached the stream on this side of the meadow, he finds only three. He explores each in its turn with single-focused intensity, but finds nothing to suggest any of them had ever been used as a campsite. Perplexed, he once again goes downstream to catch more trout.

This time, however, he goes close to the forest, where he sees a doe and her young fawn just visible within the trees. (Photo 7.13)

Stopping to test the wind's direction, he feels the warm breeze coming upslope along the stream from the valley below. With the gentle wind in his favor, he waits until the doe looks away, and then takes off his quiver lest the arrows make noise. He carefully withdraws two arrows and gets down on this stomach, a position he maintains for several minutes as he crawls slowly toward the deer. The doe moves behind a large Engelmann spruce and, head down, begins to eat. Her fawn, meanwhile, is resting on the ground a few feet from its mother, but in plain view from Storm Hawk's vantage point.

7.13 The fawn.

Convinced the doe can neither see nor smell him, Storm Hawk gets up on his hands and knees and crawls slowly, hesitantly toward the deer, all the while avoiding any direct gaze in their direction. Minutes pass until they are in range of his bow, at which time he places one of the two arrows he kept against the bow's string. Rising to a kneeling position, he waits until the doe moves just enough to cause her fawn to get up. Drawing his bow to its full tension as unobtrusively as possible, he releases the arrow, which penetrates the fawn just behind its shoulder.

Startled, the doe leaps forward a short distance, just as the second arrow strikes the stumbling fawn, sending its spirit into the land of its ancestors. Storm Hawk gets to his feet and goes to the dead fawn, as the doe disappears into the forest. Getting down on his knees, he raises his arms toward the azure sky and thanks the fawn for the gift of its life. He apologizes to the doe for having taken her baby, and he thanks the Great Spirit for the food that will nourish his body this day, when a small breeze wafts some fur of a snowshoe hare from a large limb 40 some feet up in a spruce about 30 feet away. It drifts down, landing at Storm Hawk's feet. Looking up through the boughs of several trees, he sees the faint outline of a blue-gray hawk busily plucking the fur from a freshly caught hare.

Northern Goshawk

Falconers have regarded the northern goshawk as one of the most formidable and admired birds of prey since at least medieval times. In fact, Attila, often referred to as "Atilla the Hun," even wore its image on his helmet. The Huns were a group of Eurasian nomads, of which Atilla was the ruler from 434 until his death in 453. The Hun empire stretched from the Ural River to the Rhine River and from the Danube River to the Baltic Sea.

The name "goshawk" comes from the Old English *gōsheafoc*, "goose-hawk," which, in turn, is composed of two words: *gōs*, meaning "goose," and *heafoc*, meaning "hawk." It is pronounced as if the words are still separate, *without* any "sh" sound.

The northern goshawk has short, broad wings and a long tail, both adaptations for maneuvering within its forest habitat. Adults have a distinctive black hood and white stripe above their dark-red eyes, the color of which usually develops after they are two years old. Their backs and underwings are blue-gray, and their breasts are creamy with a "chain mail" patterning of grey. Their tail feathers are barred with black. (Photo 7.14)

7.14 Northern Goshawk: (left) juvenile and (right) adult.

In addition, adults have two plumages, which they alternate: a light phase and a dark phase. The first adult molt is typically their light phase, wherein their plumage colors are a shade lighter than in their dark phase. The following year, they will be in their dark phase, wherein their same plumage colors are a shade darker than in their light phase, and so on.

Juveniles, on the other hand, are mottled-brown above with brown and buff streaking below. They have light lines over their pale-yellow eyes, and their tails are more darkly banded than those of the adults.

Female goshawks are significantly larger than males, being 23 to 27 inches long with a 43- to 50-inch wingspan, whereas males are 18 to 22 inches long and have a 35- to 41-inch wingspan. Moreover, females can weigh up to 4⁹⁄₁₀ pounds, while males weigh up to 2⁹⁄₁₀ pounds.

Although their flight is a characteristic, "flap, flap, glide," they can soar. In addition, they are capable of considerable, sustained, horizontal speeds up to 38 miles per hour in pursuit of prey. When disturbed, they utter a loud, *kak-kak-kak-kak-kak*.

As spring begins to creep up the mountain, a monogamous pair of goshawks, mated for life, follow it upward, arriving in the cirque, which has been their nesting territory for the past four years, during the first week of March. Once there, the pair begins to perform a spectacular, "undulating flight display," heralding the onset of their breeding season. This is a rare performance for such secretive forest birds, whose breeding territory includes all the habitat components of the cirque, which encompasses about 3,500 acres. Moreover, because visual displays are difficult in their forested habitat, their communication is primarily vocal.

Being aggressively territorial, especially within the vicinity of the cirque, the hawks viciously attack other raptors, sometimes over competition for food, for approaching their active nest too closely, or in a decidedly territorial-motivated behavior. At such times, they displace or even kill their perceived competitors.

Because goshawks are under the greatest threat of predation from the time they hatch until they fledge and leave the nest, the parents' fierce territorial defensiveness is probably an adaptation against such potential tree-climbing predators as black bears and martens, as well as such winged predators as golden eagles and great horned owls. Gray wolves also stalk and kill fledging goshawks on the ground, especially when larger prey is scarce.

Aside from their territorial defensiveness, most of their time is spent perched, silently waiting and watching for prey, although they switch perches after brief periods. An opportunistic predator built to move quickly and quietly, they approach a potential meal stealthily, moving unnoticed through dense cover, until close enough to overcome their intended target in mid-air with a burst of speed, such as jays, ravens, and ruffed grouse—the latter also being captured on the ground. Or they swoop out of a tree onto ground-dwelling prey so fast that it does not have time to find protective cover, such as snowshoe hares, chickarees, chipmunks, and weasels. In essence, their hunting style is marked by stealth, preferring to attack from below and behind, with the built-in factor of extraordinary persistence in their pursuit.

At other times, they fly along the interface of the forest and the meadow low and fast. The purpose is to surprise unsuspecting prey, such as mantled ground squirrels, voles, and possibly Mazama pocket gophers, as well as any unsuspecting songbirds that present themselves.

Once captured, the hawk takes its prey to a perch, where it plucks the feathers or hair. In addition, they sometimes cache prey on tree branches or wedged in a crotch between branches for up to 32 hours. This is done primarily when the parents are caring for nestlings.

During the nesting season, however, they favor tall trees with a mid-story coverage of vegetation and small openings within the forest for hunting, such as the one wherein Storm Hawk is standing as the fur floats to the forest floor. Storm Hawk is exceedingly fortunate that the hawk is so busy on his special plucking post, where he has taken the hare to be plucked clean before bringing it to the nest, that he is unaware of Storm Hawk's presence. Had he become aware of Storm Hawk, the fearless parent would have boldly attacked him for being too close to the nest, and would most likely have done considerable damage to Storm Hawk's face by raking it with the sharp, curved talons of his rear toes as he flew by, only to return and do it again, and again.

As previously mentioned, the pair's nesting territory encompasses the entire cirque, although the nest itself is situated 50 feet above the forest floor on a tight whorl of limbs near the trunk of an old Douglas-fir in the vicinity of the plucking post. The nest is a large platform of thin sticks lined with bark and fresh sprigs of Douglas-fir and mountain hemlock. The female had done most of the nest construction over the four years in which it has been annually reused, accounting for its growing size, which is now 3½ feet wide and deep.

The nest renovated for the current nesting season by April 27th, the male began feeding his mate. She, in turn, laid the first of three eggs on April 30th, the second on May 3rd, and the third on May 5th.

Whereas the male did most of the hunting and fed his mate while she incubated the eggs, he sometimes took over the duty of incubation for short stints, giving her a chance to eat. She, in turn, incubated the clutch for 33 days, until the 7th of June, when the eggs began to hatch, at which time the young were covered in white down and able to move around in the nest. Thereafter, she took constant care of the nestlings for 13 days, until the 20th of June, during which time the father provided food, and the mother generally fed the young.

As for the chicks, they are extremely vocal, using a "whistle-beg" call as a plea for food that begins with *a ke-ke-ke* and progresses to a *kakking* sound. On the other hand, when feeling well fed, they utter a high-pitched "contentment-twitter."

Two of the nestlings will venture out of the nest onto nearby branches 34 days after hatching, on the 10th of July, and the third will leave the nest 35 days after hatching, on the 11th. They will hang around the nest for 10 more days, until the 21st of July, when they will take their first, short flights. Subsequently, their parents will continue feeding them until they are 70 days old, on the 15th of August. Although the juveniles will be on their way to independence, they will remain in their parents' territory for up to a year, when they will reach sexual maturity and be truly on their own.

Meanwhile, August becomes September, and September becomes October when, by the middle of the month, the first snow begins to fall. It is not long thereafter that the goshawk family begins their downhill migration to the ancient forest along the river in the valley, where they will spend the winter, only to return to the cirque with the coming of spring.

Still thinking about the hawk, which he watched quietly for some time, Storm Hawk pulls the arrows out of the fawn, cuts it open and removes its lungs, stomach, and intestine, but leaves its liver and heart attached to the carcass, which he puts over his shoulder, and returns to camp, retrieving his quiver on the way.

Arriving at his camp, he deposits the deer on the ground, along with his bow and quiver. Turning the fawn on its back, he cuts a hindquarter off the carcass at the hip joint and lays it carefully on a patch of clean grass, after which he gathers firewood and lays his evening fire. While igniting the fire in anticipation of roasted venison, his focus becomes split between the cluster of firs that shelter his camp and the storied campsite of his quest.

Thus occupied, he skins the hindquarter and cuts off a steak through which he pokes a green alder stick from the forest. Holding the meat over the flame, he ruminates on where the fabled campsite might be and why he is so compelled to find it. He draws a blank on both counts, however, and finally manages to clear them from his mind just in time to prevent his supper from becoming overdone.

And so the day fades into history, as the curtain of stars is drawn over the land and darkness obscures all details beyond the fire's dancing light. With his fire out, Storm Hawk settles down for the night. His sleep is filled with the vision of circles of various kinds in the landscape of dreams. Moreover, the circles are all confined to the meadow east of the stream. Then he envisions a fallen subalpine fir rotting away until all that remains is a small ridge of rotten wood, like the one by which he found the Indian lettuce in the lower meadow. But, just as he approaches it, it fades away, leaving him feeling empty and lost.

June 25th

Haunted throughout the remaining night by the hidden meaning of his dream, he awakes as the first hint of light advertises the coming dawn. He rises with a sense of urgency, kindles a small fire, cooks some meat, and eats breakfast. Having a deep inner sense that his quest is sacred, he goes to the stream, awaits the sun's rise, and bathes, after which he mentally prepares to search the area of the meadow that appeared in his dreamscape.

Leaving his backpack in camp, he takes his bow and arrows and walks toward a large boulder near the cliff from which to survey the terrain. Once at the cliff, he climbs atop the boulder and sits down in a peaceful, cross-legged position. Quieting his mind, he examines the meadow's surface for any elongated irregularities that might hint of a rotten tree. Despite spending three hours observing the details of the meadow's surface, he finds nothing of interest with respect to his search.

Still atop the boulder, he once again quiets his mind. Being still and non-threatening, he is able to enjoy the company of a curious, brightly colored, male golden-mantled ground squirrel that climbs atop an adjacent boulder and watches him for some time.

Golden-Mantled Ground Squirrels

Golden-mantled ground squirrels range in length from 10 to 11½ inches and weigh from 6 to a little more than 13 ounces. Their ears are prominent, and their feet are proportionately large with naked soles and palms.

7.15 An adult golden-mantled ground squirrel.

These ground squirrels are strikingly colored, with a golden-red mantle that extends from the head down over their shoulders to the tops of their front feet. One white stripe, bordered by two black stripes, extends horizontally down each side of their back, similar to chipmunks, which are the smaller of the two. Although chipmunks have a white stripe through their eyes, golden-mantled ground squirrels have a whitish eye ring and no facial striping. (Photo 7.15)

Their backs are gray, brownish, or buff, and their undersides are whitish or yellowish-gray. Their tails are moderately bushy, brownish-black above, and reddish-brown below. Winter pelage is grayer and the mantle is duller. The underside of the tail, however, retains its bright summer coloration. As well, the squirrels exhibit a subtle, sexual dimorphism, with males having a brighter, red mantle and a significantly larger brain.

In both habits and physical structure, golden-mantled ground squirrels appear intermediate between arboreal squirrels, like the chickaree in the forest, and true ground squirrels, like the Belding ground squirrel in the meadow. Although not good climbers, golden-mantles seek refuge in a tree when no other escape is possible. The fact that they live in underground burrows is no deterrent from climbing on, running over, or sitting on fallen trees, tree stumps, boulders, and the like, a position from which they obtain an unobstructed view by remaining motionless, yet alert. These "lookouts" are an important inclusion in their daily life.

These curious squirrels are active during daylight hours, which, according to my old friend and mentor, Ken Gordon, was precisely why he enjoyed studying them. As he put it to me many years ago, both the golden-mantled ground squirrel and the yellow-pine chipmunk keep "gentlemen's hours." Ken was not by choice an early riser.

Not as quick and "nervous" as the yellow-pine chipmunk, they are, nevertheless, quick to seek their burrows when danger presents itself. The single, shrill whistle of a golden-mantled ground squirrel is seldom heard, and when it is, it is difficult to locate.

Solitary by nature, they normally dig shallow burrows in the cirque up to 100 feet long under fallen trees, stumps, and boulders or find suitable shelter in the small rockslides at the base of the cliff on the east side of the meadow. Having excavated a chamber to live in, they collect dry plant material with which to line the cavity and create a cozy nest.

A squirrel's home range varies from 1²/₁₀ to 12½ acres, depending on the density of vegetation. However, females and males have separate, 100-foot territorial areas surrounding their burrows—that is, except during the mating season, when males overlap their territories with females.

Social interactions outside the breeding season are mainly antagonistic between adults and sometimes include a threat, which may evolve into a fight. A chase, on the other hand, is normally launched without warning. The main purpose of defending a territory is to expel others of the same species.

Golden-mantled ground squirrels will ascend rocks and fallen trees as lookout stations, occasionally sitting upright for a better view. Should a would-be predator be detected, a squirrel gives an alarm call to warn of danger, whereby kin are likely to be alerted and saved, while simultaneously increasing the potential danger to the squirrel giving the warning. This particular behavior seems to be a kin preference, despite the fact that other behavior fails to indicate preferential treatment among kin. When a predator is spotted, or an alarm call heard, the squirrels dive into the nearest cover or hole, for which purpose they keep a series of burrow openings around their feeding areas.

These voracious, potbellied squirrels are omnivorous in the extreme, and literally eat almost anything they can find. In spring, much green vegetation is eaten as soon as it appears, and roots and old seeds are excavated. Later, as berries ripen, they are eagerly sought, eaten with abandon, and avidly stored. As berries wane, seeds of grasses and flowering plants, as well as the seeds of firs, pines, and spruces are harvested.

They are also fond—very fond—of truffles (the belowground fruiting bodies of mycorrhizal fungi), eating copious amounts of them, which they detect by odor and dig out in spring and autumn, thereafter spreading live spores around the forest in their feces. In addition, they plant pine trees.

In years past, I watched one of these squirrels collect pine seeds and bury them, forgetting almost instantly where they were secreted. Going back to the same location late the following spring, I was greeted by small clumps of germinating pine seedlings, which explained why, in the days of old, prior to the European invasion of North America, so many tight clumps of three, four, five, and sometimes even six old pine trees grew so close together in the same place. (Photo 7.16)

7.16 Seeds of Ponderosa pine planted by a golden-mantled ground squirrel that germinated the following spring.

Beyond vegetation, these opportunistic squirrels eat insects in all their life-cycle stages, nestling birds and eggs (such as Oregon juncos), small mammals (like montane voles), and even carrion.

Being a traditional hibernator, a mantled ground squirrel not only has to build up its body fat to survive the winter asleep but also has to store some food in its burrow to eat when it awakens in the spring. Fortunately, they are endowed with cheek pouches that allow them to transport food back to their nests and still run at full speed on all fours. When threatened by a predator, however, they have to drop the food if they want to make a quick enough getaway.

In autumn, usually by mid September or early October, depending on how mild the weather in the cirque is that year, these now-obese squirrels enter their dens and settle in for their winter's hibernation. Once sequestered, they curl into a ball, thereby minimizing their surface area and thus conserve their body heat.

In addition, their diet is high in *linoleic* acid (from the Greek *linon*, "flax" and the Latin *oleum*, "oil"). Linoleic acid is a polyunsaturated, omega-6 fatty acid, which reduces the melting point of their fat deposits, making them easier to metabolize at low temperatures.

Their hibernation is broken into short periods of torpor interspersed with wakefulness, during which they rarely eat. When aroused, a squirrel spends most of its time moving about and rearranging its nest, occasionally emerging to the surface. Females and males have the same annual period of dormancy, but females have a significantly longer period of total hibernation than males, who not only have more extensive interruptions during torpor but also longer arousals.

Although the dates for entering their dens to hibernate and emerging from their dens in spring vary to some extent with the weather, they normally reappear in early May. After emerging from hibernation, the squirrels compete with one another to establish territorial boundaries, wherein a male's territory encompasses those of several females. When females emerge from hibernation, shortly after the males, they typically copulate with the male within whose territory they find themselves.

A female was impregnated with six embryos on the 6th of May. She gave birth in her burrow under a boulder near the cliff on the 2nd of June, after a gestation period of 27 days. Born into a nest of grass and dried leaves, her litter consisted of four males and two females, each hairless except for tiny whiskers and hairs on their head, and weighing about 3½ ounces. Although their toes had not separated and their ears were closed, they could squeak and squirm around, but had little control over the position of their bodies.

Within seven days, June 9th, their fur had grown enough that their markings were clearly visible, at which time their whiskers (technically referred to as "vibrissae") were longer, and they were able to right themselves. By the 16th of June, their teeth had erupted, their ears had opened, their toes had separated, and they uttered their first adult sounds.

Their upper front teeth will not erupt, however, or their eyes open until the 28th of June, when they will also begin to groom themselves. They will begin eating solid food by the 2nd of July, after which their growth will accelerate rapidly, and they will greet the outer world in fur coats as brightly colored as those of adults.

Once out of the burrow, their mother will refuse to associate with them. The dispersing males will range farther than their female siblings, as each will establish a territory and begin to prepare for their first hibernation.

They will reach sexual maturity with their first birthday, and may live as long as seven years, but at least one or two will fall prey to northern goshawks, jays, or long-tailed weasels. Moreover, a black bear dug out two nests in the middle of June, situated under fallen trees at the forest's edge, and ate the young.

As with all the other life forms in the cirque, the golden-mantled ground squirrels perform biophysical services that enhance both the meadow and the forest in which they live. As primary consumers eating vegetation, they convert plant energy into a form useable by the predators, allowing them to reside in the cirque. They also disperse the seeds of plants and the spores of fungi obtained by way of their vegetarian dining. And further, their burrowing activities—as do those of all burrowers—both aerate the soil and aid the infiltration of water from rain and melting snow.

After half an hour of delightful company, Storm Hawk rises, sending the squirrel scurrying for its burrow as he leaves the rock and begins walking back and forth throughout the meadow's representation of his dreamscape, only to be marginally aware of a dozen or so medium-sized ground squirrels all standing up watching him, looking like so many stakes or bowling pins in the meadow. Suddenly, the meadow's silence is broken by a few short, sharp, high-pitched whistles that not only jerk Storm Hawk fully into the present moment but also send the squirrels scurrying into their burrows, which are always close at hand. For his part, Storm Hawk stops and surveys the meadow in front of him, wondering what he had just seen. After a few moments, heads begin poking out of the burrows, one at a time, checking carefully to see if the perceived danger has passed before the inhabitants come out again to feed.

Belding Ground Squirrels

Belding ground squirrels are medium sized, having a relatively short tail, short limbs, and small ears. Their bodies vary in length from 9 to 11⅘ inches, and their flattened, bushy tails are 1⁷⁄₁₀ to 3 inches long. Their upper parts are generally somewhat yellowish-gray, becoming brownish-gray on the nose and down the middle of the back. Their tails are brownish-gray above and distinctly reddish-brown below, with black margins; however, the hairs on the end have three bands of color: one black, one white, and one red. Their feet have little to no hair. Compared to other ground squirrels, their cheek pouches are moderate in size. Although they normally weigh around 10 ounces, a large male with a good accumulation of autumnal fat can weigh nearly a pound.

These ground squirrels inhabit the moist, grassy areas of the cirque's meadow, not only because they can watch for predators but also because the grass is long enough to give them some protective cover. They make well-used runways, almost little highways, through the meadow vegetation as they run from place to place, always mindful of danger. Here, they dig burrows for protection, nesting, rearing young, aestivation (dormancy during the dry, summer months), and hibernation.

Their reappearance in the spring depends on when the sun is warm enough to start the green vegetation growing, which it did this year, 1575, at the end of April. Leaving their burrows at sunrise, the first squirrel to emerge stayed at the burrow entrance until there were enough other squirrels above ground to watch for predators, thereafter moving farther afield.

Most of their activity, digging and eating, occurs in the morning, decreasing as the temperature increases, which accounts for part of the day being spent stretched out either on rocks or the ground enjoying the sun's warmth. In addition, they spend time maintaining their burrows and grooming each other. As the morning hours wane and the late-afternoon sun increasingly warms the meadow, they go back into their burrows, that is, except for juveniles engaged in play. They enter later than the adults.

For the Belding ground squirrel, social dynamics are family oriented, with most interactions occurring among the female relatives. The squirrels use scent recognition to determine one another's relatedness, which is critical for the squirrel's social interactions to function smoothly, allowing them to react properly in defense of their territories.

They recognize their kin by comparing their own biochemical characteristics with those of squirrels they encounter, each squirrel having its own archive of characteristics whereby others can recognize it. These characteristics include scents emitted though dorsal and anal glands that leave a pungent odor in the dust-bathing areas.

Such recognition is important for females because it allows them to know who to act favorably toward when defending territories or when making alarm calls. And, while females live in groups, occasionally sharing food and shelter with one another if they are related, males are mainly nomadic between seasons.

When defending a territory or sensing a threat, the squirrels emit one of two alarm calls to warn the colony of impending danger. One is as a *churr* or a *trill*, which consists of more than five notes in rapid succession, and is used primarily in conjunction with terrestrial predators, such as the long-tailed weasel, but may be given to announce predators posing little threat. Squirrels hearing this warning respond by standing erect on their hind legs, by running to a nearby rock to get a better view of the potential threat, or running into their burrows, all the while emitting this call as they flee.

The other type of alarm call is a *whistle*, an individual, high-pitched note. This call is used to alert the colony of immediate threats, usually from such aerial predators as goshawks or golden eagles. Any squirrel hearing such a whistle exhibits evasive behavior—crouching or dashing to the nearest shelter.

If running from a ground predator, only the female squirrels with kin will alert others, and then only after they have reached protection. With aerial predators, however, all squirrels give the warning. The first squirrel to send it will stand erect on hind legs while calling, watching the predator without attempting to hide.

With respect to one of their primary activities, eating, the mainly herbivorous squirrels will occasionally eat carrion, insects, and even unfortunate members of their own species. For the most part, however, their diet consists of flowers and seeds, but they will also eat nuts, roots, bulbs, green vegetation, and mushrooms. When eating, a squirrel handles food with its front paws while standing erect on its hind legs. These squirrels do not create physical food caches, as do the chipmunks and golden-mantled ground squirrels, but instead store food in the form of body fat for nourishment during aestivation (dormancy during the dry, summer months), which grades into hibernation.

They can spend up to 40 percent of the summer eating in preparation for the long months of aestivation/hibernation. In doing so, they begin unabatedly eating whatever is succulent or green from the moment they emerge in the spring until seeds become available, and thus more important in the diet. With the end of the summer glut approaching, the squirrels appear more to waddle than run down their trails, as they prepare for their long sleep.

When they disappear into their burrows for the rest of the year depends on when the summer sun becomes hot enough to dry the grasses and turn them brown, sending the squirrels below to begin aestivation and avoid the heat of late summer, which in this year of 1575 will begin in late July, after Storm Hawk has left the cirque. Old males, with copious amounts of body fat will disappear first. The last to go below ground will be the young of the year because they must put on enough body fat to see them through their dormant period. Young males will go into aestivation when they are ten weeks old, followed by the females at thirteen weeks. Even then, it may be touch and go for those born late in the year.

As autumn approaches winter, aestivation grades into hibernation. While females tend to spend their long dormancy together, males prefer to do so alone.

Males in the cirque began emerging from hibernation on April 21st of this year, whereas the time at which females emerged was spread over three weeks, with the last one to appear on May 12th. The breeding season began soon after the squirrels awoke, a period during which females were sexually receptive for less than five hours for the year. As a result, the males immediately gathered around an available female, grappling, kicking, scratching, and biting one another viciously to gain access, wherein larger, older, stronger males emerged victorious. Females thus copulated with as many as five males during their brief estrous period, thereby not only increasing the chance of pregnancy but also increasing the genetic diversity of their offspring.

The last female to emerge became pregnant with eight embryos, four males and four females, on May 13th, and began immediately digging her nesting burrow, to be used solely for giving birth and raising her young. Finished digging, she lined the chamber with grass and grass roots. This being her only litter for the year, she established a territory around her burrow, which she will defend from unrelated individuals by attacking and chasing them, a situation that will persist until her youngsters are weaned. Meanwhile, the males take their leave after mating, thus relegating to the females the sole responsibility of rearing the young.

Her nesting burrow complete, the female gives birth on the 12th of June, after a gestation period of 30 days. She will wean her offspring in 27 days, on the 9th of July, one day before Storm Hawk will have departed. (Photo 7.17) Her territorial aggressiveness is critical during this time, lest an intruding squirrel—usually an adult female or yearling male from another area—gains access to the nest and drags a squealing, squirming juvenile out of the burrow, at times for some distance before biting its head, killing it. Thereafter, the attacking squirrel will cannibalize the youngster. On the other hand, female relatives will not harm one another's young, but instead will help their kin protect them from infanticide.

7.17 A very young Belding ground squirrel.

Once weaned, the juvenile squirrels will emerge from their burrow, staying near the entrance for the first three days before commencing to explore their meadow surroundings. Males will wander away soon after weaning. Moreover, they will continue to disperse after their first successful breeding. In fact, the male that mates the most moves farthest away from the colony he mated in, whereas females rarely leave the group into which they were born.

And once again, long-tailed weasels, goshawks, and golden eagles will take a toll on the young squirrels before they have an opportunity to add their genetic diversity to that of the cirque and the generations of Belding ground squirrels to come. Nevertheless, more squirrels will survive than perish, securing the cirque's biophysical diversity throughout the coming years.

But for now, Storm Hawk is so totally engrossed in his search, he forgets about food until the light of day begins to fade. Returning to camp, he builds a fire, eats, and beds down for the night, during which he wanders the same dreamscape.

JUNE 26TH TO 30TH

And thus it is for the next three days, as his food supply

dwindles. Nevertheless, because each day intensifies the urgency of his quest, he eats less and less so he can continue his search. He is not, however, the only one causing his food to disappear. Gray jays are whisking into camp and stealing as many scraps of his food as they can when he is not looking. That is precisely why they are also known as "camp robbers."

Gray Jay

Gray jays are medium-sized, gray birds with lighter bellies: 11½ inches long; a wingspan of 18 inches; and a normal, adult weight of 2½ ounces. They have black from above the eyes to the back of the neck, a white face, ears, and forehead, and a white belly. Their gray backs have a brownish cast with fine, white streaks. Their plumage is thick and fluffy, which they puff up in cold weather, enveloping their legs and feet. Even their nostrils are covered with feathers. In addition, they have black eyes, bills, legs, and feet, as well as long tails, short-bills, and lack a crest on their heads. And, in eating, gray jays wrench, twist, and tug their food apart, as opposed to hammering it with their bills, as do other jays.

Gray jays usually fly slowly, gliding with their wings angled downward, but they are capable of fast, maneuverable flight when escaping a predator or engaged in a territorial dispute with another jay. They roost close to the trunk of an old Engelmann spruce or other large, old conifers in the cirque, and frequently sunbathe on perches that are protected from the wind.

Gregarious and often found in family groups, the jays have a clear, pleasant whistle of *wheeeooo* or *wheee-ah*; as well as a low, husky *chuf-chuf-weef*, a screeching *jaaay;* and a very rough, dry *kreh kreh kreh kreh* alarm call. And, like the Steller jay, gray jays are known to mimic sounds.

The cirque is prime habitat for gray jays because of the number of Engelmann spruce in the immediate vicinity and lodgepole pine on some of the nearby, drier slopes. Their main habitat requirements appear to be twofold: (1) sufficiently cold temperatures to ensure successful storage of perishable food and (2) trees with sufficiently pliable, scaly bark arranged in a shingle-like configuration that allows the jays to easily wedge food items under them.

In fact, they store food year 'round, thanks to unusually large glands that produce copious amounts of sticky saliva, which they use to impregnate and encase food into a rounded mass in their mouth that ultimately adheres to anything it touches. Food is thus glued up under the shingle-like scales of bark, under tufts of lichen, in conifer needles, or in the forks of trees. Consequently, they gather thousands of food items into 1,000 or more caches every day during the summer, and because the food is stored above the height of the eventual snow line, they can sustain themselves throughout bleak winters in the cirque. Furthermore, the length of such storage may be prolonged by the antibacterial properties contained in the bark and foliage of the spruce and pine.

Omnivorous, they eat just about anything, including such novel food as blood-filled winter ticks, which they get off the back of live moose, albeit far beyond the cirque. More commonly, however, they grab flying insects in the air; wade in shallow water in search of invertebrates and amphibians; kill small mammals, such as rodents and baby bats; rob the eggs and nestlings of other birds; occasionally pursue and kill such small birds as chickadees and warblers; and once in awhile eat carrion. In addition, they eat seeds; berries; fungi; slime mold, which is unrelated to fungi; and historically anything their ancestors of generations past could steal from the hunting camps of the Indigenous people who occasionally visited the area in bygone centuries.

Highly curious, they fly from tree to tree, from perch to perch, each a short distance from one another, always on the lookout for food, such as nestling birds. Such ancient thievery is clearly a genetic trait that today's generation is willingly extending to Storm Hawk's camp. In addition, the deceptively cute, intrepid thieves often abscond with the stolen food clutched in their feet, an unusual trait for songbirds in flight. With such a varied diet, coupled with the prodigious amount of food they can store and retrieve, is it any wonder they can live in the cirque throughout the winter?

Whereas resident gray jays steal food from Storm Hawk every chance they get, Steller jays and gray jays from adjacent territories follow the resident jays to steal their cached food. Therefore, resident jays carry large food items to distant caches more often than small food items. To prevent theft by other gray jays, the residents carry valuable food items further from the source before hiding them. This so-called "scatter-hoarding" discourages pilfering by competitors. At times, theft is reduced by re-caching food items into widely scattered sites.

Gray jays typically breed at two years of age and are monogamous thereafter, remaining together in their territories throughout their lives, rarely leaving each other's sides, but will find another mate if their partner disappears or dies. They breed in the cirque during the frigid conditions of February and March, which means they may be incubating eggs when there is snow on the ground and temperatures that sometimes plummet below 20 degrees Fahrenheit.

They do not, however, attempt to raise another brood in May or June like other birds in this high-mountain world, even though conditions would be warmer and seem more favorable. This evolutionary adaptation allows the jays more time for collecting and storing food to see them through the harsh winters of their snowbound cirque.

So it is that on February 17th, the resident male jay, after perching in several trees near the edge of the meadow while looking for a suitable spot, selected the site for their nest. After searching for most of the morning, he picked a site 19 feet above the ground in an Engelmann spruce on the south-facing edge of an opening in the forest, where three, old firs succumbed to heavy snow and ice in years past. This location provided the nest and its occupants with extra warmth from the sun's light.

The male was in charge of the early stages of nest building. He started by making a loose ball-like foundation of spruce and fir twigs pulled off the trees and held together with webbing from forest tent caterpillars and spiders. The initial phase completed, his mate joined him in adding a ring of twigs above the foundation, filling it in with finer twigs, strips of bark, moss, and lichens, as well as a few feathers and hair. From there on out, the female did an increasing amount of the work, and by the end of the three-week process on March 10th, she had contributed more than her partner. The finished nest was six inches high, with a cup two inches deep and three inches across. During that time, the pair had been living largely off last year's food caches.

By the 17th of March, the female had laid 5 eggs. The smooth, pale greenish-white shells were heavily speckled with dark olive spots. From then on, until they hatched on the 3rd of April, her mate brought food to the nest and fed her. The hatchlings were helpless; their eyes were closed; each pale bill had an egg tooth (a tooth-like, structure on the tip of the bill used by a baby to break out of its egg); and their pale, pink skin was sparsely covered with down feathers. Consequently, their mother stayed on the nest an additional 4 days, until the 7th of April, when she joined her mate in feeding them.

Thereafter, until they fledge on April 26th, both parents fed the nestlings a dark brown, viscous paste carried in their throats, which was comprised primarily of partially digested arthropods, such as insects and spiders, at least some of which were gleaned from cached stores of last year's food. However, the nestlings grew most rapid from the fourth through the tenth day following hatching, when they became dark-gray juveniles with gray bills and white stripes on their cheeks.

Thus, in spite of such rigorous conditions, gray jays have a high rate of success in raising their young, which typically leave the nest in late April, well before most birds begin nesting in the cirque. Their success is in part because stored food enables nesting jays to feed their young even during a mountain blizzard.

In turn, if much of the previous year's stored food lasts until the onset of cold temperatures, storing more food would mean that early-nesting jays have a better chance of making it through the long, seemingly foodless mountain winter by staying home and avoiding the dangers of migration. Moreover, early nesting, in which a single brood is produced, means more time and effort is available for storing additional food in their territory before the following winter.

The young jays initially huddled together for warmth when they left their nest on April 26th. Then, gradually, they started moving through the forest as part of a cohesive family group. But when they were 55 days old, the 28th of May (five weeks out of the nest), they began fighting among themselves for the privilege of staying with the parents beyond the breeding season, and within ten days, the 7th of June, the dominant juvenile had expelled its siblings from the home territory.

Thus, by the time Storm Hawk arrives in the cirque, the juvenile gray jays are divided into a "stayer" (the dominant sibling) and "leavers" (the subordinate, expelled siblings). In this case, the dominant juvenile will continue to accompany its parents through the first fall and winter (and perhaps longer), thereby benefiting from both their experience and protection—using its parent's territory as a safe haven, without competition, until a nearby territory becomes available.

The displaced siblings, on the other hand, went looking for unrelated adult pairs whose own nests had failed, hoping to be adopted into their own safe havens. If a young bird is still hanging around the following year, the breeding pair prevents it from approaching the nest, but may allow it to help feed the new nestlings once they fledge.

Because gray jays typically breed for the first time when they are two years old, the surviving members of this year's brood will not be raising young of their own until long after Storm Hawk has departed for home, and the essence of his sojourn forever erased from the cirque.

July 1st

Then, on the fifth day of Storm Hawk's search, something unexpected happens as he walks to the stream to wash his face and fill the deer bladder. He steps on something hard and smooth buried within many seasons of growing and dying vegetation within a few yards of the stream. Because he is focused on getting water, it does not register as anything unusual. That night, however, after a sojourn of almost two months in the cirque, his dreamscape becomes more precise in that a single circle of stones stands out from the rest.

July 2nd

Storm Hawk is jerked awake just before the last twinkling of the stars fades into the coming of day—the stone circle emblazed in his mind. Why the stone circle? What does it mean? Then he remembers the rotten tree in the lower meadow. "Stone circle. Rotten tree. Stone Circle. Rotten tree. Stone circle. Hard, smooth spot in the meadow by the stream!"

Leaping up, he grabs his bow and quiver and heads to the stream just as the sun is peeking over the eastern horizon. "I have to find that hard spot."

Reaching the stream, he realizes that he is not in the same location as yesterday; so he looks both upstream and downstream to see if there are any familiar landmarks to guide him. Seeing none, he searches upstream, then downstream, then upstream again. His hope waning, he sits on a small boulder on the stream's bank and faces his camp, when he notices one of the trees has a broken top, and he realizes that he walked next to that tree as he left camp yesterday.

Jumping to his feet, he goes just far enough downstream to align himself with the tree, after which he tries to determine exactly where he reached the stream. Then he sees the flattened spot in the vegetation, where some of the flower stems have been broken, and he remembers sitting there while contemplating how to proceed with his search.

Sitting again in the same place, he wonders why the stone circle was the only symbol in his dream and not a rotting tree as well. After all, the stories told of a group of trees surrounding the old camp.

What Storm Hawk could not know is that the camp, periodically maintained until 1483, was destroyed when lightning struck the clump of firs twice in one summer, and the resulting fire immediately destroyed most of the mature trees. The three firs that survived were so weakened that the severe windstorm of 1487 blew them over, and they lay guarding the secret of the ancient fire-ring of stones. Being small trees with soft wood, they recycled into the meadow as the decades passed. Somewhere in time they disappeared altogether, leaving behind a simple circle of stones guarded by the meadow's seasonal vegetation, where the grasses and flowers continually bear mute testimony to the daydream-like vision of a youth 575 years ago in the year 1000.

Then, the little voice in his heart tells him to consider how close to the stream he might have been when he felt the hard lump in the vegetation. Getting up, he walks a ways back toward the tree with the broken top while consciously feeling the contour of the meadow beneath his moccasins.

Thinking he has gone too far, he marks the spot by trampling the vegetation. He then turns around and walks back toward the stream, but just to the left of where he was. Reaching the stream, he turns around and repeats the procedure by walking a little to the left of his last trail. He thus continues to search for a couple of hours before he decides the stone circle must be to the right of his original path from the broken-topped tree. Again he walks back and forth, again without results. Thoroughly discouraged, he goes back toward camp.

He is about to reach the broken-topped tree when the voice of his heart tells him to turn off his mind and simply enjoy the beauty around him as he walks back to the stream. He does as his heart bids, and about three-quarters of the way back he feels a hard lump underfoot. Stopping, he gets down on his hands and knees and begins pulling out the vegetation. And there he finds the first rounded rock of the ancient fire circle.

He looks at the rock for a moment, and in that moment is overcome with a deep sense of mystical connection to the meadow. He then carefully, reverently begins to pull out the vegetation covering not only the stones but also where the fires used to burn. To his surprise, he finds bits of charcoal from the campfires that warmed his ancestors in the time of far memory.

Looking skyward, he gives thanks to the Great Spirit, and in return hears whispering voices in the ethers from those whose spirits still visit this place with love and gratitude for the times they were graced by the beauty and abundance of the meadow, stream, and forest.

So it is, on this 2nd day of July, in the year 1575, that Storm Hawk forever becomes one with the Omnipresent Spirit of the universe within him. Sensing this inner harmony, he spends the next few days visiting various parts of the meadow and its connection to the cirque, sitting often in deep inner peace and silence, as the stillness of Nature descends around him.

July 10th

Seated quietly on a rock amid a scattering of lodge pole pines near the place he has been camping, he hears a faint *chick-a-zee-zee, zee*. Looking toward the tree, he sees several tiny birds with black caps and white stripes over their eyes flitting through high branches, where they hang upside down, as they pluck insects from the pine's needles, all the while scolding *chick-a-dee-dee-dee* as they go.

Mountain Chickadee

Adults of both sexes are between 3⁴⁄₁₀ and 5½ inches long and weigh ⁴⁄₁₀ of an ounce. Males, females, and juveniles share the same plumage, which consists of a black cap joining a black stripe through their eyes almost to the beak, and a distinctive white stripe above their eyes and below the black cap. Their backs and flanks are gray, and their underparts and sides are light gray to buff. They have a short, black beak; white cheeks; and black throats. Their tails are long and narrow, and they have full, rounded wings with a typical span of about 7½ inches. (Photo 7.18)

7.18 Mountain chickadee.

Although their normal call is a hoarse *chick-a-zee-zee, zee*, at times it sounds like *cheese-bur-ger, cheese-bur-ger*. At other times it is a throaty *chick-adee-dee-dee*. Their spring song, however, is a 3-noted *fee-bee-bee*, with the *bees* at a lower pitch.

On cold, sunny mornings, which are relatively frequent in the high-mountain world of the cirque, they catch a little extra warmth by sitting in the sun on an exposed perch out of the wind. On the other hand, they typically brave cold nights, huddled in dense foliage or under big, loose flakes of bark.

The cirque's mountain chickadees forage by hopping on outer twigs and branches, gleaning the surfaces or probing into crevices for food. Quick, agile, and curious they hop and flit through the outer twigs, as they look for insects and seeds, frequently accompanied by other species. Constantly on the move, these little, acrobatic insect-gleaners often hang upside-down on the undersides of branches, cones, and needles as they search for something edible. In addition, they cling to a tree's bark while searching for tasty morsels. What's more, the chickadees are so maneuverable they can do a U-turn in a space as small as that of a large, abandoned woodpecker cavity.

During warm months in the cirque, the chickadees eat a variety of protein-rich insects, including beetles, caterpillars, wasp larvae, aphids, and leafhoppers, as well as hard-to-reach scale insects and fly larvae hidden in plant galls. In addition, they also eat spiders and their eggs, supplementing the animal food with berries, seeds, and nuts as they become available, breaking the seeds and nuts open by hammering them with their beaks.

As summer's warmth wanes, they begin collecting and storing conifer seeds just as soon as they become available, at which time the necessity of defending their caches promotes group territoriality, including hierarchical dominance within a group to dictate the social organization. This territoriality may well be critical to their survival during the winter because energetic models show that a half-ounce chickadee requires about 10 calories per day to survive, which is equivalent to about one-twentieth of an ounce of peanut butter. Nevertheless, the chickadees form feeding flocks with kinglets and nuthatches, in which the birds follow each other one by one from tree to tree.

Mountain chickadees are monogamous and territorial for the breeding season, forming pairs in September or by early spring, when those who had migrated to lower elevations for the winter begin arriving back in the cirque. Migrants not only return to the same social groups of unrelated birds in the spring but also tend to mate within these social groups year after year.

Being hole-nesters, they use the abandoned cavities of woodpeckers and nuthatches, as well as other natural cavities, although they sometimes excavate a hollow in soft, rotten wood. While they will not return to a previous, failed nest site, they may re-use successful sites in subsequent years. In this connection, the male shows his mate a number of sites, from which she selects one. Thereafter, the territorial defense around the chosen cavity encompasses 16 acres.

Having selected one of last year's, hard-walled woodpecker cavities as protection against predators, the female began building her nest on the 1st of May. Within the cavity, she made a circular base of rotten wood chips and grass, to which she added loose fur gleaned from mammal droppings. When enough materials had been accumulated, she molded a distinct cup into the material, and lastly created a fur cap with which to cover the eggs and young when she left the nest. (Incidentally, a pair of mountain chickadees further down in the forest had to settle for a large hollow in a tall, rotting stump. In this case, the female filled the cavity with several inches of rotten wood and fur to insulate the interior and help keep the temperature warm enough for her brood.)

Her nest finished on the 6th of May, she laid her first egg on the 7th, and laid one egg each day thereafter until her clutch of eight eggs was completed on the 14th. The eggs were smooth, oval, and a flat white. She incubated them for 15 days, until the 29th, when they began to hatch, at which time the babies were naked and helpless, with their eyes closed and tufts of down on their heads and along their spines. They could lift their heads when two days old, beg for food by day three, and open their eyes when they were six days old. As the chicks aged, they began quivering their wings when begging for food.

During this time, and for the first few days after the young hatch, her mate brought her food so she could remain with the chicks until they are fully feathered, when 10 and 11 days old. Then, covering them with the fur cap, she departed and joined her mate in securing food (a duty wherein the parents demonstrated significant individuality in the kinds of prey they selected) and in feeding the brood. They not only both fed the youngsters continually until they were ready to fledge and leave the nest on the 18th of June but also kept the nest clean by removing the chicks' fecal sacs, that is until a day or two prior to their fledging, when the parents allowed the feces to accumulate in the nest.

A fecal sac is a mucous membrane, which is generally white or clear with a dark end, that contains a nestling's feces. This behavior allows parent birds to keep their nest clean by removing the chicks' excrement. The nestlings, in turn, usually produce their fecal sacs within seconds after being fed. If not, a waiting adult may prod them into doing so.

Once out of the nest, the juveniles remain within their parents nesting territory until the 10th of July, when they take off on their own. As summer draws to a close in the cirque, the mountain chickadees will band together into groups of two and three pairs of adults, plus a variety of juveniles. These juveniles, having spent some time traveling in their own groups, will join a group of adults by September, at which time the group will begin to turn into a mixed-species-feeding flock that will remain together throughout most of the winter. In late winter and early spring, however, pairs will start to break away from foraging flocks and begin making their way up the mountain to the cirque, where they will commence to inspect—and claim—possible nesting sites and establish their seasonal territories.

Having completed his spiritual quest, the time has come for Storm Hawk to leave the meadow and begin his journey home. It is now late afternoon, and he is just approaching the edge of the forest, when he stops for the last time and faces the meadow and the ancient campsite it has for so long hidden within itself. Finally, he turns and follows the stream into the forest. (Photo 7.19)

7.19 The stream through the forest will lead Storm Hawk to the valley below on his way home.

Approaching the place where he shot the fawn on the 24th of June, he is momentarily drawn into the memory of another fawn, one he saw on a clear, cool night two years ago during a full Moon. Now, suddenly, he was once again lying against the large log under a small, bark lean-to at the edge of a little, grassy clearing in a virgin forest of huge, ancient trees. Since he had no fire and was downwind, the doe did not detect his presence, as she quietly crossed the small, grassy clearing and stopped within twenty feet of his head. Between them, a bright shaft of moonlight filtered through the tall firs and lighted a small place in the clearing.

As the doe started feeding, her fawn discovered the moonbeam. With head outstretched and nostrils flaring, it approached the light, its legs stiff and tucked well beneath its body for instant flight. The youngster "snorted" suddenly and fled to its mother, whose head snapped erect at the sound. The fawn nursed, and the doe returned to eating.

During the next half hour or so, the fawn alternately struck the light with its forefeet, kicked it with its hind feet while twisting sideways in the air, and raced through it. These feats of daring were often interrupted by sudden returns to its mother. At such times, the fawn went to the far side of the doe and, with its head under her belly, observed the moonbeam from safety. After a few seconds, however, it again engaged the light. As the doe gradually drifted away from the light, the fawn ceased its play.

Somewhere, a twig snaps. Storm Hawk is jerked back to the present. Shaking himself gently, he smiles and lets the memory slide into the dim light of yesteryear, after which he once again focuses on his journey.

The days pass quietly in the meadow and along the stream flowing from the lake, as Storm Hawk makes his way home. And so, the human dimension passes out of the cirque, and the fluid rhythms of Nature remain, rhythms in the eternal present without the human construct of time, rhythms that just flow without the need of an explanation to the human mind. As for Storm Hawk, wherever he goes from this day forward, his life is forever changed by the mystical connection with those who went before, those who will forever travel with him in spirit and guide the wisdom of his steps throughout the remaining years of his sojourn on Earth.

In essence, no one knows the exact instance an idea presents itself and forever changes one's life, and so the world. Just as Storm Hawk's time in the cirque forever changed his experience of life, so had his visit forever changed the cirque—if for no other reason than the animals he killed to feed himself lost their ability to further experience and thus influence the biophysical dynamics of the cirque, as they would have done had they lived to blend into its evolution and pass on generations of their kind to do the same.

Chapter 8: Life In the Cirque After Storm Hawk's Departure

FROM THE DAY STORM HAWK left the cirque on his journey home to this day, the campsite remains secreted within the protective vegetation of the meadow, which guards the sacred memories of centuries past. With Storm Hawk's departure, no human would see the meadow until I tracked the deer to its border 375 years later. From that day to this, no one has set foot in the cirque—including me. Therefore, all life within the cirque, as well as its biophysical processes, are entrained in the eternal moment—in the inviolable here and now—because that is all there is.

And so the human notion of time—wherein is contained the penchant for marking the hours, days, months, and years—passes out of the cirque and is replaced by the seasonal rhythms that have, over the multitude of centuries, guided its evolution. In essence, everything the cirque and its life have known—or ever will know—is the Eternal Moment, which transcends time. With this reality in mind, I have still incorporated our human concept of time into the narrative in a general sense so that you, the reader, will be able to relate to the seasonal changes in the sequential language you understand.

When Flowers Dance

The universal cycle of expansion and contraction becomes clearly visible throughout the seasons in the meadow with the melting of winter's snow and the awakening of plant life hidden in the earth, a cycle that dawned long ago in the dim reaches of an evolving Earth, long before the human story began. Prior to the first flower that graced the world, Earth was dominated by non-flowering, seed-bearing plants with cone-like structures, such as pine trees and ginkgos, which first appeared in the fossil record about 360 million years ago. The cones produced by these trees were either male or female, unlike the flowers of the meadow, which contain both male and female parts. Nevertheless, a male pinecone has almost everything that a flower has in terms of its genetic wiring. That said, the flower of the avocado tree is a genetic fossil, which still carries the archaic instructions that would have allowed the transformation from cones into flowers.

When flowering plants first appeared on Earth, around 240 million years ago, the atmospheric concentration of carbon dioxide was relatively low. However, the evolution of dense venation in the leaves substantially increased the effectiveness in the "plumbing system," and thus their ability to draw water from the soil. In turn, their leaves were more effective than non-flowering plants in their ability to convert sunlight, carbon dioxide, and water into energy through photosynthesis, thus providing evolutionary leverage over competing species, a self-reinforcing feedback loop. This feedback loop has profound significance for the continued evolution of flowering plants, like those painting the meadow of the cirque with a symphony of color.

Flowering plants have had, and still have, help in their evolution from the insects and birds that pollinate them in that different pollinators have preferences for distinct variations in a flower's shape. For example, large bees in the meadow prefer flowers with narrow petals. Small bees have a preference for wider flowers, whereas the bee flies select rounded flowers. Thus, depending on the type of pollinators common in an area, a flower's shape can vary significantly within different populations across a landscape. In addition, flowers create scent trails to lead pollinators, such as moths and bees, to the floral rewards of nectar and pollen. The result of such dynamic relationships between flowers and their pollinators is an ever-evolving, geographic mosaic of different floral shapes and colors (such as those of the yellow buttercup and blue gentian) augmented by the tendency of a specific plant to have a higher output of nectar and pollen, and thereby cater to the pollinator that prefers its particular shape in a given area.

Although flowers pollinated by birds, such as the hummingbirds of the meadow, initially evolved to suit the vision of insects, they have more recently shifted towards the longer wavelengths of red signals, which are inconspicuous to some insects that are poor pollinators, while simultaneously enhancing the discrimination of the bird that pollinates them.

So it is that the creativity of flowers, designed through the millennia, is written in secret within each and every seed produced by the duet of flower and pollinator. So it is that each seed brings within its coat the scripted artistry of the ages to enliven Nature's mural with the intricacy of form and to dazzle it with the primary colors of red, yellow, and blue; the secondary colors of green, orange, and purple; and every shade in between.

If you could see inside the seed of a flower in the meadow, what would you find? If you could read the encryption in the seed's DNA, you would discover the history of an unbroken chain of evolutionary trial-and-error experiments that have endured for millennia, and the seed you hold is not only the pinnacle of that experiment but also a totally unique form of life. Why? Because, each and every seed is, always has been, and always will be totally different from every other seed in the characteristics it possesses—even from seeds in the same pod. And this refers to characteristics beyond a flower's shape; palette of colors; scent trail; amount, flavor, and season of nectar; and shape and amount of pollen.

In addition, you would find that each seed includes the formula for its shape, size, consistency, and mode of dispersal: by wind, as a fleshy huckleberry eaten and defecated by a rodent or bird, or garnered and buried by a chipmunk. You would find its season of germination, the plant's growth, and demise; its physical structure and chemical composition; the odor and flavor of its leaves, stem, and roots; the viable longevity of its seeds on or in the soil; as well as the nature of the soil in which it grows. These are but a few of the genetic nuances archived in every seed throughout the corridors of time into everlasting.

In this eternal moment, however, an unusually cold stillness descends quietly over the cirque, as July 4th blends into July 5th, and the star bedecked vault of the night sky stares, winks, and twinkles. Time passes, and the day's first light, traveling 186,000 miles per second (700 million miles per hour), left the sun 8.3 minutes ago, and is just now beginning to shine on the drops of dew clinging to the yellow, red, blue, orange, pink, purple, white, and multi-colored flowers of the meadow and crowning the maturing green of the grasses.

The rising sun causes the meadow to sparkle, as the light is reflected off the drops of water, which turn into miniature rainbows as the sun's light is refracted into different wavelengths. The still mountain air begins to stir, as warm breezes make their way upslope from the valley below, causing the grasses to sway and the flowers to nod and bow in a gentle dance of delicate shapes and vibrant colors choreographed through the millennia by the finger of evolution.

Seen from above, the meadow of dancing flowers and softly swaying grasses is a vista of beauty and peace. But, under this vista of splendor, a vastly different scene meets the eye—the life and death struggle between a male wandering shrew and a Cascade earthworm. The shrew detected the worm while investigating odors amidst the slowly decomposing flowers and grasses of seasons past along the forest's edge.

Having found the worm, he pauses for a second, and then begins exploring it. Suddenly, without warning, he attacks, biting it several times along its body. The writhing of the injured worm elicits another attack. Again he pauses, but the worm's attempt to escape brings on a third lightening attack.

After several more attacks, the worm's reactions slow and the shrew starts eating it from one end, biting, chewing, and pulling off small pieces. His immediate hunger quelled, he chews the remainder of the worm into three pieces of about equal length and carries them, one at a time, to his nest in a nook under a small boulder, where they are stored for a future meal. On his last trip, however, he is distracted by a slight movement of the grass along the runway, which causes him to drop the piece of worm, but continue to his nest, where the rest of the worm is stored. Only then does he retrace his path and retrieve the last piece of worm.

The Wandering Shrew

These little shrews are usually somewhere between about 3½ and 4½ inches long and weigh between a tenth and a quarter of an ounce. (Photo 8.1) They have relatively short fur that varies on the back from a light grayish-brown in summer to a dark, grayish-brown in winter. Their undersides are usually light gray and sometimes have a silvery sheen. The tops of their feet vary from tan to brown. The hairy tails of young animals are slightly two-toned, brownish above, tannish below, and darker at the tips. The naked tails of old shrews have the same coloration. In addition, the front teeth (incisors) of both young and old individuals are dark reddish-brown.

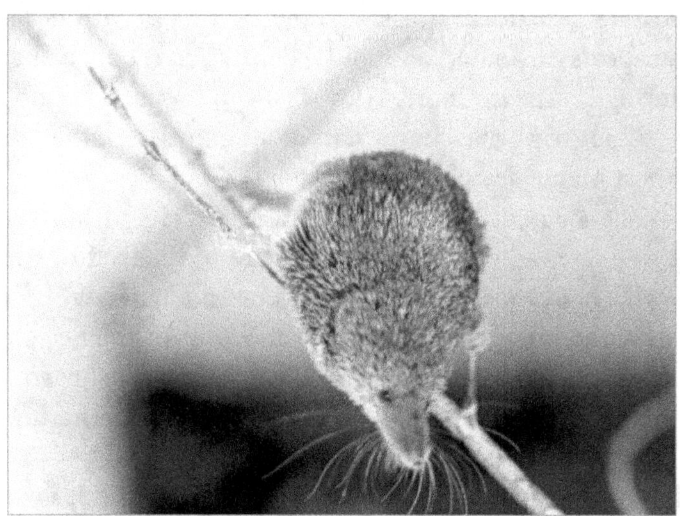

8.1 Wandering shrew.

Active both day and night, these shrews appear to be intolerant of one another and usually practice mutual avoidance, except during their breeding season, which extends in the cirque from late spring to early autumn. The rest of the year, mutual avoidance and defense of nests may facilitate spacing of individuals, and may help determine the frequency with which an individual shrew comes into contact with strangers. When contacts are frequent, a shrew tends to shift its area of activity to one that is less crowded.

Today, the 9th of July, a female shrew finds an abandoned montane vole's burrow that extends part way under a flat piece of rock that cascaded off the cliff in the vicinity of the raven's nest at the upper edge of the meadow. The burrow has been vacant ever since the female raven captured the vole on the 15th of June and took it to her nest.

After a brief exploration of the cover provided by the burrow, which extends about a foot under the rock, the female, having been bred on the 26th of June and thus conscious of the embryos within her, begins to build her nursery nest, which will contain finer materials than those used only for sleeping quarters by adults. Searching the meadow within a few feet of the rock, she collects bits of dry grass and an occasional piece of moss with her mouth and transports the material to a little depression scooped out by the vole during its short tenure. Although she drops a piece of grass on one of her trips, she simply continues empty mouthed directly to the nest before searching for more.

Having accumulated a pile of grass and bits of moss of sufficient size, she rapidly arranges them around herself by grasping pieces with her mouth and tucking them under and alongside her body. She also periodically digs into the floor of the nest, forcing material to the rear or side. By constantly turning as she works, she forms a cup, the sides of which gradually come together to create a roof over her head.

Hungry from the exertion of constructing her nest, she begins hunting along the vole's old runway. Detecting a grasshopper eating a meal of juicy vegetation along the side of the runway, she swiftly attacks, biting the hapless insect through its neck. The grasshopper is too big to easily carry, so she chews it open along its underside and eats the soft body parts, leaving the hard external skeleton as refuse.

Although she eats numerous spiders, two bugs, and several kinds of beetles over the next few days, her real boon comes four days later, on July 13th, when she chances across a dead vole. Biting and chewing, as she pushes against the carcass with her forefeet while tossing her head up and down and from side to side, she satisfies her immediate hunger. Thereafter, she returns again and again to the carcass until there is nothing edible left.

8.2 Young wandering shrews in their nest.

Since wandering shrews have high-energy requirements, they spend most of their active time searching for food. To equal a shrew's consumption of food, a 150-pound man would have to eat 250 pounds of food per day. The mutual-avoidance behavior of these shrews may therefore be beneficial, both in conserving energy that might otherwise by expended in fighting and in limiting competition for a given supply of food in a particular area.

Then, on the 15th of July, 20 days after being bred, the female gives birth to seven babies, each born naked, blind, and weighing less than $\frac{2}{100}$ of an ounce. The young grow rapidly, beginning to develop fur on their backs within two weeks and opening their eyes in three weeks. (Photo 8.2) Although the young shrews are weaned between 16 and 25 days following their birth, they remain in their nest for about a month, during which time their major activity is huddling together, thereby conserving body heat. (Photo 8.3) Once they leave their birth nest, however, few will survive their second winter and reach two years of age.

8.3 Young wandering shrews huddling together in their nest to keep warm.

Of Earthworms and the Meadow

The rocks and soil that were gouged out, chewed up, frozen, compacted, and re-deposited by the glacier 10,000 years ago, became the seedbed of the meadow, but had no earthworms in it. Thus, the plant communities that became established in the glacial till did so without the aid of Cascade earthworms. Considering that an earthworm moves at a top speed of about 5½ yards a year, it took centuries for the worms to occupy the meadow soil, and then primarily in those areas that remain moist throughout most of the year.

From front to back, the basic shape of a Cascade earthworm is a cylindrical tube a few inches long. As an invertebrate, it lacks a skeleton, but maintains its structure with internal, fluid-filled chambers that function as a hydrostatic skeleton—from the Greek *hydra* "water" and *stations* "causing to stand."

Its outer body is divided into a series of segments, each of which (except for the mouth and anus) carries claw-like bristles. Movement is achieved with the aide of an impressive muscle system that allows the worm to extend its front end, swell it to fill the circumference of its tunnel, causing the bristles to grip the soil, and then contracting its rear half. In addition, the secretion of lubricating mucus aids its movement. Be that as it may, a worm sometimes makes gurgling noises when disturbed as it moves through its lubricated tunnels, which allows an attentive raven on the ground to locate and capture it for a meal.

Although the worms mix the soil in their burrowing, thereby creating myriad passageways through which air and water infiltrate the soil to the benefit of the meadow's plants, they remain in their u-shaped tunnels during the day because the sun's ultraviolet rays immobilize them and ultimately dry out their moist, light, reddish-brown skin through which they breathe, taking in oxygen and releasing carbon dioxide. Eyeless and living in the dark, they sense light with their skin, and earless, they are extremely sensitive to vibrations. Their senses of taste and touch, however, are well developed.

The worms speed up decomposition in the cirque through consuming dead plant material and by pulling organic matter, such as a leaf, below the surface, where it is deposited either for food or used to plug the burrow. In addition, they also ingest soil particles that are small enough—including sand grains up to $\frac{1}{20}$ of an inch—into their gizzards, wherein those minute fragments of grit grind everything into a fine paste, which is then digested in the intestine. So food enters the mouth and passes into the gizzard, where strong muscular contractions grind the food with the help of mineral particles ingested along with the food. Once through the gizzard, food continues through the intestine for digestion.

Thus, when a worm defecates on the surface or deeper in the soil, minerals and plant nutrients are changed into an accessible form that nourishes plants. As such, earthworm feces are richer in available nitrogen, phosphates, and potassium than the surrounding upper six inches of soil.

Earthworms are hermaphrodites, meaning that each individual carries both male and female sexual organs. Adult earthworms develop a belt-like glandular swelling (termed a "clitellum") that covers several segments toward the front part of the animal. Mating occurs on the soil's surface, most often at night, although copulation and reproduction are separate processes. The mating pair overlaps the undersides of their front ends, and exchange sperm with each other. (Photo 8.4)

8.4 Copulating earthworms: note the belt-like glandular swelling and the white sperm the worms are exchanging at the glandular swelling, called a "clitellum."

Some time after copulation, long after the worms have separated, the belt-like swelling secretes material that forms a ring around the worm. The worm then backs out of the ring, simultaneously injecting its own eggs and the other worm's sperm into it. As the worm slips out of the ring, the ends seal to form a vaguely lemon-shaped incubator cocoon in which the embryonic worms develop. They emerge as small, fully formed worms, but lack sex structures until they are around 60 to 90 days of age. They attain full size in about one year and may live four to eight years, acting as caretakers of the meadow's soil.

The 16th of July dawns cool, but with a promise to warm quickly as the sun advances toward it zenith. Meanwhile, in the cool soil of the forest, a tiny disturbance is taking place alongside an ancient fallen tree that has lain gradually decomposing on the forest floor for more than three centuries. A little ridge of soil moves tentatively alongside the fallen tree accompanied by a tiny, reddish-pink nose that pokes through the roof of the tunnel and sniffs the air. A miniature, female mole, with the general appearance of a shrew (hence the name "shrew-mole"), appears briefly on the forest floor, only to disappear almost immediately back into the loose, sod-free topsoil from which she came and continue her rummaging for some tasty morsel of food, such as an earthworm.

Shrew-Mole

The smallest North American mole, it is often mistaken for a shrew. Thus, the common name, "shrew-mole," is apt since this little mammal has a combination of shrew-like pelage, composed of both guard hairs and underfur, and the large head, strong teeth, and broad front feet of a mole.

The shrew-mole is four to five inches long and weighs from ⅕ to ⅖ of an ounce. Its long, tapering nose is sparsely covered with fine hair, except for the tip, which is naked, reddish, and has a nostril on each side. Its ears are merely holes located near the shoulders and are seldom visible because of the dense fur, and its minute eyes are also nearly concealed by fur. Its front feet are broad with stout claws adapted for digging, like its larger cousins. The three middle claws on all feet are longer than the outer claws. (Photo 8.5)

8.5 Shrew-mole. Note the red snout, tiny eye, and slightly outward-facing front feet with their long digging claws.

Although definitely constricted at the base, the tail is relatively thick. It is encircled with rows of scales and covered with sparse, long, coarse hairs. In color, the tail resembles the pelage, which is thick, relatively soft, and almost uniform in color, varying from dark, brownish-gray to blackish-gray. In certain lights, the long, glossy guard hairs shine like metal.

At this moment, the little female is in the process of digging shallow, trough-like burrows roofed by the decaying vegetation on the forest floor by the fallen tree, forming a complex, intersecting network through which she regularly travels in search of food. As she digs, she pushes aside the earth with lateral motions of her forefeet. Using one foot at a time, she rotates her body at a 45-degree angle and forms the burrow by pressing aside and packing the loose, damp earth. She is an excellent digger because she is incredibly strong and can vertically lift almost 7 ounces, 20 times her own weight. She makes her way through loose litter on the surface of the ground by pushing the litter sideways with her forefeet and pushing her body forward with her hind feet.

Touch seems the most developed of her senses. Her flexible

nose guides her in much the same way as a blind person uses a cane. Her nose, in almost constant motion, quickly identifies each object it contacts. The gentlest contact of an object by one of the sensitive whiskers on her nose or face causes an immediate response. Debris adhering to a whisker makes her almost frantic in an effort to remove the material with her forefeet. The stiff hairs that encircle the openings of her ears are also sensitive to touch, as are the long, stiff hairs on her tail. Furthermore, her hearing is adapted to the sounds made by the invertebrates on which she feeds.

Most of her active time is spent in a ceaseless quest for food, and she may eat more than her own weight in a 12-hour period. Her greatest motivator, therefore, is her own appetite.

When hunting for food, she rummages through decaying litter, turns leaves and debris, investigates crevices, and patrols her burrows. She may climb into low vegetation and search the foliage for food, and may search both the accessible inner and outer areas of the fallen tree. Her ever-active nose, which aids her hunting, is thrown high in the air, twisted to one side or the other, rapped on the ground, or hooked under her body. Although nose rapping appears to be a characteristic of her hunting on the ground, the tapping sound made by nose rapping is not altogether beneficial. One shrew-mole, in another part of the forest, augmented its own demise by rapping its nose in dead alder leaves along the stream, thereby helping a hunting screech owl to locate it.

Encountering an earthworm along the fallen tree, the little mole strips it through her forefeet, presumably to clean off the soil, and then begins eating it from one end to the other. Once in awhile, however, she meets a large worm and simply bites off a small piece off the tail, chews and swallows it before pursuing the maimed creature for another bite, which gives the worm a chance to escape. While eating, she uses her forefeet not only to hold food but also to arrange the food in her mouth.

When insect pupae are encountered in her tunnel, she hooks them with her nose. Adult insects, on the other hand, are often struck repeated blows with her forefeet or simply covered with soil, whereas centipedes are grabbed by the head and eaten. (Photo 8.6) Beetles, ants, and slugs are refused outright. Earthworms, however, account for 40 to 50 percent of her diet.

8.6 Centipede.

Satiated from having eaten the worm, she constructs a tiny opening, too small to admit her body, in the roof of a shallow burrow just under the protective cover of the fallen tree. Immediately beneath this tiny ventilation duct, she digs a slightly larger chamber in which to sleep.

Although currently resting in a shallow chamber, she constructs deep burrows, but not as often as she does shallow ones. The deep, narrow burrows branch, intersect, and cross one another at various levels, but seldom go as deep as a foot below the surface of the soil. This burrow system contains a larger chamber built at the level of the water table between the tree and the stream along which it fell. The chamber is about five inches in diameter, with an arched ceiling about three inches high, and is close enough to the water table to have a soft, level, mud floor.

Her nest is a simple affair. She grasps small pieces of vegetation with her mouth and takes them to a selected place. When a sufficient pile of material is accumulated, she hollows out a cuplike depression in the material by moving around and tucking some of the material around herself with her mouth. To sleep, she places her feet under her body fairly close together and tucks her snout and head beneath her body between her forelegs. Her weight is thus borne by the top of her head and by her hindquarters, while her tail is placed around one side of her body. When resting, her nose is relaxed and flat against the ground. Periods of relaxation are occasionally interrupted when she raises her nose and half-heartedly sniffs the air, or scratches herself vigorously with a forefoot or hind foot.

Her periods of activity are interspersed with periods of rest and sleep. The periods of rest and sleep are longest and most frequent when her appetite is satiated, and shortest and least frequent when she is hungry. Periods of rest range from 1 to 8 minutes at irregular intervals from 2 to 18 minutes apart.

When awake, she moves in a slow walk with momentary pauses. To progress, she bends her elongated claws of her forefeet underneath the feet so that she actually walks on the backs of her foreclaws. She is not only graceful on the ground but also is a capable climber and spends time climbing about investigating the inside of an old pileated woodpecker nest cavity that now lies with its entrance near the forest floor under the fallen tree.

When frightened, she makes an incredibly swift, scuttling dash for cover, where she remains crouched and, except for rapid breathing, absolutely still. If not too badly frightened, she faces the disturbance with one forefoot raised and her mouth open.

This tiny mole is a good swimmer and sometimes explores along the edge of the stream. One day, while burrowing under the litter on the forest floor above the stream bank, she gets too close to the water and a falling branch from an ancient tree knocks her and a bit of bank into the stream. Surprised, she "flies" through the water with powerful movements of all four feet. Using the feet on each side of her body alternately, she creates an undulating motion with her body and tail. Her forward motion is so great that her head and fully two-thirds of her body are above the water.

The cirque's shrew-moles appear to be reproductively active throughout the year, but most reproduction takes place between early March and mid May. Although litters range in size from one to five, three or four is probably the norm.

So it is that by the first of May the female gives birth to four youngsters in a nest she has constructed in the soil a foot and a half below the fallen tree. The nest is made of damp willow leaves, which she collected one at a time along the stream's bank.

The babies are naked and pink at birth, lack whiskers, and weigh but a fraction of an ounce. Their eyes are merely prominent black spots under a transparent covering of skin, and their external ear openings are not yet evident. Their broad forefeet are fleshy and paddle-like, and the tops of the digits are soft and blunt, with no sign of claws.

As a baby's fur begins to grow, its skin becomes bluish to blackish with developing hair, which, upon eruption, is dark bluish-black, soft, and down-like. The fur is especially short on the upper parts, where it is almost silvery-gray. The feet and nose are still pink, and the skin of the anal region is much folded. The tail is relatively long, thick, and bluish-violet. The forefeet are turned out, with the palms away from the body. Thus it is that another generation of shrew-moles is added to the cirque's diversity of life. There is, however, yet another connoisseur of worms in the cirque, the coast mole, which is not only considerably larger than the shrew-mole but also equally at home in both the forest and the meadow along the forest's edge.

Coast Mole

While the shrew-mole is rummaging in the forest, its larger cousin, a coast mole, is extending its own burrow system in the meadow along the forest's edge, as it too searches for food. The coast mole, also known as the Pacific mole, is so named because J.G. Cooper caught the first scientific specimen on August 30, 1855, at Shoalwater Bay (= Willapa Bay), Pacific County, in the state of Washington.

Coast moles have long, tapering snouts, cylindrical bodies, and minute eyes. Their ears are simply holes near the shoulders concealed by dense fur. (Photo 8.7) A keen sense of directional ground vibrations compensate for weak sight. They have broad front feet, the toes of which terminate in stout claws adapted for digging. The forelegs and shoulders are anatomically modified in such a way that the front feet, except those of shrew-moles, are permanently turned out.

8.7 Coast mole. Note the long snout and the broad, outward-facing front feet with their strong digging claws.

The pelage is composed of soft, flexible hairs, all about the same length. The hairs become smaller in diameter near the body, making the pelage much like velvet. Such structure allows the hairs to lie in any direction, enabling a mole to go forward or backward in small burrows. Shrew-moles, on the other hand, have pelages more like those of shrews; that is, they are composed of both guard hairs and underfur directed toward the rear of the animals, so that they can only move forward in a burrow.

In addition, the upper front teeth are straight, flat, and relatively broad, similar to human teeth.

Although you would not see these moles if you were to walk in the meadow, as Storm Hawk did in the year 1575, you would see their soil mounds (usually thought of as "molehills") along the meadow's edge by the forest, which differ from those of the Mazama pocket gopher. The gopher's mounds, if you remember, are fan-like, with the burrow to one side. In contrast, the coast mole makes cone-shaped mounds of soil on the surface of the ground, with the burrow's entrance concealed in the middle of the mound.

8.8 Molehills at the lower edge of the meadow.

Coast moles, which are well adapted for a burrowing life, normally make two types of burrows: shallow surface-tunnels, especially around large, rotten fallen trees, marked by visible ridges of soil that a mole pushes up with its back and deeper tunnels that can be located by the cone-shaped mounds of soil on the surface of the ground. Although moles can traverse their burrows with surprising speed, they are relatively slow on the surface of the ground.

The molehills that dot the meadow's lower edge (Photo 8.8) are formed by soil being pushed out through a vertical tunnel, as a direct result of a mole's incredible digging strength. However, when a mole compresses the soil around a deep tunnel sufficiently to provide the required space for its body, molehills are not created.

One mound of primary importance is called the "fortress." The fortress is larger than other molehills, and it is under this particularly large mound of soil that a mole constructs its nest in a concavity about six inches below the surface and roughly eight inches in diameter. Each nest cavity has three entrances from which tunnels radiate in all directions. The nest itself is made out of relatively soft vegetation.

Whereas Cascade earthworms are their primary food, comprising 50 to 75 percent of their diet, they also eat centipedes (see photo 8.6, page 308); millipedes; snails and slugs; larval butterflies, moths, flies, and beetles; as well as adult beetles, termites, crickets, and ants.

Although coast moles are primarily nocturnal, they are also active during the day, especially around fallen, rotting trees in the forest, which may account for the strong, musky odor that probably makes them unpalatable to some would-be predators, especially other mammals.

Solitary by nature, except during late winter and early spring when they breed, a female, having become sexually mature at approximately nine to 10 months of age, will give birth to a single litter of four, naked young in early May in a deep underground nest of soft vegetation.

Somewhere in the far reaches of time, her ancestors learned to collect green grass and place it around the outside of the nursery nest after the babies were born, there to act as a heating blanket. A heating blanket? Yes. As the wet grass decays, it generates heat that is retained in the nest cavity, keeping the babies warm while their mother is off searching for food. And so it is that each generation of the coast mole's babies is so nurtured.

The Miracle of Insects

If you think about what you have read so far, you may be able to visualize insects as a vital part of Nature's sustainability, not only because the cirque's flowering plants depend on insects for pollination and thus survival but also because various animals rely on them for food: dragonflies, tiger beetles, ladybugs, trout, Cascade frogs, spotted sandpipers, bats, shrews, and moles. Their ubiquitous nature is reflected in two quotes: one by American ecologist Warder Clyde Allee, "This is not the age of man, however great his superiority ... it is the age of insects," and the other by American author Anthony Doerr, "Insects Will Not Take Over The World.

They Already Own It."

I once heard it said that God was inordinately fond of beetles. I'd say God was inordinately fond of insects in general, as judged by their astonishing array of sizes, colors, shapes, habitats, abilities, and behaviors.

Although I marveled at the few insects I was aware of along the roadside ditch I played in as a child, I had no inkling of the magnitude of the insects' world. I knew about the water skippers in the ditch, for example, but had no idea that a member of the family, known as "sea skaters," had long ago decided to navigate the open seas. And I knew about grasshoppers because I not only used them as bait to catch fish but also ate them for survival during my solo treks in the mountains of Oregon and Washington. However, I had no concept of their incredible variety, as I have since discovered in Egypt, Nepal, Japan, Malaysia, and throughout much of Europe, the United States, and Canada.

So, if you will permit me, we will digress for a moment to a discussion of insects that will have brief examples from outside the boundaries of the cirque in other parts of the world. And, because of the subject's vastness, this glimpse into the insect's world will have a slightly generalized scope.

Insects vary in size from the minute aphid to the dragonfly, the latter being several inches long. They also range from a dull white (a termite), to the brilliant hues of the rainbow (a tiger beetle), to glorious primary colors and all combinations thereof (butterflies), whereas others are so camouflaged they are difficult to see (an assortment of moths, bugs, and beetles). Some insects are blind (various termites and such strict cave-dwellers as specialized spring-tails and scarab beetles), whereas others have five eyes (bees) that are arranged as three, small, simple eyes set in a triangle between two, large compound eyes.

Insects also come in every conceivable shape, including round (ladybugs), oblong (click beetles), vertically flat (fleas), horizontally flat (flat bark beetles), long and skinny (walking sticks), fat (scarabs), smooth (leaf beetles), long-snouted (weevils), frilly (tropical "praying" mantis), plainly visible (yellow jackets), well camouflaged (a small scarab beetle in the Egyptian desert that mimics a pebble), and so on. They live below ground, inside leaves, in bushes and trees, inside dead wood, and in water. Beyond the cirque, insects occur from the Arctic to the tropics, from the jungle to the desert, from the open ocean to above timberline in the Himalayas, in every kind of water, soil, and vegetation.

Insects fly, hop, crawl, climb, swim, walk on water, burrow, and snap their necks to right themselves. The dragonfly, for instance, can hover, fly forward and backward, up and down, to this side and that. The springtail, flea, flea beetle, grasshopper, and cricket, among others, can hop. In fact, if you could jump proportionately as high as a flea, you could leap over a very tall building. Then again, if you could pick up and carry a load proportional to that of an ant, you would be the strongest person in the world. If you could dig with speed proportional to the crickets I saw in southern Nepal, you could, with your bare hands, out-dig anyone with a shovel. If you could lie on your back and simply snap your neck to right yourself, like a click beetle, you would astound whoever witnessed your accomplishment.

Although people think of most insects as crawling, if you could cover the terrain with the speed and endurance of an ant, you would easily walk fifty miles in an eight-hour day without tiring. If you could leap a distance equivalent to that of a grasshopper, you would forever be the world's broad-jumping champion by a very wide margin. If you could climb up a vertical surface like a housefly, you could safely walk up the side of a twenty-story building. If you could emulate a water skater or sea skater, you could literally "walk on water." If you could swim as fast as a water boatman (a bug), you would be the fastest swimming human on Earth. If you could maneuver in the water like a whirligig beetle, you would be little more than a blur of motion. If you were as light and well engineered as an ant, you could fall from a ten-story building and sustain not a single injury. If you could fly and navigate like a monarch butterfly, you could ride the winds to distant lands anytime you wished.

Insects pollinate flowers, cut leaves, produce honey, produce acid, eat wood, eat every conceivable kind of plant and all of their parts, eat meat and suck blood, cultivate fungi, make silk, make wax, metamorphose, carry a cold light in their bodies that is blinked for communication at night, "herd" and "milk" other insects as though they were cows, recycle decomposing vegetation and flesh, chew up wood and spit out paper, sting, bite, suck, spit, keep blood from clotting, live totally under water at one stage of their lives and on land in another, and make music.

Some insects are social and construct elaborate homes in the ground, in wood, and even build huge, vertical, colonial homes of soil. Others make more modest homes of mud with arched entryways. Although many insects are single in lifestyle, there is a scarab that lives as a guest in ant colonies.

Insects are predaceous, vegetarian, fungivorous (fungi eaters), frugivorous (fruit eaters), parasitic, mutualistic, and cannibalistic. There are as well adult insects, such as adult mayflies, that do not eat at all; in fact, some even lack mouthparts. In addition, insects transmit diseases among themselves and to other animals, plants, and humans. Some wasps even make paper, and have done so long before humans learned how. If all of the truly miraculous aspects of the world's insects were incorporated into you as a single person, you would be the most amazing and adaptable creature on Earth, although not always socially acceptable.

That insects have so many abilities we humans lack and could never emulate, and so are physically superior to us in many ways, it is imperative that we pause to contemplate our place in the scheme of things and gain a little humility. Then, perhaps, we would treat all life on our home planet with more respect.

"Simple-minded" as insects may be by our reckoning, at the rate we are destroying our global environment, they will likely be around well after we humans have made planet Earth uninhabitable for ourselves.

However simple we may think insects to be, Ralph Waldo Emerson pointed out that, "The invariable mark of wisdom is to see the miraculous in the common." Perhaps a closer look at some of the cirque's insect occupants will help us to better appreciate them as fellow travelers on our home planet.

The Meadow's Tripartite Script

While the moles are going about their daily activities in the forest and the meadow along the forest's edge, flowers of the meadow are playing host to a drama that is characteristic of the insect's world throughout planet Earth. Although the actors change with geographic location, the script is the same. In this case, Nature has dictated a millennial evolutionary script between aphids, ants, and ladybugs, with aphids playing the lead roles.

Aphids

Of all the insects that feed on the meadow's plants, aphids are perhaps the most ubiquitous. Aphids are small, sap-sucking insects that are actually related to true bugs.

The aphids in the meadow have soft, green bodies that are roughly $\frac{4}{100}$ of an inch long and thus easily blend into the background color of the plants from even a short distance away. They have two antennae and two compound eyes. Their mouthparts are designed for piercing plants and sucking the plant's sap. They have long, thin legs and two-jointed, two-clawed "feet." They also have a pair of narrow tubes situated at the end of their abdomen (termed "cornicle tubes") through which they secrete a quick-drying wax that helps to protect them from predators and parasites. (Photo 8.9)

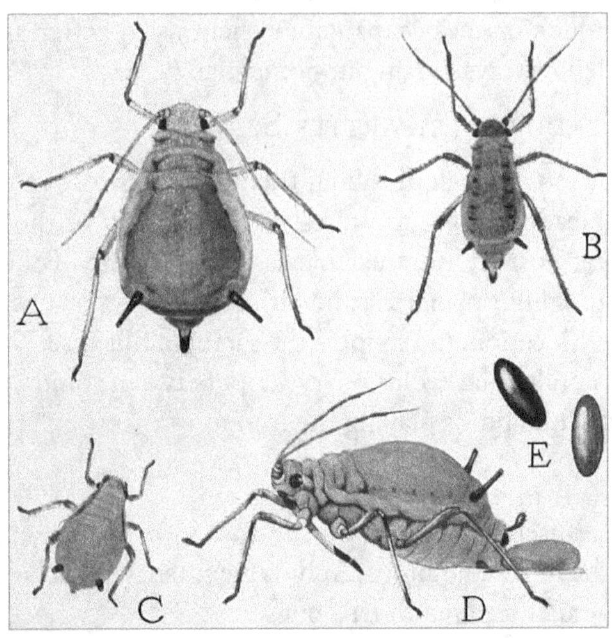

8.9 *Aphids: A, adult sexual female; B, adult male; C, young female; D, female laying an egg; E, eggs. Note the pair of "cornicle tubes."*

Aphids feed passively on the sap of the meadow's flowering plants, as well as some other plants, by puncturing the vessels that carry the sap, of which there are two kinds: *concentrated* and *diluted*. Once a vessel containing a high concentration of sugars is punctured, the sap, which is under elevated pressure, is forced into the aphid's food canal. On the other hand, when a vessel that is primarily a transporter of water and a more dilute solution of sugars is penetrated, aphids must actively suck the fluid out because these vessels are mediated by low internal pressure.

As it turns out, aphids must ingest the watery kind of sap to balance the amount of sugar ingested in the concentrated portion, thereby balancing the overall sugar content in their "hemolymph," which is the insect equivalent of human blood (from the Greek *haîma* "blood" plus the Latin *lympha*, "water nymph"). Then, because the sap is an unbalanced diet due to its lack of essential amino acids, which aphids, like all animals, cannot produce, they depend on internal-symbiotic bacteria to recycle their bodily waste and turn it into the missing amino acids.

All reproduction in aphids is parthenogenetic, meaning asexual reproduction resulting in the offspring being clones of their mother (from Greek *parthenos*, meaning "virgin" and *genesis*, meaning "birth"). Therefore, all of the eggs that survive the winter produce females. In turn, the females again produce young through parthenogenesis, only this time the embryos develop within their mother and are born alive, termed "viviparous" (from the Latin *vivus* "alive" and *parus* "giving birth"). The offspring resemble their parent in every way except size. This reproductive process reiterates throughout the summer, producing multiple generations that typically live 20 to 40 days. So it is that one female, hatched in the spring, may produce many generations resulting in thousands of female descendants.

In autumn, however, aphids undergo sexual, egg-laying reproduction. A change in the length of daylight hours and temperature, or perhaps a lower quantity and quality of food, causes females to produce sexual females and males parthenogenetically. The males are genetically identical to their mothers except that they have one fewer sex chromosome. These sexual aphids may lack wings or even mouthparts. When sexual females and males mate, the females lay eggs that develop outside the mother, and the young aphids emerge as winged or wingless females the following spring. (Photo 8.10)

As aphids feed, some transmit viruses to the cirque's plants, killing them. Plants exhibiting aphid damage have a variety of symptoms, such as a decrease in their rate of growth, mottled leaves, yellowing, stunted growth, curled leaves, browning, wilting, low yields, and death. In addition, the removal of sap creates a loss in a plant's vigor; what's more, aphid saliva is toxic to plants.

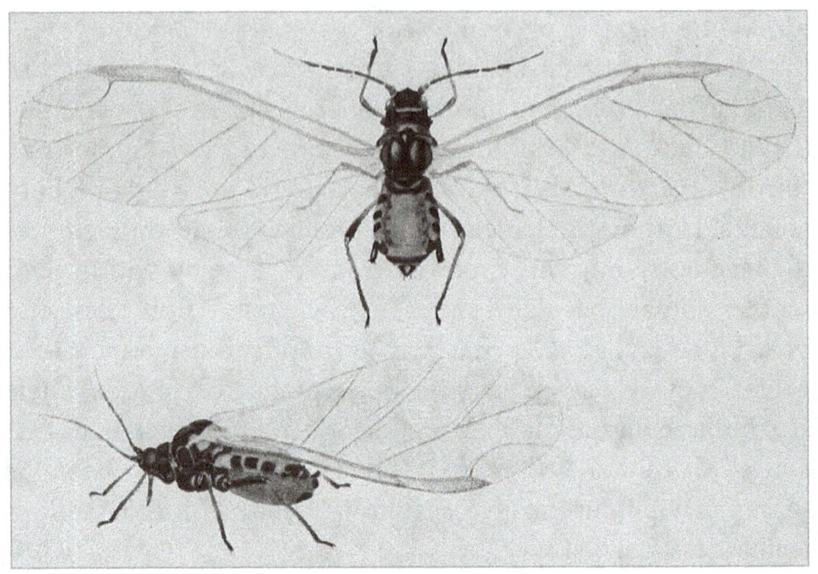

8.10 Winged female aphids.

The Ants

As another member of the script, some species of ants actually "farm" aphids. (Photo 8.11) Because the liquid aphids draw from plants is low in nitrogen, they must consume large quantities to gain adequate nutrition. The aphids then excrete equally large quantities of sugary liquid, called "honeydew," which the ants ingest. The ants, in turn, have chemicals on their feet, which tranquilizes the aphids, allowing the ants to keep them close by as a source of food. Then, using their antennae to stroke the aphids, the ants stimulate them to release the honeydew. As a result, some species of aphids have even lost the ability to eliminate their own bodily waste, and must now depend on the ants to "milk" them.

8.11 Ants.

Ants not only make sure "their" aphids stay well fed and safe but also carry their aphids to a new food source when the host plant is depleted of nutrients. Some species of ants continue to care for their aphids during winter, carrying aphid eggs home, protecting them in their nests throughout the cold months. The eggs are stored where the temperature and humidity are optimal, and are moved as needed when conditions change. In spring, when the aphids hatch, the ants carry them to a host plant to feed. Moreover, ants will aggressively defend their "herd" of aphids if predatory insects or parasites attempt to harm them. Ants will even go so far as to destroy the eggs of known aphid predators, such as ladybugs—properly known as *ladybeetles,* because they have biting-chewing mouthparts, as opposed to bugs, which have piercing-sucking mouthparts.

Although aphids are almost always wingless, certain environmental conditions, such as too dense a population or a decline in their source of food, will trigger them to develop wings and fly to a new location. Not wanting to lose their source of food, the ants prevent aphids from dispersing either by tearing off their wings before they can become airborne or by using an allelochemical to stop them from developing wings in the first place, thus impeding their ability to leave. (An "allelochemical" is a chemical emitted by one species that affects individuals of a different species—from the Greek *allēlōn*, "reciprocally.")

Despite being taken care of by ants, the soft-bodied aphids have a wide variety of insect predators, such as crab spiders, "aphid lions" (the larvae of green lacewings), and ladybeetles.

LADYBEETLES

The name, "ladybug," which originated in North America, is not an accurate reflection of their true nature because they are actually beetles—not true bugs. The convergent lady beetle is between ¼ and ⅜ inch in length, and females are larger than males. It has a semi-hemispherical shape. Two wing covers, known as "elytra," protect its sides and back, under which is a pair of delicate wings. The wing covers are yellowish-red or tannish-red with 12 black spots, three large ones on the posterior of each wing cover and three small ones on each shoulder: bright colors, termed "aposematic" (from the Greek *apo*, "away" and *sēma*, "sign").

Aposematic coloration is used to warn would-be predators, such as insect-eating birds, frogs, and dragonflies, that the lady beetle is unpalatable. To this end, a lady beetle's hemolymph (the fluid in the body tissues and cavities of insects, which transports nutrients—analogous to our blood) is both toxic and rank. When startled, an adult lady beetle emits the foul-smelling fluid from its leg joints, known as "reflex bleeding," leaving yellow stains on the surface below. Potential predators are likely deterred by the vile mix of alkaloids, and equally repulsed by the sight of a seemingly sickly beetle. Larvae, on the other hand, can ooze these alkaloids from their abdomens.

A lady beetle's legs and underside are all black, and both its legs and antennae are short. The front part of the thorax is black with a white border and white lines that are directed inward, converging as it were, toward one another and the abdomen, hence the species name, *convergens*. (The thorax, which is the midsection of the beetle's body, holds its head, legs, wings, and abdomen in place.)

During the warm summer months, the lady beetles live on flowers, branches, and bushes because their prey is easy to find in these places. At other times, such as inclement weather or to avoid predators, they seek shelter under leaves and branches.

A solitary species most of the year, when temperatures begin to drop in the autumn, lady beetles seek shelter for the winter, aggregating on the south sides of large objects, such as the trees along the meadow's edge, sometimes numbering in the hundreds or thousands. Here, they enter "diapause," which is a physiological state of dormancy or stasis wherein they can survive such conditions as temperature extremes, drought, or reduced food availability. ("Diapause" means their metabolism slows down.) Thus, they are often among the first insects to appear in the spring.

Active primarily during daylight hours, adults fly from plant to plant searching for prey (Photo 8.12), while larvae move from plant to plant by walking across overlapping leaves, often following leaf veins until they either detect odor-based cues or simply bump into their aphid prey. Plants with flowers that produce lots of pollen and nectar, such as asters, as well as harboring aphids, are crucial for attracting lady beetles.

8.12 A lady beetle devours an aphid.

Prey is located visually, through a sense of smell, and other chemical cues. Convergent lady beetles typically eat aphids, scale insects, and plant mites. Although both larvae and adults prey mostly on aphids, they also consume the eggs and larvae of other insects, such as stinkbugs. Moreover, they have a prodigious appetite and may consume between 40 to 75 aphids per day or as many as 5,000 aphids over a lifetime. Not only that, but they eat the most aphids in a day when the temperature is around 73 degrees Fahrenheit.

On the other hand, when aphids are scarce, the adults can eat honeydew, nectar and pollen, or even petals and other soft parts of plants. If food is really scarce, they tend to become cannibalistic, and eat their own larvae and eggs. During the autumn, adults will feed on pollen to gain extra fat in preparation for hibernation.

Although the cirque's female lady beetles normally produce two generations a year, one in the spring and the other in the autumn, they are able to enter into reproductive diapause during dry seasons or times of extreme temperature, when food resources are not plentiful enough to allow successful reproduction. Be that as it may, lady beetles go through a complete life cycle, known as metamorphosis, from egg to adult, a process that usually takes about three to four weeks.

Females generally lay their eggs in concert with the population cycles of the aphids, not only laying most of their eggs when the aphid cycle is at its peak but also laying them near the aphids, to increase the likelihood that the larvae will easily find food. A female normally lays 200 to 300 small (4/100 to 5/100 of an inch long), spindle-shaped, yellowish eggs near her prey in upright batches of 15 to 30 over several months during spring and early summer.

The eggs hatch into dark-colored larvae resembling miniature alligators that are about 1/25 to 3/8 of an inch long with distinct orange spots on the leading edge of their thorax. Like alligators, they have bumpy skin, as well as long, pointed abdomens; spiny bodies; and legs that protrude from their sides.

On hatching, the first larvae in each group of eggs may start by eating the unhatched ones, thus obtaining required energy until they find aphids. Once found, the larvae consume hundreds of aphids or other insects for 20 to 30 days, during which they grow and molt (shed their skin) several times. Next, the larvae enter a pupal stage (similar to a moth's cocoon or butterfly's chrysalis) that is orange and black and hemispherical in shape. This "resting" stage usually lasts 3 to 12 days, during which time feeding ceases. Finally, an adult emerges and the search for food and a mate begins.

Mating takes place soon after emerging from the pupa. Once mated, a female must consume aphids in order to reproduce. Therefore, if the supply of aphids is abundant, she may start laying eggs within about a week of mating, but if the supply is scanty, she may wait for up to nine months. Depending on her circumstances, a female can lay up to 1,000 eggs during her life.

While the trio of insects is playing its role in helping to maintain yet another facet of the predator-prey dynamics within the meadow and its cirque, the heat of summer is gradually increasing. In doing so, it is encouraging the ripening huckleberries to offer their invitation to all berry-loving animals: from ants and yellowjackets to gray jays, Steller jays, robins, Townsend chipmunks, yellow-pine chipmunks, mantled ground squirrels, black bears, and Pacific jumping mice. Of all these inhabitants of the cirque, only the jumping mice reside primarily in the areas that qualify as meadow. In fact, as dusk deepens on this day, July 20, 1575, a handful of jumping mice are staining their mouths with the purple juice of ripe huckleberries that have fallen to the ground. Were you, perchance, to be picking huckleberries in the same patch, however, the likelihood of your seeing a jumping mouse would be slim indeed because they are primarily nocturnal, though they are also active during twilight.

Pacific Jumping Mouse

Jumping mice are about 9½ inches long, most of which is a long, slender, sparsely haired, tapering (4⁹⁄₁₀- to 6-inch) tail that is distinctly bicolored: brown above and white below. In addition, the rear portion of the body is much heavier than the front part, and the hind limbs are much larger and more powerful than the forelimbs.

8.13 Pacific jumping mouse: note the long hind feet and the long tail.

Their brightly colored fur is composed of stiff, bristly hairs that lie close to the body and are strongly tricolored, with a distinct separation of colors on the back, sides, and the underside. Their backs are brown with an infusion of many yellowish-tipped hairs. Their sides are yellowish-orange with numerous scattered brownish-tipped and blackish-tipped hairs, and their undersides vary from clear white to a white washed with light orange. The color of their fur becomes paler as autumn approaches.

Their hind legs are much longer than their forelegs. The soles of their feet are naked, and the hind feet are long and narrow with long, slender toes. They have small, slightly elongated heads with small eyes located midway between the nose and ears. The ears are short, but longer than the surrounding fur. (Photo 8.13)

The jumping mice of the cirque are associated primarily with areas of the meadow's vegetation along the edge of the forest (Photo 8.14) and wherever the forest interdigitates within the meadow, such as the area of Storm Hawk's first camp, which was a short way into the finger of trees. They also live a short way into the forest, where the meadow's vegetation occupies the stream banks.

8.14 Typical habitat for the jumping mice of the meadow.

Although the mice occasionally walk on all four feet (Photo 8.15), they normally progress by pushing off with their hind feet and land on both of their forefeet together. When leaping, they steady themselves by using their long, strong tails as braces. Their tails also act as a counterbalance that compensate for the vigorous thrust of their long hind limbs. If a mouse looses most or all of its tail, it somersaults when trying to land.

8.15 Tracks of a Pacific jumping mouse: note the impression of the long, hind foot.

When pursued, they propel themselves through the air in long leaps, covering from three to almost six feet in a bound. After a few rapid leaps, they stop suddenly, crouch slightly, remaining motionless, relying on their pelage as camouflage, and then move to dense cover when the danger passes. In this case, the mice not only have the aforementioned counter-shading, where they are darker above and lighter below but also have sides that are yellowish-orange with many scattered brownish-tipped and blackish-tipped hairs that blend in with the multi-colored vegetation of the changing seasons.

If pursued further, however, they take flight in earnest. At the height of a jump, a mouse turns its head down while arching its back, and dives headlong into vegetation, at which time their rustlings can be heard for several feet. Even though it may strike thick vegetation, it lands on its forefeet; then, bringing the long hind legs well forward beneath its body, it leaps again.

Good swimmers and divers, the stream poses no barrier to the jumping mice, although they use branches and fallen trees for bridges when they are available. Because most of them live along the forest-meadow interface, they can go almost anywhere they choose without having to swim. Within the meadow, however, there are occasions when a mouse must navigate the streams by swimming if it wants to reach the opposite bank.

Jumping mice cut the stems of grass to get at the seeds, which comprise more than half their diet. In doing so, they leave neat piles of stalks behind. When eating, they seize food with their forepaws, sit back on their haunches, and nibble it. They also eat fungi, fruit, insects, and even snails and fish. However, they do not store food.

Although they normally forage on the surface of the ground, they will climb into huckleberry bushes, often six inches or more above the ground, in search of selected berries, at which time they are particularly noisy. The dense, shrubby nature of tightly packed thickets, as well as their long hind feet and long tails, allows them to move relatively freely in or on a thicket. When startled, they either dive headfirst into the thicket or escape by leaping across the surface of the thicket's springy top. When resting on top of a thicket, the mice normally have their tails braced across the upper surface of a dense grouping of leaves.

During summer, jumping mice construct well-hidden, fragile, dome-shaped nests on the ground, although some are in slight depressions dug by the mice. Summer nests are composed of coarse, broad-leaved grasses that are loosely interwoven, and are about six inches in diameter and about four inches high. Each nest has a single opening in the side and appears to belong to one or two individuals. (Photo 8.16) Throughout the remainder of the year, they are snug in nests of mosses, grasses, and plant fibers in chambers from a few inches to about six feet below the surface of the ground.

8.16 The summer nest of a Pacific jumping mouse.

Whereas jumping mice are usually silent, they squeak when disagreeing with each other and vibrate their tails rapidly against some resonant body, such as dry leaves, to produce a drumming sound. They also jump wildly from side to side when irritated.

Most male jumping mice become sexually mature in June, but a sexually mature individual may occasionally occur in late May. Some individuals still have maximum-sized, descended testes as late as the first half of August. Females are also receptive in May and June.

They give birth to a single litter of four to eight young in July or August, after a gestation period of 18 to 23 days. The babies are born pink, naked, and helpless in a well-hidden nest of July grasses and weigh between 2½ and 3 ounces. Their eyes are closed, their ears are folded over, and their vibrissae, or whiskers, are not yet visible. They have short, stubby heads, and relatively long tails. Weaned and independent in roughly a month, they attain sexual maturity the following year, and can occupy the meadow for at least four years before dying of old age.

As autumn approaches, the mice begin to accumulate layers of fat under the skin, over the muscles of the body, and throughout their body cavity. Having doubled their weight with fat, they enter hibernation in their warm, dry, belowground nests with the onset of freezing weather. During hibernation, as the winter winds howl, the snow accumulates, and the sun seems to be held hostage in the southerly latitudes, the jumping mice of summer are rolled up in little, furry balls with their noses and feet tucked against their bellies and their tails curled around their bodies, at which time they appear to be dead. While in torpor for the winter, their body temperatures drop to 32.6 degrees Fahrenheit.

If, however, a mouse were to be given warmth, the latent spark of life in its body would soon respond, and in half an hour it would be fully awake. But remove the warmth and it would again doze off. Thus, the jumping mice will remain in hibernation until released by the warmth of the late spring sun, when they will again grace the aboveground world of the cirque.

Deer Mouse

While the jumping mice are limited in the areas of the cirque they inhabit, there is one little denizen, called the deer mouse, that is virtually ubiquitous, apparently dwelling wherever it chooses. On several occasions in years past, I disturbed these mice in their daytime nests as high as 80 feet above the ground in Douglas-fir trees, where they raced along the branches and up and down the trunks with seeming reckless abandon.

Moreover, this little creature is a bundle of curiosity that cannot refrain from the seemingly constant urge to explore. To give you an example, in the summer of 1958 when, at the age of 18, I got a job as a counselor in a YMCA forest camp for boys at Spirit Lake at the base of Mount St. Helens in the Cascade Mountains of Washington.

My job was that of "Hike Master," which meant I was in charge of the hiking program and was out on trails much of the time. When not out on trails, I was in camp, where I slept in a three-sided shelter made of logs and cedar shakes. Inside the shelter was a low, wooden pallet on which I rolled out my sleeping bag.

Ancient western hemlocks and western redcedars, through whose high crowns the wind blew in soft, swooshing sighs, surrounded the shelter. As darkness crept into the forest, many small mammals began their nightly activities; one of these was a deer mouse.

One night, shortly after I arrived in camp to begin my summer duties, a plump, female deer mouse scrabbled about on my sleeping bag. Over the course of an hour or so, she rummaged here and there, nibbling on my bar of soap, and generally keeping me awake with her hustling and bustling. I did not think too much about it, because deer mice were everywhere scurrying hither and yon in the night, which is exactly what deer mice are supposed to do!

But the next night she was back, and the night after that, and the following night. By the fourth night, I decided I wanted to get a good look at this wee mouse that seemed to enjoy disturbing me just as soon as I got settled for sleep, so I left a candle burning. At first nothing happened. Then, just as I decided the gently-flickering light was keeping the mouse away, she suddenly appeared out of the shadows and scampered onto my chest, where she "screeched" to a halt. With pointed nose twitching; large, dark eyes glistening; and big, sensitive ears straining forward, she inspected me, all the while having everything in reverse for an instant get away.

Neither of us moved; I even held my breath until I was sure my lungs would burst. When I could not hold it any longer, I began breathing as quietly and slowly as possible. But instead of dashing away, she relaxed also. In fact, sitting on my chest about six inches from my face, she began washing her face and ears. She was most fastidious in her grooming, which ended only when she had cleaned her body right down to the very tip of her long, slender tail. I, who at 18—having spent most of my free time alone wandering the forested mountain trails—had never had a date with a girl, not even to the movies, and most certainly had never before been privy to such an open display of a female's toilette!

Finished with her grooming, she ventured closer and closer

to my face until she almost touched me. That, however, was quite enough bravery for one night, so she scurried away, but not without plotting a return engagement.

She appeared regularly whenever I was in camp, and performed her nightly toilette in the dancing light of my candle while sitting on my sleeping bag only inches from my face. I loved it when she came to see me. Her visits made each night a special, private time, a time I thought about on and off all day, and looked forward to with increasing anticipation, as the shadows of evening began stealing the light of day from the forest.

She became quite trusting and seemed to enjoy the little snacks I left for her on the small, wooden ledge alongside my bed. Not knowing at first what she would like, I left an assortment of shelled peanuts, rolled oats, raisins, and pieces of apple. Although over the course of a night she either ate whatever I left or packed it away to her pantry, her favorite food was raisins, which she consumed on the spot.

Camp lasted about three months, and it was toward the end of the summer that I first saw the short-tailed weasel near my sleeping shelter. A short-tailed weasel (also called an ermine when in winter white) is a small, lithe carnivorous mammal that catches, among other things, deer mice for food. And so, while I was greatly saddened when my little friend, whom I dubbed "the washing deer mouse," suddenly vanished, I was not surprised. Her disappearance was attested by the fact that she both failed to visit me, as she had so faithfully done, and her snacks were left untouched—even the raisins. I could not, however, blame the weasel for simply doing what weasels do, which is eat deer mice should they get a chance.

Thinking back, I am still deeply touched that so small a mouse would trust me enough to perform her nightly toilette on top of me as I lay in my sleeping bag during those soft, quiet summer nights over 50 years ago. That indeed was an honor!

Beyond that, I had participated in a new kind of relationship, one in which a wild animal befriended me of its own accord, in its own habitat. Thus I experienced another dimension of the joy and sorrow embodied in the constantly changing relationships we call life.

So named because they have the agility of deer, these mice are only three to four inches long from the tip of their noses to the base of their tails, which in turn are 2⅖ to 5 inches in length. Adults weigh from ⅖ of an ounce to ⅘ of an ounce.

The deer mouse is slender in form with large, black, beady eyes; big, scantily furred, thin ears; long, prominent whiskers; and a long, finely haired tail. In addition, its front legs are shorter than its hind legs.

In summer, the fur on its back varies from brown to dark brown, but is darkest along the midline from the top of the head to the base of the tail. Some individuals are reddish-brown, others grayish-brown. The top of its tail is light brown to dark brown. The tops of its feet, the underside of its body, and the underside of its tail are clear white. There is a sharp line of demarcation between the dark upper parts and the white under parts—the aforementioned counter-shading, which gives the mice a flat appearance on moon-lit nights, helping them blend into the dark, earthy tones of their surroundings. In winter, the long, soft pelage is slightly brighter in color. Moreover, the sexes are similar in appearance throughout the year. (Photo 8.17)

8.17 Deer mouse.

Almost strictly nocturnal, deer mice become active at twilight, as darkness claims the cirque—that is, with the exception of moonlit nights, when most aboveground activity ceases because the brightness makes them vulnerable to predation. Even though they are graceful and agile in the extreme, they can be exceedingly noisy scampering about in dry vegetation, causing a commotion that would indicate a much-larger animal is abroad.

Although their usual means of locomotion is walking or running, when pursued, they leap. These mice are also good swimmers, so, while they readily cross over streams using rocks or fallen trees as bridges, they are not opposed to swimming or even foraging in shallow water.

Deer mice are relatively social and have home ranges that shift about and loosely overlap, usually with a mouse of the opposite sex. Within these parameters, an adult male, a few adult females, and several young make up their basic social unit, wherein they tend to recognize one another and interact a lot. That is, until females have young, at which time they are more aggressive in their territorial defense because an unknown, intruding mouse may kill an unattended youngster.

Adults tend to be relatively sedentary and occupy small home ranges, which average 1¼ acre for males and ¾ of an acre for females. Males use their home ranges for access to food, nests, and reproductively receptive females within their overlapping home ranges. Females, on the other hand, use their home ranges for feeding, nesting, and rearing young. In both cases, however, their activity centers on their nest and stockpile of food.

These beautiful mice nest in burrows dug in the ground or nests constructed in raised areas, such as fallen trees, hollows in trees and stumps, under loose bark, or crevices in the cliff and its talus. Their nests are made with a variety of materials, such as grasses, mosses, plant fibers, roots, and even thistledown, and may be as much as four inches in diameter. Whereas most deer mice nest alone, they will sometimes reside with a mouse of the opposite sex.

Deer mice are active above ground in the cirque during spring, summer, and autumn. In cold, wet weather, however, their activity is curtailed on the surface, although perhaps not below ground. On the other hand, winter in the cirque causes the mice to shift most of their activities under the insulating cover of snow. Severe cold may restrict their travel to the vicinity of their nest, or even sequester them within it for a few days. At such times, a group of 15 or more mice of mixed sexes and ages may huddle together in a nest to conserve heat. They may also enter a sluggish period, or torpor, to reduce their body temperature and conserve energy. As the weather moderates with the coming of spring, they once again resume their aboveground explorations. (Photo 8.18)

8.18 A deer mouse peering out of its burrow in spring.

Usually considered vegetarians, deer mice are really omnivorous, finding their food by odor rather than sight. Once found, they use their sharp, front teeth to gnaw through the hard seeds and the tough, outer skeleton of beetles, as well as to gnaw on the shed antlers of deer (see photo 6.45, page 181) and elk, and the bones of dead animals, from which they derive calcium. (Photo 8.19)

8.19 The leg bone of deer chewed by a deer mouse to get calcium.

Throughout the year, deer mice in the cirque change their eating habits to access whatever is available during that season. In winter, for example, they capitalize on spiders, caterpillars, beetles, and bugs, most of which are inactive under the snow, where the mice concentrate their activity. On occasion, a mouse finds carrion with which to supplement its winter diet. At times, they even ingest their own feces, a practice called "coprophage," from the Greek *copros*, "feces" and *phagein*, "to eat."

During the spring, seeds and young leaves become available, along with earthworms and insects, which the mice consume in large quantities. In addition, they eat a variety of mycorrhizal fungi (truffles), serving the same type of ecological function as that described earlier for the northern flying squirrel and chickaree.

In summer, they dine on such seeds as those of Douglas fir, lodgepole pine, Engelmann spruce, and vine maple, as well as huckleberries and truffles of various kinds. With the advent of autumn, however, they slowly shift their eating habits to resemble those of winter. In addition, they cache seeds in holes in the ground, in tree cavities, and even in bird nests, storing up to a pint in each location. However, despite their deposition of autumnal fat and stockpiles of food, starvation during severe winters in the cirque is a chief cause of mortality.

Even though March in the cirque can still be a brutal winter month, the breeding season of the deer mice can begin, but the timing depends more on the availability of food than the time of year. Because less than half of the mice, of both sexes, leave their original home ranges to reproduce, mating within families (incest) limits the gene flow among the cirque's deer-mouse population.

Nevertheless, deer mice reproduce profusely, with three to four litters of one to nine young being produced annually. In the lower, warmer elevations at the foot of the Western Cascades, for example, the mice breed every three to four weeks during the warmer months and less frequently during the winter. And the size of a litter increases each time a female gives birth, until the fifth or sixth litter, then decreases.

While most males mate with more than one female, a monogamous pair may live in the same nest, or the female may drive her mate away, caring for the young by herself. At other times, the male remains with older youngsters while the female moves to a new nest to give birth to her next litter.

To give an example, the mice begin to breed during the third week in April. But it is not until the 23rd day of the month that a yearling female becomes pregnant with a litter of seven babies, five females and two males. After a gestation period of 24 days, the babies are born in a cozy, belowground nest of dried grasses, moss, and thistledown under a boulder, where the talus meets the meadow.

The babies are born helpless, naked, and wrinkled with pink skin, each weighing about $\frac{9}{100}$ of an ounce. Their eyes are closed, and their ears are folded over. Juvenile hair begins to develop when they are two days old. Their ears unfold on day three; their ear canals open on their tenth day, and their eyes open when they are 14 days old. While nursing her babies, the mother carries them clinging to her nipples as she moves about, or picks them up one at a time in her mouth.

Her youngsters grow rapidly, and are finally weaned when they are 32 days old. They disperse 500 to 600 feet from their nest shortly thereafter to establish their own home ranges. At times, however, a mother will tolerate the presence of her offspring for longer periods. That is, until she has a second litter, at which time she forces them out of the nest.

Although the juveniles, now gray above and white below, will not have reached their adult size until the beginning of July, thereafter gaining weight slowly, they will become sexually mature some time between late June and mid July. Meanwhile, their mother, who was bred again within days of giving birth, already has another litter. As for the young females, they may well produce their first litters before summer's end.

Like other rodents in the cirque, deer mice are important for spreading the seeds of numerous plants and the spores of fungi. They are also an important staple for several of the cirque's inhabitants, including weasels, bobcats, and owls, among others. Thus, most of the mice will live less than a year, many of them consumed by predators.

BOBCAT

Bobcats stand 21 inches high at the shoulder and are 30 to 50 inches long. They weigh from 12 to 30 pounds, with males being slightly larger than females.

They are muscular, short-tailed, long-legged cats with relatively small feet. Because their hind legs are longer than their front legs, they have a bobbing gait. In addition, they have yellow eyes and black pupils, which widen into black circles to maximize the reception of light during their nocturnal activities. Their ears are slightly tufted and blackish with a white spot near each tip. They have white eyelids and a pinkish-red nose. The hairs along the sides of their face, from the ears to the throat, are long and form a ruff, somewhat like sideburns. (Photo 8.20) The upper parts of their body are grayish, tannish, or reddish, usually with irregular black spots, the color being intense along the middle of the back, becoming lighter on the sides. Their rump and hind legs are tannish, and their underparts, including the inner sides of the legs, are whitish with black spots. There are indistinct black rings on their tail, but the tip is black above and whitish below. The "bobbed" appearance of their tail is what gives them the name "bobcat."(Photo 8.21)

8.20 Bobcat, note the "sideburns."

8.21 Bobcat; note the short tail.

With respect to their temperament, Ernest Thompson Seton wrote in 1928, "Shy as any wild thing is the Bobcat, rarely seen except by accident, and then is quite ready to forgo all battle honours and retreat in search of peace. Nevertheless, like many a timid, law-abiding citizen, he can be terrible when put to it by desperation."

Mainly active from three hours before sunset until about midnight, and then again from before dawn until three hours after sunrise, they may, on occasion, be abroad during midday. Their sight, hearing, and sense of smell are particularly well developed, but while they can see in the dark, they cannot see in total darkness. However, they possess exceptionally sensitive whiskers that help them gain a "feel" of their surroundings. Like other cats, they have excellent balance, in addition to which they are good climbers. The most notable evidence of this quiet cat in the cirque is its tracks (Photo 8.22), droppings, and scrapes, as well as clawing prominent trees in the area. (Photo 8.23)

8.22 Fresh bobcat tracks in mud.

8.23 A bobcat's clawing on a tree along its hunting route.

The usual gait of these medium-sized predators is a stiff-legged walk, but, when in a hurry, they can cover the ground in bounds of six to eight feet. Bobcats are quick, active, and lithe. Although their endurance does not seem great, they are exceedingly well coordinated and strong.

Silent, retiring cats under normal circumstances, there is no mistaking their intention to fight for survival when cornered. With ears laid back flat against their heads and eyes flashing, they snarl and spit their defiance.

These solitary cats occupy home ranges/territories that vary widely in this mountainous terrain from 25 to 30 square miles for males and about 5 square miles for females, which they delineate by using urine, feces (Photo 8.24), scrapes in the soil and snow (Photo 8.25), and anal gland secretions to repel intruders. Whereas home ranges/territories of males will overlap those of many females, and even to some extent another male's, females are intolerant of one another; thus, their territories are strictly exclusive.

8.24 Typical bobcat droppings; note the segmentation.

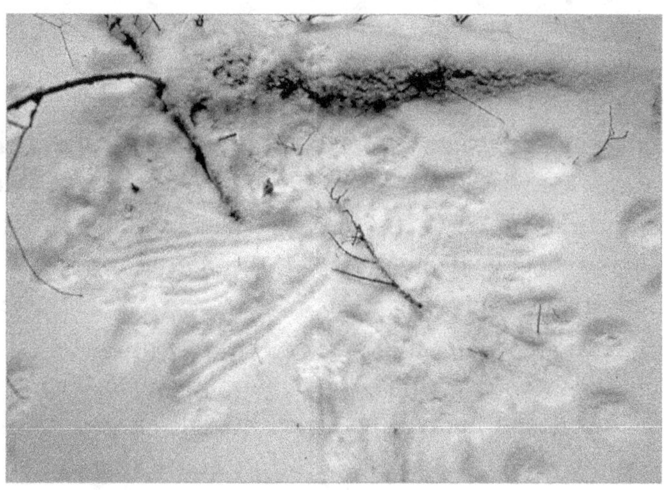

8.25 A bobcat's territorial scrape in the snow.

These highly mobile cats have several dens within various parts of their home ranges/territories. The main den of the female, whose territorial center is the cirque, is located in a small cave just above the base of the cliff near a seep toward the eastern side of the meadow. This den, which has a strong odor of its occupant, is the one in which she rears her young, and the one she lined with a shallow layer of leaves, mosses, and other vegetation, which she scratched into a shape that suited her.

This is not, however, her only den or shelter. She has one in a hollow of a fallen tree close to the place where Storm Hawk killed the deer on the 24th of June in 1575. She has another deeper in the forest under a fallen tree, and one in a large space formed centuries ago in the talus when a large boulder came to rest on top of two other boulders with a space between them. Elsewhere, in the far reaches of her territory, she has temporary shelters in dense vegetation, wherein she rests unseen during fair weather.

Hunting bobcats are not only stealthy and patient but also masters of the ambush. Because they hunt primarily by sight and sound, they spend much of their time sitting, crouching, watching, and listening. Anything attracting their attention is investigated. Moreover, they tend to travel the same general routes over and over again when they hunt, but not necessarily in a particular number of days, as evidenced by their tracks and feces.

The female in the cirque, for example, travels from two to seven miles along her habitual route. However, she adjusts her behavior seasonally, becoming more active during daylight hours in autumn and winter in response to the activity of her available prey, which in turn is more active during the day in colder months.

Strictly a carnivore (meat eater), snowshoe hares are the female's main prey in the cirque and its surrounding landscape. She also eats montane voles, deer mice, Pacific jumping mice, bushy-trailed woodrats, pikas, chipmunks, northern flying squirrels, chickarees, ruffed grouse, trout, and young deer. In essence, these tough little cats eat almost anything, including insects and carrion. Natural-born survivors, they can go for long periods without food, but will eat heavily when prey is abundant.

The female adjusts her hunting techniques according to the different sizes of her prey. With small animals, such as insects, deer mice, and squirrels, she hunts in areas of known abundance, where she lies or crouches, waiting for her quarry to wander within 10 feet so she can pounce and grab it with her sharp, retractable claws. For slightly larger animals, those weighing about 1½ to 12½ pounds, such as hares and grouse, she stalks them from cover and waits until they come within 20 to 35 feet before rushing to attack.

In winter, when her smaller prey is scarce or when the opportunity presents itself, she stalks deer, most often when the deer, usually a fawn or yearling, is lying down. When close enough, she rushes in and grabs it by the neck before biting the throat, base of the skull, or chest. Then, having eaten her fill, she covers the carcass with snow or leaves, often returning several times to dine.

As the time approaches March, the area's dominant male, among others, enters the female's territory to mate during her 44-day estrous cycle (from the Latin *oestrus*, meaning "sexual desire"). This is the only time of the year in which the two interact. Now, the pair travels together within her territory, and these otherwise silent, solitary cats engage in purring, hissing, snarling, and growling amid playfully bumping, chasing, and ambushing each other.

Being not only the last male but also the dominant male to enter her territory, just before she becomes receptive, which lasts for seven days, he grasps her in the typical, felid-neck grip and copulates with her several times. Finally, on the 11th of March, their mating consummated, she conceives six kittens, three females and three males.

Mating over, he leaves, and she begins a 67-day gestation period, which will last until the 17th of May, when her kittens are born in her den in the cliff. An excellent mother, she will raise them by herself.

Well clothed in short hair and eyes closed, the newly born young range from 7 to 7⅖ inches long and weigh from 3 to 3⅕ ounces. Their eyes open when they are nine days old. By mid-June, the kittens are beginning to explore their surroundings. And it so happens that, on the last day of June, a curious female's desire to explore led her to barely exit the den—and never return, being carried off by a male golden eagle intent on feeding his nestlings. By the end of July, the remaining kittens are weaned, and begin eating meat secured by their mother. It is end of October, however, before they are large enough to follow their mother and commence learning to hunt.

Time passes, and the youngsters, now juveniles, begin to disperse the following March, the males going the farthest, at which time their home ranges, once established, will be around three square miles. The five surviving cats weigh about 10 pounds by their first birthday, at which time the two females become sexually mature.

Thereafter, two of the males lose their lives, as they, on separate occasions, are discovered eating carrion claimed by the cirque's pack of wolves—one during a severe cold spell in December, the other in early February. With respect to the surviving male, it will take until the next May for him to reach the sexual maturity.

Of the six kittens born in the cirque that year on the 17th of May, the remaining three will live between 12 and 13 years to pass on the genetic legacy archived in each generation that survives to ensure its continuity through the millennia. Further, during their lives and those of their offspring and their offspring's offspring, the bobcats of the cirque and its surrounding terrain will play a critical role in helping to control the populations of their prey, lest the various species over-populate their habitat and alter it to their detriment.

Golden Eagle

The Golden Eagle is one of the largest, fastest, nimblest birds of prey (raptor) in North America. Adults are dark brown with a paler, but lustrous, golden sheen on the back of the head and neck, and some grey on their inner-wings and tail. Moreover, while their legs are entirely encased in feathers, the bare parts of their feet are yellow. The adult eagles residing in the cirque have whitish patches on the undersides of their wings. Their beak is dark at the tip, fading to yellowish near their head. (Photo 8.26)

8.26 Golden Eagle.

Juveniles less than a year old tend to have the most extensive amount of white in their plumage. However, because of the considerable variability in the plumage of different individuals, juvenile eagles cannot be reliably differentiated from adults on sight alone, including those attempting to nest for the first time. The final, adult plumage is attained when the birds are between 5½ and 6½ years old.

When seen at a distance, their head appears relatively small and their tail to be long, projecting farther behind their body than the head sticks out in front. They are about three feet long from the tip of their beak to the end of their tail. They have broad wings that vary in length from just over two feet to a little over three feet, and a wingspan that goes from 6 feet to 7¾ feet. Adult females, which are considerably larger than adult males, can weigh 10 to 16 pounds, whereas males weigh about 25 percent less than females, or around 4 to 6 pounds.

Eagles can rotate their head approximately 180 degrees in each direction, as opposed to humans, who can typically rotate their heads just 70 to 90 degrees in either direction. In addition, eagles' beaks and talons are made of keratin (like human finger nails), which are constantly growing, but a wild eagle's normal life maintains their proper length.

Although a single golden eagle is a solitary bird, the pair living in the cirque is mated for life. Their home range, which at times is more like a hunting territory, encompasses 59 square miles of cliffs, talus, a small lake, snowmelt ponds, streams, meadows, and various configurations of forest.

As far as territoriality is concerned, it is the primary cause of confrontations between non-paired individuals, which, as a species, maintain some of the largest-known home ranges (or territories) of any bird, the size of which may be dictated by the supply of available food and the preferred landscape. Thus, when one of the cirque's eagles sees an interloper within their territory, it treats the invader aggressively.

When the interloper is met, usually at the edge of the pair's territory, the cirque's resident eagle may precede, or follow, its direct confrontation (which consists of aggressive, direct, flapping flight with exaggerated downstrokes) with intense bouts of undulating displays, lessening the need for physical confrontations, which can be fatal. An undulating flight pattern consists of a rapid series of up to 20 steep dives at speeds up to 200 miles an hour from great height, culminating in upward swoops, with the eagle beating its wings three or four times at the apex of each rise.

For its part, the invader often responds by rolling over and presenting its talons to the territory's owner. Rarely, however, will one of the resident eagles lock talons with an interloper and tumble through the air, sometimes falling several revolutions before releasing their grip.

Another way the eagles express their aggression is through body language while perched, particularly the adult female when confronted by an intruding eagle. She holds her head and body upright, with the feathers on her head and neck erected, her wings slightly spread, and her beak open. Her intense gaze often accompanies this display.

Alternately, one of the pair engages in a similar posture with wings spread wide and oriented toward the interloper, sometimes rocking back on its tail and even flopping over onto its back with talons extended upward in defense. At times this behavior is accompanied by a wing slap against the threatening intruder. Still another approach, when confronted by an outsider, is for the defending eagle to turn away, partially spread its tail, lower its head, and remain still. Yet another tactic, one used by adults on the nest, is for them to lower their heads and "freeze" when approached by an interloper.

Superlative fliers, golden eagles are equipped with long, broad wings and a somewhat finger-like spreading of their wingtip-feathers. When they soar or glide, which they often do, their wings are lifted into a slight "V," the wingtip-feathers spread apart like fingers, and the wings and tail are held in one plane. The speed of an unhurried eagle soaring is around 28 to 32 miles an hour.

On the other hand, when they must engage in flapping, they appear at their most labored. Flapping flight generally consists of six to eight deep wing beats, interspersed with two- to three-second glides.

When hunting or displaying, an eagle is capable of gliding at speeds of 120 miles an hour. Beyond that, when aiming at prey or engaging in a territorial dispute, an eagle holds its wings partially closed, tight against its body, with its legs up against its tail. In a full dive toward prey, a golden eagle can reach speeds of 150 to 200 miles per hour, making it one of the two fastest moving animals on earth—the fastest being the peregrine falcon, which can reach speeds of 242 miles per hour.

Despite the dramatic ways in which golden eagles attain food and interact with others of their kind or raptors of other species, their daily life is often rather uneventful. For example, the adult male of the cirque frequently sits awake on a perch for 78 percent of the daylight hours, whereas his mate either sits on the nest during the breeding season or perches an average of 85 percent of the daylight hours. During the height of summer, most of the pair's hunting and territorial flights occur between 9:00 and 11:00 am and 4:00 and 6:00 pm, whereas the remaining 15 or so hours of daylight is spent perching or resting. While the pair sleeps in each other's company through much of the night, exceptionally cold winter weather may cause single, highly independent individuals to drop their usual guard and perch together.

With respect to their voice, golden eagles have a particular penchant for silence, even while breeding. Although vocalizations normally center on the nesting period, when the parents call to their offspring, one of the adults may occasionally accost an intruder, but rarely do the pair communicate vocally with each other. Vocalizations, when they do occur, include: a *chirp*, a *seeir*, a *pssa*, a *skonk*, a *cluck*, a *wonk*, a *honk*, and a *hiss*.

The pair in the cirque, like all others of their kind, have stomachs about the size of a walnut. Nevertheless, they can eat up to ⅓ of their own body weight because they have an area called the "crop" in which to store food, allowing them to survive without having to eat every day. The crop is an expanded, muscular pouch in the esophagus near the throat. In essence, it is an enlarged part of the esophagus, which, in turn, is that part of the digestive canal that connects the throat to the stomach. The crop's function is to temporarily store extra food for later consumption.

The crop is vital to an eagle's life because, while a golden eagle is one of the most powerful predatory birds in the world, its success rate in actually capturing prey is about 20 percent. In addition to which, a fully grown eagle requires from eight to almost nine ounces of food a day, but in a world where there are cycles of feast and famine, an individual may go without food for up to a week, and then gorge on two pounds at one sitting, the excess being relegated to temporary storage in its crop.

Albeit, the pair in the cirque normally hunts during daylight hours, they occasionally hunt from one hour before sunrise to one hour after sunset during the breeding season to fulfill the extra demands of their nestlings. Regardless of when they hunt, their powerful talons ensure that prey seldom escapes once it is grabbed. Why? Because the talons exert approximately 440 pounds of pressure per square inch, around 15 times more pressure than a human hand can exert.

Moreover, the eagles have seven primary hunting techniques, with many individual variations, which they can quickly employ to accommodate changing circumstances:

In the first method, the eagle soars at least 160 feet above the cirque. Once prey is sighted, it partially closes its wings and enters a long, low-angled glide that can carry it over half a mile with increasing speed, as it progressively closes its wings. Just prior to impact, the eagle opens its wings, fans it tail, and thrusts it feet forward with talons extended to grab the prey, which creates a booming sound as its wings whip against the wind, sounding like a clap of thunder in the instant before the strike. This technique is used in openings on solitary or widely dispersed prey, such as a ruffed grouse that ventured outside the forest some distance into the meadow. In this situation, a variation of the technique may be used, where a bird sits on a lofty perch and simply waits for the prey to expose itself.

The second technique is exemplified by a high soar with a vertical dive, or "stoop," which is used to attack birds in flight. Since the hunting eagle is out-paced and out-maneuvered by swift-flying birds, it can only succeed in attacking slower-flying species, such as the Barrow's goldeneye, a duck that visits the lake during the snow-free seasons. However, this method requires the eagle to have the advantage of height above its prey, if its capture is to succeed.

The third and most common method is employed by an eagle flying along a contour with a short glide, as a prelude to the attack. This tactic consists of a low-level quartering flight, often just 16 to 50 feet above the ground, a maneuver that prevents the hunting eagle from becoming visible against the sky when viewed from below, a feat accomplished by hugging the contours of the landscape. This method is useful for hunting colonial, burrowing prey, such as the Belding ground squirrels in the eastern side of the meadow. In this case, the individual squirrel is selected in a matter of seconds before the strike. If the first attempt fails, the eagle may fly around again, attempting to ambush another squirrel.

The fourth strategy commences with a low-angled dive some distance from the quarry, which is then closely chased by a gliding eagle, whether an evasively running hare or a grouse in flight. The key to success is the eagle's agility balanced by the prey's inability to reach cover.

The fifth approach is used for slow-moving prey, or any prey with little behavior geared toward escape. This includes any potentially dangerous animal, such as a young bobcat. In this case, the low-flying eagle quarters below the skyline and gradually swoops down on its intended meal. However, when hunting mammalian carnivores, such as a bobcat, the eagle may hover for some time over the potential prey and not pursue the attack unless the mammal looks down.

The sixth way of hunting is used to secure the cirque's deer. Here, the eagle flies over a family group, causing them to freeze, huddle, or break into a run. The eagle then selects it prey (typically a fawn or yearling), flies in low, and lands on the deer's back or neck, which it grips firmly in an attempt to pierce vital organs or cause shock with a crushing hold on bone and cartilage. Next, the eagle rides the deer for several minutes with its wings outstretched and flapping to maintain its balance until the deer collapses from exhaustion, shock, or internal injury.

In the seventh method of solo hunting, the eagle simply walks on the ground and attempts to grab a snowshoe hare and pull it out of the cover in which it is hiding. At other times, the eagle may even grab a small fawn and literally pull it out from between its mother's legs.

And then there is cooperative hunting by the mated pair, in which one individual follows the other at different elevations above the ground. The initial pursuer diverts the prey's attention, such as that of a young, bewildered fawn, by diving, while the second bird flies in unseen to make the kill. However, the eagles have greater success when hunting alone than when hunting as a pair.

There are times, especially during the winter months, when the ground squirrels are in hibernation and snowshoe hares and grouse tend to remain closer to cover within the forest, that the eagles scavenge for carrion. In fact, carrion can account for a significant portion (even a majority) of the eagles' diet in winter, most frequently from carcasses of such animals as elk and deer killed by the wolves, puma, and even occasionally by a bobcat. The eagles usually discover such bounty by following the ravens as they patrol the cirque for available carcasses.

The eagles in the cirque stay within their nesting territory until winter weather or snow depths get too severe, at which time they move downslope into the forest, but remain within their home range. As winter finally begins to wind down with the approach of May, the pair begins its breeding season, but do not, at this point in their relationship, repeat courtship displays and rarely engage in talon-locking, downward spirals.

Their original bond was formed six years ago when, at the age of four, they performed their first and only "sky dance," through which they both bonded for life and claimed the cirque as their original nesting territory. One form of their sky dancing was the aforementioned undulating flight pattern in which they performed a rapid series of up to 20 steep dives at speeds up to 200 miles an hour from great height, culminating in upward swoops, beating their wings three or four times at the top of each rise. In another form, known as "pendulum flight," the eagles dove and rose, then turned over to retrace their path.

Even so, the pair still engages in aerial play with objects such as rocks, sticks, or small clumps of earth. For example, the male picks up a rock or piece of wood and drops it only to enter into a steep dive and catch it in mid-air, repeating the maneuver three or more times. Meanwhile, the female takes a clump of earth, drops it, and catches it in the same fashion.

Over the years, they have built three nests (termed "eyries"), regularly spaced at seven miles apart in different areas of their territory, and used them alternately. This means one of their nests is built in an ancient tree within the forest.

This year, however, they are using their original nest for the fourth time, having done so for the last two years. It is on a ledge ¾ of the way up a largely sheer part of the cliff face, and provides them not only with an unobstructed view of the cirque and its surrounding landscape but also with maximum protection from mammalian predators.

Their nest, which they began building three months before the female laid her first clutch of eggs, has undergone several repairs over the years, each time becoming slightly larger. It was originally constructed with large sticks gleaned along the edge of the forest, some of which were around 70 inches long, about 2 inches in diameter, and weighed as much as 2 pounds. Today, their nest is 4 feet long by 4½ feet wide by 4 feet high, with an enclosed cup 3 feet wide and 1½ feet deep. The bottom of the cup is cushioned with an accumulating layer of grasses.

The nests of older mated pairs in other parts of the surrounding country, however, have reached over 10 feet in length, 7 feet in width, 14 feet in height, and 3 feet in depth, and now weigh well over 550 pounds. These nests, having been used repeatedly through the years, were repaired and enlarged with each occupation.

Today, the 23rd of April, the pair copulates for 20 seconds, but the female will not lay her eggs until the 2nd of June, at which time she lays the first, the second three days later, and the third two days after that. The eggs are white with brown spots and blotches.

The female will do most, but not all, of the incubating, which will last 44 days until the 16th of July. Prior to this time, both eagles will do their own hunting, but thereafter the male begins to feed her.

Around three o'clock in the afternoon on the 15th, the chick in the first egg laid can be heard within it. Fifteen hours later, at six o'clock in the morning on the 16th, the first chip is being broken off of the egg, after which the male chick is quiescent for around 27 hours, until nine o'clock in the morning of July 17th. The hatching activity accelerates thereafter, and the shell is broken apart by five o'clock on the 17th, 35 hours after hatching commenced. From then on, it requires only two hours, and the chick is completely free by seven o'clock, 37 hours after hatching commenced. Then comes the hatching of number two (a female) and number three (a male), upon which each chick is covered in fluffy, white down, and its eyes are partially open.

Although the chicks will weigh close to four ounces when they hatch, the first will weigh 12%10 ounces one day after hatching, the second 8%10 ounces, and the third and last 3½ ounces, easily making the largest chick the dominant one. By the time the third egg hatches, the oldest chick begins to act aggressively toward his younger siblings.

The chicks spend the first 10 days mainly lying in the bottom of the nest. Despite being covered by the body of their mother to keep them warm, they are capable of preening by the time they are two days old. Within 10 days, the first chick to hatch weighs a little over one pound—the others somewhat less—and they begin to sit up, even though their mother will now brood them until they are 20 days old.

Nevertheless, within the first two days of the younger siblings' hatching, the aggression escalates into "bill-stabbing," wherein the oldest chick jabs its younger siblings around their necks or the middle of their bodies with the intent of creating fatal wounds. Although not directly killed, the youngest chick starves to death by the time it is 15 days old, in part because it stopped begging for food once the aggression escalated, and the parents only feed begging chicks. Although their mother provides excellent parental care, and is fully aware of the aggression, she does not intervene.

In this case, however, the second-oldest chick survived. Shortly after the young are 20 days old, the amount of aggression between the two siblings decreases, and both chicks fledge, though in other nests the aggression may again increase shortly before fledging. During this time, the chick's voices grow from a soft *chirp* to a disyllabic (two-syllable) *seeir* at around 15 days of age. From then on, their voices grow louder, clearer, and into a conspicuously harsher *psaa* from about 20 days of age to as late as several weeks after fledging.

Around this time, the chicks begin standing, which becomes their main position over the next 40 days, the beginning of October. Nevertheless, the whitish down remains the nestlings' sole body cover until they are around 25 days old, at which point it is gradually replaced by dark feathers that outline their shape and create a color pattern of dark areas scattered within an overall background of whitish down.

During this time, their father captured and brought 90 percent of food to the nest. On the other hand, he perched away from the nest about 74 percent of the time, whereas their mother stayed on the nest most of the time prior to the chicks fledging. When the chicks were around 29 days old, however, she began perching off the nest, and will stop perching on the nest platform altogether when they become 40 days old.

From the age of 10 days to 45 days, the nestlings eat large quantities of food and grow considerably. As the nesting season progresses, the meals increase in size. For the first 30 days or so, the nestlings are fully dependent on their parents to feed them, but thereafter they begin standing around the edge of the nest and practice tearing their food apart. In addition, they start "mantling" over their own portion of food at around 14 days old, which means they stand over a piece of food with their wings partially open, their tails fanned, and their heads bowed, to completely cover and thus protect their food. This competitive behavior occurs only in nests with more than one chick, like the one on the cliff. Here, despite the fact that the female's daily consumption of food is greater than her male sibling's, the male will develop sooner and fledge more quickly than his sister.

With respect to sanitation, the young eagles attempt to defecate over the edge of the nest shortly after their first few meals, but they will not be competent at it until they are around 20 days old.

From 50 days of age onward, their dark-brown plumage sprouts from the same sockets as did the down, and changes in the plumage become subtler. Their feet go from flesh-colored at hatching, to grey, and then black, finally becoming yellow. As the structure of their wings develops, they start flapping their wings when they are around 20 days or so old. Thereafter, the frequency and intensity increases dramatically until they are 40 days old, after which the male fledges when he is 69 days old, September 24th, and the female fledges four days later, when she is 73 days old.

The male's first attempted flight is an abrupt departure in which he jumps off the nest and uses a series of short, stiff wing-beats to glide downward. His female sibling, on the other hand, is blown out of nest while flapping her wings. Both of their initial flights are short, on unsteady wings, and followed by uncontrolled landings.

The siblings stay within 330 feet of the nest for the first few weeks after fledging. During this time, they have a favorite perch, where their parents bring them food, which seldom requires them to take wing. Within 18 to 20 days after their first flight, the young eagles will take their first circling flight, but cannot gain height as efficiently as their parents for approximately 60 days. Then, around the time they are four months old, November 17th, they commence to shun the attention of their parents, even if offered shelter from rain.

They stay within three miles of their nest for the first 100 days after fledging, but begin dispersing over nine miles in the following 40 days. As seen from below while in flight, they have distinct white patches at the base of their primary wing feathers, and their tails are white with a distinct, dark, terminal band.

During this time, the brother-sister pair become mutually

caring, as they fly together, perch together, and preen each other for months after declaring independence. With time, they will separate, move farther apart, acquire adult plumage, find their own mates, and establish their own breeding territories.

Although 70 to 80 percent of the golden eagles hatched this year will die before they reach adulthood, between four and five years of age, the pair from the cirque will not only survive but also live to be 19 and 21 years old.

But for now, with the bobcat roaming the forest and the golden eagles patrolling the sky, autumn begins its reign in this high mountain world, as the onset of the elk's breeding season is heralded throughout the cirque by the space-piercing bugles of sexually stimulated bulls. (Photo 8.27)

8.27 Bull elk bugling.

When Roosevelt Elk Visit the Meadow

Roosevelt elk are slender-legged animals with necks that are thick in proportion to their heads. Adults grow up to 10 feet in length and stand up to 5 feet tall at the shoulders. Males, referred to as "bulls," are some 40 percent larger than females, termed "cows," at maturity and generally weigh between 700 and 1,200 pounds, while cows weigh 575 and 625 pounds. Elk, as all deer, lack upper front teeth, but they do have a pair of upper "canine teeth," or "ivories," that wear down with age. The ivories are thought to be saber-like tusks that ancestral species of elk used in combat in the receding horizon of ages past. (Photo 8.28)

8.28 Cow and bull Roosevelt elk.

There are whitish glands (metatarsal glands) below the hocks on the outsides of the hind legs. (A "hock" is equivalent to a human ankle.) Females lack antlers, but the males develop large, widely branched antlers.

The hair along the sides of the neck is long and dark, forming a dark-brown mane on the throat. The hair on the back and sides is shorter and varies from light grayish, yellowish-gray, yellowish-brown, to brown. The head, neck, mane, and legs are dark brown to almost blackish; the underparts are darker than the back. The clearly defined rump patch and short tail vary from light yellowish to dark yellowish or tannish-yellow. Cows and calves are darker than the bulls. Young calves are brownish with large yellowish-white blotches.

Over the course of a year, elk may experience temperatures ranging from 100 degrees Fahrenheit in summer to 40 degrees below zero Fahrenheit in winter. Thus, they grow a thicker coat of hair during the autumn, which helps to insulate them during the winter. The winter coat, consisting of two layers of thick, long, guard hairs and a dense, woolly undercoat, is five times warmer than their summer coat.

How, you might wonder, *is such a difference possible?* Well, the inside of each of the long, winter guard hairs resembles a bee's honeycomb, with thousands of tiny air pockets filling it. These "dead airspaces" make guard hairs both warm and waterproof. In addition, elk can make their hair stand on end, creating a thicker coat by trapping more air within it. In fact, their winter coat is so thick it allows falling snow to accumulate on their back without melting. Beyond that, they can also tuck their legs beneath them when they lie down, thus losing less heat through their legs, chest, and belly.

With the onset of warm weather, they begin rubbing against trees and other objects to help remove their heavy winter coat. The demise of their winter coat is clearly visible as ragged tatters with the old, winter hair dangling like long, scraggly beards from their necks and sides. (Photo 8.29) By July, their winter coat has been completely replaced by a thin, sleek layer of short hair, which lasts a scant two months. Although they do not look like they are shedding in September, their summer hair is falling out, as the long, thick winter coat begins replacing it.

8.29 Bull elk shedding their winter coat.

The stimulus for each year's growing/shedding of their summer and winter coats is driven by the seasonal shift in the photoperiod, the increasing or decreasing amount of light available each day. This is the same biophysical signal that causes the leaves to grow in spring and drop in autumn.

Although adult elk usually stay in single-sex groups much of the year (Photo 8.30), bulls that retain their antlers for more than half the year are unlikely to form a "bachelor group" with other antlered males, and thus live alone. Antlers are not only a secondary sex characteristic but also a means of defense, as is a strong, front-leg kick, which is performed by both sexes when provoked.

8.30 Post-breeding-season bachelor group.

Once the antlers are shed, however, bulls tend to form a bachelor group, which allows them to work cooperatively in fending off predators, such as a puma or wolves. In addition, herds tend to employ one or more scouts, whose duty it is to detect predators, thereby giving the other members time to eat and rest.

When feeling threatened by the suspected presence of a predator, an alarmed elk raises its head high, opens its eyes wide, moves stiffly, and rotates its ears to listen. Once agitated, as by the actual approach of a predator, it holds its head high while laying its ears back and flaring its nostrils. Sometimes it even punches with its front hooves. On the other hand, elk threaten one another by curling back their upper lip, grinding their teeth, and hissing softly.

The vocalization of bulls, called "bugling,"—a sound as distinctive as the howl of a gray wolf—is loud enough to be heard for miles, and is an adaptation to open environments, such as the cirque's meadow, where sound can travel great distances.

Unlike the cirque's deer, which are mainly browsers, elk are primarily grazers; but like other deer, they also browse. Moreover, elk, like cows, are ruminants, and thus not only have four-chambered stomachs but also chew their cud. It works like this:

When an elk first takes a bite of grass in the meadow, it chews just enough to moisten the food. Once swallowed, the food goes into the first section of the stomach, which is a large chamber that helps to store the food after it is eaten. Here, the initial fermentation process takes place.

The liquid resulting from this process trickles down into the second chamber, where further fermentation occurs, but the solid food is partially regurgitated up into the mouth for a second round of chewing. This process is known as "chewing the cud," and helps to further break down the food. This stomach is lined with small compartments in the shape of a honeycomb, and is known as the "Hardware Stomach" because it is the main compartment where objects, like stones, are collected and degraded by the gastric juices of the elk's intestinal tract.

The chewed cud, accompanied by the fermented liquid, then passes directly into the third chamber, which, like the first two chambers, has no digestive glands. Its function is to continue mashing up the food between its many folds, but it is the smallest of the three chambers, and soon passes the food into the fourth chamber.

It is here, in the fourth and final chamber, that the digestive glands are located. They, in turn, secrete the acid and enzymes required to break down the food, and thus form the only "real" stomach. Beyond this, the intestinal tracts of elk function much like those of the deer.

I do not know what the direct comparison between elk and domestic cows might be, but cows spend nearly eight hours out of every day chewing their cud. This duration, plus normal chewing of food, can total upwards of 40,000 jaw movements per day. Due to the similarity between elk and cows with respect to their stomachs, it is not surprising that elk tend to feed primarily in the mornings and evenings, seeking sheltered areas in between to chew their cud and digest their food.

Elk consume an average of 20 pounds of various kinds of

vegetation daily. From late spring to summer, they feed on grasses and sedges, adding various forbs to the mix in summer, going back primarily to grasses in the autumn. In winter, the scarcity of grasses causes them to add shrubs, such as elderberry and devil's club, as well as tree bark and twigs, to their diet. However, they also eat mushrooms and lichens.

Because the grasses and forbs are 80 percent digestible, the elk need to put on enough weight while on their summer range in the cirque to carry them through the winter, when much of their food is only 50 percent digestible. This means the elk need a third of their winter's diet stored in body fat accumulated during the summer and autumn, which explains why they seem to be constantly engaged in some form of eating while in the cirque.

Clearly, the breeding season, known as "rut," is now under way, as attested by the occasional frosty night and the bugling of sexually oriented bulls within the cirque and beyond. Cows, in turn, are attracted to males that bugle more often and have the loudest call.

This is the time when bulls compete for the attention of the cows and will try to defend females in their harem, which is here defined as a group of cows and calves associated with one or two mature bulls for purposes of breeding. If a harem cow wanders, the bull stretches his neck out low, tips up his nose, tilts his antlers back and circles her, thus keeping her under control from August into early winter.

On the other hand, rival bulls challenge opponents by bellowing and by paralleling each other, walking back and forth. This allows potential combatants to assess the size of each other's antlers and body as a hallmark of their fighting prowess.

Only mature bulls have harems. Bulls between two to four years old, and over 11 years of age, rarely have harems, and spend most of the rut on the harem's periphery. However, young bulls and old bulls that do acquire a harem keep it together later in the breeding season than bulls in their prime, which lasts from four until eight years of age.

A bull that wins a harem rarely eats, and so may lose up to 20 percent of his body weight. Moreover, a bull entering the rut in poor condition is not only less likely to make it through to the peak period of conception but also less likely to possess the strength to survive the rigors of the oncoming winter.

Although Storm Hawk has already been gone for some time, the story told by the elders of his tribe, which brought him to the cirque in the first place, echoes in the bugling of the elk. The story begins in the year 1301, when a father and two sons from his tribe pause at the edge of a high meadow on the slopes of a mountain that, one day in the centuries ahead, a young Indian teen will visit on a spiritual quest for the site of his ancestor's ancient hunting camp, but for now, it is a balmy September afternoon. The man leads the boys to a small clump of subalpine fir in the upper part of the meadow and instructs them to make camp. The boys gather wood, build a small lean-to shelter of dead sapling poles and fir boughs, and then explore the small stream rushing its way through the meadow.

The man leaves and walks quietly along the edge of the meadow toward the forest looking for signs of elk, which they have come to hunt. He pauses, climbs a small, rocky promontory, and surveys the forest. He is glad that he brought his sons to this place.

Morning arrives cold and clear. After completing their duties, they take their short, heavy elk bows and quivers of stout arrows and leave camp. They move along the edge of the meadow toward an area of the forest recovering from a fire in the year 987. The boys are going to learn how to hunt elk, and they are excited.

Hunting elk is a critical event in the life of a boy because it takes a stronger bow than it does to kill a deer. To hunt elk is therefore an important step toward manhood, a rite of passage, and a lesson in humility because elk, the second largest deer in what will, at some future time, be called the "New World," can be elusive and dangerous, especially the bulls during the breeding season.

The father leads his sons to the edge of the forest with its interspersed openings, which are characteristic of this subalpine area. Here they begin to follow a well-used elk trail through the thickets toward the coolness of the ancient forest. They walk in silence for three and a half hours and come to a spring, where they drink and rest.

They follow the elk trail further into the ancient forest. It goes steeply up to the base of a cliff. Here they find the disarticulated, partly eaten skeleton of a cow elk. They stop to examine it. The father points to what is left of the ribs and tells his sons wolves have eaten on them.

"You can tell by the way the softer parts of the bones have been chewed off."

"What killed the elk?" asks the younger son.

"I don't know," answers the father, "the bones are too scattered to tell even though it has only been here since last winter. You can tell that by these small pieces of tough sinew that still cling to the spine."

The older son brings the skull to his father. He looks at it and says, "She was very old; look how her special teeth are worn down."

They move on without unraveling the history of last winter's incident when, during the first snows before migration, a pack of seven wolves chased the cow along the ridge until she panicked and ran toward the cliff, where she slipped in the snow and fell over the edge, breaking her neck. The wolves and ravens had done the rest.

They climb up a steep trail at the end of the cliff and come to a small pass leading down into the next basin and headwater stream. Here they find a fir sapling completely shredded from the ground up to seven feet, where a large bull elk had thrashed his antlers. Next to it is a larger sapling with its bark scraped off one side. The father points to it and tells his sons how the cows marked the area with their lower, front teeth by scraping them upward against the trunk of the tree, letting the shavings drop to the ground.

They follow the elk trail, periodically coming to bull rubs and cow scrapes. The boys learn that a mature, breeding bull usually holds a small basin as his breeding territory, and that he marks its boundaries with signposts alongside of which the cows scrape. They learn that each territory has at least one pass into another drainage that serves as an escape route, and that each territory has at least one well-concealed, well-protected, high spot, where the bull can rest in safety and know what goes on around him without exposing himself.

"Sometimes," their father tells them, "if a wise, old bull wants to watch the world, he will back his rear into lower limbs of a young fir tree and so hide his light yellowish rump. This leaves his head and dark forequarters to protrude, which makes him seem to disappear. In this way, he can watch the world and still be very difficult to see."

They learn that elk are noisy when undisturbed, the cows and calves calling back and forth, rustling branches, breaking twigs, snorting and wheezing as they breathe, and that these huge animals can suddenly become as spirits, moving silently and swiftly with nothing but their tracks and a warm, musky odor to attest their passage.

"Elk," their father explains, "have a female (matriarchal) society in which the adult bulls live separately from the adult cows during the non-breeding season. A matriarchal herd (cow herd) is composed of cows, their calves, and subadults (adolescents) of both sexes.

The degree to which a member of a particular sex and age class associates with the central cow-calf unit is determined by the behavioral interrelationships of that individual with the other members of the herd. Yearling bulls, for example, show a strong cow-herd attachment at those times of the year when they are not driven out by an adult bull during the breeding season or when the cows are not giving birth to calves.

The composition of a cow herd dominated by an old "lead" cow seems most stable from November to May, and the association of subadult bulls with the cow herd reaches a peak during the winter. The duration of these visits decreases annually, however, as the bulls approach maturity.

Adult bulls join a cow herd only temporarily during the breeding season. When not accompanying the cows, they gather into bachelor groups.

A cohesive herd has a central area that it uses to the exclusion of other individuals or herds even though the area is not actively defended. As the distance from the central area increases, use by the resident herd decreases, and competition with other groups intensifies.

A herd's strong orientation toward its central area is probably based on the area's availability of preferred food, water, cover, and knowledge of the escape routes. Although precise boundaries do not exist, there is seldom an overlap between closely adjoining herds and little trespassing, perhaps because the resident herd "sign posts" trees more frequently within its central area than it does outside it, communicating its monopoly of the area.

The herd uses the lower portion of the meadow as its primary feeding area. It also uses the ancient forest, which has cool temperatures on hot days and has a good ground cover of herbs and some grasses. In addition, the stream within the ancient forest has several places to drink.

Thus the herd's central area has water, food, and both hiding cover and thermal cover. Hiding cover is used for escape, to see without being seen, and is capable of concealing 90 percent of a standing elk at a distance of 200 feet or less. Thermal cover, on the other hand, can act as hiding cover, but also is large enough in size and dense enough to produce its own internal climate—cool in summer and warm in winter—that allows an elk to maintain a nearly constant core-body temperature, which conserves its energy.

The boys learned about thermal cover on the second to the last day of their stay with the elk. It was a very hot afternoon when they crawled into the coolness of a dense thicket and saw nothing but the legs of elk moving among the young trees.

They also watched a cow "sign posting" along the edge of the thicket. She started by carefully drawing her nose several times up and down a small tree, as though sniffing it. She then scraped the tree with her lower front teeth, drawing them in deliberate, vertical strokes from the bottom to the top of the area she had marked with her nose. The shavings simply fell and accumulated on the ground. She then deliberately rubbed the sides of her muzzle and chin against her flanks.

When they told their father what they had seen, he said, "Bulls of five summers and older do the same thing, but they use the base of their antlers to scrape the trees."

The boys had heard from other boys in their village that bulls rub the skin off their antlers because it itches. They asked if what the other boys had said was true because all the bulls they had thus far seen already had shining antlers without skin. Their father told them he had seen bulls go for many days with bothersome masses of stripped skin hanging over their eyes without making any attempt to remove it, even though it was obvious that it was causing them a great deal of annoyance.

"The skin does not itch," he said, "because the antlers are dead and hard when the skin begins to come off. It comes off by accident or when the bulls start to sign post early enough to rub it off before it simply falls off by itself."

After a pause to see if his sons were following what he was saying, he continued, "Such early rubbing is always rather gentle and hesitant as though the antlers are not yet completely hardened and capable of withstanding the heavy pressure and rough use we have seen in the last few days. The antlers are a dingy brown when the skin has just dropped off, but as breeding intensifies, and bulls begin to thrash vegetation, like we saw yesterday, their antlers become even more polished and gleaming than they are now. But not all bulls have antlers of the same color because they become stained by whatever vegetation they most frequently attack."

The boys remembered the bull they watched the day before. It was a big, light-tan bull with a dark-brown head and long, dark-brown mane; in fact, he was so big that he had thrust his head against a young tree, just over two inches in diameter, and shook his head so vigorously that the tree broke.

The bull had then attacked a shrub, and while attacking it, had unsheathed his penis and eliminated copious amounts of urine in spurts that had carried over three feet. He had directed the urine along his belly, thoroughly soaking the dark-brown hair, and had then lowered his head and saturated the long, dark mane on his throat and the sides of his face. He backed out of the shrub after a few minutes and dug his antlers into the urine-soaked grass and herbs, flinging them over his back. Finally, he lay down in the urine-soaked area and rolled several times before leaving.

They watched another bull wade into the stagnant water and foul-smelling mud of a wallow and submerge his head and neck in the water. He then knelt and rubbed his chest, neck, and face in the slimy mud on the bottom.

After having watched the bulls, the boys decided they were glad men didn't have to go through all this just to interest girls. If they did, the boys would have remained bachelors.

"Do bulls get killed very often when they fight?" the younger boy asked his father.

"No. They do get hurt, and even killed, but not so many as die in the winter of hunger," his father answered. "I remember watching one fight many seasons ago. A young bull approached a herd of cows that belonged to a large bull. Each of the bulls called out several times in a loud voice (bugled) and circled the other about 50 feet away. Suddenly, they stopped and charged, their antlers coming together with a terrific crash. They pushed and twisted. Finally, with a sudden twist of his head, the big bull threw the young bull to one side, and taking advantage of the opening, charged into the young bull's right side with his antlers, knocking him off his feet. When he got up, he left in a hurry!"

There is much to learn. So the father and sons spend several days among the elk because the tribe will hunt the elk when they move to lower elevations for winter. And a successful hunt depends on a hunter's knowledge, for this is in the days before horses, when The People of the Land had to carry everything on their backs.

The father allows his sons to kill one calf so they might learn how to hunt and feed their families, and eventually their parents in the seasons to come. He allows them to kill only a calf because that is all they can use until the tribal hunt. The father is pleased with his sons, and they are wiser boys who leave the meadow and the forest and the elk, who travel through a land of yellows, reds, browns, and oranges of vine maple in the waning days of September.

Like their father before them, they leave something of themselves, of their youth, in this high country. And, in turn, they take a measure of adulthood, a measure of dignity and of humility back to their village at the base of the great mountains.

The land again belongs to the elk and to the wolves and puma that hunt the elk year round for food. For now, the elk continue to live as elk live without human presence.

What their father did not tell them, because he did not know, is that on top of each bull's head are two specialized bone follicles covered with skin. Antlers grow out of these follicles every spring and summer, triggered by the increasing daylight, which in turn elevates the level of the hormone "testosterone" in the elk's blood, stimulating the growth of antlers.

Antlers begin as layer upon layer of cartilage that slowly mineralizes into bone. A soft, tender covering, called "velvet," both protects the developing antlers and carries blood to the growing bone tissue. (Photo 8.31) If you were to look closely at a hardened antler, you would see grooves and ridges on it, marking the paths of veins that carried blood throughout the velvet during the antler's development.

8.31 Bull elk in velvet antlers.

Because the velvet is easily damaged, injuries can cause a bull to have malformed antlers for a given year or sometimes for the rest of his life. Antler-cells grow faster than any other kind of bone, up to one inch per day during the summer. When, however, the blood stops flowing in August, the antlers mineralize and harden, and the velvet both falls off on its own and is rubbed off by the bull. The hardened antlers are composed of calcium, phosphorous, and as much as 50 percent water.

Testosterone continues to build within the bulls well into September, prompting them to seek receptive cows, fight other bulls, and mate. But then the level of testosterone begins to slowly drop by October and continues to decline until early spring, when the antlers drop off. The follicles out of which the antlers grew bleed a little, but soon heal. Then comes the spring green-up, and the cycle commences again, as a new set of antlers begins to sprout.

A bull usually grows slim, 10- to 20-inch long, unbranched antlers, called spikes, in his second year. By the third year, his antlers begin developing tines that branch from the main beam, and by his seventh summer, his antlers may have six tines each, weigh as much as 40 pounds, and grow to a length and spread of more than four feet. A large set of antlers identifies a bull that is successful not only in finding food but also in eating a lot.

Both the quantity and quality of the food a bull consumes is critical because an enormous amount of nutrients is required to obtain the energy and minerals needed to grow antlers, as well as the energy to carry them. In addition, large antlers identify a bull that is able to defend himself against other bulls and predators. This information is of great interest to the cows, because they normally choose to mate with the strongest, most successful bulls—those with the biggest antlers.

The last day of September becomes the first day of October, and by the end of October, most of the cows are bred and on the way to the winter range. Some of the bulls will follow the cows to lower elevations, but the biggest ones will stay in the high country until the snow is so deep they are forced to leave or die.

Cows have a short estrous cycle of only a day or two, and mating usually involves a dozen or more attempts. The cows will carry their calves for 255 to 275 days and will give birth in and around the cirque during the last week in May and the first week in June. Just before giving birth, a cow leaves the herd and selects a place where she will give birth to a single young, seldom two, weighing between 33 and 35 pounds. The newly born calf can stand by the time it is 20 minutes old. The mother and her new offspring will rejoin the herd in a week or so, at which time the calf is well coordinated and able to keep up with its mother.

When alarmed or frightened, cows emit a call similar to the bark of a dog; this call warns the calves, especially before a mother and her new offspring return to the safety of the herd. The newborn calf reacts immediately to the bark of a cow. It conceals itself in any available vegetation by dropping to its belly, stretching its head out flat on the ground, and remaining motionless. (Photo 8.32) The light blotches on its overall dark coat help to disrupt its outline, making it difficult to see, and the fact that it is odorless makes it virtually impossible to detect. Once a mother and her calf return to the herd, however, a bark does not cause the youngster to hide, but it does direct its attention to whatever made the cow give the alarm.

8.32 Recently born elk calf in defensive posture.

Calves depend mainly on their mothers' milk for the first four to six weeks and may nurse five or six times a day. They are tended by a "babysitter" cow, who keeps them together while their mothers feed. Young calves are kept close by a series of vocalizations, which means that within the "nursery" is an ongoing and constant chatter during the daytime hours.

When it is time for a youngster to nurse, its mother calls her baby with a high-pitched "neigh." The nursing period over, the calf's mother simply walks away and starts to eat. Further attempts by the calf to nurse may bring a resounding whack across its back from a front hoof or a butt from the side of her head, but her youngster normally returns to the babysitter without hesitation.

As the calves become less dependent on milk, the babysitter becomes more lax in her efforts to keep them together. By autumn the calves have not only lost their spots but also are feeding with the herd and have outgrown the need for a babysitter, but they still tend to remain together. Although some of the young will fall to predation and injury throughout the passage of seasons, others will live 10 to 13 years.

As September passes into October, the days and nights grow increasingly colder. In its turn, December is very cold and the snows are deep, forcing the elk into the ancient forest at lower elevations along the big river. Here, protected from the snow by the huge trees, they have good thermal cover and food. Although not all will survive until spring, the cows will add new life to the herd when the sun is again warm, the breezes gentle, and they are once more on their summer range in the cirque.

So, my friend, we come to the end of our journey. While we have glimpsed an infinitesimal part of the life and biophysical dynamics that make up this high-mountain world, I could not—in many lifetimes—reveal it all to you. I say this because, as you may remember, the cirque is at once a historical archive; a dynamic, living system; and a present encyclopedia of knowledge. The magnificence and wonder of its ongoing creation is, to me, beyond words, beyond thought. With that, I must leave you. It is, however, with deep, abiding joy that I have been able to spend a few days in the cirque with you.

APPENDIX: COMMON AND SCIENTIFIC NAMES OF PLANTS AND ANIMALS

FUNGI
Amanita	*Amanita* spp.
Fungi	Zygomycota
Mushrooms	Agaricomycetes
Root-rot fungus	*Phytophthora cinnamomi*
Slime mold	*Fuligo septica*

LICHENS
Fremont's lichen	*Bryoria fremontii*
Lichens	Mycophycophyta

ALGAE
Algae	Protista

FERNS
Deer fern	*Blechnum spicant*
Parsley fern	*Cryptogramma crispa*

GRASSES AND GRASS-LIKE PLANTS
Grasses	Gramineae
Sedge	*Carex* spp.
Tufted hairgrass	*Deschampsia cespitosa*

FORBES
Alpine shooting star	*Dodecatheon alpinum*
American twinflower	*Linnea borealis*
Aster	*Aster* spp.
Avalanche lily	*Erythronium montanum*
Bear grass	*Xerophyllum tenax*
Bedstraw	*Galium* spp.
Beggar-tick	*Bidens* spp.
Buttercup	Ranunculus spp.
Cinquefoil	*Potentilla* spp.
Coltsfoot	*Petasites frigidus*
Common monkey flower	*Mimulus guttatus*
Davidson's penstemon	*Penstemon davidsonii*

Fireweed	*Epilobium* spp.
Gentian	*Gentiana sceptrum*
Glacier lily	*Erythronium grandiflorum*
Indian lettuce	*Claytonia perfoliata*
Lupine	*Lupinus* spp.
Oregon oxalis	*Oxalis oregana*
Oregon sedum	*Sedum oregonense*
Paintbrush	*Castilleja* spp.
Penstemon	Penstemon spp.
Pink monkey flower	*Mimulus lewisii*
Scarlet gilia	*Ipomopsis aggregata*
Stonecrop	*Sedum* spp.
Subalpine lupine	*Lupinus latifolius*
White marsh marigold	*Caltha leptosepala*
Woolly sunflower	*Eriophyllum lanatum*

TREES AND SHRUBS

Alders	*Alnus* spp.
Avocado	*Persea americana*
Colorado piñon pine	*Pinus edulis*
Devil's club	*Oplopanax horridum*
Douglas-fir	*Pseudotsuga menziesiis*
Dwarf willow	*Salix herbacea*
Elderberry	*Sambucus* spp.
Engelmann spruce	*Picea engelmannii*
Ginkgo	*Ginkgo biloba*
Grand fir	*Abies grandis*
Huckleberries	*Vaccinium* spp.
Limber pine	*Pinus flexilis*
Lodgepole pine	*Pinus contorta*
Mountain hemlock	*Tsuga mertensiana*
Mountain huckleberry	*Vaccinium membranaceum*
Mountain willow	*Salix eastwoodiae*
Noble fir	*Abies procera*
Salal	Gaultheria shallon
Silver fir	*Abies amabilis*
Single-leaf piñon pine	*Pinus monophylla*
Sitka alder	*Alnus viridis*
Southwestern white pine	*Pinus strobiformis*
Subalpine fir	*Abies lasiocarpa*

Vine maple   *Acer circinatum*
Western spring beauty   *Montia sibirica*
Whitebark pine   *Pinus albicaulis*
Willow   *Salix* spp.

INVERTEBRATES: BACTERIA

Bacteria   Prokaryotes

PROTOZOA

Protozoa   Eukaryotes

WORMS

Cascade earthworm   *Megascolides cascadensis*
Earthworms   Annelida

MOLLUSKS

Slugs   Molluska
Snails   Molluska

CRUSTACEANS

Signal crayfish   *Pacifastacus leniusculus*

ISOPODS

Pillbugs   *Armadillidium vulgare*
Sowbugs   *Porcellio scaber*

MILLIPEDES AND CENTIPEDES

Centipedes   Chilopoda
Millipedes   Diplopoda

SPIDERS AND TICKS

Crab spiders   Thomisidae
Spiders   Arachnida
Spider mites   Tetranychidae
Winter tick   *Dermacentor albipictus*

INSECTS

Alderfly   Sialidae
Ancient dragonfly (extant)   *Epiophlebia* spp.

Ants	Formicidae
Aphids	Aphididae
Bees	Hymenoptera
Bee fly	Bombyliidae
Beetles	Coleoptera
Bugs	Hemiptera
Bumblebees	*Bombus* spp.
Butterflies	Lepidoptera
Caddisflies	Trichoptera
Carpenter ants	*Camponotus* spp.
Cascade tiger beetle	*Cicindela longilabris ostenta*
Click beetle	Elateridae
Convergent lady beetle	*Hippodamia convergens*
Craneflies	Tipulidae
Crickets	Gryllidae
Damp-wood termite	*Zootermopsis angusticollis*
Damselflies	Odonata
Dragonfly	Odonata
Flat bark beetles	Cucujidae
Fleas	Siphonaptra
Flea beetle	Chrysomclidac
Flies	Diptera
Forest tent caterpillar	*Malacosoma disstria*
Grasshoppers	Orthoptera
Green lacewing	Chrysopidae
Ground beetles	Carabidae
Housefly	*Musca domesticas*
Lacewing	Chrysopidae
Lady beetle	Coccinellidae
Leaf beetle	Chrysomelidae
Lightning bugs (aka firefly)	Lampyridae
Mantids	Mantidaes
Mayfly	Ephemeroptera
Midges	Chironomidae
Monarch butterfly	*Danaus plexippus*
Mosquitoes	Culicidae
Moths	Lepidoptera
Northern Caddisfly	*Ecclisocosmoecus scylla*
Predacious diving beetle	*Dytiscus* spp.
Sea skaters	*Halobates* spp.

Scale insects   Hemiptera
Scarab beetles   Scarabaeidae
Springtails   Collembola
Stinkbug   Pentatomidae
Stonefly   Plecoptera
Syrphid fly   Syrphidae
Walking sticks   Phasmatodea
Wasps   Hymenoptera
Water strider   Gerridae
Weevils   Curculionidae
Whirligig beetle   Gyrinidae
Wood-eating cranefly *Lipsothrix* spp.
Yellowjacket   *Vespula maculifrons*

VERTEBRATES:
FISH
Rainbow trout   *Oncorhynchus mykiss*

AMPHIBIANS
Cascade frog   *Rana cascadae*
Long-toed salamander *Ambystoma macrodactylum*
Western toad   *Bufo boreas*

REPTILES
Western terrestrial garter snake *Thamnophis elegans*

BIRDS
Barrow's goldeneye   *Bucephala islandica*
Black-chinned hummingbird *Archilochus alexandri*
Broad-billed hummingbird *Cynanthus latirostris*
Broad-tailed hummingbird *Selasphorus platycercus*
Burrowing owl   *Athene cunicularia*
Canada goose   *Branta canadensis*
Chickadees   *Poecile* spp.
Clark's nutcracker   *Nucifraga columbiana*
Cliff swallows   *Petrochelidon pyrrhonota*
Common raven   *Corvus corax*
Dark-eyed junco   *Junco hyemalis*
European common cuckoo *Cuculus canorus*
Flammulated owl   *Psiloscops flammeolus*

Golden eagle	*Aquila chrysaetos*
Gray-crowned rosy-finch	*Leucosticte tephrocotis*
Gray jay	*Perisoreus canadensis*
Great horned owl	*Bubo virginianus*
Hummingbirds	Trochilidae
Kinglet	*Regulus* spp.
Killdeer	*Charadrius vociferus*
Mountain chickadee	*Poecile gambeli*
North African ostrich	*Struthio camelus camelus*
Northern goshawk	*Accipiter gentilis*
Nuthatch	*Sitta* spp.
Oregon junco	*Junco hyemalis oreganus*
Owls	Strigiformes
Peregrine falcon	*Falco peregrinus*
Pileated woodpecker	*Dryocopus pileatus*
Red-breasted nuthatch	*Sitta canadensis*
Ruffed grouse	*Bonasa umbellus*
Rufous hummingbird	*Selasphorus rufus*
Sapsucker	*Sphyrapicus* spp.
Sharp-shinned hawk	*Accipiter striatus*
Spotted sandpiper	*Actitis macularia*
Steller's jay	*Cyanocitta stelleri*
Swainson's thrush	*Catharus ustulatus*
Tree swallows	*Tachycineta bicolor*
Turkey vulture	*Cathartes aura*
Varied thrush	*Ixoreus naevius*
Vaux's swift	*Chaetura vauxi*
Violet-crowned hummingbird	*Amazilia violiceps*
Wablers	Parulidae
Western screech owl	*Megascops kennicottii*
Wilson's warbler	*Wilsonia pusilla*
Winter wren	*Troglodytes troglodytes*

MAMMALS

Big brown bat	*Eptesicus fuscus*
Black bear	*Ursus americanius*
Black-tailed deer	*Odocoileus hemionus columbianus*
Bobcat	*Felis rufus*
Bushy-tailed woodrat	*Neotoma cinerea*
California bat	*Myotis californicus*

Cascade red fox	*Vulpes vulpes cascadensis*
Chickaree (aka Douglas squirrel)	*Tamiasicurus douglasi*
Coast mole	*Scapanus orarius*
Coyote	*Canis latrans*
Deer mouse	*Peromyscus maniculatus*
Douglas squirrel (aka chickaree)	*Tamiasicurus douglasi*
German shepherd	*Canis lupus familiaris*
Gray wolf	*Canis lupus*
Heather vole	*Phenacomys intermedius*
Hoary bat	*Lasiurus cinereus*
Hyenas	Hyaenidae
Little brown bat	*Myotis lucifigus*
Long-eared bat	*Myotis evotis*
Long-legged bat	*Myotis volans*
Long-tailed weasel	*Mustela frenata*
Mantled ground squirrel	*Callospermophilus lateralis*
Marsh shrew	*Sorex bendirii*
Marten	*Martes americana*
Mazama pocket gopher	*Thomomys mazama*
Montane vole	*Microtus montanus*
Mule deer	*Odocoileus hemionus*
North American black bear	*Ursus americanus*
North American elk	*Cervus elaphus*
North American pika	*Ochotona princeps*
Northern flying squirrel	*Glaucomys sabrinus*
Northern water shrew	*Sorex palustris*
Pacific jumping mouse	*Zapus trinotatus*
Puma (aka mountain lion)	*Puma concolor*
Rock rabbit (aka pika)	*Ochotona princeps*
Roosevelt elk	*Cervus elaphus roosevelti*
Shrew-mole	*Neürotrichus gibbsi*
Short-tail weasel	*Mustela erminea*
Silver-haired bat	*Lasionycteris noctivagans*
Snowshoe hare	*Lepus americanus*
Townsend big-eared bat	*Plecotus townsendii*
Townsend chipmunk	*Tamias townsendii*
Water vole	*Microtus richardsoni*
Western red-backed vole	*Clethrionomys californicus*
Yellow-pine chipmunk	*Tamias amoenus*

REFERENCES

Ackerman B.B., F.G. Lindzey, T.P. Hemker. 1984. Cougar food habits in southern Utah. *Journal of Wildlife Management*, 48:147–155.

Acquisto, A-C. Townsend's chipmunk. http://animaldiversity.ummz.umich.edu/accounts/Tamias_townsendii/ (accessed September 13, 2014).

Addison, E.M., R.D. Strickland, and D.J.H. Fraser. 1989. Gray Jays, *Perisoreus canadensis*, and common ravens, *Corvus corax*, as predators of winter ticks, *Dermacentor albipictus. The Canadian Field-Naturalist*, 103:406–408.

Ali, S. 1936. Do birds employ ants to rid themselves of ectoparasites? *Journal of the Bombay Natural History Society*, 38:628–631.

Allee, W.C. http://en.wikipedia.org/wiki/Warder_Clyde_Allee (accessed June 11, 2014).

Allen, D.L. 1938. Notes on the killing technique of the New York weasel. *Journal of Mammalogy*, 19:225–229.

Allen, G.M. 1939. Bats. Harvard University Press, Cambridge, MA. 368 pp.

Allen, J.A. 1890. A Review of some of the North American ground squirrels of the genus *Tamias. Bulletin of the American Museum of Natural History*, 3:45-116.

Alsop, F. J., III. 2001. Smithsonian Birds of North America, Western Region. DK Publishing, Inc., New York, NY. 752 pp.

Alt, D.D. and D.W. Hyndman. 1978. Roadside Geology of Oregon. Mountain Press Publishing Co., Missoula, MT. 280 pp.

Altmann, M. 1952. Social behavior of elk, *Cervus canadensis nelsoni*, in the Jackson Hole area of Wyoming. *Behavior*, 4:116–143.

American Black Bear. http://www.nwf.org/wildlife/wildlife-library/mammals/black-bear.aspx (accessed September 24, 2014).

American Black Bear. http://en.wikipedia.org/wiki/American_black_bear (accessed September 24, 2014).

Andersen, N.M. and L. Cheng. 2004. The Marine Insect Halobates (Heteroptera: Gerridae): Biology, Adaptations, Distribution, And Phylogeny. *Oceanography and Marine Biology: an Annual Review*, 42:119–180.

Anderson, V. Creation of the Cascade Mountains. http://highonadventure.com/Hoa08apr/Vicki/creation%20of%20the%20cascade%20mountains.htm. (accessed January 13, 2014).

Anting (bird activity). http://en.wikipedia.org/wiki/Anting_(bird_activity) (accessed December 1, 2014).

Aphid. http://en.wikipedia.org/wiki/Aphid (accessed June 15, 2014).

Ar, A., C.V. Paganelli, R.B. Reeves, and others. 1974. The avian egg: water-vapor conductance, shell thickness, and functional pore area. *The Condor*, 76:153–158.

Ar, A. and H. Rahn. 1985. Pores in avian eggshells: gas conductance, gas exchange and embryonic growth rate. *Respiration Physiology*, 61:1–20.

Armitage, K.B. 1981. Sociality as a life-history tactic of ground squirrels. *Oecologia*, 48:36–49.

Armstrong, D., J.P. Fitzgerald, and C.A. Meaney. 2011. Mammals of Colorado, Second Edition. University Press of Colorado. Boulder, CO. 704 pp.

Asa, C.S., L.D. Mech, U.S. Seal, and E.D. Plotka. 1990. The influence of social and endocrine factors on urine-marking by captive wolves (*Canis lupus*). *Hormones and Behavior*, 24:497–509.

Ashford, D.A., W.A. Smith, and A.E. Douglas. 2000. Living on a high sugar diet: the fate of sucrose ingested by a phloem-feeding insect, the pea aphid *Acyrthosiphon pisum*. *Journal of Insect Physiology*, 46:335–341.

Astronomy 161. http://csep10.phys.utk.edu/astr161/lect/earth/tectonics. html (accessed on April 5, 2013).

Attila. http://en.wikipedia.org/wiki/Attila (accessed September 8, 2014).

Atzet, T. and L.A. McCrimmon. 1990. Preliminary plant associations of the southern Oregon Cascade Mountain province. Grants Pass, OR: U.S. Department of Agriculture, Forest Service, Siskiyou National Forest. 330 pp.

Bailey, V. 1936. The Mammals and Life Zones of Oregon. *North American Fauna*, 55:1–416.

Bak, P. and K. Chen. 1991. Self-organizing criticality. *Scientific American*, January:46–53.

Baker, L.A., R.J. Warrena, D.R. Diefenbacha, and others. 2001. Prey Selection by Reintroduced Bobcats (*Lynx rufus*) on Cumberland Island, Georgia. *The American Midland Naturalist*, 145:80–93.

Bakken, G.S., V.C. Vanderbilt, W.A. Buttemer, and W.R. Dawson. 1978. Avian eggs—thermoregulatory value of very high near-infrared reflectance. *Science*, 200:321–323.

Bakker, V.J., and K. Hastings, K. 2002. Den trees used by northern flying squirrels (*Glaucomys sabrinus*) in southeastern Alaska. *Canadian Journal of Zoology*, 80:1623–1633.

Balda R. and C. Kamil. 1992. Long-term spatial memory in Clark's nutcracker, *Nucifraga columbiana*. *Animal Behavior*, 44:761–769.

Balda R. and C. Kamil. 2002. Spatial and social cognition in corvids: An evolutionary approach. Pp. 129–134. *In*: The cognitive animal. (Bekoff, M., C. Allen, and G. M. Burghardt eds.). MIT Press, Cambridge, MA.

Banfield, A.W.F. 1974. The Mammals of Canada. University of Toronto Press, Toronto, CA. 438 pp.

Barbour, R.W. and W.H. Davis. 1969. Bats of America. University of Kentucky Press, Lexington, KY. 286 pp.

Barnard, W.H. 1996. Juvenile Grey Jay preys upon magnolia warbler. *Journal of Field Ornithology*, 67:252–253.

Basic Facts About Black Bears. http://www.defenders.org/black-bear/basic-facts (accessed September 24, 2014).

Basic Facts About Bobcats. http://www.defenders.org/bobcat/bobcats (accessed October 24, 2014).

Bartels, M.A. and D.P. Thompson.1993. Spermohilus lateralis. *Mammalian Species*, 440:1–8.

Bauer, J.W., K.A. Logan, L.L. Sweanor, and W.M. Boyce. 2005. Scavenging Behavior in Puma. *The Southwestern Naturalist*, 50:466–471.

Bear Smart Society. Reproduction. http://www.bearsmart.com/resources/north-american-bears/reproduction (accessed September 27, 2014).

Beever, E.A., P.F. Brussard and J. Berger. 2003. Patterns of apparent extirpation among isolated populations of pikas (*Ochotona princeps*) in the Great Basin. *Journal of Mammalogy*, 84:37–54.

Behnke, R. 1992. Native trout of western North America. American Fisheries Society, Bethesda, Md. 275pp.

Behrend, D.F. and R.W. Sage Jr. 1974. Unusual feeding behavior by black bears. *Journal of Wildlife Management*, 38:570.

Beiswenger, R.E. 1981. Predation by gray jays on aggregating tadpoles of the boreal toad *Bufo boreas*. *Copeia*, 1981:459–460.

Belding's ground squirrel. http://en.wikipedia.org/wiki/Belding's_ground_squirrel (accessed October 6, 2014).

Belding's Ground Squirrel, (*Urocitellus beldingi*). http://www.redorbit.com/education/reference_library/animal_kingdom/mammalia/1112518983/belding's-ground-squirrel-urocitellus-beldingi/ (accessed October 6, 2014).

Belltawn, M. *Spermophilus lateralis*. http://animaldiversity.ummz.umich.edu/accounts/Spermophilus_lateralis/ (accessed September 29, 2014).

Beneski, J. and D. Stinson.1987. Sorex palustris. *Mammalian Species*, 296:1–6.

Beng, S.E. and A. Dornhaus. 2014. Be meek or be bold? A colony-level behavioural syndrome in ants. *Proceeding of the Royal Society B*, 281 no. 1791 (2014) doi: 10.1098/rspb.2014.0518.

Berendse, B. and M. Scheffer. 2009. The angiosperm radiation revisited, an ecological explanation for Darwin's 'abominable mystery'. *Ecology Letters*, 12:865–872.

Bhullar, B-A.S., J. Marugán-Lobón, F. Racimo, and others. 2012. Birds have paedomorphic dinosaur skulls. *Nature*, 487:223–226.

Bihr, K. and R. Smith. 1998. Location, structure and contents of burrows of *Spermophulus lateralis* and *Tamias minimus*, two ground-dwelling sciurids. *Southwestern Naturalist*, 43:352–362.

Birchard, G.F. and D.C. Deeming. 2009. Avian eggshell thickness: scaling and maximum body mass in birds. *Journal of Zoology*, 279:95–101.

Blanckenhorn, W. 1991. Fitness consequences of foraging success in water striders (*Gerris remigis*; Heteroptera: Gerridae). *Behavioral Ecology*, 2:46–55.

Bloom, P.H. and S.J. Hawks. 1982. Food habits of nesting Golden Eagles in northeast California and northwest Nevada. *Raptor Research*, 16:110–115.

Boag, D.A. 1977. Summer food habits of Golden Eagles in southwestern Alberta. *Canadian Field-Naturalist*, 91:296–298.

Bobcat. http://en.wikipedia.org/wiki/Bobcat (accessed October 24, 2014).

Bobcat. http://animals.nationalgeographic.com/animals/mammals/bobcat/ (accessed October 24, 2014).

Bobcat. http://bigcatrescue.org/bobcat-facts/ (accessed October 24, 2014).

Bogan, M.A. 1972. Observations on parturition and development in the hoary bat, *Lasiurus cinereus*. *Journal of Mammalogy*, 53:611–614.

Bookhout, T.A. 1965. Breeding biology of snowshoe hares in Michigan's upper peninsula. *Journal of Wildlife Management*, 29:296–303.

Brady, N.C. and R.R. Weil. 2009. Elements of the Nature and Properties of Soils (3rd Edition). Prentice Hall, Upper Saddle River, NJ. 624 pp.

Broadbooks, H.E. 1970. Home ranges and territorial behavior of the yellow pine chipmunk (*Eutamias amoenus*). *Journal of Mammalogy*, 51:310–326.

Brothers, D.R. 1994. Bufo boreas (Western Toad) Predation. Herpetological Review, 25:117.

Brown, B.T. 1992. Golden Eagles feeding on fish. *Journal of Raptor*

Research, 26:36–37.

Brown, J.L. 1964. The integration of agonistic behavior in the Steller's jay, *Cyanocitta stelleri* (Gmelin). *University of California Publications in Zoology*, 60:223–328.

Bruck, J.N. and J.M. Mateo. 2010. How Habitat Features Shape Ground Squirrel (*Urocitellus beldingi*) Navigation. *Journal of Comparative Psychology*, 124:176 –186.

Bryant, L.D. and C. Maser. 1982. Classification and distribution. Pp. 1–59. *In*: Elk of North America, Ecology and management. (J.W. Thomas and D.E. Toweill, eds). Stackpole Books, Harrisburg, PA.

Burley, R.W. and D.V. Vadehra. 1989. The Avian Egg: Chemistry and Biology. John Wiley & Sons, New York. 472 pp.

Burnell, K.L. and D.F. Tomback. 1985. Steller'S (sic) Jays Steal Gray Jay Caches: Field and Laboratory Observations. *The Auk*, 102:417–419.

Bushy-tailed woodrat. http://en.wikipedia.org/wiki/Bushy-tailed_woodrat (accessed January 30, 2014).

Byers, C., J. Curson, and U. Olsson. 1995. Sparrows and Buntings: A Guide to the Sparrows and Buntings of North America and the World. Houghton Mifflin Harcourt, Boston, MA. 334 pp.

Calder, W. 1969. Temperature relations and under water endurance of the smallest homeothermic diver, the water shrew. *Comparative Biochemistry and Physiology*, 30A:1075–1082.

Cameron, E.S. 1908. Observations on the Golden Eagle in Montana. *The Auk*, 25:251–268.

Campbell, J.B. 1970. Hibernacula of a population of *Bufo boreas boreas* in the Colorado Front Range. *Herpetologica*, 26:278–282.

Carcamo, H.A and J.R. Spence. 1994. Kin Discrimination and Cannibalism in Water Striders (Heteroptera: Gerridae): Another Look. *Oikos*, 70:412–416.

Carey, A.B., T.M. Wilson, C.C. Maguire, and B.L. Biswell. 1997. Dens of northern flying squirrels in the Pacific northwest. *Journal of Wildlife Management*, 61:684–699.

Carey, C. 1978. Factors Affecting Body Temperatures of Toads. *Oecologia*, 35:197–219.

Carnie, S.K. 1954. Food habits of Golden Eagles in the coastal ranges of California. *The Condor*, 56:3–12.

Cassey, P., G.H. Thomas, S.J. Portugal, and others. 2012. Why are birds' eggs colourful? Eggshell pigments co-vary with life-history and nesting ecology among British breeding non-passerine birds. *Biological Journal of the Linnean Society*, 106:657–672.

Cave insect. http://en.wikipedia.org/wiki/Cave_insect (accessed June 9, 2014).

Chamala, S., A.S Chanderbali, J.P. Der, and others. 2013. Assembly and Validation of the Genome of the Nonmodel Basal Angiosperm *Amborella*. *Science*, 342:1516–1517.

Chamberlain, M.I., B.D. Leopold, and L.M. Conner. 2003. Space use, movements and habitat selection of adult Bobcats (*Lynx rufus*) in Central Mississippi. *The American Midland Naturalist*, 149:395–405.

Chanderbali, A.S., V.A. Albert, J. Leebens-Mack, and others. 2009. Transcriptional signatures of ancient floral developmental genetics in avocado (*Persea americana*; Lauraceae). *Proceedings of the National Academy of Sciences*, 106:8929–8934.

Cheng, Y-C. and G.R. Fleming. 2009. Dynamics of Light Harvesting in Photosynthesis. *Annual Review of Physical Chemistry*, 60:241–262.

Cherry, M. and S. Kratville. Effects of winter recreation on subnivean fauna. http://beringiasouth.org/effects-of-winter-recreation-on-subnivean-fauna (accessed July 19, 2013).

Cialdini, R. and G. Orians. 1994. Nesting studies of the Spotted Sandpiper. *Passenger Pigeon*, 6:79–81.

Ciszek, D. Lynx rufus. http://animaldiversity.ummz.umich.edu/accounts/Lynx_rufus/ (accessed October 24, 2014).

Clark's Nutcracker. http://birdweb.org/Birdweb/bird/clarks_nutcracker?tab=1 (accessed July 23, 2014).

Clark's Nutcracker. http://en.wikipedia.org/wiki/Clark's_nutcracker (accessed July 23, 2014).

Clark's Nutcracker. http://www.allaboutbirds.org/guide/clarks_nutcracker/lifehistory (accessed July 23, 2014).

Cliff Swallow. http://www.allaboutbirds.org/guide/cliff_swallow/lifehistory (accessed July 5, 2014).

Cliff Swallow. http://en.wikipedia.org/wiki/American_cliff_swallow (accessed July 5, 2014).

Cliff Swallow. http://animals.nationalgeographic.com/animals/birding/cliff-swallow/ (accessed July 5, 2014).

Cliff Swallow. http://birds.audubon.org/birds/cliff-swallow (accessed July 5, 2014).

Cliff Swallow. http://birdweb.org/birdweb/bird/cliff_swallow (accessed July 5, 2014).

Clothier, R.R. 1955. Contribution to the life history of *Sorex vagrans* in

Montana. *Journal of Mammalogy*, 36:214–221.

Coccinellidae. http://en.wikipedia.org/wiki/Coccinellidae (accessed June 15, 2014).

Collopy, M.W. 1983. Foraging Behavior and Success of Golden Eagles. *The Auk*, 100:747–749.

Conaway, C. 1952. Life history of the water shrew (Sorex palustris). American Midland Naturalist, 48: 219–248.

Conner, M.M. and M.W. Miller. 2004. Movement patterns and spatial epidemiology of a prion disease in mule deer population units. *Ecological Applications*, 14:1870–1881.

Constantine, D.G. 1958. Ecological observations on lasiurine bats in Georgia. *Journal of Mammalogy*, 39:64–70.

Constantine, D.G. 1959. Ecological observations on lasiurine bats in the North Bay area of California. *Journal of Mammalogy*, 40:13–15.

Constantine, D.G. 1966. Ecological observations on lasiurine bats in Iowa. *Journal of Mammalogy*, 47:34–41.

Corn, P.S. 1993. Bufo boreas (boreal toad) predation. Herpetological Review, 24:57.

Cotton, C.L., and K.L. Parker. 2000. Winter activity patterns of northern flying squirrels in sub-boreal forests. *Canadian Journal of Zoology*, 78:1896–1901.

Cowan, I.McT. and C.J. Guiguet. 1965. The mammals of British Columbia. *British Columbia Provincial Museum*, 11:1–141.

Craighead, L. 2003. Bears of the World. Voyageur Press, Stillwater, MN. 132 pp.

Crandel, D.R. 1965. The Glacial History of Western Washington and Oregon. Pp. 341–353. *In*: The Quaternary of the United States. J.E. Wright, Jr., and David G. Frey (eds.). Princeton Univ. Press, Princeton, NJ. (1965).

Csuti, B.A., T.A. O☒Neil, M.M. Shaugh-nessy, E.P. Gaines, and J.C. Hak. 2001. Atlas of Oregon Wildlife: Distribution, Habitat, and Natural History. Oregon State University Press, Corvallis, OR. 544 pp.

Cuckoo. http://en.wikipedia.org/wiki/Cuckoo (accessed July 31, 2014).

Culver, M., W.E. Johnson, J. Pecon-Slattery, and S.J O'Brien. 2000. Genomic ancestry of the American puma (*Puma concolor*). *Journal of Heredity*, 91:186–97.

Dalquest, W.W. 1942. Geographic variation in northwestern snowshoe hares. *Journal of Mammalogy*, 23:166–183.

Dalquest, W.W. 1943. Seasonal distribution of the hoary bat along the

Pacific coast. *The Murrelet*, 24:20–24.

Dalquest, W.W. 1947. Notes on the natural history of the bat, *Myotis yumanensis*, in California, with a description of a new race. *American Midland Naturalist*, 38:224–247.

Dalquest, W.W. 1947. Notes on the natural history of the bat *Corynorhinus rafinesquii* in California. *Journal of Mammalogy*, 28:17–30.

Dalquest, W.W. 1948. Mammals of Washington. *University of Kansas Museum of Natural History Publication*, 2:1–444.

Dalquest, W.W. and D.R. Orcutt. 1942. The biology of the least shrew-mole, *Neurotrichus gibbsii minor*. *American Midland Naturalist*, 27:387–401.

Darby, A., B. Raymond, and A. Douglas. 2003. The olfactory response of coccinellids to aphids on plants. *Entomologia Experimentalis et Applicata*, 95:113–117.

Dark-eyed Junco. http://www.birdweb.org/birdweb/bird/dark-eyed_junco (accessed September 5, 2014).

Dark-eyed Junco. http://en.wikipedia.org/wiki/Dark-eyed_junco (accessed September 5, 2014).

Dark-eyed Junco. http://www.allaboutbirds.org/guide/dark-eyed_junco/id (accessed September 5, 2014).

Dark-eyed Junco, *Junco hyemalis*. http://birds.audubon.org/birds/dark-eyed-junco (accessed September 5, 2014).

Darwin, C. 1998. On The Origin of Species. Modern Library, a Division of Random House Publishers, New York, NY. 689 pp.

Dasmann, R.F. and R.D. Taber. 1956. Behavior of Columbian black-tailed deer with reference to population ecology. *Journal Mammalogy*, 37:143–164.

Davis, W.H., R.W. Barbour, and M.D. Hassell. 1968. Colonial behavior of *Eptesicus fuscus*. *Journal of Mammalogy*, 49:44–50.

Dearing, M.D. 1997. The Function of Haypiles of Pikas (*Ochotona princeps*). *Journal of Mammalogy*, 78:1156–1163.

Deblinger, R.D. and A.W. Alldredge. 1996. Golden Eagle predation on pronghorns in Wyoming's Great Divide Basin. *Journal of Raptor Research*, 30:157–159.

Deer Mouse. http://www.esf.edu/aec/adks/mammals/deer_mouse.htm (accessed October 6, 2014).

Deer Mouse. http://www.biokids.umich.edu/critters/Peromyscus_maniculatus/ (accessed October 6, 2014).

Dekker, D. 1985. Hunting behavior of Golden Eagle *Aquila chrysae-*

tos migrating in southwestern Alberta. *Canadian Field Naturalist*, 49:383–385.

del Moral, R. and A.F. Watson. 1978. Gradient structure of forest vegetation in the central Washington Cascades. *Vegetatio*, 38:29–48.

Dewsbury, D. 1988. Kinship, Familiarity, Aggression, and Dominance in Deer Mice (*Peromyscus maniculatus*) in Seminatural Enclosures. *Journal of Comparative Psychology*, 102:124–128.

Dice, L.R. 1932. The songs of mice. *Journal of Mammalogy*, 13:187–196.

Dice, L.R. 1933. Longevity in *Peromyscus maniculatus gracilis*. *Journal of Mammalogy*, 14:147–148.

Dice, L.R. 1949. Variations of *Peromyscus maniculatus* in parts of western Washington and adjacent Oregon. *Contribution of the Laboratory of Vertebrate Biology University of Michigan*, 44:1–33.

Dicken, E.F. and S.N. Dicken 1979. The making of Oregon: A Study In Historical Geography, Vol. 1. Oregon Historical Society, Portland, OR. 222 pp.

Dietary biology of the golden eagle. http://en.wikipedia.org/wiki/Dietary_biology_of_the_golden_eagle (accessed October 28, 2014).

Dietz, M. *Perisoreus canadensis*, gray jay. http://animaldiversity.ummz.umich.edu/accounts/Perisoreus_canadensis/ (accessed July 23, 2014).

Dimick, R.E. and D.C Mote. 1934. A Preliminary Survey of the Food of Oregon Trout. Agricultural Experiment Station, Oregon State Agricultural College and Oregon State Game Commission Cooperating, Corvallis. *Station Bulletin*, 323:5–23.

Dixon, A.F.G. 1997. Aphid Ecology, An optimization approach. (second edition). Chapman and Hall, London, UK. 300 pp.

Dixon, J. 1919. Notes on the natural history of the bushy-tailed woodrats of California. *University of California Publication in Zoology*, 21:49–74.

Dixon, J. 1934. A study of the life history and food habits of mule deer in California. *California Fish and Game*, 20:6–144.

Dolenska, M., O. Nedved, P. Vesely, and others. 2009. What constitutes optical warning signals of ladybirds (Coleoptera Coccinellidae) towards bird predators: colour, pattern or general look? *Biological Journal of The Linnaen Society*, 98:234–242.

Douglas, A.E. 1998. Nutritional Interactions in Insect-Microbial Symbioses: Aphids and Their Symbiotic Bacteria *Buchnera*. *Annual Review of Entomology*, 43:17–37.

Douglas, G.W. 1972. Subalpine plant communities of the western North Cascades, Washington. *Arctic and Alpine Research*, 4:147–166.

Douglas Squirrel. http://en.wikipedia.org/wiki/Douglas_squirrel (accessed November 15, 2014).

Dow, D. 1965. The role of saliva in food storage by the Gray Jay. *The Auk*, 82:139–154.

Eagle Biology. http://www.nationaleaglecenter.org/learn/biology/ (accessed October 28, 2014).

Earthworm. http://en.wikipedia.org/wiki/Earthworm (accessed May 8, 2014).

Earthworm (Family Lumbricidae). https://www4.uwm.edu/fieldstation/ naturalhistory/bugoftheweek/earthworms.cfm (accessed May 8, 2014).

Edelman, A. and J. Koprowski. 2006. Influence of female-biased sexual size dimorphism on dominance of female Townsend's chipmunks. *Canadian Journal of Zoology*, 84:1859–1863.

Edge, W.D., C.L. Marcum, and S.L. Olson-Edge. 1988. Summer forage and feeding site selection by elk. *Journal of Wildlife Management*, 52:573–577.

Edson, J.M. 1933. A visitation of weasels. *The Murrelet*, 14:76–77.

Edwards, C.A. and P.J. Bohlen. 1996. Biology and Ecology of Earthworms, 3rd Edition. Chapman & Hall, London, UK. 426 pp.

Ehrlich, P., D. Dobkin, and D. Wheye. 1988. The Birders Handbook: A Field Guide to the Natural History of North American Birds. New York: Simon and Schuster Inc., New York, NY. 785 pp

Eisenberg, J.F. 1964. Studies on the behavior of *Sorex vagrans*. *American Midland Naturalist*, 72:417–425.

Eisner, T. and D. Aneshansley, D. 2008. "Anting" in Blue Jays, evidence in support of a food-preparatory function. *Chemoecology*, 18:197–203.

Elk. http://en.wikipedia.org/wiki/Elk (accessed August 20, 2014).

Elk Facts. http://www.rmef.org/ElkFacts.aspx (accessed August 20, 2014).

Emerson, D.O. and W.E. Howard. 1978. Mineralogy of woodrat, *Neotoma cinerea*, urine deposits from northeastern California. *Journal of Mammalogy*, 59:424–425.

Engel, K.A. and L.S. Young. 1989. Spatial and temporal patterns in the diet of Common Ravens in southwestern Idaho. *The Condor*, 91:372–378.

Erickson, A.W. and J.E. Nellor. 1964. Breeding biology of the black bear. *Michigan State University Research Bulletin*, 4:1–45.

Erickson, A.W., J.E. Nellor, and G.A. Petrides. 1964. The black bear in Michigan. *Michigan State University Research Bulletin*, 4:1–102.

Evans, S.T. 2013. How the Cascade Mountains were Created. http://www.sciences360.com/index.php/how-the-cascade-mountains-were-created-2068/ (accessed January 13, 2014).

Febvay, G., I. Liadouze, J. Guillaud, and G. Bonnot. 1995. Analysis of Energetic Amino Acid Metabolism in *Acyrthosiphon Pisum*: A Multidimensional Approach To Amino Acid Metabolism in Aphids. *Archives of Insect Biochemistry and Physiology*, 29:45–69.

Fecal sac. http://en.wikipedia.org/wiki/Fecal_sac (accessed September 12, 2014).

Fedriani, J.M., T.K. Fuller, R.M. Sauvajot, and E.C. York. 2000. Competition and intraguild predation among three sympatric carnivores. *Oecologia*, 125:258–270.

Feldhamer, G.A., B.C. Thompson and J.A. Chapman. 2004. Wild Mammals of North America (second ed.). Johns Hopkins University Press, Baltimore, MD. 1,232 pp.

Feldman, C. R. and K.E. Omland. 2005. Phylogenetics of the common raven complex (*Corvus*: Corvidae) and the utility of ND4, COI and intron 7 of the ⊠-fibrinogen gene in avian molecular systematics. *Zoologica Scripta*, 34:145–146.

Ferguson-Lees, J., and D.A. Christie. 2001. Raptors of the World. Houghton Mifflin Harcourt, Boston, MA. 992 pp.

Ferns, M. 1995. Geologic Evolution of the Blue Mountains Region, The Role of Geology in Soil Formation. *Natural Resource News*, 5:2–3,17.

Ferron, J. 1985. Social behaviour of the golden-mantled ground squirrel (*Spermophilus lateralis*). *Canadian Journal of Zoology*, 63:2529–2533.

Findley, J.S. and C. Jones. 1964. Seasonal distribution of the hoary bat. *Journal of Mammalogy*, 45:461–470.

Findley, J.S., E.H. Studier, and D.E. Wilson. 1972. Morphologic properties of bat wings. *Journal of Mammalogy*, 53:429–444.

Forbes, R.B. and L.W. Turner. 1972. Notes on two litters of Townsend's chipmunks. *Journal of Mammalogy*, 53:355–359.

Forsman, E.D., I.A. Otto, D. Aubuchon, and others. 1994. Reproductive chronology of the northern flying squirrel on the Olympic peninsula, Washington. *Northwest Science*, 68:273–276.

Fraley, J. Clark's Nutcracker. *Montana Outdoors*, http://fwp.mt.gov/mtoutdoors/HTML/articles/portraits/nutcracker.htm (accessed July 25, 2014).

Frank, C. and K. Storey. 1995. Optimal depot fat composition for hibernation by golden-mantled ground squirrels (*Spermophilus lateralis*).

Journal of Comparative Physiology, 164:536–542.

Franklin, J.F. and C.T. Dyrness. 1973. Natural vegetation of Oregon and Washington. Gen. Tech. Rep. PNW-8. Portland, OR: U.S. Department of Agriculture, Forest Service, Pacific Northwest Forest and Range Experiment Station. 417 pp.

Franklin, W.L. 1968. Herd organization, territoriality, movements and home ranges in Roosevelt elk. M.S. Thesis. Humboldt State College, Arcata, CA. 89 pp.

Franklin, W.L., A.S. Mossman, and M. Dole. 1975. Social organization and home range of Roosevelt elk. *Journal of Mammalogy*, 56:102–118.

Fuller, C. and A. Blaustein. 1990. An investigation of sibling recognition in a solitary sciurid, Townsend's Chipmunk, *Tamias townsendii. Behaviour*, 112:36–52.

Fuller, T.K., L.B. Stephen, T.A. Decker, and J.E. Cardoza. 1995. Survival and Cause-Specific Mortality Rates of Adult Bobcats (*Lynx rufus*). *American Midland Naturalist*, 134:404–408.

Gabrielson, I.N. 1923. Notes on *Thomomys* in Oregon. *Journal of Mammalogy*, 4:189–190.

Gall, G.A.E. and P.A. Crandell. 1992. The Rainbow Trout. *Aquaculture*, 100:1–10.

Gannon, W.L. 1988. Zapus trinotatus. *Mammalian Species*, 315:1–5.

Gashwiler, J.S. 1959. Small mammal study in west-central Oregon. *Journal of Mammalogy*, 40:128–139.

Gashwiler, J.S. 1971. Deer mouse movement in forest habitat. *Northwest Science*, 45:163–170.

Gashwiler, J.S., W.L. Robinette, and O.W. Morris. 1961. Breeding habits of bobcats in Utah. *Journal of Mammalogy*, 42:76–84.

Geist, V. 1998. Deer of the World: Their Evolution, Behavior, and Ecology. Stackpole Books, Mechanicsburg, PA. 421 pp.

General Info on the Elk Industry. http://www.wapiti.net/general.cfm (accessed August 21, 2014).

Gerridae. http://en.wikipedia.org/wiki/Gerridae (accessed June 11, 2014).

Ghatpande, A., S. Ghatpande, and M. Khan.1995. Effect of different intensities of fluorescent light on the early development of chick embryos in ovo. *Cellular and Molecular Biology Research*, 41:613–621.

Gibbons, A. 2007. Food For Thought. *Science*, 316:1558–1560.

Gillihan, S.W. and K.R. Foresman. 2004. Sorex vagrans. *Mammalian Species*, 744:1–5.

Glendenning, R. 1959. Biology and control of the coast mole, *Scapanus orarius orarius* True, in British Columbia. *Canadian Journal of Animal Science*, 39:34–44.

Goehring, H.H. 1972. Twenty-year study of *Eptesicus fuscus* in Minnesota. *Journal of Mammalogy*, 53:201–207.

Golden Eagle. http://www.baldeagleinfo.com/eagle/eagle7.html (accessed October 25, 2014).

Golden Eagle. http://www.allaboutbirds.org/guide/golden_eagle/lifehistory (accessed October 25, 2014).

Golden Eagle. http://en.wikipedia.org/wiki/Golden_eagle (accessed October 25, 2014).

Golden-mantled Ground Squirrel. http://www.nps.gov/brca/nature-science/groundsquirrel.htm (accessed September 29, 2014).

Golley, F.B. 1957. Gestation Period, Breeding and Fawning Behavior of Columbian Black-Tailed Deer. *Journal of Mammalogy*, 38:116–120.

Gordon, K L. 1936. Territorial behavior and social dominance among Sciuridae. *Journal of Mammalogy*, 17:171–172.

Gordon, K. L. 1938. Observations on the behavior of *Callospermophilus* and *Eutamias*. *Journal of Mammalogy*, 19:78–84.

Gordon, K.L. 1943. The natural history and behavior of the western chipmunk and mantled ground squirrel. *Oregon State Monographs, Studies in Zoology*, No. 5, Oregon State College Press.

Goss, R.J. 1963. The deciduous nature of deer antlers. Pp. 339–369. *In*: Mechanisms of hard tissue destruction. R. Sognnaes (ed). *American Academy for the Advancement of Science Publication*, 75, Washington, D.C.

Goss, R.J. 1968. Inhibition of growth and shedding of antlers by sex hormones. *Nature*, 220:83–95.

Goss, R.J. 1969. Photoperiodic control of antler cycles in deer. I. Phase shift and frequency changes. *Journal of Experimental Zoology*, 170:311–324.

Goss, R.J. 1970. Photoperiodic control of antler cycles in deer. II. Alterations in amplitude. *Journal of Experimental Zoology*, 171:223–234.

Gough, Z. Dinosaurs 'shrank' regularly to become birds. http://www.bbc.co.uk/nature/28563682 (accessed August 1, 2014).

Gould, E. 1955. The feeding efficiency of insectivorous bats. *Journal of Mammalogy*, 36:399–407.

Graf, W. 1955. The Roosevelt elk. Port Angeles Evening News, Port Angeles, Washington. 105 pp.

Graf, W. 1956. Territorialism in deer. *Journal of Mammalogy*, 37:165–170.

Graham, R.E. 1966. Observations on the roosting habits of the big-eared bat, *Plecotus townsendii*, in California limestone caves. *Cave Notes*, 8:17–22.

Grange, W.B. 1932. Observations on the snowshoe hare, *Lepus americanus phaeonotus* Allen. *Journal of Mammalogy*, 13:1–19.

Gray-crowned rosy finch. http://en.wikipedia.org/wiki/Gray-crowned_rosy_finch (accessed June 30, 2014).

Gray-crowned rosy finch. http://www.allaboutbirds.org/guide/Gray-crowned_Rosy-Finch/lifehistorys (accessed June 30, 2014).

Gray-crowned rosy finch. http://birding.about.com/od/birdprofiles/p/Gray-Crowned-Rosy-Finch.htm (accessed June 30, 2014).

Gray-crowned rosy finch. http://birdweb.org/birdweb/bird/gray-crowned_rosy-finch (accessed June 30, 2014).

Gray jay. http://www.allaboutbirds.org/guide/gray_jay/id (accessed July 23, 2014).

Gray jay. http://birdweb.org/Birdweb/bird/gray_jay?tab=1 (accessed July 23, 2014).

Gray jay. http://en.wikipedia.org/wiki/Gray_jay (accessed July 23, 2014).

Gray wolf. http://en.wikipedia.org/wiki/Gray_wolf (accessed August 8, 2014).

Grouse Facts. http://www.ruffedgrousesociety.org/grouse-facts#.U8G_6ByuSAs (accessed July 13, 2014).

Grubb, T.C., Jr. 2003. The Mind of the Trout: A Cognitive Ecology for Biologists and Anglers. The University of Wisconsin Press, Madison, WI. 208 pp.

Ha, J. C. and P.N. Lehner. 1990. Notes on Gray Jay Demographics in Colorado. *The Wilson Bulletin*, 102: 698–702.

Habeck, J.R. 1967. Mountain hemlock communities in western Montana. *Northwest Science*, 41:169–177.

Habitat Management For Black-Tailed Deer. http://www.nrcs.usda.gov/Internet/FSE_DOCUMENTS/nrcs142p2_042116.pdf (accessed July 18, 2014).

Hadley, D. Aphid-Herding Ants: How Ants and Aphids Help Each Other. http://insects.about.com/od/coolandunusualinsects/f/antsandaphids.htm (accessed June 17, 2014).

Hadley, D. 10 Fascinating Facts About Ladybugs http://insects.about.com/od/beetles/a/10-facts-ladybugs.htm (accessed June 21, 2014).

Hafner, D.J. 1993. North American pika (*Ochotona princeps*) as a late Quaternary biogeographic indicator species. *Quaternary Research*,

39:373–380.

Hagen, K.S. 1060. Biological Control with Lady Beetles. *Plants and Gardens: the Brooklyn Botanic Garden Record*, 16:28–35.

Hales, D.F., A.C.C. Wilson, M.A. Sloane, and others. 2002. Lack of Detectable Genetic Recombination on the X Chromosome During the Parthenogenetic Production of Female and Male Aphids. *Genetics Research*, 79:203–209.

Hall, E.R. 1951. American weasels. *University of Kansas Museum of Natural History Publication*, 4:1–446.

Hamilton, W.J., Jr. 1933. The weasels of New York. *American Midland Naturalist*, 14:289–344.

Hanken, J. and P.W. Sherman. 1981. Multiple Paternity in Belding's Ground Squirrel Litters. *Science*, 212:351–353.

Harada, T., R. Tabuchi, and J. Koura. 1997. Migratory syndrome in the water strider *Aquarius paludum* (Heteroptera: Gerridae) reared in high versus low nymphal densities. *European Journal of Entomology*, 94:445–452.

Harestad, A. 1991. Spatial behaviour of Townsend's chipmunks and habitat structure. *Acta theoriologica*, 36:247–254.

Harper, J.A. 1964. Movement and associated behavior of Roosevelt elk in southwestern Oregon. *Proceedings of the Western Association of State Game and Fish Commissions*, 44:139–141.

Harper, J.A. 1971. Ecology of Roosevelt elk. Oregon State Game Commission, Portland, OR. 44 pp.

Harper, J.A., J.H. Harn, W.W. Bentley, and C.F. Yocom. 1967. The status and ecology of the Roosevelt elk in California. *Wildlife Monographs*, 16:1–49.

Harrington, F.H. 1981. Urine-Marking and Caching Behavior in the Wolf. *Behaviour*, 76:280–288.

Harris, C.E., J.W. Beals, and K. Geier-Hayes. 1994. Deer mouse and yellow-pine chipmunk density and food habits in three central Idaho shrub communities. Idaho Department of Fish & Game, Boise. 23 pp.

Harrison, H.H. 1975. Eastern Birds' Nests. Peterson Field Guide Series, Houghton Mifflin, New York. 288 pp.

Hartman, G.D. and T.L. Yates. Scapanus orarius. *Mammalian Species*, 253. (1985):1–5.

Hatch, D.R.M. 1968. Golden Eagle hunting tactics. *Blue Jay*, 26:78–80.

Hauer, F.R., J.A. Stanford, and R.L. Newell (editors). 2008. International Advances in the Ecology, Zoogeography, and Systematics of Mayflies and Stoneflies. University of California Publications in Entomology 128. 422 pp.

Haug, G.W. 1938. Rearing the Coccinellid *Hippodamia convergens* on Frozen Aphids. *Annals of the Entomological Society of America*, 31: 240–248.

Hayes, J.P., E.G. Horvath, and P. Hounihan. 1995. Townsend's chipmunk populations in Douglas-fir plantations and mature forests in the Oregon Coast Range. *Canadian Journal of Zoology*, 73:67–73.

Hays, H. 1972. Polyandry in the Spotted Sandpiper. *Living Bird*, 11:43–57.

Headley, S.K. and S. Sells. Townsend's Chipmunk. (2005) http://osuext. intermountaintech.org/download/ec%201580.pdf (accessed September 13, 2014).

Heinrich, B. 1988. Winter foraging at carcasses by three sympatric corvids, with emphasis on recruitment by the raven, *Corvus corax*. *Behavioral Ecology and Sociobiology*, 23:141–156.

Helgen, K.M., F.R. Cole, L.E. Helgen, and D.E. Wilson. 2009. Generic Revision in the Holarctic Ground Squirrel Genus *Spermophilus*. *Journal of Mammalogy*, 90:270–305.

Hibben, R.C. 1937. A preliminary study of the mountain lion, *Felis oregonensis*. *University of New Mexico Biological Series*, 5:1–59.

Hindelang, M. The Science of Winter Ecology. http://www.ed.mtu.edu/ esmis/winter/ecology.html (accessed July 19, 2013).

Hippodamia convergens http://en.wikipedia.org/wiki/Hippodamia_convergens (accessed June 21, 2014).

Hoagland, C.S. Basic Facts About Mountain Lions. http://www.defenders.org/mountain-lion/basic-facts (accessed August 3, 2014).

Hochuli, P.A. and S. Feist-Burkhardt. 2013. Angiosperm-like pollen and *Afropollis* from the Middle Triassic (Anisian) of the Germanic Basin (Northern Switzerland). *Frontiers in Plant Science*, DOI: 10.3389/fpls.2013.00344.

Hodek, I., A. Honek, and H.F. van Emden (editors). 2012. Ecology and Behaviour of the Ladybird Beetles. Wiley-Blackwell Publisher, Hoboken, NJ. 600 pp.

Hodek, I. and P. Cerngier. 2000. Sexual activity in Coccinellidae (Coleoptera): a review. *European Journal of Entomology*, 97:449–456.

Holekamp, K.E. 1984. Natal dispersal in Belding's ground squirrels (*Spermophilus beldingi*). *Behavioral Ecology and Sociobiology*, 16:21–30.

Holekamp, K.E. 1986. Proximal Causes of Natal Dispersal in Belding's

Ground Squirrels. *Ecological Monographs*, 56:365–391.

Holmes, W. 1995. The ontogeny of littermate preferences in juvenile golden-mantled ground squirrels: effects of rearing and relatedness. *Animal Behaviour*, 50:309–322.

Honek, A., Z. Martinkova, and S. Pekar. 2007. Aggregation characteristics of three species of Coccinellidae (Coleoptera) at hibernation sites. *European Journal of Entomology*, 104: 51–56.

Hooven, E.F., R.F. Hoyer, and R.M. Storm. 1975. Notes on the vagrant shrew, *Sorex vagrans*, in the Willamette Valley of western Oregon. *Northwest Science*, 49:163–173.

Hornocker, M.G. 1969. Winter territoriality in mountain lions. *Journal of Wildlife Management*, 33:457–464.

Hornocker, M.G. 1970. An analysis of mountain lion predation upon mule deer and elk in the Idaho Primitive Area. *Wildlife Monograph*, 21:1–39 pp.

Hornocker, M.G. and S. Negri (editors). 2010. Cougar ecology and conservation. University of Chicago Press, Chicago, IL. 304 pp.

Horvath, O. 1966. Observation of parturition and maternal care of the bushy-tailed woodrat (*Neotoma cinerea occidentalis* Baird). *The Murrelet*, 47:6 8.

Howell, A.B. 1920. A study of the California jumping mouse of the genus *Zapus*. *University of California Publications in Zoology*, 21:225–238.

Howell, A.B. 1926. Voles of the genus *Phenacomys*. North American Fauna, 48:1–66.

Huntly, N.J., A.T. Smith, and B.L. Ivins. 1968. Foraging behavior of a refuging herbivore, the pika (*Ochotona princeps*), with comparisons of grazing and haying. *Journal of Mammalogy*, 67:139–48.

Huntly, N.J., A.T. Smith, and B.L. Ivins. 1987. Influence of refuging consumers (pikas: *Ochotona princeps*) on subalpine meadow vegetation. *Journal of Ecology*, 68:274–283.

Hutchins, H.E. and F.M. Lanner. 1982. The central role of Clark's nutcracker in the dispersal and establishment of whitebark pine. *Oecologia*, 55:192–201.

Imperial College London. 2007. Herding Aphids: How 'Farmer' Ants Keep Control Of Their Food. ScienceDaily, www.sciencedaily.com/releases/2007/10/071009212548.htm (accessed June 17, 2014).

Ingham, E.R. 1995. Organisms in the Soil: The Functions of Bacteria, Fungi, Protozoa, Nematodes, and Arthropods. *Natural Resource News*, 5:10–12, 16–17.

Ingles, L.G. 1956. Mammals of the Pacific States. Stanford University Press, Stanford, CA. 506 pp.

Ingles, L.G. 1961. Home range and habitats of the wandering shrew. *Journal of Mammalogy*, 42:455–462.

Innes, D.G.L. and J.S. Millar. 1982. Life history notes on the heather vole, *Phenacomys intermedius levis*, in the Canadian Rocky Mountains. *Canadian Field-Naturalist*, 96:307–311.

Iriarte, J.A., W.L. Franklin, W.E. Johnson, and K.H. Redford. 1990. Biogeographic variation of food habits and body size of the America puma. *Oecologia*, 85:185–190.

Iwaniuk, A. 2001. Interspecific variation in sexual dimorphism in brain size in Nearctic ground squirrels (*Spermophilus* spp.). *Canadian Journal of Zoology*, 79:759–765.

Jackson, H. 1928. A taxonomic review of the American long tailed shrews. *North American Fauna*, 51:1–238.

Jamal, E. and G. Brown. 2001. Orientation of *Hippodamia convergens* (Coleoptera: Coccinellidae) larvae to volatile chemicals associated with *Myzus nicotianae* (Homoptera: Aphididae). *Environmental Entomology*, 30:1012–1016.

Jameson, E.W. 1952. Food of Deer Mice, *Peromyscus maniculatus* and *P. boylei*, in the Northern Sierra Nevada, California. *Journal of Mammalogy*, 33:50–60.

Janečka, J.E., T.L. Blankenship, D.H. Hirth, and others. 2006. Kinship and social structure of Bobcats (*Lynx rufus*) inferred from microsatellite and radio-telemetry data. *Journal of Zoology*, 269:494–501.

Janes, S.W. 1976. The apparent use of rocks by a raven in nest defense. *The Condor*, 78:409.

Jędrzejewski, W., K. Schmidt, J. Theuerkauf, and others. 2007. Territory size of wolves *Canis lupus*: linking local (Białowieża Primeval Forest, Poland) and Holarctic-scale patterns. *Ecography*, 30:66–76.

Jerkins, S.H. and B. Eshelman. 1984. Spermophilus beldingi. *Mammalian Species*, 221:1-8.

Johnsgard, P. 1990. Hawks, Eagles, & Falcons of North America: Biology and Natural History. Smithsonian Institution Press, Washington, D.C. 408 pp.

Johnson, D.R. 1989. Body Size of Northern Goshawks on Coastal Islands of British Columbia. *Wilson Bulletin*, 101:637–639.

Johnson, Jr., C.G. 1998. Vegetation Response after Wildfires in National Forests of Northeastern Oregon. USDA Forest Service, Pacific Northwest Region. R6-NR-ECOL-TP-06-98. 128 pp.

Johnson, M. L. 1973. Characters of the heather vole, Phenacomys, and the red tree vole, *Arborimus*. *Journal of Mammalogy*, 54:239–244.

Jones, G.S., J.O. Whitaker, Jr., and C. Maser. 1978. Food habits of jumping mice (*Zapus trinotatus* and *Z. princeps*) in western North America. *Northwest Science*, 52:57–60.

Jonkel, C.J. and I.McT. Cowan. 1971. The black bear in the spruce-fir forest. *Wildlife Monographs*, 27:1–57.

Juan de Fuca Plate. http://en.wikipedia.org/wiki/Juan_de_Fuca_Plate (accessed January 21, 2014).

Julia Smith. *Canis lupus*, gray wolf. http://animaldiversity.ummz.umich. edu/accounts/Canis_lupus/ (accessed August 8, 2014).

Kaiser, J. 2004. Wounding Earth's Fragile Skin. *Science*, 304:1616–1618.

Kamler, J.F. and P.S. Gipson. 2000. Home range, habitat selection, and survival of bobcats, *Lynx rufus*, in a prairie ecosystem in Kansas. *Canadian Field-Naturalist*, 114:388–94.

Kelso, L. and M.M. Nice. 1963. A Russian contribution to anting and feather mites. *The Wilson Bulletin*, 75:23–26.

Kilner, R.M. 2006. The evolution of egg colour and patterning in birds. *Biological Reviews*, 81:383–406.

King, J.A. (Editor). 1968. Biology of *Peromyscus* (Rodentia). *The American Society of Mammalogists Special Publication*, 2:1–593.

Kirschbaum, K., J. Roof, and M.S. Harris. *Tachycineta bicolor*. http:// animaldiversity.ummz.umich.edu/accounts/Tachycineta_bicolor/ (accessed July 9, 2014).

Kirschbaum, K. and K. Moore. *Actitis macularius*. http://animaldiversity. ummz.umich.edu/accounts/Actitis_macularius/ (accessed November 28, 2014).

Koch, E.D. 2012. Juvenile Golden Eagle (*Aquila chrysaetos*) Drops Rock near Dusky Grouse (*Dendragapus obscurus*). *Journal of Raptor Research*, 46:407–407.

Koga, T. and Hayashi, K. 1991. Territorial behavior of both sexes in the water strider *Metrocoris histrio* (Hemiptera: Gerridae) during the mating season. *Journal of Insect Behavior*, 6:65–77.

Krumm, C.E., M.M. Conner, N.T. Hobbs, and others. 2010. Mountain lions prey selectively on prion-infected mule deer. *Biological Letters*, 6:209–211.

Krutzsch, P.H. 1954. Notes on the habits of the bat *Myotis californicus*. *Journal of Mammalogy*, 35:539–545.

Krutzsch, P.H. 1954. North American jumping mice (genus *Zapus*). *University of Kansas Museum of Natural History Publication*, 7:349–472.

Krystek, L. The Speed of Light. http://www.unmuseum.org/speed.htm (accessed on April 17, 2014).

Lancaster, J.B. and R. Briers (editors). 2008. Aquatic insects: challenges to populations. *Proceedings of the Royal Entomological Society's 24th Symposium*. 332 pp.

Lanner, R.M. 1996. Made for each other: a symbiosis of birds and pines. Oxford University Press, New York, NY. 160 pp.

Larivière, S. and L.R. Walton. 1997. Lynx rufus. *Mammalian Species*, 563:1–8.

Lee, C. Powerful feet and talons help birds of prey make their living. *Lubbock Avalanche-Journal*, http://lubbockonline.com/stories/032606/gue_032606062.shtml (accessed October 25,2014).

Lee, M.S.Y., A. Cau, D. Naish, and G.J. Dyke. 2014. Sustained miniaturization and anatomical innovation in the dinosaurian ancestors of birds. *Science*, 345:562–566.

Leng, R.A. 2008. Digestion in the rabbit—a new look at the effects of their feeding and digestive strategies. Pp. 25–27. *In*: Proceedings MEKARN Rabbit Conference: Organic rabbit production from forages. (Reg Preston and Nnguyen Van Thu, Eds.) Cantho University, Vietnam.

Lesher, F. and J. Lesher. 1984. Gray Jay takes live mammal. *The Loon*, 56:72–73.

Lewis, S.B., K. Titus, M.R. Fuller. 2006. Northern Goshawk Diet During the Nesting Season in Southeast Alaska. *Journal of Wildlife Management*, 70:1151–1160.

Liao, J.C., D.N. Beal, G.V. Lauder, and M. S. Triantafyllou. 2003. Fish exploiting vortices decrease muscle activity. *Science*, 302:1566–1569.

Linsdale, J.M., and Q.P. Tomich. 1953. A herd of mule deer. University of California Press, Berkeley, CA. 567 pp.

Lissaman, P.B. and C.A. Schollenberger. 1970. Formation flight of birds. *Science*, 168:1003–1005.

Loehr, K.A. and A.C. Risser, Jr. 1977. Daily and Seasonal Activity Patterns of the Belding Ground Squirrel in the Sierra Nevada. *Journal of Mammology*, 58:445–448.

Loomis, J. and H. Stone. Lady Beetle *Hippodamia convergens* http://ir.library.oregonstate.edu/xmlui/bitstream/handle/1957/19819/ec1604.pdf (accessed June 21, 2014).

Looney, M. *Tamias amoenus*. http://animaldiversity.ummz.umich.edu/accounts/Tamias_amoenus/ (accessed October 5, 2014).

Louie, J.N. http://www.seismo.unr.edu/ftp/pub/louie/class/100/plate-tectonics.html (accessed on April 5, 2012).

Lovallo, M.J. and E.M. Anderson. 1996. Bobcat (*Lynx rufus*) Home Range Size and Habitat Use in Northwest Wisconsin. *American Midland Naturalist*, 135:247–8.

Maccarone, A.D. and W.A. Montevecchi. 1986. Factors affecting food choice by Gray Jays. *Bird Behavior*, 6:90–92.

Macnab, J.A. and D. McKey-Fender. 1947. An Introduction To Oregon Earthworms With Additions To The Washington List. *Northwest Science*, 21:69–75.

Magnuson, J.J. 1990. Long-Term Ecological Research And the Invisible Present. *BioScience*, 40:495–501.

Malamuth, E. and M. Mulheisen. Northern flying squirrel, *Glaucomys sabrinus*. http://animaldiversity.ummz.umich.edu/accounts/Glaucomys_sabrinus/ (accessed November 16, 2014).

Marr, N.V. and R.L. Knight. 1983. Food Habits of Golden Eagles in Eastern Washington. *The Murrelet*, 64:73–77.

Marshall, A.D. and J.H Jenkins. 1966. Movements and home ranges of bobcats as determined by radio-tracking in the upper coastal plain of west-central South Carolina. *Proceedings of the Conference of the Southeastern Association of Game and Fish Commissions*, 20:206–214.

Maser, C. 1966. Notes on a Captive *Sorex vagrans*. *The Murrelet*, 47:51–53.

Maser, C. 1967. Black Bear Damage to Douglas-fir in Oregon. *The Murrelet*, 48:34–38.

Maser, C. 1989. Forest Primeval: The Natural History of an Ancient Forest. Sierra Club Books, San Francisco, CA. 282 pp.

Maser, C. 1998. Mammals of the Pacific Northwest: From the Coast to the High Cascades. Oregon State University Press, Corvallis, OR. 406 pp.

Maser, C. 2004. Of Ditches And Ponds: A Journey Through The Metaphors Of Childhood And Maturity. Woven Strings Publishing, Amarillo, TX. 184 pp.

Maser, C. 2005. Our Forest Legacy: Today's Decisions, Tomorrow's Consequences. Maisonneuve Press, Washington, D.C. 255 pp

Maser, C. 2009. Earth in Our Care: Ecology, Economy, and Sustainability. Rutgers University Press, Piscataway, New Jersey. 262 pp.

Maser, C. 2015. Interactions of Land, Ocean, and Humans: A Global

Perspective. CRC Press, Boca Raton, FL. 332 pp.

Maser, C. and R.M. Storm. 1970. A Key to Microtinae of the Pacific Northwest (Oregon, Washington, Idaho). Oregon State University Book Stores, Inc., Corvallis, OR. 162 pp.

Maser, C., J.M. Trappe, and R.A. Nussbaum. 1978. Fungal-Small Mammal Interrelationships with Emphasis on Oregon Coniferous Forests. *Ecology*, 59:799–809.

Maser, C., R. Anderson, and E. Bull. 1981. Aggregation and Sex Segregation in Northern Flying Squirrels in Northeastern Oregon, an Observation. *The Murrelet*, 62:54–55.

Maser, C. and R.S. Rohweder. 1983. Winter food habits of cougars from northeastern Oregon. *Great Basin Naturalist*, 43:425–427.

Maser, C. and F.M. Beer. 1984. Notes on Cicindelid Habitats in Oregon. *Cicindela*, 16:39–60.

Maser, C., Z. Maser, J.W. Witt, and G. Hunt. 1986. The northern flying squirrel: a mycophagist in southwestern Oregon. *Canadian Journal of Zoology*, 64:2086–2089.

Maser, C. and Z. Maser. 1987. Notes on mycophagy in four species of mice in the genus *Peromyscus*. *Great Basin Naturalist*, 47:308–312.

Maser, C. and Z. Maser. 1988. Interactions among squirrels, mycorrhizal fungi, and coniferous forests in Oregon. *Great Basin Naturalist*, 48:358–369.

Maser, C., A.W. Claridge, and J.M. Trappe. 2008. Trees, Truffles, and Beasts: How Forests Function. Rutgers University Press, New Brunswick, NJ. 288 pp.

Maser, Z. and C. Maser. 1987. Notes on mycophagy of the yellow-pine chipmunk (*Eutamias amoenus*) in northeastern Oregon. *The Murrelet*, 68:24–27.

Mateo, J. M. 1996. The development of alarm-call response behavior in free-living juvenile Belding's ground squirrels. *Animal Behavior*, 52:489–505.

Mateo, J.M. 2010. Alarm calls elicit predator-specific physiological responses. *Biology Letters*, 6:623–625.

Mateo, J.M. and W.G. Holmes. 1999. How rearing history affects alarm-call responses of Belding's ground squirrels (*Spermophilus beldingi*, Sciuridae). *Ethology*, 105:207–222.

Maurer, G., S.J. Portugal, M.E. Hauber, and others. 2014. First light for avian embryos: eggshell thickness and pigmentation mediate variation in development and UV exposure in wild bird eggs. *Functional Ecology*,

DOI: 10.1111/1365-2435.12314.

May, M. Gray-Crowned Rosy-Finch. http://birding.about.com/od/birdprofiles/p/Gray-Crowned-Rosy-Finch.htm (accessed June 30, 2014).

May, P. Chlorophyll. http://www.chm.bris.ac.uk/3motm/chlorophyll/chlorophyll_h.htm (accessed on 5 January, 2013).

May, R.M. 1970. Flight formations in geese and other birds. *Nature*, 282:778–780.

Maxson, S. and L. Oring. 1980. Breeding season time and energy budgets of the polyandrous Spotted Sandpiper. *Behaviour*, 74:200–263.

Mayntz, M. Cliff Swallow. http://birding.about.com/od/birdprofiles/p/Cliff-Swallow.htm (accessed July 3, 2014).

Mazama pocket gopher. http://en.wikipedia.org/wiki/Mazama_pocket_gopher (accessed February 9, 2014).

McAllister, J.A. and R.S. Hoffmann. 1988. Phenacomys intermedius. *Mammalian Species*, 305:1–8.

McCallum, D.A., R. Grundel, and D.L. Dahlsten. 1999. Mountain Chickadee (*Poecile gambeli*). In: The Birds of North America, No. 453 (A. Poole, Ed.). The Birds of North America Online, Ithaca, New York. (accessed September 9, 2014).

McFrederick, Q.S., J.C. Kathilankal, and J.D. Fuentes. 2008. Air Pollution Modifies floral Scent Trails. *Atmospheric Environment*, 42:2336–2348.

McGahan, J. 1968. Ecology of the Golden Eagle. *The Auk*, 85:1–12.

McIntyre, C.L. 2002. Patterns in nesting area occupancy and reproductive success of Golden Eagles (*Aquila chrysaetos*) in Denali National Park and Preserve, Alaska, 1989-99. *Journal of Raptor Research*, 36:50–54.

Mech, L.D. 1974. Canis lupus. *Mammalian Species*, 37:1–6.

Mech, L.D. 1977. Wolf-Pack Buffer Zones as Prey Reservoirs. *Science*, 198:320–321.

Mech, L.D. 1999. Alpha status, dominance, and division of labor in wolf packs. *Canadian Journal of Zoology*, 77:1196–1203.

Mech, L.D. and L. Boitani (Editors). 2001. Wolves: Behavior, Ecology and Conservation. University of Chicago Press, Chicago, IL. 472 pp.

Meinertzhagen, R. 1940. How do larger raptorial birds hunt their prey? *Ibis*, 4:530–535.

Meredith, D.H. 1972. Subalpine cover associations of *Eutamias amoenus* and *Eutamias townsendii* in the Washington Cascades. *American Midland Naturalist*, 88:348–357.

Merriam, C. H. 1889. Description of a new genus, Phenacomys and four new species of Arvicolinae. North American Fauna, 2:27–45.

Merritt, J.F. (Editor). 1984. Winter Ecology of Small Mammals. *Carnegie Museum of Natural History, Special Publication*, No. 10, Carnegie-Mellon University Press, Pittsburgh, Pennsylvania. 380 pp.

Mertl-Millhollen, A.S., P.A. Goodmann, and E. Klinghammer. 1986. Wolf scent marking with raised-leg urination. *Zoo Biology*, 5:7.

Millburn, M. Black-Tailed Deer Feeding Habits. http://animals.pawnation.com/blacktailed-deer-feeding-habits-5706.html (accessed July 18, 2014).

Miller, F.L. 1965. Behavior associated with parturition in black-tailed deer. *Journal of Wildlife Management*, 29:629–631.

Miller, F.L. 1970. Distribution patterns of black-tailed deer (*Odocoileus hemionus columbianus*) in relation to environment. *Journal of Mammalogy*, 51:248–260.

Miller, F.L. 1971. Mutual grooming by black-tailed deer in northwestern Oregon. *Canadian Field-Naturalist*, 85:295–301.

Miller, F.W. 1930. The spring moult of *Mustela longicauda*. *Journal of Mammalogy*, 11:471–473.

Miller, F.W. 1931. A feeding habit of the long-tailed weasel. *Journal of Mammalogy*, 12:164.

Miller, F.W. 1931. The fall moult of *Mustela longicauda*. *Journal of Mammalogy*, 12:150–152.

Miller M.W., H.M. Swanson, L.L. Wolfe, and others. 2008. Lions and Prions and Deer Demise. PLoS ONE 3(12): e4019. doi:10.1371/journal.pone.0004019

Minnesota Department of Natural Resources. Ruffed Grouse. http://www.dnr.state.mn.us/birds/ruffedgrouse.html (accessed July 13, 2014).

Morrison, P.H. and F.J. Swanson. 1990. Fire History and Pattern in a Cascade Range Landscape. USDA Forest Service General Technical Report. PNW-GTR-254. Pacific Northwest Research Station, Portland, OR. 77 pp.

Morton, M.L. and. J.S. Gallup. 1975. Reproductive Cycle of the Belding Ground Squirrel (*Spermophilus beldingi*): Seasonal and Age Differences. *Great Basin Naturalist*, 35:427–433.

Mountain Chickadee. http://www.allaboutbirds.org/guide/mountain_chickadee/id (accessed September 9, 2014).

Mountain Chickadee. http://birdweb.org/birdweb/bird/mountain_chickadee (accessed September 9, 2014).

Mountain Chickadee. http://en.wikipedia.org/wiki/Mountain_chickadee

(accessed September 9, 2014).

Mountain Chickadee, *Poecile gambeli*. http://birds.audubon.org/birds/mountain-chickadee (accessed September 9, 2014).

Müller-Schwarze, D. 1969. Pheromone function of deer urine. *American Zoologist*, 9:21.

Müller-Schwarze, D. Social significance of forehead rubbing in black-tailed deer (*Odocoileus hemionus columbianus*). *Animal Behaviour*, 20 (1972):788–797.

Muñoz-Fuentes V., C.T. Darimont, R.K. Wayne, and others. 2009. Ecological factors drive differentiation in wolves from British Columbia. *Journal of Biogeography*, 36:1516-1531.

Murie, A. 1944. The Wolves of Mt. McKinley. Fauna of the National Parks of the United States. *Fauna Series No 5*. U.S. Government Printing Office, Washington, D.C. 251 pp.

Murphy, K.M., G.S. Felzien, M.G. Hornocker, and T.K. Ruth.1998. Encounter Competition between Bears and Cougars: Some Ecological Implications. *Ursus*, 10:55–60.

Muths, E. and P. Nanjappa. *Anaxyrus boreas*. http://amphibiaweb.org/cgi/amphib_query?where-genus=Anaxyrus&where-species=boreas (accessed August 27, 2014).

Muul, I. 1969. Mating behavior, gestation period, and development of *Glaucomys sabrinus*. *Journal of Mammalogy*, 50:121.

Nagorsen, D.W. 1987. Summer and winter food caches of the heather vole, *Phenacomys intermedius*, in Quetico Provincial Park, Ontario. *Canadian Field-Naturalist*, 101:82–85.

Naylor, B.J., J.F. Bendell, and L. Spires. 1985. High densities of Heather Voles, *Phenacomys intermedius*, in Jack Pine, *Pinus banksiana*, forests in Ontario. *Canadian Field-Naturalist*, 99:494–497.

Nelson, A.L. 1934. Some Early Summer Food Preferences of the American. Raven in Southeastern Oregon. *The Condor*, 36:10–15.

Nette, T., D. Burles, and M. Hoefs. 1984. Observation of Golden Eagle, *Aquila chrysaetos*, predation Dall Sheep, *Ovis dalli dalli*, lambs. *Canadian Field Naturalist*, 98:252–254.

Nielsen, C.K. and A. Woolf. 2001. Spatial Organization of Bobcats (*Lynx rufus*) in Southern Illinois. *The American Midland Naturalist*, 146:43–52.

North American Cougar. http://en.wikipedia.org/wiki/North_American_cougar (accessed August 3, 2014).

Northern flying squirrel. http://en.wikipedia.org/wiki/Northern_flying_squirrel (accessed November 16, 2014).

Northern Goshawk, *Accipiter gentiles*. http://birds.audubon.org/birds/northern-goshawk (accessed September 6, 2014).

Northern Goshawk. http://birdweb.org/birdweb/bird/northern_goshawk (accessed September 6, 2014).

Northern Goshawk. http://www.allaboutbirds.org/guide/northern_goshawk/lifehistory (accessed September 6, 2014).

Northern Goshawk. http://en.wikipedia.org/wiki/Northern_goshawk (accessed September 6, 2014).

Northern Goshawk—Esteemed Bird of Prey. http://birdnote.org/show/northern-goshawk-esteemed-bird-prey (accessed September 6, 2014).

Nowak, R.M. 1995. Another look at wolf taxonomy, Pp. 375–397. *In*: Ecology and conservation of wolves in a changing world. Carbyn, L.N., S.H. Fritts, and D.R. Seip (eds). *Proceedings of the Second North American Symposium on Wolves*, Edmonton, Canada.

Nussbaum, R.A. and C. Maser. 1969. Observations of *Sorex palustris* Preying on *Dicamptodon ensatus*. *The Murrelet*, 50:23.

Nussbaum, R.A. and C. Maser. 1975. Food Habits of the Bobcat, *Lynx rufus*, in the Coast and Cascade Ranges of Western Oregon in Relation to Present Management Policies. *Northwest Science*, 49:261–266.

Nussbaum, R.A., E.D. Brodie, Jr., and R.M. Storm. 1983. Amphibians & Reptiles of the Pacific Northwest. The University Press of Idaho, Moscow, ID. 332 pp.

Oberski, I.M. and J.D. Wilson. 1991. Territoriality and site-related dominance: on two related concepts in avian social organization. *Ethology*, 87:225–236.

Ocean Temperatures. http://oceanservice.noaa.gov/facts/ninonina.html (accessed May 6, 2014).

Olendorff, R.R. 1976. The Food Habits of North American Golden Eagles. *American Midland Naturalist*, 95:231–236.

Olson, D. 1989. Predation on breeding western toads (*Bufo boreas*). *Copeia*, 2:391–397.

Orlando, C. Quaking aspen are a visual feast. http://www.oregon.gov/odf/urbanforests/docs/featuredtreequakingaspen.pdf (accessed July 14, 2014).

Ostrich. http://en.wikipedia.org/wiki/Ostrich (accessed July 31, 2014).

Panet, I., G. Pajot-Métivier, M. Greff-Leffdtz, and others. 2014. Mapping the mass distribution of Earth's mantle using satellite-derived gravity gradients. *Nature Geoscience*, doi:10.1038/ngeo2063.

Pangaea. http://en.wikipedia.org/wiki/Pangaea (accessed January 15,

2014).

Paquet, P.C. 1991. Scent-marking behavior of sympatric wolves (*Canis lupus*) and coyotes (*C. latrans*) in Riding Mountain National Park. *Canadian Journal of Zoology*, 69:1721–1727.

Pauli, J.N., B. Zuckerberg, J.P. Whiteman, and W. Porter. 2013. The subnivium: a deteriorating seasonal refugium. *Frontiers in Ecology and the Environment*, 11:260–267.

Peacock, M.M. 1997. Determining natal dispersal patterns in a population of North American pikas (*Ochotona princeps*) using direct mark-resight and indirect genetic methods. *Behavioral Ecology*, 8:340–350.

Pearson, O.P., M.R. Koford, and A.K. Pearson. 1952. Reproduction of the lump-nosed bat (*Corynorhinus rafinesquii*) in California. *Journal of Mammalogy*, 33:273–320.

Pennisi, E. 2004. The Secret Life of Fungi. *Science*, 304:1620–1622.

Peromyscus maniculatus. http://en.wikipedia.org/wiki/Peromyscus_maniculatus (accessed October 6, 2014).

Perry, J and B. Roitberg. 2005. Ladybird mothers mitigate offspring starvation risk by laying trophic eggs. *Behavioral Ecology and Sociobiology*, 58:578–586.

Pfau, J. Douglas's squirrel, *Tamiasciurus douglasii*. http://animaldiversity.ummz.umich.edu/accounts/Tamiasciurus_douglasii/ (accessed November 15, 2014).

Pierce B.M., V.C. Bleich, and R.T. Bower. 2000. Selection of mule deer by mountain lions and coyotes: effects of hunting style, body size and reproductive state. *Journal of Mammalogy*, 81:462–472.

Platnick, J. *Zapus trinotatus*. http://animaldiversity.ummz.umich.edu/accounts/Zapus_trinotatus/ (accessed June 27, 2014).

Poelker, R.J. and H.D. Hartwell. 1973. Black bear of Washington. *Washington State Game Department Biological Bulletin*, 14:1–180.

Polderboer, E.B., L.W. Kuhn, and G.O. Hendrickson. 1941. Winter and spring habits of weasels in central Iowa. *Journal of Wildlife Management*, 5:115–119.

Pompon, J., D. Quiring, P. Giordanengo, and Y. Pelletier. 2010. Role of xylem consumption on osmoregulation in *Macrosiphum euphorbiae* (Thomas). *Journal of Insect Physiology*, 56:610–615.

Portugal, S.J., T.Y. Hubel, J. Fritz, and others. 2014. Upwash exploitation and downwash avoidance by flap phasing in ibis formation flight. *Nature*, 505:399–402.

Power, E.E and D.C. Hauser. 1974. Relationship of Anting and Sunbathing to Moulting in Wild Birds. *The Auk*, 91:537–563.

Preble, E.A. 1899. Revision of the Jumping mice of the genus *Zapus*. *North American Fauna*, 15:1–43.

Purandare, S. and B. Tenhumberg. 2012. Influence of aphid honeydew on the foraging behaviour of *Hippodamia convergens* larvae. *Ecological Entomology*, 37:18–192.

Purdic, K.L., A.K. Skemp, and D.R. Papaj. 2007. Aposematic coloration, luminance contrast, and the benefits of conspicuousness. *Behavioral Ecology*, 18:41–46.

Putz, B. Western Heather Vole, *Phenacomys intermedius*. http://animal-diversity.ummz.umich.edu/accounts/Phenacomys_intermedius/ (accessed November 21, 2014).

Pyare, S. and W. Longland. 2001. Patterns of ectomycorrhizal-fungi consumption by small mammals in remnant old-growth forests of the Sierra Nevada. *Journal of Mammology*, 82: 681.

Pyare, S. and W. Longland. 2001. Mechanisms of truffle detection by northern flying squirrels. *Canadian Journal of Zoology*, 79:1007–1015.

Pyare, S., W.P. Smith, J.V. Nicholls, and J.A. Cook. 2002. Diets of northern flying squirrels, *Glaucomys sabrinus*, in southeast Alaska. *Canadian Field Naturalist*, 116:98–103.

Pyle, P. Identification Guide to North American Birds. Part 1. 1997. Slate Creek Press, Bolinas, CA. 732 pp.

Quaternary extinction event. http://en.wikipedia.org/wiki/Quaternary_extinction_event (accessed August 4, 2014).

Quick, H.F. 1944. Habits and economics of the New York weasel in Michigan. *Journal of Wildlife Management*, 8:71–78.

Rainbow Trout (*Oncorhynchus mykiss*). http://www.tpwd.state.tx.us/huntwild/wild/species/rbt/ (accessed July 15, 2014).

Rainbow-Trout-or-Steelhead. http://www.nwf.org/wildlife/wildlife-library/amphibians-reptiles-and-fish/rainbow-trout-or-steelhead.aspx (accessed July 15, 2014).

Revis, H.C. and D.A. Waller. 2004. Bactericidal and Fungicidal Activity of ant chemicals on feather parasites: an evaluation of anting behavior as a Method of Self-medication in Songbirds. *The Auk*, 121:1262–1268.

Rhoads, S.N. 1894. A new jumping mouse from the Pacific slope. *Proceedings of the Academy of Natural Sciences of Philadelphia*, 46:421–422.

Ridolfi, K. Rainbow Trout. http://animaldiversity.ummz.umich.edu/accounts/Oncorhynchus_mykiss/ (accessed July 15, 2014).

Rising, J.D., and D.D. Beadle. 1996. A guide to the identification and natural history of the sparrows of the United States and Canada. Academic Press, Boston, MA. 365 pp.

Rising, J.D. 2010. A Guide to the Identification and Natural History of the Sparrows of the United States and Canada. Christopher Helm Publishers, London, UK. 379 pp.

Roache, L.C. 1960. Ladybug, Ladybug: What's in a Name? *The Coleopterists Bulletin*, 14:21–25.

Robertson, R., B. Stutchbury, and R. Cohen. 1992. Tree Swallow (*Tachycineta bicolor*). Pp. 1–28. *In*: A. Poole, P. Stettenheim, and F. Gill (editors). The Birds of North America, 11 (1). *The Academy of Natural Sciences*, Philadelphia, PA; The American Ornithologists' Union, Washington, DC.

Robertson, S. How do Chipmunks communicate? http://www.ehow.com/info_10069070_chipmunks-communicate.html. (accessed September 23, 2014).

Robinson, S. R. 1980. Anti-predator Behavior and Predator Recognition in Belding's Ground Squirrels. *Animal Behavior*, 28:840–852.

Robson, D. Proto-Humans Mastered Fire 790,000 Years Ago. *ABC News*, October 28, 2008 (accessed 27 February 27, 2009).

Rogers, L.L. 1974. Shedding of foot pads by black bears during denning. *Journal of Mammalogy*, 55:672–674.

Rogers, L.L. 1980. Inheritance Of Coat Color And Changes in Pelage Coloration in Black Bears in Northeastern Minnesota. *Journal of Mammalogy*, 61:324–327.

Roosevelt elk. http://en.wikipedia.org/wiki/Roosevelt_Elk (accessed August 20, 2014).

Root, L. Rainbow Trout (*Oncorhynchus mykiss*). http://www3.northern.edu/natsource/FISH/Rainbo1.htm (accessed July 17, 2014).

Roger, C. 1999. Mechanisms of Prey Selection in the Ladybeetle *Coleomegilla Maculata Lengi* Timb (Coleoptera:Coccinellidae). PhD Thesis. Department of Natural Resource Sciences. MacDonald Campus of McGill University, Montréal, Canada. 168 pp.

Ruffed Grouse. http://www.allaboutbirds.org/guide/ruffed_grouse/id (accessed July 13, 2014).

Ruffed Grouse. http://en.wikipedia.org/wiki/Ruffed_grouse (accessed July 13, 2014).

Ruffed Grouse. http://birds.audubon.org/birds/ruffed-grouse (accessed July 13, 2014).

Ruffed Grouse. http://www.dec.ny.gov/animals/45436.html (accessed

July 13, 2014).

Rufous Hummingbird. http://www.allaboutbirds.org/guide/rufous_hummingbird/lifehistory (accessed November 26, 2014).

Rutter, R.J. 1969. A contribution to the biology of the Grey Jay (*Perisoreus canadensis*). *Canadian Field-Naturalist*, 83:300–316.

Sanchez-Zapata, J.A., S. Eguia, M. Blazquez, and others. 2010. Unexpected role of ungulate carcasses in the diet of Golden Eagles *Aquila chrysaetos* in Mediterranean mountains. *Bird Study*, 57:352–360.

Saroki, A. *Hippodamia convergens*, convergent lady beetle. http://animaldiversity.ummz.umich.edu/accounts/Hippodamia_convergens/ (accessed, June 21, 2014).

Schlegal, M. 1976. Factor affecting calf elk survival in north central Idaho. *Western Association of State Game and Fish Commission*, 56:342–355.

Schmidt, P. and J.A. Lockwood. 1992. Subnivean Arthropod Faunas of Southeastern Wyoming: Habitat and Seasonal Effects on Population Density. *American Midland Naturalist*, 127:66–76.

Schulte-Hostedde, A., J. Millar, and L. Gibbs. 2002. Female-biased sexual size dimorphism in the yellow-pine chipmunk (*Tamias amoenus*): sex-specific patterns of annual reproductive success and survival. *Evolution*, 56:2519–2529.

ScienceDaily. For birds, red means 'go': Some flowers evolved red hues favored by birds. http://www.sciencedaily.com/releases/2013/03/130305100957.htm (accessed April 17, 2014).

ScienceDaily. Insight Into Evolution Of First Flowers. http://www.sciencedaily.com/releases/2009/05/090518172453.htm (accessed April 17, 2014).

Seidensticker, J.C., IV; M.G. Hornocker, W.V. Wiles, and J.P. Messick. 1973. Mountain lion social organization in the Idaho Primitive Area. *Wildlife Monograph*, 35:1–60.

Seton, E.T. 1928. Animals Worth Knowing. Doubleday, Doran, and Co., New York, NY. 299 pp.

Shefferly, N. Snowshoe hare. http://animaldiversity.org/accounts/Lepus_americanus/ (accessed December 1, 2014).

Sherman, P.W. 1977. Nepotism and the evolution of alarm calls. *Science*, 197:1246–1253.

Sherman, P.W. 1981. Reproductive Competition and Infanticide in Belding's Ground Squirrels and Other Animals. Pp. 311–331. *In*: Natural Selection and Social Behavior. Alexander R.D.A. and D. W. Tinkle (editors). Chiron Press, New York.

Sherman, P.W. 1981. Kinship, Demography, and Belding's Ground Squirrel Nepotism. *Behavioral Ecology and Sociobiology*, 8:251–259.

Sherman, P.W. and. M.L. Morton. 1984. Demography of Belding's ground squirrels. *Ecology*, 65:1617–1628.

Shivaraju, A. *Puma concolor*. http://animaldiversity.ummz.umich.edu/site/accounts/information/Puma_concolor.html (accessed August 3, 2014).

Shrestha, M., A.G. Dyer, S. Boyd-Gerny, and others. 2013. Shades of red: bird-pollinated flowers target the specific colour discrimination abilities of avian vision. *New Phytologist*, 198:301–310.

Shriner, W. 1998. Yellow-bellied marmot and golden-mantled ground squirrel responses to heterospecific alarm calls. *Animal Behaviour*, 55:529–536.

Sieving, K.E. and M.F. Willson. 1998. Nest predation and avian species diversity in northwestern forest understory. *Ecology*, 79:2391–2402.

Sikes, R.S. and M.L. Kennedy. 1992. Morphologic Variation of the Bobcat (*Felis rufus*) in the Eastern United States and Its Association with Selected Environmental Variables. *American Midland Naturalist*, 128:313–324.

Smith, A.T. 1974. The Distribution and Dispersal of Pikas: Influences of Behavior and Climate. *Journal of Ecology*, 55:1368–1376.

Smith, A.T. and M.L. Weston. 1990. Ochotona princeps. *Mammalian Species*, 352:1–8.

Smith, C.C. 1970. The coevolution of pine squirrels (*Tamiasciurus*) and conifers. *Ecological Monographs*, 40:349–371.

Smith, D.G. 1982. Spatial Relationships Of Nesting Golden Eagles In Central Utah. *Journal of Raptor Research*, 16:127–132.

Smith, D.G. and J.R. Murphy. 1973. Breeding ecology of raptors in the eastern Great Basin of Utah. *Brigham Young University Science Bulletin, Biological Series*, 18:1–76.

Smith, F.A. 1997. Neotoma cinerea. *Mammalian Species*, 564:1–8.

Smith, R. 1991. Rainbow Trout (*Oncorhynchus mykiss*). Pp. 304–323. *In*: Trout: The Wildlife Series. (J. Stoltz and J. Schnell, eds.). Stackpole Books, Harrisburg, PA. 370 pp.

Smithers, B.L., C.W. Boal, and D.E. Andersen. 2005. Northern Goshawk diet in Minnesota: An Analysis using video recording systems. *Journal of Raptor Research*, 39:264–273.

Sorenson, M. 1962. Some aspects of water shrew behavior. *American Midland Naturalist*, 68:445–462.

Spalding, D.J. Cougar in British Columbia. *British Columbia Fish and*

Wildlife Branch. http://www.env.gov.bc.ca/wld/documents/cougar.htm (accessed August 3, 2014).

Spiller, N.J., L. Koenders, and W.F. Tjallingii. 1990. Xylem ingestion by aphids—a strategy for maintaining water balance. *Entomologia Experimentalis et Applicata*, 55:101–104.

Spotted Sandpiper. http://www.allaboutbirds.org/guide/spotted_sandpiper/lifehistory (accessed June 21, 2014).

Spotted Sandpiper. http://en.wikipedia.org/wiki/Spotted_sandpiper (Accessed June 22, 2014).

Spotted Sandpiper, *Actitis macularius*. http://birds.audubon.org/birds/spotted-sandpiper (accessed June 21, 2014).

Squires, J.R., and R.T. Reynolds. 1997. Northern Goshawk (*Accipiter gentilis*). Pp. 2–27. *In*: Birds of North America, No. 298 (A. Poole and F. Gill, eds.). The Academy of Natural Sciences, Philadelphia, PA, and the American Ornithologists' Union, Washington, D.C.

Stahlecker, D.H., D.G. Mikesic, J.N. White, and others. 2009. Prey remains in nests of Four Corners Golden Eagles: 1998-2008. *Western Birds*, 40:301–306.

Stahler, D., B. Heinrich, and D. Smith. 2002. Common ravens, *Corvus corax*, preferentially associate with grey wolves, *Canis lupus*, as a foraging strategy in winter. *Animal Behaviour*, 64:283–290.

Staley, K. and J. Mueller. 2000. Rainbow Trout (*Oncorhynchus mykiss*). *Fish and Wildlife Habitat Management Leaflet*, 13:1–11.

Stebbins, R.C. 1985. A Field Guide to Western Reptiles and Amphibians. Second Edition. Houghton Mifflin Company, Boston, MA. 336 pp.

Stonedahl, L. and J.D. Lattin. 1982. The Gerridae or Water Striders of Oregon and Washington (Hemiptera:Heteroptera). *Oregon State University Technical Bulletin*, 144:1–36.

Steller's Jay. http://www.allaboutbirds.org/guide/stellers_jay/id (accessed July 21, 2014).

Steller's Jay. http://en.wikipedia.org/wiki/Steller's_jay (accessed July 21, 2014).

Steller's Jay. http://birdweb.org/birdweb/bird/stellers_jay (accessed July 21, 2014).

Steller's Jay. http://www.birdinginformation.com/birds/ravens-crows-magpies-jays/stellers-jay/ (accessed July 22, 2014).

Strickland, D. 1991. Juvenile dispersal in Gray Jays: dominant brood member expels siblings from natal territory. *Canadian Journal of Zoology*, 69:2935–2945.

Strickland, D. and T.A. Waite. 2001. Does initial suppression of allofeeding in small jays help to conceal their nests? *Canadian Journal of Zoology*, 79:2128–2146.

Subnivean climate. http://en.wikipedia.org/wiki/Subnivean_climate (accessed July 19, 2013).

Sugden, A., R. Stone, and C. Ash. 2004. Ecology in the Underworld. *Science*, 304:1613.

Suplee, C. El Niño/La Niña. http://www.nationalgeographic.com/elnino/mainpage.html (accessed May 6, 2014).

Sutherland, J.B. and R.L. Crawford. 1979. Gray Jay feeding on slime mold. *The Murrelet*, 60:28.

Sutton, D.A. 1992. Tamias amoenus. *Mammalian Species*, 390:1–8.

Sutton, D.A. 2003. Tamias Townsendii. *Mammalian Species*, 432:1–8.

Suzuki, I.S., K. Fukuda, E. Arihara, and others. 2010. Photodynamic antimicrobial activity of avian eggshell pigments. *FEBS Letters*, 584:770–774.

Svihla, A., and R.D. Svihla. 1933. Notes on the jumping mouse, *Zapus trinotatus trinotatus* Rhoads. *Journal of Mammalogy*, 14:131–134.

Sweanor, L., K.A. Logan, and M.G. Hornocker. 2000. Cougar Dispersal Patterns, Metapopulation Dynamics, and Conservation. *Conservation Biology*, 14:798–808.

Swenson, R. 1989. Emergent Evolution and the Global Attractor: The Evolutionary Epistemology of Entropy Production Maximization. *Proceedings of the 33rd Annual Meeting of The International Society for the Systems Sciences*, 33:46–53.

Swenson, R. 1991. Order, evolution, and natural law: Fundamental relations in complex system theory. Pp 125–148. *In*: Cybernetics and Applied Systems. (C. Negoita, ed.). Marcel Dekker Inc., New York, NY.

Swenson, R. and M.T. Turvey. 1991. Thermodynamic reasons for perception-action cycles. *Ecological Psychology*, 3:317–348.

Tamias amoenus. http://www.mnh.si.edu/mna/full_image.cfm?image_id=1509 (accessed October 5, 2014).

Tamias amoenus. http://imnh.isu.edu/digitalatlas/bio/mammal/rod/squir/ypch/ypchfrm.htm (accessed October 5, 2014).

Taylor, M. *Nucifraga columbiana*, Clark's nutcracker. http://animaldiversity.ummz.umich.edu/accounts/Nucifraga_columbiana/ (accessed July 23, 2014).

Temple, S.A. 1974. Winter Food Habits of Ravens on the Arctic Slope of Alaska. *Arctic*, 27:41–46.

Temple, S.A. 1987. Do predators always capture substandard individuals disproportionately from prey populations? *Ecology*, 68:669–674.

The Earth. http://www.enchantedlearning.com/subjects/astronomy/planets/earth/Inside.shtml (accessed on April 5, 2010).

The Northern Water Shrew. *West Virginia Wildlife Magazine.* 2004. http://www.wvdnr.gov/wildlife/magazine/archive/04Winter/wildlife_diversity_notebook.shtm (accessed February 3, 2014).

Thomas, J.W., H. Black, Jr., R.J. Scherzinger, and R.J. Pederson. 1979. Chapter 8, Deer and Elk. Pp. 104–127. *In*: Wildlife Habitats in Managed Forests: The Blue Mountains of Oregon and Washington. (Jack Ward Thomas, Technical Editor). U.S. Department of Agriculture, Forest Service, Pacific Northwest Range and Experiment Station, Portland, Oregon. Agricultural Handbook No. 553.

Thompson, S.P., R.S. Johnstone, and C.D. Littlefield. 1982. Nesting history of Golden Eagles in Malheur-Harney Lakes Basin, southeastern Oregon. *The Raptor Research Foundation*, 16:116–122.

Tomback, D.F. 1978. Foraging strategies of Clark's Nutcracker. *Living Bird*, 16:123–161.

Tomback, D.F. 1982. Dispersal of whitebark pine seeds by Clark's Nutcracker: A mutualism hypothesis. *Journal of Animal Ecology*, 51:451–467.

Tomback, D.F., S.F. Arno, and R.E. Keane. 2001. Whitebark Pine Communities: Ecology and Restoration. Island Press, Washington, DC. 440 pp.

Toweill, D.E. and C. Maser. 1985. Food of cougars in the Cascade Range of Oregon. *Great Basin Naturalist*, 45:77–80.

Toweill, D.E., C. Maser, L.D. Bryant, and M.L. Johnson. 1988. Reproductive characteristics of Eastern Oregon cougars. *Northwest Science*, 62:147–149.

Toweill, D. E. and J. W. Thomas (editors). 2002. North American elk: Ecology and Management. Smithsonian Institution Press, Washington, D.C. 962 pp.

Townsend's chipmunk. http://en.wikipedia.org/wiki/Townsend's_chipmunk (accessed September 13, 2014).

Toynbee, A. 1958. Civilization on Trial and the World and the West. Meridian Books, Inc. New York, NY. 348 pp.

Trainer, C.E. 1971. The relationship of physical condition and fertility of female Roosevelt elk (*Cervus canadensis roosevelti*) in Oregon. M.S. Thesis. Oregon State University, Corvallis, OR. 93 pp.

Tree Swallow. http://www.allaboutbirds.org/guide/tree_swallow/id (accessed July 9, 2014).

Tree Swallow. http://en.wikipedia.org/wiki/Tree_swallow (accessed July 9, 2014).

Tree Swallow. http://birdweb.org/birdweb/bird/tree_swallow (accessed July 9, 2014).

Tree Swallow, *Tachycineta bicolor*. http://birds.audubon.org/birds/tree-swallow (accessed July 9, 2014).

Tsuchida, T., R. Koga, X.Y. Meng, T. Matsumoto, and T. Fukatsu. 2005. Characterization of a Facultative Endosymbiotic Bacterium of the Pea Aphid *Acyrthosiphon pisum*. *Microbial Ecology*, 49:126–133.

Turner, L.W. 1972. Autecology of the Belding ground squirrel in Oregon. Ph.D. Dissertation. Department of Biological Sciences, University of Arizona, Tuscon. 149 pp.

Turner, L.W. 1973. Vocal and Escape Response of *Spermophilus beldingi* to Predators. *Journal of Mammology*, 54:990–993.

Tyler, T., W.J. Liss, L.M. Ganio, and others. 1998. Interaction between Introduced Trout and Larval Salamanders (*Ambystoma macrodactylum*) in High-Elevation Lakes. *Conservation Biology*, 12:94–105.

Ulmer, Jr., F.A. 1941. Melanism in the Felidae, with Special Reference to the Genus *Lynx*. *Journal of Mammalogy*, 22:285–288.

USGS Patuxent Wildlife Research Center. 2014. Longevity Records of North American Birds. http://www.pwrc.usgs.gov/bbl/longevity/longvrec.cfm (accessed July 21, 2014).

Valutis, L.L. and J.M. Marzluff. 1977. A Golden Eagle Eats wild Canada Goose Eggs. *The Raptor Research Foundation*, 31:288–289.

Vargas, G., J. Michaud, and J. Nechols. 2012. Cryptic maternal effects in *Hippodamia convergens* vary with maternal age and body size. *Entomologia Experimentalis et Applicata*, 146:302–311.

Vaughan, T. and P. Krutzsch. 1954. Seasonal distribution of the hoary bat in southern California. *Journal of Mammalogy*, 35:431–432.

Veghte, J. 1964. Thermal and metabolic responses of the Gray Jay to cold stress. *Physiological Zoology*, 37:316–328.

Vernes, K. 2001. Gliding performance of the northern flying squirrel (*Glaucomys sabrinus*) in mature mixed forest of eastern Canada. *Journal of Mammalogy*, 82:1026–1033.

Vernes, K. 2004. Breeding biology and seasonal capture success of northern flying squirrels and red squirrels in southern New Brunswick. *Northeastern Naturalist*, 11:123–137.

Verts, B.J. and L.N. Carraway. 1998. Land Mammals of Oregon. University of California Press, Berkeley, CA. 668 pp.

Vigallon, S.M. and J.M. Marzluff. 2005. Abundance, Nest Sites, and Nesting Success of Steller's Jays Along a Gradient of Urbanization in Western Washington. *Northwest Science*, 79:22–27.

Voelkl, B., S.J. Portugal, M. Unsöld, and others. Matching times of leading and following suggest cooperation through direct reciprocity during V-formation flight in ibis. *Proceedings of the National Academy of Sciences of the United States of America*. February 2, 2015, doi: 10.1073/pnas.1413589112.

Waite, T.A. 1992. Social Hoarding and a Load Size-Distance Relationship in Gray Jays. *The Condor*, 94:995–998.

Waite, T.A. and D. Strickland. 1977. Cooperative Breeding in Gray Jays: Philopatric Offspring Provision Juvenile Siblings. *The Condor*, 99:523–525.

Waite, T.A. and J.D. Reeve. 1997. Multistage scatter-hoarding decisions in the Gray Jay (*Perisoreus canadensis*). *Bird Behavior*, 12:7–14.

Waldien, D., J. Hayseb, and M. Husob. 2006. Use of downed wood by Townsend's Chipmunks (*Tamias townsendii*) in Western Oregon. *Journal of Mammalogy*, 87:454–460.

Walker, K.M. 1955. Distribution and taxonomy of the small pocket gophers of northwestern Oregon. Ph. D. Thesis. Oregon State College [University], Corvallis, OR. 200 pp.

Ward, J.V. 1992. Aquatic Insect Ecology: 1. Biology and habitat. New York: Wiley & Sons, New York, NY. 438 pp.

Wardle, D.A., R.D. Bardgett, J.N. Klironomos, and others. 2004. Ecological Linkages Between Aboveground and Belowground Biota. *Science*, 304:1629–1633.

Waring, R.H. and J.F. Franklin. 1979. Evergreen coniferous forest of the Pacific Northwest. *Science*, 204:1380–1386.

Warwicker, M. Eggshells act like 'sunblock', study suggests. http://www.bbc.co.uk/nature/28492239 (accessed July 30, 2014).

Water Strider. http://www.nwf.org/Wildlife/Wildlife-Library/Invertebrates/Water-Strider.aspx (accessed June 11, 2014).

Watson, J. 2011. The Golden Eagle (Second Edition). T. & A.D. Poyser, London, UK. 448 pp.

Webb, J. Ant colony 'personalities' shaped by environment. http://www.bbc.com/news/science-environment-28658268 (accessed August 8, 2014).

Weckworth B.V., S.L. Talbot, and J.A. Cook. 2010. Phylogeography of wolves (*Canis lupus*) in the Pacific Northwest. *Journal of Mammalogy*, 91:363–375.

Wells-Gosling, N. and L.R. Heany. 1984. Glaucomys sabrinus. *Mammalian Species*, 229:1–8.

Western Toad. http://www1.dnr.wa.gov/nhp/refdesk/herp/html/4bubo.html (accessed August 27, 2014).

Western Toad. http://en.wikipedia.org/wiki/Western_toad (accessed August 27, 2014).

What is cud, and why do cattle chew it? http://www.cattle-empire.net/blog/115/what-cud-and-why-do-cattle-chew-it (accessed August 21, 2014).

Whitaker, Jr., J.O. 1962. *Endogone, Hymenogaster,* and *Melanogaster* as small mammals foods. *American Midland Naturalist*, 67:152–156.

Whitaker, Jr., J.O. 1995. Food availability and opportunistic versus selective feeding in insectivorous bats. *Bat Research News*, 1995:75–77.

Whitaker, Jr., J.O. 1996. National Audubon Society Field Guide to North American Mammals. Alfred A Knopf, Inc., New York, NY. 937 pp.

Whitaker, Jr., J.O. and C. Maser. 1976. Food Habits of Five Western Oregon Shrews. *Northwest Science*, 50:102–107.

Whitaker, Jr., J.O., C. Maser, and L.E. Keller. 1977. Food habits of bats of western Oregon. *Northwest Science*, 51:46–55.

Whitaker, Jr., J.O., C. Maser, and R.J. Pedersen. 1979. Food and ectoparasitic mites of Oregon moles. *Northwest Science*, 53: 268–273.

Whitaker, Jr., J.O., C. Maser, and S.P. Cross. 1981. Foods of Oregon silver-haired bats, *Lasionycteris noctivagans. Northwest Science*, 55:75–77.

Whitaker, Jr., J.O., S.P. Cross, and C. Maser. 1983. Food of vagrant shrews (*Sorex vagrans*) from Grant County, Oregon, as related to livestock grazing procedures. *Northwest Science*, 57:102–111.

Whitaker, Jr., J.O. and W.J. Hamilton, Jr. 1998. Mammals of the Eastern United States. Cornell University Press, Ithaca, NY. 583 pp.

Whitaker, L. M. 1957. A Résumé of Anting, with Particular Reference to a Captive Orchard Oriole. *The Wilson Bulletin*, 69:195–262.

Whitehead, L.F. and A.E. Douglas. 1993. A Metabolic Study of *Buchnera,* the Intracellular Bacterial Symbionts of the Pea Aphid *Acyrthosiphon pisum. Journal of General Microbiology*, 139:821–826.

Why Cows Have Four Stomachs. http://synapsida.blogspot.com/2011/08/why-cows-have-four-stomachs.html (accessed August 21, 2014).

Wilkinson, T.L., D.A. Ashfors, J. Pritchard, and A.E. Douglas. 1997. Honeydew Sugars and Osmoregulation in the Pea Aphid *Acyrthosiphon pisum*. *The Journal of Experimental Biology*, 200:2137–2143.

Williams, D.D. and B.W. Feltmate. 1992. Aquatic Insects. CAB International, Wallingford, Oxfordshire, UK. 360 pp.

Williams, E.S. 2005. Chronic Wasting Disease. *Veterinary Pathology*, 42:530–549.

Williams, E.S., and S. Young. 1980. Chronic wasting disease of captive mule deer: a spongiform encephalopathy. *Journal of Wildlife Disease*, 16:89–98.

Williams, O. and B. A. Finney. 1964. *Endogone*—Food for mice. *Journal of Mammalogy*, 45:265–271.

Wilmers, C.C., D.R. Stahler, R.L. Crabtree, and others. 2003. Resource dispersion and consumer dominance: scavenging at wolf-and hunter-killed carcasses in Greater Yellowstone, USA. *Ecology Letters*, 6:996–1003.

Wimsatt, W.A. 1944. Further studies on the survival of spermatozoa in the female reproductive tract of the bat. *Anatomical Record*, 88:193–204.

Wimsatt, W.A. 1960. An analysis of parturition in Chiroptera, including new observations on *Myotis l. lucifugus*. *Journal of Mammalogy*, 41:183–200.

Wolff, J. and D. Durr. 1986. Winter Nesting Behavior of *Peromyscus leucopus* and *Peromyscus maniculatus*. *Journal of Mammalogy*, 67:409–12.

Wright, P.L. 1942. Delayed implantation in the long-tailed weasel (*Mustela frenata*), the short-tailed weasel (*Mustela ciognani*), and the marten (*Martes americana*). *Anatomical Record*, 83:341–353.

Wright, P.L. 1942. A correlation between the spring moult and spring changes in the sexual cycle in the weasel. *Journal of Experimental Zoology*, 91:103–110.

Wright, P.L. 1947. The sexual cycle of the male long-tailed weasel (*Mustela frenata*). *Journal of Mammalogy*, 28:343–352.

Wright, P.L. 1948. Breeding habits of captive long-tailed weasels (*Mustela frenata*). *American Midland Naturalist*, 39:338–344.

Wright, P.L. 1948. Preimplantation stages in the long-tailed weasel (*Mustela frenata*). *Anatomical Record*, 100:593–608.

Young, I.M. and J.W. Crawford. 2004. Interactions and Self-Organization in the Soil-Microbe Complex. *Science*, 304:1634–1637.

Young, S.P. 1958. The bobcat of North America. Stackpole Co., Harrisburg, PA. 193 pp.

Yuan-Chug, C. and G.R. Fleming. 2009. Dynamics of Light Harvesting in Photosynthesis. *Annual Review of Physical Chemistry*, 60:241–262.

Zeveloff, S.I., F.R. Collett. 1988. Mammals of the Intermountain West. University of Utah Press, Salt Lake City. 351 pp.

Zwickel, F.G.J. and H. Brent. 1953. Movement of Columbian black-tailed deer in the Willapa Hills area, Washington. *The Murrelet*, 34:41–46.

Photo Credits

Photos not noted below, credit Chris Maser

Photo 2.7. Photograph by Chris Maser and Michael Castellano, USDA Forest Service.

Photo 2.9 Photograph by R. B. Forbes, U.S. Department of Agriculture http://commons.wikimedia.org/wiki/File:Neotoma_cinerea_bushy_tailed_woodrat.jpg

Photo 2.11 Photograph by Jim W. Grace, USDA Forest Service.

Photo 3.1 Photograph by Mberg http://commons.wikimedia.org/wiki/File:Western_Toad_1.JPG

Photo 4.8. U.S. Fish and Wildlife Service.

Photo 4.9. Photograph by John Anderson, USDI Bureau of Land Management.

Photo 5.1 Photograph by and courtesy of Sue Johnston.

Photo 5.2 Photograph by Marcelochal. http://commons.wikimedia.org/wiki/File:Libelula_070.jpg

Photo 5.3 Photograph by Tim Bekaert, http://commons.wikimedia.org/wiki/File:Anax_imperator_female.jpg

Photo 5.4 Photograph by Jim Conrad, http://commons.wikimedia.org/wiki/File:Dragonfly-nymph-exoskeleton.jpg

Photo 5.5. Photograph by and courtesy of Dr. Norman Anderson, Department of Entomology, Oregon State University.

Photo 5.6. Photograph by and courtesy of Dr. Norman Anderson, Department of Entomology, Oregon State University.

Photo 5.7. Photograph by "Pudding4brains," http://commons.wikimedia.org/wiki/File:Schietmot_buiten_zijaanzicht_R_compositie.jpg.

Photo 5.8 Photograph by Trépas, http://commons.wikimedia.org/wiki/File:Pteronarcyidae.jpg.

Photo 5.9 Photograph by Aung, shttp://commons.wikimedia.org/wiki/File:Ephemeridae1pl.jpg.

Photo 6.1 Photograph by Scott, http://commons.wikimedia.org/wiki/File:Ruffed_Grouse_1.jpg

Photo 6.16 Photograph by Donna Dewhurst, U.S. Fish and Wildlife Service.

Photo 6.17 Photograph by Ralph Anderson, USDA Forest Service.

Photo 6.20 Oregon Department of Fish and Wildlife photograph by

Donovan A. Leckenby.

Photo 6.21 Photograph by Stan Canter, National Park Service.

Photo 6.22 Photograph by Donovan A. Leckenby, Oregon Department of Fish and Wildlife.

Photo 6.23 Photograph by Donovan A. Leckenby, Oregon Department of Fish and Wildlife.

Photo 6.24 U.S. Government photographer unknown.

Photo 6.25 Photograph by Paul Cryan, U.S. Geological Survey.

Photo 6.27 Photograph by James M. Trappe, USDA Forest Service.

Photo 6.28 Photograph by Ronald S. Rohweder, Oregon Department of Fish and Wildlife.

Photo 6.32 Photograph by Jim W. Grace, USDA Forest Service.

Photo 6.33 Photograph by Jim W. Grace, USDA Forest Service.

Photo 6.35 Photograph by Jim W. Grace, USDA Forest Service.

Photo 6.37 Photograph by James M. Trappe, USDA Forest Service.

Photo 6.43 Oregon Department of Fish and Wildlife photograph.

Photo 6.44 Oregon Department of Fish and Wildlife photograph.

Photo 6.47 Photograph by Chris Maser and Jan Henderson, USDA Forest Service.

Photo 6.50 Oregon Department of Fish and Wildlife photograph.

Photo 6.51 National Park Service photograph.

Photo 6.52 Oregon Department of Fish and Wildlife photograph.

Photo 6.53 Photograph by W. L. Miller, National Park Service.

Photo 6.54 Painting by Bob Hines, U.S. Fish and Wildlife Service. http://commons.wikimedia.org/wiki/File:Cyanocitta_stelleriFJ03P04CA.JP

Photo 6.55 U.S. Fish and Wildlife Service photograph.

Photo 6.62 Photograph by "BeijingWolf." http://commons.wikimedia.org/w/index.php?title=User:BeijingWolf&action=edit&redlink=1

Photo 6.63 Photograph by Brooks Tracy, U.S. Fish and Wildlife Service.

Photo 7.1 Photograph by Ken Hammond, U.S. Department of Agriculture.

Photo 7.2 Photograph by Jim W. Grace, USDA, Forest Service.

Photo 7.4 Photograph by Robert Smith and Chris Maser.

Photo 7.12 Photograph by Dave Menke, U.S. Fish and Wildlife Service.

Photo 7.13 Oregon Department of Fish and Wildlife photograph.

Photo 7.14 Elon Howard Eaton, author, 1866-1935 and Louis Agassiz Fuertes artist, 1874-1927. Birds of New York. New York State Museum Memoir 12, Volume 2. Albany, NY. 1914. 719 pp. http://commons.

wikimedia.org/wiki/File:Accipiter_gentilisAAP045CA.jpg

Photo 7.18 Photograph by Dave Menke, U.S. Fish and Wildlife Service.

Photo 8.1 Photograph by Robert M. Storm and Chris Maser.

Photo 8.2 Photograph by and courtesy of my late friend, Kenneth L. Gordon.

Photo 8.3 Photograph by and courtesy of Kenneth L. Gordon.

Photo 8.4 Photograph by Jack Hynes. http://commons.wikimedia.org/wiki/File:Mating_earthworms.jpg

Photo 8.9 Plate 2 from *Insects, Their Way and Means of Living*, by Robert E. Snodgrass, U.S. Bureau of Entomology. Smithsonian Scientific Series, Volume five. Published by the Smithsonian Institution Series. Inc. , New York, NY. 1930. 362 pp.

Photo 8.10 Plate 4 from *Insects, Their Way and Means of Living*, by Robert E. Snodgrass, U.S. Bureau of Entomology. Smithsonian Scientific Series, Volume five. Published by the Smithsonian Institution Series. Inc. , New York, NY. 1930. 362 pp.

Photo 8.11 Photograph by © Leandro Gomes Moreira. http://commons.wikimedia.org/wiki/File:Ant_at_work_03.jpg

Photo 8.12 Photograph by Scott Bauer, USDA, Agricultural Research Service.

Photo 8.13 Photograph by and courtesy of my friend, Robert M. Storm.

Photo 8.17 Photograph by James Gathany, Center of Disease Control and Prevention.

Photo 8.18 National Park Service photograph.

Photo 8.20 Photograph by and courtesy of my late friend, E. Wayne Hammer.

Photo 8.21 U.S. Fish and Wildlife Service photograph.

Photo 8.25 Oregon Department of Fish and Wildlife photograph.

Photo 8.26 Painting by Joseph Wolf, 1820-1899. In the U.S. National Museum of Wildlife Art. http://commons.wikimedia.org/wiki/File:Wolf_golden_eagle.jpg

Photo 8.27 Photograph by Erwin and Peggy Bauer, U.S. Fish and Wildlife Service.

Photo 8.28 Photograph by Kirk Heims, U.S. Army Corps of Engineers.

Photo 8.29 Photograph by Mongo. http://commons.wikimedia.org/wiki/File:Elk_Stags.jpg

Photo 8.30 Photograph by Smart Glen, U.S. Fish and Wildlife Service.

Photo 8.31 Photograph by Jon Sullivan. http://commons.wikimedia.org/

wiki/File:Elk_at_Gibbon_meadow.jpg
Photo 8.32 Oregon Department of Fish and Wildlife photograph.
Photos part II
Photo Part II.1 Photograph by Wayne Raphael.
Photo Part II.2 Photograph by Harvey Thorstad.